DIALECTS, ENGLISHES, CREOLES, AND EDUCATION

ESL & APPLIED LINGUISTICS PROFESSIONAL SERIES
Eli Hinkel, Series Editor

Nero, Ed. • *Dialects, Englishes, Creoles, and Education*

Basturkmen • *Ideas and Options in English for Specific Purposes*

Kumaravadivelu • *Understanding Language Teaching: From Method to Postmethod*

McKay • *Researching Second Language Classrooms*

Egbert/Petrie, Eds. • *CALL Research Perspectives*

Canagarajah, Ed. • *Reclaiming the Local in Language Policy and Practice*

Adamson • *Language Minority Students in American Schools: An Education in English*

Fotos/Browne, Eds. • *New Perspectives on CALL for Second Language Classrooms*

Hinkel • *Teaching Academic ESL Writing: Practical Techniques in Vocabulary and Grammar*

Hinkel/Fotos, Eds. • *New Perspectives on Grammar Teaching in School Language Classrooms*

Birch • *English L2 Reading: Getting to the Bottom*

Hinkel • *Second Language Writers' Text: Linguistic and Rhetorical Features*

For more information on LEA titles please contact
Lawrence Erlbaum Associates, Publishers, at www.erlbaum.com.

DIALECTS, ENGLISHES, CREOLES, AND EDUCATION

Edited by

Shondel J. Nero
St. John's University

LEA
LAWRENCE ERLBAUM ASSOCIATES, PUBLISHERS
2006   Mahwah, New Jersey   London

Lawrence Erlbaum Associates, Inc., Publishers
10 Industrial Avenue
Mahwah, New Jersey 07430
www.erlbaum.com

Cover design by Kathryn Houghtaling Lacey

Library of Congress Cataloging-in-Publication Data

Dialects, Englishes, Creoles, and education / edited by Shondel J. Nero
    p. cm. — (ESL & applied linguistics professional series)
  Includes bibliographical references and indexes.
  ISBN 0-8058-4658-1 (alk. paper)
  ISBN 0-8058-4659-X (pbk. : alk. paper)
  1. English language—Study and teaching—Foreign speakers. 2. English
language—Variation—English-speaking countries. 3. English language—
Dialects—English-speaking countries. 4. Languages in contact—English-speaking
countries. 5. Creole dialects, English. I. Nero, Shondel J. II. Series: ESL and
applied linguistics professional series.

PE1128.A2.D444 2005
427—dc22
                                     2005051013
                                         CIP

Printed in the United States of America
10 9 8 7 6 5 4 3 2 1

Contents

Foreword
When the Margins Are at the Center

Peter Elbow
Professor of English Emeritus
University of Massachusetts, Amherst

The authors of this much-needed book raise more questions than they answer. This is appropriate, given the complex topic. But there's a big question they do answer: Should teachers and citizens recognize that the various dialects, Englishes, and creoles we find around us—widely felt as wrong, broken, and bad—are in fact full, valid, sophisticated languages? The authors agree that the answer is Yes.

We badly need this strong affirmation. Language prejudice runs startlingly deep—in some ways deeper than racial prejudice. When I encounter tolerant people who are remarkable for their openness to dangerous ideas and wrong practices that mainstream society rejects—people who above all sincerely reject racism—I find that a good number of them are deeply intolerant of language they call wrong or bad. They welcome all people and ideas—as long as they are "well spoken."

Yet when the authors agree on the validity and sophistication of dialects and creoles, they cannot help but raise another question—perhaps larger and more difficult: How can teachers affirm, value, respect, and cherish these dialects and creoles, while nevertheless at the same time helping student speakers gain control of the "standard" or prestige mainstream variety of English that they need for success in school and in most jobs?

This difficult question seems to me the driving force in the book. Virtually all the authors chew on it; they suggest answers of various sorts—sometimes tentatively, sometimes confidently. As a result, the book offers a wide range of thought-provoking ideas—and many concrete, practical, classroom-based suggestions—suggestions that teachers all over the country are looking for.

Across the variety of suggestions and approaches, I sense one main theme: *build on strength.* That is, when teachers want to help students get control of the prestige mainstream variety of English, they will do best by building on the sophisticated linguistic command of their home language that all students bring to the classroom. Indeed, most students who speak a nonmainstream variety of English have been negotiating dual languages for much of their lives. For this reason they tend to be more linguistically so-phisticated than most mainstream students in their understanding of how language varies and how it is a site of power and influence. It is possible for teachers to build on this rich linguistic strength in order to help them at-tain command over the standard variety. (This is the theme that has driven the two essays I've written about varieties of English; see Elbow, 1999, 2002.)

There's another large theme hovering over this book: *what looks marginal can turn out to be central.* What looks normal is really a parochial special case, and what looks special or odd or "other" is actually a fuller and more accu-rate picture of how things are.

The first time I became aware of this theme—and how it can turn one's head around—was in my reading about the history of science. For example:

• It looks as though we earthlings are at the center and the sun revolves around us from a peripheral position; indeed when Galileo argued against this view—at his peril—most of the empirical evidence was against him. His breakthrough consisted of imaginative model-making that was hard to support empirically. (See Burtt's, 1955, splendid important book on this story.)

• It looks as though every moving object—bicycle or billiard ball—even-tually slows down and stops once we stop pushing it (unless it's rolling downhill). But actually, all bodies in motion keep going forever unless something gets in their way. In order to come up with this odd but true uni-versal law, Galileo had to start by thinking of the planets as a special case—heavenly bodies moving in a "heavenly space"—completely unlike earthly bodies in our dull heavy "sublunar" realm. By thinking about what seemed marginal beyond the borders of the earth, he and others were able to work out crucial counterintuitive insights about everything on earth. (See Burtt on this story, too.)

• As we fly in fast airplanes, it looks as though our watches work fine and objects stay the same size. But experiments have confirmed the counter-intuitive principles of relativity and demonstrated that objects at high veloc-ities actually get smaller and heavier—and time slows down. Our sense of constancy is misleading: It's a "parochial" special case that applies only to what we see in our small "parish" (the root of the word *parochial*).

• It looks as though we cannot destroy matter even if we burn it: All the bits are still there in the smoke and ashes; all the atoms or molecules are "conserved." But again, relativity shows that matter is *not* conserved and can in fact be transformed into energy. Again, our local parochial view misleads us about the larger real picture.

If we turn from physics to language we will see that the same principle often applies: What looks odd or marginal or local can give us a better picture of how things really work:

• It looks as though monolingual groups are the norm and multilingual folk who live at the margins of these groups are the exception. Illich (1980) and Pratt (1987, 1991) both show that this view is parochial and misleading: "Communities in which monolingual people prevail are rare. . . . To take it for granted that most people are monolingual is typical of the members of the middle class" (Illich, p. 46).

• It looks as though each individual's spoken language is a kind of local, imperfect approximation or imitation of the *real* collective language that he or she is using—whether it's English or Chinese. But actually, the truth is the other way around. In *The Linguistic Individual,* Johnstone (1996) points out that languages

> are treated as if they were superorganic, existing outside the individual and available for logging into, like mainframe linguistic computers. . . . But no two people do in fact have exactly the same history of linguistic experience, so no two grammars can be exactly alike. . . . [E]ach individual's grammar is distinct. . . . [G]rammar and cultures are never completely shared. . . . (pp. 173–174)

What we think of as real languages are fictional imitations, convenient abstract constructs. What's most real is what appears peripheral and marginal—the unique and separate languages spoken by different individuals. Our parochial thinking *works* if we are content to look at language through a gross lens—just as the gross lens of Newtonian physics works for most objects we actually have to handle. (Interestingly, our parochial thinking about language is just like Plato's theory that the *idea* of a bed is real, while individual physical beds are imperfect imitations.)

* * *

It's clear, I trust, how these stories apply to the book you hold in your hand. Dialects and creoles are widely assumed to be marginal—in comparison to "real languages." Schools develop curricula that are "special" and "other" for speakers of dialects and creoles. But if linguistic individualism and uniqueness are the reality, and if multilingualism and contact among languages are the norm—i.e., *mixture and hybridity*—then it turns out that this book is crucial for helping us correct our parochial misunderstandings about how language actually works. We need to have our heads turned around in order to "re-see" or "re-understand" the learning and teaching of language. We need to look at dialects, creoles, and pidgins in order to correct our mistaken assumptions about what is truly normal or truly mainstream in language—and to try to think more carefully about what a normal mainstream classroom might actually need.

Here are four concrete examples of parochial assumptions about "normality" and how they need to be reinterpreted through a process of looking more closely at dialects and creoles:

1. It looks as though dialects and creoles change while standard languages are stable. The very concept of *standard* means there is a fixed model and individual usage tends toward it. (Consider the history and etymology of the word *standard*. Originally it was the flag held aloft by a soldier at the head of the troops—someone whose job was to keep it aloft even as everyone around him was struck down or starting to retreat.) But we need to turn our heads around on this matter. In fact the "standard" itself is constantly changing. Our teaching and curricular planning would improve if we paid more attention to the fact that change is the norm. For example, both mainstream and dialect-speaking students would find the study of "standard correct grammar" more interesting and memorable if it were presented as drifting—especially when it can be shown how this drift is almost always toward what is considered "wrong"—which is usually towards what's more common and comfortable for them. (Even linguistic researchers sometimes buttress the misleading idea of an unchanging standard with their research about how dialects and creoles tend to drift toward the standard or sometimes move away from it).

2. It looks to most people as though dialects and creoles are hybrid while "regular" languages are more pure. But we will understand and teach "pure" languages better if we learn from dialects and hybrids about the hybridity in all languages.[1]

---

[1] Renato Rosaldo (1995) puts it succinctly:

> On the one hand, hybridity can imply a space betwixt and between two zones of purity in a manner that follows biological usage that distinguishes two discreet species and the hybrid pseudo species that results from their combination. . . . On the other hand, hybridity can be understood as the ongoing condition of all human cultures, which contain no zones of purity because they undergo continuous processes of transculturation (two-way borrowing and lending between cultures). Instead of hybridity versus purity, it is hybridity all the way down. (p. xv)

3. It looks as though "regular" "mainstream" students grow up with a language appropriate for writing, whereas dialect and creole speakers are disadvantaged because their languages are not. Yet of course the constant experience of mainstream students is that even their "standard," sanctioned version of English is inappropriate for writing. In fact, standard *written* English is *no one's* mother tongue. Everyone has to learn writing as a new language.

This fact is important because in schools, writing trumps speaking. "Competence in English" in a school context tends to mean command over syntax and writing. A student who has problems there will be called "deficient in English" even if he or she has good competence in speaking and wields a large vocabulary. Stephen Krashen (2003) points out an odd asymmetry that makes matters worse: Our culture seems to insist on virtually 100% accuracy in writing, but nothing like this high standard for speaking, reading, or listening. In short, our parochial assumptions lead people to focus on a "dialect problem for marginal students when they write," whereas in fact *all* students face a speech/writing problem they must learn to overcome.

4. It looks to many in the general public as though mainstream speakers have a language whereas others have a dialect. Of course lots of others *are* aware of a central insight from linguistics, namely that every language is a dialect and every dialect a language. But there's another parochial misunderstanding that is widespread even among scholars, policymakers, and teachers. That is, it looks as though mainstream speakers operate safely from within the "standard" language whereas speakers of dialects and creoles feel a pressure that comes from operating outside it—the pressure that comes from the difference between how they actually speak and how they "ought to speak." But in fact, mainstream speakers too (especially in school) characteristically have the same experience of finding that the language that comes most naturally to their mouths and minds is considered wrong and in need of correction. Virtually all students in a culture like ours—where the culture of schooling and the culture of literacy are strong—are constantly experiencing a pressure from "the standard." Illich (1980) recounts for us the remarkable history of how this situation came about.

It turns out that what we take for granted as normal—classrooms that teach "proper English" to everyone—is in fact exceptional and stems from an amazing historical event. In the same year that Columbus persuaded Queen Isabella of not-yet-Spain to fund his adventure, a grammarian persuaded her to fund an equally pregnant adventure. Nebrija was the first man to write the grammar of a European national language—and probably the first ever to write a grammar of any current vernacular spoken language. He persuaded Isabella that her reputation would soon wither unless the current Castilian dialect were regularized and preserved (to become what we call Spanish). In addition, Spain was in the process of expelling all Moors and Jews and enlarging its territory, and Nebrija also argued that "language has always been the consort of empire, and forever shall remain its mate" (from his *Gramatica Castellana*, quoted in Illich, p. 33).

But Nebrija didn't write a grammar of Castilian as it was spoken; he "fixed" it—in both senses of the word. "[T]his our language has been left loose and unruly. . . . By means of my grammar, [the people] shall learn artificial Castilian, not difficult to do, since it is built up on the base of a language they know; and, then, Latin will come easily . . ." (Nebrija, quoted in Illich, pp. 43 & 37). Illich comments:

> Outside of those societies that we now call Modern European, no attempt was [ever] made to impose on entire populations an everyday language that would be subject to the control of paid teachers or announcers. Everyday language, until recently [the Renaissance], was nowhere the product of design; it was nowhere paid for and delivered like a commodity. (p. 47)

Illich argues that throughout most of human history and throughout most of the world, people have not been considered needful of *instruction in their mother tongue.* Only in our parochial culture are we somehow tricked into thinking that people cannot possess their mother tongue without being taught in school.

> Formerly there had been no salvation outside the Church; now, there would be no reading, no writing—if possible, no speaking—outside the educational sphere. . . . (p. 37)

Thanks to the exceptional events Nebrija set in motion, no one in our culture operates safely from within the "standard" language, and the experience of "dialect" speakers highlights what we need to understand as the experience of mainstream speakers.

* * *

In short, this helpful book about what the culture defines as "other"—dialects and creoles and alternative versions of English—serves in fact to give us a better window on the subtle realities of all human language. These realities are ignored by most teachers and most curriculum planners because they concentrate parochially on mainstream classrooms and mainstream languages. In planning mainstream classrooms, they think they are "leaving out the exceptions," when in fact they are leaving out what's central but hidden from them. We are accustomed to thinking of science as the realm of subtle realities that are hidden but powerful, but a book like this one helps us see subtle hidden but powerful realities of language that we need to understand for *all* good language teaching and language policy.

REFERENCES

Burtt, E. A. (1955). *The metaphysical foundations of modern physical science.* Garden City, NY: Doubleday.

Elbow, P. (1999). Inviting the mother tongue: Beyond "mistakes," "bad English," and "wrong language." *Journal of Advanced Composition, 19*(2), 359–388. (Reprinted in *Everyone can write: Essays toward a hopeful theory of writing and teaching writing,* 2000, Oxford: Oxford University Press)

Elbow, P. (2002). Vernacular Englishes in the writing classroom: Probing the culture of literacy. In C. Schroeder, P. Bizzell, & H. Fox (Eds.), *ALT DIS: Alternative discourses and the academy* (pp. 126–138). Portsmouth: Heinemann.

Illich, I. (1980). Vernacular values. *Co-Evolution Quarterly,* 24–49.

Johnstone, B. (1996). *The linguistic individual: Self-expression in language and linguistics.* New York: Oxford University Press.

Krashen, S. D. (2003). *Explorations in language acquisition.* Portsmouth, NH: Heinemann.

Pratt, M. L. (1987). Linguistic utopias. In N. Fabb, D. Attridge, A. Durant, & C. MacCabe (Eds.), *The linguistics of writing* (pp. 48–66). Manchester: Manchester University Press.

Pratt, M. L. (1991). The arts of the contact zone. *Profession 91.* New York: Modern Language Association.

Rosaldo, R. (1995). Foreword. In N. G. Canclini (Ed.), *Hybrid cultures: Strategies for entering and leaving modernity* (C. L. Chiappari & S. L. Lopez, Trans.). Minneapolis: University of Minnesota Press.

Preface

This volume brings together a multiplicity of voices, both theoretical and practical, on the politics, challenges, and strategies of educating students who speak and/or write in dialects of English or related language systems that are at variance with academic discourse. The volume focuses specifically on the increasing number of speakers of diverse or nonstandard varieties of English, creoles, and hybrid varieties of English that teachers confront daily in classrooms in North America and worldwide as a result of the spread of English, internal and global migration, and increased educational access. The students affected typically speak language varieties such as African American Vernacular English, Caribbean Creole English, Tex Mex, West African Pidgin English, Indian English, among others, and many educators are often unsure how to respond to the unique linguistic needs of these students given their "English-speaking" classification or affiliation.

The purpose of this collection is to assist educators in confronting the complex questions and challenges of teaching speakers of diverse varieties of English by offering a sociohistorical perspective on language spread and variation, analysis of related issues such as language attitudes, linguistic identities and prescribed versus actual language use, and practical suggestions for pedagogy. Collectively, the chapters invite educators and scholars to begin to consider and adopt policies and practices appropriate to their specific sociolinguistic contexts to improve the language development and academic performance of linguistically diverse students.

Although the volume builds on previous work on varieties of English and creoles, what sets it apart is: (a) its unique focus on the educational implications of the spread and use of diverse varieties of English and related creoles within one text; (b) a comprehensive introduction providing a theoretical framework for the chosen pieces; and (c) the breadth and depth of perspective of the contributors, who are researchers and practitioners in diverse fields such as applied linguistics, sociolinguistics, TESOL, bilingual education, anthropology, composition, literacy, and English studies.

The intended audience for this volume are graduate students of TESOL, applied linguistics, English, and language education; teachers of English as a Second Language (ESL); teachers of speakers of diverse and nonstandard varieties of English; teachers and scholars of English, composition, literacy, applied linguistics, and sociolinguistics; and general readers with an interest in language diversity.

OVERVIEW

The volume is comprised of an introduction, providing an overview of the issues, 12 chapters that cover a broad range of issues on varieties of English and related language systems, and a brief concluding chapter. Drawing on theories of linguistic imperialism, macroacquisition, and creolization, the introduction discusses the far-reaching linguistic and attitudinal consequences of linguistic imperialism, the language debates that have ensued as a result of language spread, and the ambivalent attitudes towards identification with standard and nonstandard varieties of English. This is followed by a discussion of the implications of the overarching themes of the chapters for education.

The chapters are arranged in seven parts, each containing two chapters, except Part IV and Part VI, which have one chapter each. The two chapters in Part I on *World Englishes, Creoles, and Education* orient the reader to the broad questions of the goals of English language teaching and the role of the vernacular in the classroom. This is followed by six parts, each focused on one of the following language varieties: African American Vernacular English (AAVE)/Ebonics, Caribbean Creole English (CCE), Hawai'i Creole English (HCE), Hispanized English, West African Pidgin English (WAPE), and Asian Englishes. The grouping of the chapters into parts allows the reader to gain a deeper understanding of the unique development, features, and issues relative to a specific variety of English within the theoretical framework of the book, and to address the needs of speakers of these particular varieties in schools. At the same time, it offers a clearer perspective from which to compare and contrast one variety of English with another.

All of the chapters are first published in this volume, except the two on AAVE. These two pieces are included with permission because they offer critical insights into the last great debate of the 20th century on language and education—Ebonics and its role in education—and thus they remain seminal to the field.

The chapters are so designed that they may be read sequentially or as individual pieces, although there's a high degree of intertextuality among them. Each chapter is preceded by a list of key points to help focus the reader and provide a framework for reading, writing, reflection, and discussion. Each one is also followed by a list of questions for discussion and reflective writing, which are designed to both engage and challenge the ideas presented in the chapter as well as to encourage a range of approaches in dealing with language diversity. As such, questions may be answered individually, in pairs, small groups, or as a whole class.

The conclusion sums up the pivotal themes and tensions in the preceding chapters, and suggests directions for future research. It is hoped that this volume will begin to address the ongoing questions of how best to respond to the increasing linguistic diversity in 21st-century classrooms.

Acknowledgments

The idea for this volume was spawned about five years ago. It seemed to me then that I was spending a tremendous amount of time culling and xeroxing articles and book chapters on dialects of English from a variety of sources every time I wanted to talk to my graduate students about English language diversity and education. So it occurred to me that I ought to put together a volume that would speak to the educational impact of the spread of English in the broadest possible way. Many thanks to Naomi Silverman, Senior Editor at Lawrence Erlbaum Associates (LEA), for having the wisdom to wholeheartedly endorse such an idea from the beginning. From her prompt and enthusiastic response to my initial query about publishing a volume such as this, to her steadfast support and guidance in shepherding this project to the end, she's been a force. Thanks to the entire LEA production staff for expediting the publishing process with care and efficiency, and especially to Erica Kica, Assistant Editor, for her attention to detail and for answering my never-ending questions. Ditto to the copyeditors for their hard work in finetuning the manuscript.

Thanks to Eli Hinkel, Series Editor, for her support, unwavering belief in the project, her refreshing honesty, and her close reading of the chapters and constructive criticism. She's helped to make this a much better product.

Much appreciation to the reviewers of the manuscript for their careful reading and helpful feedback and suggestions.

I am greatly indebted to all of the contributors to this volume without whom I could not have done this. The breadth and depth of their ideas and perspectives have made this a richer volume. I thank them all for their patience and professionalism throughout this project.

To Peter Elbow, who convened a group of scholars at the University of Massachusetts, Amherst, in summer 2001 to talk about language diversity and education. That spirited symposium reinforced the need for this volume. Thanks to Peter for his vision and endorsement of the project.

This work could not have been completed without the financial and moral support of the administration, faculty, and staff at St. John's University. My deep appreciation to: Provost Julia Upton, Dean Jerrold Ross of the School of Education, Richard Sinatra, my department chair, and my colleagues on the department's personnel and budget committee for approving a research leave that allowed me to complete the manuscript; my colleagues in the School of Education Faculty Forum, especially Rene Parmar and Mary Ann Maslak, for reading early drafts of the introduction and offering constructive criticism; my former graduate students, Timothy Becker and Penny Pavlatos, for reading and "field testing" the introduction.

To all of my friends, especially Sonia Bacchus, Jennifer Joe, and Brynmor Bowen, who have always supported my work—thank you for caring, listening, and believing in me.

To my siblings, Trevor Nero, Cherryl Cooper, Kwesi Nero, and Dara Nero, and their families; to Mom and Dad—thank you all for your constant love and support.

Finally, to my husband, Louis Parascandola, for being my greatest champion, my in-house editor, my sounding board—my heartfelt appreciation for your amazing and unflinching love and support.

Introduction

Shondel J. Nero
St. John's University

> *Language is primarily what people do rather than what they say or think they do,*
> *or what they are told to do, say or think—although these social aspects have their*
> *place in both everyday life and scholarly debates.*
> —McArthur (1998, p. 202)

The latter half of the 20th century witnessed an unprecedented spread of the English language worldwide. This proliferation can be attributed to a combination of historical, political, social, economic, cultural, and technological factors. The result is the emergence of new varieties of English and related language systems, multiple linguistic identities, challenges to the construct of the native speaker, and the need for a critical reexamination of the nature and goals of English language teaching and learning. The chapters in this volume address these complex issues and their concomitant challenges from diverse perspectives, with particular emphasis on the implications for education. Although the volume builds on previous work on varieties of English and creoles (Burns & Coffin, 2001; Cheshire, 1991; Crystal, 1997; Kachru, 1992; Mufwene, 1993; Rickford, 1999; Roberts, 1988), what sets it apart is its unique focus on the educational implications of the spread and use of diverse varieties of English and related creoles.

The populations discussed in the chapters have in one way or another come into contact with and shaped a variety of English, taking ownership of the language in the process. As a consequence, schools have had to address the language use, needs, and attitudes of a wide range of English speakers within the larger sociopolitical context of the spread of the language. Two primary bases were used for selecting the populations: First, as speech communities, they have an historical identification or connection with English through Anglo-American domination (the cases of African Americans, U.S.-based Latinos, Hawaiians,[1] and Filipinos) or through British colonization (the cases of Caribbeans, West Africans, and Indians). Secondly, the populations are in the U.S. in sufficiently high numbers, particularly in urban centers, such that teachers are likely to encounter speakers from these populations in their classes.[2]

In order to place the chapters in their proper sociohistorical context, I begin with a discussion of the genesis and spread of diverse varieties of English and related creoles within three theoretical frameworks: (1) Phillipson's (1992) notion of *linguistic imperialism*; (2) Brutt-Griffler's (2002) theory of *macroacquisition*; and (3) *pidginization and creolization* as proposed by scholars such as Holm (1988). It is argued that English language spread and variation have implications for the ownership of the language, questions of language standards, and linguistic identity, among others. A major contention of this volume is that language spread and variation have also raised several questions and challenges for educators which are discussed in the chapters, such as: Which models and/or varieties of English are appropriate in various educational contexts? What is the role of the vernacular in school? How can teachers reconcile the privileging of standard English while trying to validate students' vernacular in school? How can teachers and students address the ambivalent (often negative) attitudes vis-à-vis nonstandard dialects of English and their speakers? What are the appropriate placement, assessment, and strategies for teaching students who claim multiple linguistic identities or those who claim to be native speakers of English but whose spoken/written language is at variance with school-based English and discourse? How can teachers identify and address the different needs of speakers of English-based creoles, New Englishes, and traditional second language learners? The purpose of this volume is not to propose definitive answers or solutions to the issues and questions raised, but rather to heighten awareness of the complexity of the evolution and use of language, and to provide a context within which educators might begin to adopt policies and practices appropriate to their specific sociolinguistic and teaching contexts.

---

[1]The adjective *Hawaiian* normally refers to indigenous Hawaiians. Here, however, I am using it in the broader sense to also include residents of the state of Hawai'i who are primarily Hawai'i Creole English speakers.

[2]See Appendix for Census 2000 data and additional information on ethnic populations in the U.S.

BACKGROUND

The proliferation of varieties of English around the world can be traced to two primary phenomena: first, the migration of English-speaking peoples from the United Kingdom to the United States, Canada, Australia, and New Zealand (referred to by Brutt-Griffler, 2002 as *speaker migration*); and secondly, the encounters of English-speaking Europeans with ethnic populations who spoke various non-European languages in places like the United States, the Caribbean, Africa, and Asia. In the latter case, the majority of these encounters were in exploitive conditions, most notably, slavery. The abolition of slavery or similar conditions (such as indentured labor) gave way to new, equally exploitive, sociopolitical and economic arrangements, namely colonialism, neocolonialism, and now, globalization. In all of these various systems, the underlying common factor is an uneven distribution of power between the groups that are in contact with each other. Phillipson (1992) argues that such an asymmetrical power relationship is the essence of imperialism, and that one of the most effective ways to sustain this relationship is through what he calls *linguistic imperialism*. Phillipson offers a working definition of *English linguistic imperialism* as "the dominance of English . . . asserted and maintained by the establishment and continuous reconstitution of structural and cultural inequalities between English and other languages" (p. 47). He explains further that *structural* refers to concrete properties such as financial resources or institutions (e.g., school), and *cultural* refers to intangible factors such as language attitudes or pedagogical principles. In practice, for example, this might mean that continued power of English is ensured by the institutionalization of systems that privilege English over local vernaculars in school and the wider culture by giving material rewards to those who develop proficiency in a standardized form of English. Furthermore, the success of this practice is premised on two basic tenets:

1. Enforcing the superiority of the English spoken by the group who has power, and by extension, the superiority of the speakers themselves.
2. Denigrating the mass vernacular, or worse, not recognizing it as a language at all (and therefore devaluing its speakers).

The spread of English, however, has not been a simple unidirectional phenomenon, with one group imposing its language on another. Nor has the center of gravity of the language remained fixed as is widely presumed (McArthur, 1998). Languages in contact take on lives of their own, that is to say, new and distinct forms that reflect the sociolinguistic and political realities of the particular sites of contact. In the case of English, a range of related language varieties has emerged as a result of contact—pidgins, creoles, African American Vernacular English (AAVE), Hispanized English, Indian English, West African Pidgin English (WAPE), and so forth—and with this emergence, a parallel set of ambivalent language attitudes by their speakers and the wider community.

Brutt-Griffler's (2002) theory of *macroacquisition* has been one of the most comprehensive conceptual frameworks thus far to address the spread and change of English by entire speech communities. Responding to what she perceives as Phillipson's Euro-centered theory of linguistic imperialism, particularly to explain the spread of English, Brutt-Griffler contends that macroacquisition, defined as "the acquisition of a second language by a speech community" (p. 138) as opposed to an individual, offers a counterpoint to linguistic imperialism. Her theory is premised on the notion that English owes its existence as a world language in large part to the struggle against imperialism and not to imperialism alone; hence, speech communities around the world and in the United States have not only acquired the language but have made it their own, changing it in the process.

Brutt-Griffler posits two types of macroacquisition, both of which result in bilingual speech communities: *Type A macroacquisition*, in which speakers of different mother tongues within the same environment simultaneously acquire a common second language that serves as a unifying linguistic resource (e.g., English in Nigeria, India or the Philippines), termed *indigenized* or *nativized* varieties in the literature (Bokamba, 1991; Cheshire, 1991; Kachru, 1986). A unique feature of Type A is that the second language acquisition (SLA) process takes place in a nonnative setting with little input from native speakers; hence, Brutt-Griffler argues, there is no fixed target language to aspire to. Rather, the language variety emerges through the SLA process itself, characteristically defined by its own lexical items, idioms, and transformed meanings. *Type B macroacquisition*, on the other hand, is evidenced when a largely monolingual speech community is transformed into a bilingual speech community by virtue of being in an environment in which another mother tongue dominates (e.g., Hispanized English of U.S.-based Latinos).

While macroacquisition focuses on the emergence of bilingual speech communities, especially in Asia and Africa, it does not sufficiently address speakers of other varieties of English such as Caribbean Creole English (CCE), Hawai'i Creole English (HCE) or AAVE,[3] who do not necessarily

---

[3]The abbreviations *AAVE* and *AAE* (African American Vernacular English and African American English respectively) are used interchangeably in some chapters in this volume to refer to the everyday language of many African Americans. The term *Ebonics* is also used to refer to the language of this group. The term came to prominence in national discourse in 1996 in the wake of the Oakland School Board Resolution, although it was created some 23 years earlier.

perceive themselves as bilingual or part of a bilingual speech community in any strict sense. The development of CCE and HCE have been explained through language contact theories of *pidginization* and *creolization*. *Pidgins* are linguistic systems that develop where two groups who speak different languages come into contact. Pidgins are characterized by reduced syntax and lexicon, and are native to neither group. It is further argued that over time pidgins, suitably expanded, become *creoles*, where the language is used by the next generation and becomes native to them. In the case of creoles,[4] the lexicon is typically provided by the *superstrate* language (or the language spoken by the group in power in the specific context, namely English, in the case of former British or American colonies), while the syntax is influenced by the local ethnic language(s). It should be noted that the terms pidgin and creoles themselves have been broadly used. For example, in Hawai'i, Pidgin and Hawai'i Creole English are often used synonymously (see Eades, Jacobs, Hargrove, & Menacker, chap. 7, this volume).

Mufwene (1994) argues persuasively that indigenized Englishes and creoles (which, together, he broadly labels as *New Englishes*) have a few characteristics in common, the most obvious of which is the fact that they emerged from language contact situations. In addition, they all emerged from exploitive situations and are primarily spoken by non-Europeans, the latter fact having a direct perceptual impact in schools. Their differences, notes Mufwene, "lie primarily in ethnographic status (high for indigenized Englishes and low for creoles), in the nature of the lexifier (nonstandard for creoles and standard for indigenized English) and in the medium of transmission (casual contact in the case of creoles, but formalized through the school system in the case of indigenized Englishes)" (p. 24).

Another critical difference is noteworthy here. In the case of the Anglophone Caribbean, a creole continuum has developed that ranges from a strict Creole to Creole English to a local standardized form of English, all of which have *vernacularized* to various degrees. That is because the majority of the Caribbean population today are descendants of transplanted and enslaved peoples whose original ethnic languages were largely eradicated during their enslavement. Thus, the Creole English developed and spoken in the region is, for most, the only language they can lay claim to and the primary one used. It is publicly labeled English due to the stigmatization of creolized varieties. The perception in the mind of the Caribbean native, then, is that English is their only language, however different it may be in

---

The same interchangeable use is true for *CCE* and *CEC* (Caribbean Creole English and Caribbean English Creole respectively). In each case, the abbreviations merely indicate the author's preference for describing the language variety.

[4]Throughout this introduction, *creoles* is spelled with a lowercase "c" to describe linguistic systems emanating from language contact. *Creoles* is spelled with an uppercase "C" whenever I refer to a specific variety, e.g., Caribbean Creole English.

terms of structure, lexicon, pronunciation, and usage from a standard variety of English. The perception precludes the Anglophone Caribbean native from thinking of him or herself as a bilingual or of English as a second language, a perception that has implications for placement and assessment in schools (see Winer, chap. 5 and Pratt-Johnson, chap. 6, this volume). Compare this to someone from Nigeria, for example, who might first speak and identify with Igbo or Yoruba and only secondarily with English—a more clearcut bilingual case.

The CCE speaker can also be compared and contrasted to the AAVE speaker. Although the languages of both emerged from the sociolinguistic conditions of plantation slavery, the CCE speaker's language has been influenced by a proportionally larger number of Creole and nonstandard English speakers compared to an AAVE speaker; hence, the language of the CCE speaker is generally more creolized or nonstandard than the AAVE speaker even though they both claim to be, and are generally considered, native speakers of English. Still, the AAVE speaker's language is sufficiently different from standardized American English such that it can be a serious factor in their performance in school. This issue will be taken up later. Language contact has also accounted for the emergence of varieties such as Tex Mex, a rule governed linguistic code consisting of Spanish and English spoken by many Mexican Americans in South Texas (see Hall Kells, chap. 9, this volume).

LANGUAGE DIVERSITY DEBATES

The diversity among the language varieties discussed so far calls into question the unitary view of English, the ownership of English, the construct of the native speaker, and linguistic identity. It is clear that the spread and change of English defies a unitary model of the language. McArthur (1998), for example, argues for a dynamic model where variation, heterogeneity, flux, and language change are an integral part of the language—of any language—and for this reason, he describes the existence of the "English languages." Still, McArthur acknowledges that for both practical and social reasons we set boundaries on the language and continue to perceive of it as monolithic, underscoring a paradox that, he contends, is at the heart of most languages: "they are monolithic and multiple at the same time" (p. 201). The paradox articulated by McArthur is one of several issues raised by linguists in recent years in regard to the spread of English. First, the question might be asked, at what point does English evolve into what might be considered another language? Furthermore, the definition of language itself, and the difference between a language and a dialect continue to be an unresolved debate among linguists. Often, the distinction is more political than linguistic. Linguistics teaches us that all human languages as systems of communication are equally valid, and to speak a language is, by definition, to speak a dialect of that language. Many linguists have opted for the term *language variety* instead of *dialect* to avoid the negative connotations of *dialect* (Wolfram, Adger, & Christian, 1999).

Related to the debate on language versus dialect is the question as to whether or not pidgins and creoles should be considered dialects of English or separate languages. In the strictest sense, most linguists consider creoles to be separate languages, and several progressive language policies and movements by linguists and creole speakers alike have tried, with varying degrees of success, to argue for recognition of creoles as autonomous languages. For example, there has been a growing movement in Hawai'i to consider Pidgin or HCE as a separate language (Eades, Jacobs, Hargrove, & Menacker, chap. 7, this volume).

In the Anglophone Caribbean, there has been a range of positions on the status of Creole. The most extreme creolist position would argue that Creole English or, more specifically, Creole, is the mother tongue in the Caribbean (Devonish, 1986; Folkes, 1993) and therefore standard English is, in fact, a second language in the region. Linguists who take a more moderate position readily acknowledge the blurriness of the creole continuum in the Caribbean, complicating as it sometimes does the boundaries and definition of a language itself. Roberts (1988), for instance, cites the case of Jamaica where "[t]he wide spectrum [of varieties] challenges the definition of a language and calls into question the extent to which two speech varieties in a society can differ and still be treated as belonging to the same language" (p. 9).

In the United States, one of the most controversial events in the last decade in regard to language recognition was the 1996 Oakland California School Board Resolution which called for the recognition of *Ebonics* (a synonym for AAVE) as "the primary *language*" of African American children, and to take this into account in their language arts lessons (see Rickford, chap. 3, and Delpit, chap. 4, this volume). The Resolution set in motion a spirited national debate on language versus dialect, language stigmatization, language and race, and the education and academic performance of African Americans and other speakers of nonmainstream languages. It also underscored the fact that language attitudes and practices in the real world still view AAVE and English-lexified creoles as bad, or broken or deformed English rather than separate languages, and hold tenaciously to a prescriptivist, hierarchical model of language which does not give equal status to all languages or all varieties thereof. The very notion of a standard or standardized form of a language (as in *standard English*) connotes a privileging of one variety or dialect of a language over another, and raises a host of related and challenging questions for educators that are the thrust of the discussion in this volume.

Another very important issue for educators in North America and England is how to place speakers of so-called nativized varieties of English in school. The fact that English has nativized in various parts of the world has allowed its speakers in those regions to claim nativeness to the language, or at least to a particular variety of it. Higgins (2003) correctly calls for a "pluricentric understanding" (p. 619) of English norms that would allow us to accept someone as a native speaker of Indian English or Caribbean English. I have noted elsewhere (Nero, 2002), however, that speakers of such varieties of English are often perceived as "not quite native" by other speakers who claim exclusive ownership of English or who consider themselves the "real" native speakers. In other words, there seems to be a qualitative difference (and judgment) between a *native* and a *nativized* speaker.[5] Widdowson (1994) cautions against the tendency by British or European American speakers to claim exclusive ownership of English: "The very fact that English is an international language means that no nation can have custody over it. . . . It is not a possession which they (so-called native speakers) lease out to others while still retaining the freehold. Other people actually own it" (p. 385). Widdowson defies what Leung, Harris, and Rampton (1997) call the "idealised[6] native speaker." This construct not only privileges a perceived native speaker, but also a particular type of native speaker, one that is typically middle class, educated, and of European heritage. Leung et al. observe that the notion of the idealized native speaker ignores classroom realities where students may claim dual or multiple linguistic identities and affiliations, complicating the tendency by educators to construct second language speakers as a monolithic group for ease of placement and instruction.

Finally, there are two common characteristics emanating from the spread, development, and use of diverse varieties of English: The first is the fact that they are all stigmatized, particularly in school; secondly, a number of ambivalent attitudes toward them have emerged, all of which might be viewed through the lens of linguistic imperialism. The paradox that inheres in language structure (e.g., one can argue that AAVE is both a dialect of English and another language at the same time; Palacas, 2001) extends to language attitudes. Kachru (1977) notes that in many countries where English has nativized, the language is seen as simultaneously the great unifier and divider. On the one hand, in areas of the world such as South Asia and

---

[5]A substantial body of work has challenged the native speaker construct (Brutt-Griffler & Samimy, 2001; Canagarajah, 1999; Cook, 1999; Davies, 1991; Ferguson, 1992; B. Kachru, 1986; Y. Kachru, 1994; Kramsch, 1997; Leung, Harris, & Rampton, 1997; Nayar, 1994; Paikeday, 1985; Pennycook, 1994; Rampton, 1990; Sridhar, 1994; Widdowson, 1994).

[6]The British spelling, *idealised*, is quoted in the first instance to maintain the integrity of the original text. Subsequent uses of the word in this introduction adhere to the American spelling, *idealized*.

West Africa where multiple ethnic dialects are spoken, English was imposed as the colonial language. English, then, has come to serve in these locales as the common language uniting the nation-state, assuming its own structure, flavor, and norms of usage. On the other hand, English is mainly enforced or learned through schooling, and only those who have access to schooling and who develop proficiency in the language would be accorded privilege in the society at large (Ngugi, 1986). This state of affairs perpetuates the social stratification of language, economic, and political power, and exacerbates the class divide in already rigidly stratified societies.

The stigmatization of vernacular speakers is also one of the principal tenets of linguistic imperialism. Unfortunately, many speakers of ethnic languages within former British colonies or speakers of nonstandard dialects of English within English-dominant countries have internalized the stigma. Attitudes towards the vernacular, however, are also ambivalent. Most vernacular speakers simultaneously celebrate and denigrate their language, aptly characterized by Kachru and Nelson (2001) as "attitudinal schizophrenia" (p. 14). The celebration of the vernacular reflects one aspect of what LePage and Tabouret-Keller (1985) call "acts of identity," where the speaker uses the language to affirm his/her linguistic heritage and in-group solidarity (see Delpit, chap. 4, for more on group identity and language use). At the same time, the language is denigrated as it suggests low socioeconomic status, and even lack of education. The same ambivalence is demonstrated towards standard English. Smitherman (1977) gives the example of the push–pull phenomenon in the African American community—a simultaneous push towards gaining proficiency in standard English as the language of access and power, and a pull away from it for fear of sounding or acting white.

The push–pull phenomenon noted by Smitherman is not unique to the African American community. The chapters in this volume dealing with Caribbean, Hawai'i, and Latino students also speak to the tension between students' assimilating into mainstream culture while maintaining in-group identity, most palpably manifested through language use and affiliation. Many contributors suggest practical and sensitive strategies to socialize students into mainstream discourse without compromising respect for their vernaculars.

IMPLICATIONS FOR EDUCATION

Given the foregoing discussion, what then are the implications of English language spread and variation for education? The chapters in this volume address this critical question from a range of perspectives. The first two chapters raise some broad issues such as the reconceptualization of English

Language Teaching (ELT), and the need to examine the resources, methodologies, materials, curricula, and expertise in ELT (Kachru, chap. 1); attitudes towards the use of the vernacular in the classroom, and approaches in different types of language programs that focus on the vernacular (Siegel, chap. 2). Other chapters examine issues such as language attitudes, standard language ideology, placement, assessment (particularly high stakes testing), bilingualism and bidialectalism, features of particular language varieties, strategies for teaching dialect speakers, academic performance of speakers of vernaculars or other Englishes, and culturally responsive curricula.

Before examining these issues, some broader classroom realities must be addressed. First, the diversity of Englishes and creoles around the world suggests that educators will encounter an increasing number of speakers of these varieties in their classrooms. In the last two decades, public and private schools and colleges in New York City, for example, have witnessed a rapidly growing number of students who are speakers of Caribbean Creole English, Spanglish, Indian English, and West African English, in addition to the more traditional population of AAVE speakers. The same phenomenon has been occurring in other major urban centers in the United States, Canada, and England. Many speakers of these varieties identify English as their only or primary language—English, that is, as they have perceived, known, and used it. This may be the case even when the students' receptive competence is not paralleled by productive competence in the kind of English privileged in school.

The extent to which the language produced by such students is accepted in school depends on the degree to which it approximates or deviates from educators' perception of what is acceptable English for school purposes. Since most schools give primacy to written language, students tend to (and are encouraged to) de-emphasize features of their orality in school, lest they interfere with their acquisition of literate discourse. In this regard, schools have been the chief custodians of linguistic imperialism, manifested in the privileging of English over other vernacular languages as mentioned earlier, and within English, focusing on a narrow form known as the standard that adheres to prescriptivist rules of grammar and Western essayist rhetorical conventions. The privileging of this particular standard in school, especially in writing, is both overt, as evidenced in practices of placement, assessment, reading and writing instruction, and covert, in terms of negative attitudes towards students whose spoken and/or written language deviate from it. Implicit in these practices are the asymmetrical power relations within classrooms (reflective of the society at large), the notion that English in school and beyond automatically means standard English, and that a speaker or writer who is not proficient in standard English has compromised a legitimate claim to the language and to ultimate school success.

The power dynamic in the classroom and beyond, characterized by Delpit (1995) as the *culture of power*, is critical in understanding how we determine the goals of ELT, how we enact language policies and programs in schools, and how we teach and assess language. Kachru in chap. 1, for instance, raises the fundamental question, what should be the goal(s) of ELT? The question is both broad and specific—broad, in the sense that the target variety of English is different in various contexts because the language has spread and changed. Yet, Kachru asserts that American and British standardized varieties of English dominate the ELT market worldwide in all spheres because of the power of the U.S. and the U.K., sending a message that proficiency in these varieties is the (most valued) goal, a position she challenges.

Actual language use, however, often defies this goal. Students typically speak and/or write the language variety that developed in their particular milieu (e.g., Indian or Filipino English), despite schooling efforts to the contrary. In the case of non-American English-speaking students, for example, only if and when they migrate to the U.S. do they confront the difference (see Govardhan, chap. 11, this volume, on the difference in essay writing between American and Indian students; also, Tayao in chap. 12 notes that many educators in the U.S. find the language of their Philippine English-speaking students "bookish"). In the same manner, AAVE-speaking students confront the difference between their vernacular and standard English when they enter school.

In a more specific sense, many language teachers see preparing students to develop proficiency in standard English as one of their primary goals. This includes grammar, pronunciation, lexicon, and discourse conventions with respect to the four language skills—speaking, listening, reading and writing. In this regard, Widdowson (1994) contends that, historically, grammar has been singled out as the *shibboleth*. Teachers tend to be generally tolerant of diversity in pronunciation and lexicon, but not grammar. Therefore, as alluded to earlier, students whose language does not adhere to the prescriptive rules of standard English grammar, especially in writing, tend to fare poorly in school. This suggests that vernacular speakers such AAVE, HCE, CCE or WAPE speakers who come to school with a different grammar system (albeit equally logical) are likely to encounter difficulties in language arts lessons unless an attempt is made to bridge the gap sensitively. De Kleine (chap. 10, this volume) discusses the disproportionate focus on grammar in placement and assessment, and its effect on WAPE speakers.

Just as a disproportionate amount of significance and power is given to grammar as compared to other aspects of language, so too is a strong preference given to writing over speech in school. This is largely due to the fact that the vast majority of assessment instruments that really matter in school are based on writing, and are written, administered, and judged on standard English norms. Here again, students whose writing exhibits dialect features or those who are not proficient in standard English are unlikely to fare well. García and Menken (chap. 8, this volume) address the disparity between the language of high-stakes testing and actual language use.

The primacy given to standard English in school because of its real and perceived benefits is aptly captured in Lippi-Green's (1997) notion of *standard language ideology*. Because this ideology strongly influences the goals of ELT, many teachers not only make teaching standard English an important goal, but do so with a particular focus on preparing students for standardized assessment, a focus that puts an undue burden on teachers in an era of high-stakes testing, and perpetuates the reductive view of language assessment as premised on grammatical correctness rather than communicative effectiveness (Matsuda, 2003).

As Lippi-Green contends, standard language ideology is often euphemistically framed under the *appropriateness* argument, that is to say, standard English is appropriate for school, work, and formal domains, whereas all other varieties of English are appropriate for informal domains or less serious topics (see also Eades et al., chap. 7, this volume). Notwithstanding the bifurcated language use suggested by this argument, the reality is that students do not simply drop their home language at the school door. Educators are thus challenged to find ways to constructively build on the language students bring to school, and, given the widely accepted, albeit arbitrary, power accorded standard English, teach this variety to students at the same time.

Delpit (1995) suggests that the power dynamics in the classroom must be openly addressed in order to accomplish this dual task, and give students from nonmainstream language backgrounds a fair chance at success. She argues for making the culture of power explicit in the classroom. In practice, this might mean openly acknowledging the arbitrary power of standard English and explicitly teaching the rules and uses of literate discourse. At the same time, she makes a persuasive argument for validating students' vernaculars. The idea here is reconciling the privileging of standard English while validating students' home language (chap. 4 in this volume offers concrete suggestions on how to do this). It must be noted, however, that Delpit's suggestions are no panacea (they constitute one approach to a complex issue), and are only viable in a classroom environment that allows for honest, open dialogue on language-related issues, in particular the question of language attitudes.

Many schools have also attempted to accomplish this dual task for vernacular speakers by implementing various language programs that promote bidialectalism as the goal (this is discussed at length in chapters 2–5). As noted earlier, depending on whether one perceives a student's vernacular as a separate language or a dialect of English, a student might be best served in either a bilingual or bidialectal program. But even in making such a distinction, power dynamics are at play. For example, it is less difficult for a school to make a case for implementing a bilingual program as opposed to a bidialectal one. That is because bilingual programs recognize students who speak autonomous languages such as Spanish or Chinese. The autonomy of a language gives it authenticity. Dialects, by contrast, are unfairly perceived as inferior versions of the standard variety, lacking autonomy, and therefore authenticity. Dialect programs are thus less likely to be funded and/or supported. Witness the misguided perception during the Oakland School Board Ebonics controversy that the Board was calling Ebonics a language as a ploy to get bilingual funding.

The placement of students in appropriate language programs continues to be a challenge for educators, who must differentiate among the needs of traditional ESL students (e.g., speakers of Chinese, Spanish, or Haitian), speakers of nativized varieties such as Indian English, and Creole speakers such as speakers of CCE. I and others have argued elsewhere (Adger, 1997; Nero, 2001) that speakers of varieties such as CCE are not well served in traditional ESL classes precisely because they perceive themselves as already knowing and speaking English, so they do not see it as a second language in the way that a Spanish speaker would. They also generally have more receptive knowledge in standard English (although not necessarily paralleled by productive competence) compared to traditional ESL students. De Kleine's study of West African Pidgin English–speaking students herein shows a similar phenomenon. I would argue that such students are best served in classes where their receptive knowledge of English can be used as a base for literacy development. They might benefit from a bidialectal program or contrastive approach that, among other things, raises awareness of the real differences between their actual and perceived language competence and standard English, differences that are often masked by superficial similarities. In the absence of a firmly established bidialectal program, one might reasonably argue that ESL teachers are certainly better equipped (because of their linguistic training) than other teachers to respond to the needs of this population. Ultimately, appropriate placement and assessment for linguistically diverse students requires familiarity with their actual language use, acceptance of students' self-ascribed linguistic identities, and alternative assessments that go beyond standardized testing.

Once students who speak diverse varieties of English and creoles are in the classroom, teachers are faced with choosing effective resources, materials, and strategies for teaching them. Their choices will be influenced by the needs and demographics of their student populations, the goals of ELT in their particular environment, and the resources at their disposal. Kachru (chap. 1, this volume) criticizes the anglocentric curriculum, resources, and materials that dominate ELT, a sentiment echoed by Matsuda (2003).

Pratt-Johnson (chap. 6), Delpit (chap. 4), Hall Kells (chap. 9), and other authors in this volume offer a counterpoint to this dominance by suggesting ways to implement culturally relevant curriculum and pedagogy for the populations being discussed.

It is clear that such implementation involves confronting language attitudes in a constructive manner in the classroom, raising awareness of the salient features and legitimacy of diverse language varieties, and using this knowledge to develop cultural and linguistic sensitivity. Pratt-Johnson (chap. 6) and Winer (chap. 5), among others, propose several concrete strategies to achieve this, even addressing specifics such as error correction.

The chapters in this volume reflect and seek to revise attitudes, policies, and practices that have emanated from the spread of English. The authors problematize notions of language ownership, language boundaries, linguistic identity, and language ideologies that sustain imperialist models. At the same time, through their research and problem posing, the authors offer concrete strategies for a pedagogy of inclusion, one that seeks to validate all varieties of language and speakers with the ultimate goal of educational equity.

APPENDIX

The following data for the populations discussed in this volume were taken from the U.S. Census Bureau, Census 2000 (www.census.gov):

Total U.S. Population: 281,421,906

Latinos: 35,305,818

African Americans: 34,658,190

West Indians (Anglophone Caribbean): 1,914,410

Top two Asian countries where English is an official language:

Philippines: 1,850,314

India: 1,678,765

Top four Anglophone West African countries:

Nigeria: 161,705

Ghana: 149,434

Liberia: 25,140

Sierra Leone: 12,239

Most of the populations above are concentrated in five urban centers: Los Angeles, New York, San Francisco, Miami, and Chicago. To a lesser degree, they are also in Houston, Dallas, Washington, DC, and Detroit.

It is noteworthy that Latinos are now the leading and fastest growing minority group in the U.S., a trend that is likely to continue well into this century. It is for this reason that the variety of English spoken by this group was included in this volume.

The West Indian population is significant (disproportionately high) given that the total population for the region is approximately 5,000,000. The data point to heavy migration from the region, most notably from Jamaica (689,001 at this census count). It is for this reason that an entire chapter in this volume focuses on Jamaicans. Most West Indians in the U.S. reside on the East Coast, especially in New York City, Washington, DC, and Miami.

The two Asian countries represented both have historical ties with English. The Filipino population, which is the largest, is heavily concentrated in California, and has often been neglected in the literature. This volume attempts to redress that neglect.

REFERENCES

Adger, C. T. (1997). *Issues and implications of English dialects for teaching English as a second language* (TESOL Professional Papers No. 3). Alexandria, VA: TESOL.

Bokamba, E. G. (1991). West Africa. In J. Cheshire (Ed.), *English around the world: Sociolinguistic perspectives* (pp. 493–508). Cambridge: Cambridge University Press.

Brutt-Griffler, J. (2002). *World English: A study of its development.* Clevedon, UK: Multilingual Matters.

Brutt-Griffler, J., & Samimy, K. (2001). Transcending the nativeness paradigm. *World Englishes, 20*(1), 99–106.

Burns, A., & Coffin, C. (Eds.). (2001). *Analysing English in a global context.* New York: Routledge.

Canagarajah, S. (1999). Interrogating the "native speaker fallacy": Non-linguistic roots, non-pedagogical results. In G. Braine (Ed.), *Non-native educators in English language teaching* (pp. 77–92). Mahwah, NJ: Lawrence Erlbaum Associates.

Cheshire, J. (1991). *English around the world: Sociolinguistic perspectives.* Cambridge: Cambridge University Press.

Cook, V. (1999). Going beyond the native speaker in language teaching. *TESOL Quarterly, 33*(2), 185–209.

Crystal, D. (1997). *English as a global language.* Cambridge: Cambridge University Press.

Davies, A. (1991). *The native speaker in applied linguistics.* Edinburgh, UK: Edinburgh University Press.

Delpit, L. (1995). The silenced dialogue: Power and pedagogy in educating other people's children. In L. Delpit, *Other people's children* (pp. 21–47). New York: The New Press.

Devonish, H. (1986). *Language and liberation: Creole language politics in the Caribbean.* London: Karia Press.

Ferguson, C. (1992). Foreword. In B. Kachru (Ed.), *The other tongue: English across cultures* (2nd ed., pp. xiii–xvii). Urbana: University of Illinois Press.

Folkes, K. (1993). *Issues of assessment and identification of Anglo-Caribbean students in a migratory educational environment.* (ERIC Document Reproduction Service No. ED 367 170)

Higgins, C. (2003). "Ownership" of English in the Outer Circle: An alternative to the NS–NNS dichotomy. *TESOL Quarterly, 37*(4), 615–644.

Holm, J. (1988). *Pidgins and creoles* (Vol. I). Cambridge: Cambridge University Press.

Kachru, B. (1977). The new Englishes and the old models. *English Teaching Forum, 15,* 29–35.

Kachru, B. (1986). *The alchemy of English: The spread, functions, and models of non-native Englishes.* Oxford: Pergamon Press. (Reprinted 1990, University of Illinois Press)

Kachru, B. (1992). *The other tongue: English across cultures* (2nd ed.). Urbana: University of Illinois Press.

Kachru, B., & Nelson, C. (2001). World Englishes. In A. Burns & C. Coffin (Eds.), *Analysing English in a global context* (pp. 9–25). London: Routledge.

Kachru, Y. (1994). Monolingual bias in SLA research. *TESOL Quarterly, 28,* 795–800.

Kramsch, C. (1997). The privilege of the nonnative speaker. *Publication of the Modern Language Association, 112,* 359–369.

LePage, R., & Tabouret-Keller, A. (1985). *Acts of identity: Creole-based approaches to language and ethnicity.* Cambridge: Cambridge University Press.

Leung, C., Harris, R., & Rampton, B. (1997). The idealised native speaker, reified ethnicities, and classroom realities. *TESOL Quarterly, 31*(3), 543–560.

Lippi-Green, R. (1997). *English with an accent.* New York: Routledge.

Matsuda, A. (2003). Incorporating World Englishes in Teaching English as an international language. *TESOL Quarterly, 37*(4), 719–729.

McArthur, T. (1998). *The English languages.* Cambridge: Cambridge University Press.

Mufwene, S. (Ed.). (1993). *Africanisms in Afro-American language varieties.* Athens: University of Georgia Press.

Mufwene, S. (1994). New Englishes and criteria for naming them. *World Englishes, 13*(1), 21–31.

Nayar, P. (1994). Whose English is it? *TESL-EJ, 1*(1), F-1. Retrieved November 6, 1999, from http://www-writing.berkeley.edu/TESL-EJ/ej01/f.1.html

Nero, S. (2001). *Englishes in contact: Anglophone Caribbean students in an urban college.* Cresskill, NJ: Hampton Press.

Nero, S. (2002). Englishes, attitudes, education. *English Today, 18*(1), 53–56.

Ngugi. (1986). *Decolonising the mind: The politics of language in African literature.* Portsmouth, NH: Heinemann.

Paikeday, T. (1985). *The native speaker is dead!* Toronto: Paikeday.

Palacas, A. (2001). Liberating American Ebonics from Euro-English. *College English, 63*(3), 326–352.

Pennycook, A. (1994). *The cultural politics of English as an international language.* London: Longman.

Phillipson, R. (1992). *Linguistic imperialism.* Oxford: Oxford University Press.

Rampton, B. (1990). Displacing the "native speaker": Expertise, affiliation and inheritance. *English Language Teaching Journal, 44,* 97–101.

Rickford, J. (1999). *African American Vernacular English.* Malden, MA: Blackwell.

Roberts, P. (1988). *West Indians and their language.* Cambridge: Cambridge University Press.

Smitherman, G. (1977). *Talkin and testifyin: The language of Black America.* Boston: Houghton Mifflin.

Sridhar, S. (1994). A reality check for SLA theories. *TESOL Quarterly, 28,* 800–805.

Widdowson, H. G. (1994). The ownership of English. *TESOL Quarterly, 28,* 377–392.

Wolfram, W., Adger, C. T., & Christian, D. (1999). *Dialects in schools and communities.* Mahwah, NJ: Lawrence Erlbaum Associates.

Part I

WORLD ENGLISHES, CREOLES, AND EDUCATION

Chapter 1

World Englishes and Language Education

Yamuna Kachru
University of Illinois at Urbana-Champaign

KEY POINTS

- Reconceptualization of English Language Teaching (ELT) worldwide.
- Examination of methodologies, resources, sociolinguistic, and ideological concerns in ELT.
- Overreliance on Anglo-American models and expertise in language teaching and written language inappropriate for Asia and Africa.
- Need for openness and acceptance of language variation among educators.
- Call for implementation of more inclusive methodologies, materials, and curricula in ELT worldwide.

INTRODUCTION

One consequence of the unprecedented worldwide spread of English is that when we think of teaching English as a second, foreign or international language, we are confronted with two major questions: the conceptualization of what it means to teach English and the resources available for the enterprise (Kachru, 1997b).

There are two key issues in the area of determining what one means by English language education in any context. The crucial process of language education originates, as Strevens (1980) observes, ". . . in 'the public will'—in the sociolinguistic situation. The languages systematically taught in a given country are a reflection of the wishes and expectations of society" (p. 11). This is true of the demand for English language teaching worldwide as it is true of Chinese, Hindi, or French within its own national or regional context.

Since English is the most widely learned and taught language, this naturally raises the first issue, namely, that of which model of English teachers and texts are to be presented to the learners in a given situation. The second issue has to do with the implications of the choice of the model for the teaching and learning of English. These two bring in a host of related topics, including those of ownership of English (e.g., Widdowson, 1994), the relevance of the native speaker (e.g., Cook, 1999), questions of standard (e.g., Kachru, 1985; Quirk, 1985, 1988), competing ideologies (e.g., Ricento, 2000), and identity construction (e.g., Kachru, 2002; Ooi, 2001; Stubbe & Holmes, 1999).

As regards the resources for teaching English, there are three issues that need attention: contextually appropriate syllabus, methodologies, and materials. It may be useful to look at resources for two different contexts of language education, that of teacher training and that of language instruction. I will discuss both contexts briefly.[1]

Before I get into the discussion of issues raised above, a slight digression is necessary. The worldwide spread of English has been described in terms of three Circles of English: the Inner Circle, the Outer Circle and the Expanding Circle (Kachru, 1985). The Inner Circle refers to the mother country of English, England, and subsequently, the British Isles, North America, Australia and New Zealand where colonial administration and population migration took the language. The Outer Circle consists of the former colonies or territories of Britain and the US in Africa, South Asia, Southeast Asia and elsewhere; in these cases, large scale population migration of English speakers from Britain was not involved. The Expanding Circle characterizes Asian, European, Latin American and other countries that are adopting English increasingly for political and economic reasons. The labels Inner, Outer and Expanding are not meant to establish a hierarchy; they simply reflect the historical context of the origin and spread of the English language.[2] I will use the term Circles to refer to these regions in the subsequent discussion.

---

[1]Englishes spoken in the Caribbean, Melanesia, Polynesia, South America as well as the so-called non-standard varieties spoken in North America, the UK and other parts of the world are also part of World Englishes. The issues relevant to these varieties have been addressed elsewhere in this volume.

[2]Ghana, India, Kenya, Nigeria, Pakistan, the Philippines, Singapore, Sri Lanka, and others in this category are characterized as members of the Outer Circle whereas Brazil, China, Egypt, France, Germany, Italy, Japan, Korea, Malaysia, Saudi Arabia, Thailand, Turkey, Russia, Venezuela, and others that were British or American colonies are members of the Expanding Circle.

There are attempts to label a singular entity such as World English (Brutt-Griffler, 2002) or International English (Jenkins, 2000). These labels deny the pluricentricity of the medium and misdirect the research efforts at standardization of an abstraction (e.g., the phonology of International English as in Jenkins, 2000) at the cost of understanding the phenomenon of wide distribution and deep penetration of the medium across cultures. McArthur's (1998) characterization of monolithic models is worth repeating here:

> The monolithic, linear model that takes us from Old English through Middle English to Modern English (culminating with Darwinian elegance in the standard international language of newspapers and airports) has, it seems to me, been asked to bear more weight than it can reasonably support. The emergence, therefore, of plural, non-linear models is a positive development, among whose advantages are a more accurate depiction of the diversity in which we are embedded and also a more democratic approach to the social realities of English at the end of the twentieth century. (p. xvi)

ENGLISHES IN LANGUAGE EDUCATION

Linguists are well aware of the fact that terms such as language and dialect, though familiar, are difficult to define. What may be perceived as a language by one group may be considered a dialect by another, and what may be considered dialects may indeed be different languages in reality. The first case is illustrated by the example of Hindi and Urdu in India. They are mutually intelligible, share a basic phonology, grammar and vocabulary, and yet are considered two languages based primarily on the religious identities associated with the two labels and the two orthographies for writing—Devanagari for Hindi and Perso-Arabic for Urdu. The same is true of Norwegian and Swedish in Europe; they are mutually intelligible and share a great deal of their grammar, but are considered two separate languages. The second is exemplified by the so-called Chinese dialects that differ considerably from each other at all linguistic levels and are not mutually intelligible, and yet are considered the same language as they are united by a common civilization and writing system—the Chinese characters.

The diffusion of English beyond the British Isles in the past raised the issue of a separate identity for American English, hence the title of Mencken's description of American English, *The American Language* (1936). More recently, Australian English (AusE) has declared its independent identity with the publication of the *Macquarie Dictionary* and a number of grammatical descriptions of Australian English (e.g., Collins & Blair, 1989) and varieties within it (e.g., Horvath, 1985). Grammatical descriptions and dictionaries are arms of codification that firmly establish the existence of a language in society. Judging by the efforts under way for descriptions of other international varieties of English in Asia and Africa, especially in the Outer Circle countries, it is expected that a number of these will gain more recognition in the near future in spite of all the current controversies surrounding their emergence.

As varieties are codified and emerge as legitimate standard languages within their own national/regional boundaries, they are used in education, publication, print and audio-visual media and other domains of public and intellectual life. It would seem illogical even to suggest, for example, that Standard British English be taught in American schools or be adopted for publication of US books, newspapers, in broadcast journalism, etc.

THE QUESTION OF MODEL

The profession of English language teaching (ELT) has not had to face this issue seriously so far. Institutions of teacher education and publishing in the two powerful centers—the UK and the US—have relied on their own models of General American English (GAE) and Standard British English (BE). When English education was introduced in Asia, Africa and other parts of the world following colonization and military occupation, British and American authorities relied on their own countries' resources for starting the ELT ventures.[3] Recently, following trade-related expansion, Australia has been making inroads into ELT by providing facilities for teacher education in Australian institutions and sending its own model, material and ELT experts to different parts of the world.

Since the models of English teaching—especially the British and American English norms—are well-established, a question may arise as to why these should not continue. After all, they are well-established, with a tradition of codification in grammars and dictionaries, and there is a wealth of textbooks and educational resources already available in them. In addition, judging from the pronouncements of educational policymakers in many parts of the world, e.g., in India, Japan, Singapore, they are in favor of maintaining the status quo in their own countries anyway (see Quirk, 1985 & 1988, for an articulation of this position).

There is, however, increasing realization among ELT professionals and the users of English of the gap that has appeared between the traditional

---

[3]This is what happened when American forces occupied the Philippines in late nineteenth century and Japan following World War II. Following the Korean War, English education was revived in Korea under the American influence. In the colonies of Africa and Asia, English education was imposed by the British empire and was later adopted and adapted by the independent nations of the regions as a result of their own internal needs and aspirations. For a detailed discussion of these historical facts, see Baik (1995), Bamgbose (1971), Gonzalez (1997), Ike (1995), B. Kachru (1983), Rahman (1990), among others.

practices and new sociolinguistic realities of English language education in many parts of the world. Reliance on the models of GAE, BE, and AusE are understandable in their own contexts in view of the sociolinguistic reality of the US, the UK and Australia. It becomes problematic when the models are transported to Asia and Africa and there is expectation that India, Nigeria and Singapore will somehow become GAE, BE or AusE-speaking countries forgetting their own histories of English language and literature that are at least as old as that of America, and certainly older than that of Australia (see Ashcroft, Griffiths & Tiffin, 1989; Baumgardner, 1996; B. Kachru, 1986a, 1986b; Talib, 2002; Thumboo, 2001, among others).

In this connection, it is worth remembering what Marckwardt (1942) observed: The acceptance of one type of speech over another as standard is not based upon linguistic considerations; it is based upon political, cultural, and economic factors, and ". . . it is a mistaken attitude to ascribe to the standard any logical, aesthetic, or functional virtue which it does not possess" (p. 310). Furthermore, London English may be a satisfactory standard for most Southern English speakers, but "there is no excuse for its adoption in New York, Chicago, Atlanta, or San Francisco, when these cities in themselves constitute powerful centers which affect in many ways the behavior of the inhabitants within their sphere of influence" (p. 309). The same is true of Delhi, Lagos and Singapore. They are powerful centers in their own region and are quite capable of evaluating what is better, more correct or more appropriate for their own purposes. That is to say, if the new contexts of America and Australia led to the development of distinct Englishes in these regions in spite of shared ethnicity, culture and civilization, it is reasonable to conclude that the same will apply in the very different sociocultural contexts of Asia, Africa and other parts of the world that have their own distinct ethnicities, cultures and civilizations.

The fact that there are distinct varieties of Indian, Nigerian, Philippine and Singaporean Englishes has been established beyond a doubt by users of these varieties.[4] In addition, there are well-established creoles such as Jamaican Creole in the Caribbean and Tok Pisin in Melanesia, and nonstandard languages such as African American English in the US that are recognized for their vital role in the national life of their respective regions and

---

[4]Not only have these varieties been described, there has been a long tradition of literary creativity in these varieties. The list of prestigious prizes and awards to writers from these regions includes: the Nobel prize in literature to Wole Soyinka (Nigeria) in 1986, Derek Alton Walcott (St. Lucia) in 1992, V. S. Naipaul (Trinidad) in 2001. The Booker Prize has been awarded to Keri Hulme (Maori writer, New Zealand 1985), Chinua Achebe (Nigeria) in 1987, Micahel Ondaatje (Sri Lanka) in 1992, Ben Okri (Nigeria) in 1991, Salman Rushdie (India) in 1995, and Arundhati Roy (India) in 1997. The Pulitzer Prize has been awarded to Jhumpa Lahiri (India) in 2001, and the Neustadt Prize to Raja Rao (India) in 1988. See Kachru (1992), Schneider (1997b), Thumboo (2001), among others for references.

the education of their children. What are the implications of this reality for the ELT profession? ELT professionals and linguists have been interested in creoles and their educational implications for some time now (e.g., works such as Nero, 2001, in the US and much earlier and continuing work of linguists and educators in the Caribbean and the Pacific regions with respect to nonstandard dialects in Australia). The same cannot be said for world varieties of English except for researchers interested in studying the Englishes of the Outer and Expanding Circles (see, however, Brown, 1995; Brown, 2001; Brown & Baumgardner, 2001; Brown & Peterson, 1997; Kachru, 1997b).

IMPLICATIONS FOR ELT

Resolving the issue of model is not as simple as deciding whether General American English (GAE) is appropriate for the US and Singaporean English (SgE) is appropriate for Singapore. There are a host of other issues that arise: sociolinguistic, educational, and ideological. And then there is the pragmatic issue of implementation of decisions that are taken in view of the above considerations.

Sociolinguistic Concerns

When we talk of GAE or BE or Indian English (IE), it is clear that these represent abstractions. Within the United States, there are various regional, social and ethnic dialects. One ethnic dialect that has gained a great deal of attention over the years and has recently led to a visible impact on education in several regions of the US is the variety known variously as African American Vernacular English (AAVE), Ebonics, or African American Language (AAL), (see Pandey, 2000b, for references). The distinctness of AAL has been well established in linguistic descriptions and literary creativity (see, e.g., Green, 2002; Labov, 1972; Lanehart, 2001; Lippi-Green, 1997; Mufwene, Rickford, Bailey, & Baugh, 1998; Smitherman, 1977). As AAL-speaking children are socialized within their speech community, it is difficult for them to make a sudden transition to GAE when they enter school. And yet, they have to become proficient in this variety in order to function effectively in national life. As Pandey (2000a) argues, there is considerable justification for teaching GAE to speakers of AAL as a second language *employing a bilingual method* of teaching in order to facilitate the transition. The phrase emphasized above is crucial, but I will come back to this later.

The same situation applies to speakers of world Englishes with a difference. As was said before, for AAL speakers, it is essential to become proficient in GAE as they have to interact with other ethnic groups in all spheres of economic and political activity. For users of Indian, Nigerian, Pakistani, Philippine, Singaporean or other Outer and Expanding Circle Englishes, it is not necessary that everyone become familiar with GAE or BE. Most of the users of these varieties need English to interact with their own compatriots or within their own region such as Asia, South Asia, Southeast Asia, East Africa, or West Africa, depending on the sphere of their activity. Only a section of the population engaged in international activities need be familiar with other varieties, including varieties such as Euro-English, the emerging variety in the European Union (Cenoz & Jessner, 2000; Modiano, 1996).

In fact, in China, Japan, Malaysia, Korea and other Expanding Circle countries in Asia, just as in the Outer Circle countries such as India, Pakistan, the Philippines and Singapore, there is growing realization that they have their own distinct varieties of English (e.g., see Honna & Takeshita, 1998, 2000; Kachru, 1997a; Matsuda, 2003; Shim, 1999; Takeshita, 2000; Zhang, 2003). And deliberations by linguists, creative writers and educators show awareness of their own creative potential in language and confidence in recommending the teaching of their own varieties with transition to the other Asian and world varieties such as IE, SgE, Euro-English, GAE or BE where necessary. For instance, Takeshita (2001) observes:

There is a need for English teachers with various linguistic and cultural backgrounds who will prepare students for the multilingual and multicultural experiences that they will definitely encounter in the future if they wish to utilize their English ability as educated Japanese citizens in the global community. (p. 38)

There is also greater assertion of identities of regional varieties. For instance, the Philippine writer Jose (1997) emphasizes using material that writers know firsthand and asserts:

I have expunged the word "summer" from my writing unless it is in the context of four seasons. . . . Because there is no summer in this country. We have a dry season, wet season, rainy season, dusty season, but never, never "summer." (p. 168)

The Malaysian writer Raslan (2000) observes:

We can appropriate and reinvent the language to our own ends. . . . The rhythm of things—you have to get that. . . . If the Indians can do it in Indian English, I don't see why we can't do it in Malaysian English. It is all a matter of confidence. . . . It is rather like an artificial limb which you turn to your own advantage. We should not be so constrained by the fact that it was the language of our oppressors. If we want to think of it as the language of our oppressors, then it will oppress us. (pp. 188–189)

Writers from South Asia and Africa declared their independence from the Anglo-American linguistic hegemony and literary canonicity beginning in the early decades of the 20th century (see Ashcroft et al., 1989; Kachru, 1986a, 1998, 2001; Talib, 2002, among others for references).

Educational Concerns

It is true that increasingly English teaching materials are produced locally in India, Pakistan, and other Outer Circle countries. There is, still, however, reliance on Inner Circle Experts, especially agencies such as the British Council, for feedback of various sorts. And almost all reference materials are being produced in the West. This is partly due to lack of confidence among policymakers and ELT professionals of the Outer Circle trained in the Anglo-American institutions of ELT education, and partly due to the enormous amount of investment by the Inner Circle in maintaining the ELT Market. After all, ELT, with teacher education programs, experts for exports and publications of teaching and reference materials has immense potential for the sluggish economies of the Anglo-American complex. As pointed out in *EFL Gazette* of March 1989, "the worldwide market for EFL training is worth a massive 6.25 billion pounds sterling a year, according to a new report from the Economic Intelligence Unit." Promotion of Inner Circle models for teaching and learning English thus is of vital economic importance to the UK, the US, and Australia.

The people of the Outer and Expanding Circle, as has been mentioned above, have realized the limitations of the existing paradigms of ELT. It is now the responsibility of the ELT profession to evaluate the ethical aspect of existing ELT practices and fulfill the global needs of the people.

Ideological Concerns

Ethical considerations lead to ideological issues involved in ELT. One of the problems in promoting effective ELT in the Outer and Expanding Circle is the ethnocentricism of the applied linguistics and ELT professions. This is reflected in the approaches and methodologies of communicative language teaching and language for special purposes instructions. The goals of these approaches have always emphasized the competence of native speaker–hearer, i.e., speaker–hearer of GAE or BE. As the Puerto Rican writer Pedro Pietri comments, this has led to most multilingual learners of English feeling that "[they] were not educated in those schools; [they] came out semiliterate. Sometimes totally illiterate" (Hernandez, 1997). In the context of Asia, as Honna and Takeshita (1998) note:

> The unrealistic English teaching model of expecting American English as the outcome of English instruction in Japan prevents students from taking an active part in real communication in English—they are afraid of not speaking "correctly" and "appropriately" like native speakers of English. (p. 136)

There is very little to no awareness that most Japanese now interact with Chinese, Singaporean, Korean, Thai and Indian speakers of English in their business dealings, or that most Indian, Pakistani, Bangladeshi and Sri Lankan speakers interact in English within their own region of South Asia.[5] Native speaker competence for them means competence in their own varieties and the goal of effective communication for them is to successfully interact within their own sphere(s) of activity. Their interaction may not involve any Anglo-American speaker–hearer of English at all. They need to be comfortable with the conventions of language use within their own context—Asian, African, or whatever. Anglo-American, Australian or European conventions of language use is thus not of exclusive importance in most of Asia, Africa or Latin America.

Implications for Practice

The implications are several: change in attitudes and perceptions, emphasis on more openness and acceptance of variation among educators, search for suitable methodologies and materials, and pragmatic aspects of implementation of the new curricula at all levels of English education. Above all, the profession has to rise beyond the Anglo-American ethnocentricism in ELT.

The first task is for institutions of teacher education in the Inner Circle centers of ELT to adopt a curriculum that encourages respect for all varieties of English (Brown, 1995; Brown, 2001; Brown & Baumgardner, 2003; Brown & Peterson, 1997). As a Japanese Executive of the International Energy Agency demanded in a piece published in *International Herald Tribune*, November 3, 1995:

---

[5]According to the figures published by the Ministry of Public Management, Home Affairs, Posts and Telecommunication of Japan, Japan's trade with Asian countries is more than double that of its trade with the US and the European Union combined. China, rather than the US, is its single largest trade partner.

We non-natives are desperately learning English; each word pronounced by us represents our blood, sweat and tears. Our English proficiency is tangible evidence of our achievement of will, not an accident. Dear Anglo-Americans, please show us you are also taking pains to make yourselves understood in an international setting. (Mikie Kiyoi, cited in McArthur, 1998, p. 211)

In this connection, let us look at some powerful arms of control of the profession. The first powerful arm of the profession is the ELT graduate programs in the US and UK. In the US alone there are about 150 such programs, varying widely in terms of academic excellence. A number of them award Master's degrees; a small number, about twenty-five, award Bachelor's degrees. However, increasingly, such programs are initiating interdisciplinary Ph.D. programs; there are about thirty such Ph.D. programs. A study by Vavrus (1991) explored whether "teacher trainees are receiving information about IVEs [Institutionalized Varieties of English]" (p. 185). On the basis of a restricted survey, she found that ". . . only UH and UIUC [Universities of Hawai'i and Illinois at Urbana-Champaign] have elective courses that emphasize non-native varieties of English" (p. 186).[6]

The second arm of control is the publishing industry. Professional journals occupy a central position in the continuing education of teachers and provide crucial information about the state of the art of the profession to all sectors involved in English language-related activities. B. Kachru (1997a) surveyed two leading professional journals, one British and one North American, for five years (1986–1990): *Applied Linguistics* and *TESOL Quarterly*. The results of his rather quick content analysis of the two journals are in Table 1.1.

The attitude seems to be that the Inner Circle provides the expertise and the rest of the world is only fit to consume what is produced in the Inner Circle. There are centers of English language publication in Hong Kong, India, Singapore, and other parts of the world, which have been contributing to the general scholarship in English studies for decades. By not reviewing what is produced in these parts of the world in the journals of the profession, by not inviting Asian, African and other scholars to serve on the editorial boards of the journals, by not publishing their submissions of research on the pretext of their writing conventions being circular or not conforming to the argumentative writing in the Anglo-American tradition, applied linguistics in general and English studies in

---

[6]Since the 1991 survey, many more universities in the US and elsewhere have started independent courses in World Englishes or incorporated the concept in other courses, e.g., Indiana State University at Terre Haute, State University of New York at Stony Brook, Purdue University, Portland State University, St. John's University in New York, University of Hawai'i at Honolulu, among others. Chukyo University at Nagoya, Japan has recently established a College of World Englishes and a Department of World Englishes within the College.

TABLE 1.1
Representation of Regions in Journals

Item	TESOL Quarterly	Applied Linguistics
1. Total articles published	118	106
2. Articles from Asia/Africa	2	7
3. Total book reviews/notices	117	18
4. Reviews of books published in Asia/Africa		
5. Review of books by Asian/African authors	1	
6. Books reviewed on topics related to world Englishes/nonnative Englishes/world literatures in English (Asian/African)		

particular misses out on the breadth and depth of perspectives from scholars outside of the Inner Circle.

What is true of journals is also true of reference materials such as encyclopedias and handbooks. International for most publications by American and British publishers means scholars from the UK, the US, occasionally from Western Europe, and a token or two, if that, from Japan or some part of Asia or Africa. As Kachru (2002) points out, one such encyclopedia on a major branch of applied linguistics is a 758-page volume entitled the *Encyclopedia of Bilingualism and Bilingual Education* edited by Colin Baker and Sylvia Prys Jones, published by Multilingual Matters (1998). This project was considered "an internationally significant event" (p. vii), its significance enhanced by its scope as ". . . around two-thirds of the world's population are bilingual" (p. vii). The volume is intended for international readership "to share *different perspectives* . . . the *views* of language minorities and language majorities *faithfully,* and to *represent* different political agendas" (p. viii).

The international goals of the encyclopedia are discussed in four major sections and appendices and the sections include a total of over 130 subsections. In addition, "for those who wish to dig deeper a Bibliography of over 2000 entries is provided . . ." (p. viii). As Kachru says, "This volume then is an ambitious source of knowledge on one of the most vibrant issues in contemporary societies in practically every part of the world." The question arises: how representative is this particular source of knowledge of the bilingual world of Asia and Africa that comprises over four billion people (two thirds of the world population) out of a total population of over six billion? In other words, who is assigned the representational power of defining the African and Asian bilingual world, their visions and voices, and the constructs of their societies? What representational power is, for example, in the hands of African and Asian scholars of multilingualism? What representation is given to the scholars from the regions with a long tradition of

TABLE 1.2
Profile of Volume on Bilingualism and Bilingual Education

Editors	2, both from UK
Consulting Editors	16, none from Africa, 1 Japanese
Experts ("Who gave their expertise with particular topics, queries or requests . . .")	Over 94% non-African/non-Asian
Experts (Organizations)	All non-African/non-Asian
Authors (A significant number cited for further reading)	580: an overwhelming number non-African/non-Asian
Bibliography (over 2000 items)	90% non-African/non-Asian

bilingualism who have worked on its role in education, language policies and planning, literary creativity, and social interaction?

The architects of such volumes work at different levels, as editors, consulting editors and as contributors or experts. It is they who have the representational and interpretive power. They determine the authentication and appropriateness of the sources on which analyses are made and a speech community is constructed and defined. They determine the methodological and conceptual frameworks.

The profile of the encyclopedia shown in Table 1.2 is illuminating. This profile gives us some indication of the underlying voices that represent, interpret and authenticate the knowledge embodied in this international resource on bilingualism. Note that even the 6–10% in experts consulted or scholars cited in the volumes from Asia and Africa may not be Asian or African at all; they may be expatriate Anglo-American/European scholars working in these regions.

A recently published resource for applied linguistics, *The Oxford Handbook of Applied Linguistics,* edited by Kaplan (2002) provides yet another telling example of the power of (re)interpreting knowledge: in this case applied linguistics. The contributors "are drawn from diverse backgrounds" that reflect "diversity," of which "45 percent are drawn from countries other than the United States." These countries are: Australia, Belgium, Canada, Hungary, the Netherlands, and the United Kingdom (p. vi). This then is the vision of the global world applied linguistics and the ELT profession share! The profession needs to be reminded of Widdowson's warning (1994): "I think we need to be cautious about the designs we have on other people's worlds when we are busy designing our own."[7]

One consequence of the narrow perspective evident in formulating the global in this manner is that the theories and methodologies developed in the field lack universality and legitimacy and remain culture and context-

---

[7]The discussion of the Encyclopedia and Handbook is based on B. Kachru (2002). See also B. Kachru (in press, and forthcoming).

bound. For instance, conceptualizations such as interlanguage, fossiliza-
tion, error, pragmatic failure, ESP-propelled genre analysis, etc. have no validity or application in the context of world Englishes, and in the contexts
of legitimate ethnic varieties such as AAL, or Caribbean and Melanesian
Englishes, and yet these are the reigning paradigms of research in the field.

In teaching methodologies, it is time to revive the bilingual method of
teaching to facilitate transition between languages or varieties as the case
may be. Code-mixing and switching have a legitimate place in the multilingual's repertoire just as switching between registers and styles has its functions in a monolingual's linguistic behavior. There is no reason to stigma-
tize mixing and switching; in fact, these can be exploited for effective
language teaching as can translation between languages and varieties. The
experiences of Caribbean communities, Mexican Americans, AAL-speakers
and others are rich sources to draw upon for teaching materials. Encouraging language awareness is a methodologically sound practice in language
teaching within the USA. The same applies in Asian and African contexts
where local varieties need to be juxtaposed with Inner Circle varieties to
create language awareness and strengthen identity construction in terms of
Chinese, Indian, Japanese, Nigerian, Philippine or Singaporean English
speakers. The success of the ELT operation has to be measured in terms of
what Baxter (1980) says about the Japanese context:

> [S]peaking English Japanese-ly goes beyond strictly linguistic elements; it is a
> manner of speaking English that does not threaten the speaker nor come into
> conflict with this person's identity as a Japanese. It is also the means by which
> a Japanese can say, 'I'm an English speaker.' (p. 52)

This is what the World Englishes paradigm means by the term communicative competence.

Resources for Curriculum Development

Five components of World Englishes curriculum are worth considering.
The topics are for both English language classrooms, depending on the
level of instruction, and teacher education programs. The topics under
"Pedagogical concerns" are of two types: the topics listed under both a and
b are for teacher education programs whereas only the ones listed under a
are for the English language classrooms.

1. The concept World Englishes: motivations for a pluralistic model—
   linguistic, sociolinguistic, pragmatic, pedagogical.
2. Historical, political, and economic background of the spread of English.

3. Processes of acculturation, nativization and Englishization and their impact on English and local languages (for impact of English on local languages, see Kachru, 1986a; Smith, 1987; Thumboo, 2001, among others).

4. The medium and the message: one medium adapted to varied messages conforming to local sociocultural contexts; the relevance of society and culture to linguistic structure and language use.

5. Pedagogical concerns:

   a. Choice of norms and models.

      Attitudes toward varieties and norms.

      Issues in standards and codification.

      The lectal range in Englishes.

      Effect of attitudes and other external factors on policy decisions.

      Goals of instruction.

      Definitions of linguistic proficiency and communicative competence.

      Issues of intelligibility across varieties.

   b. Qualification of teachers.

      Choice of methods: English only or bilingual, including code-mixing and switching.

      Communicative Language Teaching, Language for Special Purposes, Genre-based, and other such approaches.

      Appropriacy of materials.

      Issues in teaching, textbooks, and classroom practices.

      Goals of testing.

      Instruments of testing.

CONCLUSION

Bringing world Englishes into the classroom may be a challenging task, but its rewards are obvious: a more just and equal partnership between the Circles. We already have a group of well-trained and experienced educators of Englishes around the world who are ready to share their expertise (Braine, 1999; Seidlhofer, 1999). And we have resources in terms of linguistic descriptions and other reference materials, including considerations in test constructions (Lowenberg, 1992, 1993). As in the spheres of economics, diplomacy and politics, in education, too, the world has to become truly global. English language educators are in a unique position to play a crucial role in this arena if the ELT profession shows willingness to shed its ethnocentrism and adopt a global perspective.

Suggested Further Readings

The following anthologies cover most of these topics and additional resources are available in journals such as *Asian Englishes, English Today, English World Wide and World Englishes*: Bailey and Görlach (1982), Bamgbose, Banjo & Thomas (1995), Baumgardner (1993, 1996), Bautista (1997), Bolton (2002, 2003), Cheshire (1991), B. Kachru (1982, 1992, 1986a, 1986b, 1997b), Jenkins (2003), Y. Kachru & Nelson (in press), McArthur (1992), Melcher & Shaw (2003), Newbrook (1999), Pakir (1993), Platt, Weber, & Ho (1984), Said & Ng (2000), Schneider (1997a, 1997b), Smith (1981, 1987), Smith & Forman (1997), Stanlaw (2003), Tay (1993), Thumboo (2001), Tickoo (1995a, 1995b), among others.

QUESTIONS FOR DISCUSSION AND REFLECTIVE WRITING

1. Kachru raises the critical question of which models of English are appropriate in various contexts. With a partner, discuss this question in light of Phillipson's notion of linguistic imperialism alluded to in the introduction to this volume.

2. The author raises sociolinguistic, educational, and ideological concerns in ELT. Which of these concerns are most important in your particular teaching context, and what steps can be taken to address them?

3. Write a reflective journal in response to any one of the various sections of this chapter (use the section headings as your guide). What questions does this section raise for you? What new knowledge have you gained?

REFERENCES

Ashcroft, B., Griffiths, G., & Tiffin, H. (1989). *The empire writes back: Theory and practice in postcolonial literature. New accents.* London: Routledge.

Baik, M. J. (1995). *Language, ideology, and power: English textbooks of two Koreas.* Seoul: Thaehaksa.

Bailey, R. W., & Görlach, M. (Eds.). (1982). *English as a world language.* Ann Arbor: University of Michigan Press.

Baker, C., & Jones, S. P. (Eds.). (1998). *Encyclopedia of bilingualism and bilingual education.* Clevedon, England: Multilingual Matters.

Bamgbose, A. (1971). The English language in Nigeria. In J. Spencer (Ed.), *The English language in West Africa* (pp. 35–48). London: Longman.

Bamgbose, A., Banjo, A., & Thomas, A. (Eds.). (1995). *New Englishes: A West African perspective.* Ibadan: Mosuro.

Baumgardner, R. J. (Ed.). (1993). *The English language in Pakistan*. Karachi: Oxford University Press.

Baumgardner, R. J. (Ed.). (1996). *South Asian English: Structure, use, and users*. Urbana: University of Illinois Press.

Bautista, M. L. S. (Ed.). (1997). *English is an Asian language: The Philippine context*. Sydney, Australia: Macquarie Library.

Baxter, J. (1980). How should I speak English? American-ly, Japanese-ly or internationally? *The Japan Association for Language Teaching Journal*, 2, 31–61.

Bolton, K. (Ed.). (2002). *Hong Kong English: Autonomy and creativity*. In K. Bolton (Series Ed.), *Asian Englishes today*. Hong Kong: Hong Kong University Press.

Bolton, K. (2003). *Chinese Englishes: A sociolinguistic history*. In the series *Studies in English language*. Cambridge: Cambridge University Press.

Braine, G. (Ed.). (1999). *Non-native educators in English language teaching*. Mahwah, NJ: Lawrence Erlbaum Associates.

Brown, K. (1995). World Englishes: To teach? Or not to teach? *World Englishes*, *14*(2), 233–245.

Brown, K. (2001). World Englishes and the classroom: Research and practice agendas for 2000. In E. Thumboo (Ed.), *The three circles of English* (pp. 371–382). Singapore: UniPress.

Brown, K., & Baumgardner, R. J. (2003). World Englishes: Ethics and pedagogy. *World Englishes*, *22*(3), 245–251.

Brown, K., & Peterson, J. (1997). Exploring conceptual frameworks: Framing a world Englishes paradigm. In L. Smith & M. Forman (Eds.), *World Englishes 2000* (pp. 32–47). Honolulu: University of Hawai'i Press.

Brutt-Griffler, J. (2002). *World English: A study of its development*. Clevedon, UK: Multilingual Matters.

Cenoz, J., & Jessner, U. (Eds.). (2000). *English in Europe: The acquisition of a third language*. Clevedon: Multilingual Matters.

Cheshire, J. (Ed.). (1991). *English around the world: Sociolinguistic perspectives*. Cambridge: Cambridge University Press.

Collins, P., & Blair, D. (Eds.). (1989). *Australian English: The language of new society*. St. Lucia: University of Queensland Press. (Reprinted in the series on *Varieties of English around the world*, Vol. 15, Amsterdam: John Benjamins)

Cook, V. (1999). Going beyond the native speaker in language teaching. *TESOL Quarterly*, *33*(2), 185–209.

Gonzalez, A. (1997). The history of English in the Philippines. In M. L. S. Bautista (Ed.), *English is an Asian language: The Philippine context* (pp. 25–40). Sydney, Australia: Macquarie Library.

Green, L. J. (2002). *African American English: A linguistic introduction*. Cambridge: Cambridge University Press.

Hernandez, C. D. (1997). *Puerto Rican voices in English: Interviews with writers*. Westport, CT: Praeger.

Honna, N., & Takeshita, Y. (1998). On Japan's propensity for native speaker English: A change in sight. *Asian Englishes*, *1*(1), 117–137.

Honna, N., & Takeshita, Y. (2000). English language teaching for international understanding in Japan. *EA Journal*, *18*(1), 60–78.

Horvath, B. (1985). *Variation in Australian English: The sociolects of Sydney*. Cambridge: Cambridge University Press.

Ike, M. (1995). A historical review of English in Japan. *World Englishes*, *14*(1), 3–11.

Jenkins, J. (2000). *The phonology of English as an international language*. Oxford University Press.

Jenkins, J. (2003). *World Englishes: A resource book for students*. London: Routledge.

Jose, F. S. (1997). Standards in Philippine English: The writer's forum. In M. L. S. Bautista (Ed.), *English is an Asian language: The Philippine context* (pp. 167–169). Sydney, Australia: Macquarie Library.

Kachru, B. (Ed.). (1982). *The other tongue: English across cultures.* Urbana, IL: University of Illinois Press. (Paperback by Pergamon Press, Oxford, UK, 1983)

Kachru, B. (1983). *The Indianization of English: The English language in India.* New Delhi: Oxford University Press.

Kachru, B. (1985). Standards, codification and sociolinguistic realism: The English language in the outer circle. In R. Quirk & H. Widdowson (Eds.), *English in the world: Teaching and learning the language and literatures* (pp. 11–30). Cambridge: Cambridge University Press.

Kachru, B. (1986a). *The alchemy of English: The spread, functions and models of non-native Englishes.* Oxford, UK: Pergamon Press. (South Asian edition by Oxford University Press, New Delhi; reprinted by University of Illinois Press, Urbana-Champaign. In the series *English in the global contexts,* 1990)

Kachru, B. (1986b). Non-native literatures in English as a resource for language teaching. In R. Carter & C. Brumfit (Eds.), *Literature and language teaching* (pp. 140–149). London: Oxford University Press.

Kachru, B. (Ed.). (1992). *The other tongue: English across cultures* (2nd rev. ed.). Urbana: University of Illinois Press.

Kachru, B. (1996). The paradigms of marginality. *World Englishes, 15*(3), 241–255.

Kachru, B. (1997a). Past-imperfect: The other side of English in Asia. In L. Smith & M. Forman (Eds.), *World Englishes 2000* (pp. 68–89). Honolulu: University of Hawai'i Press.

Kachru, B. (1997b). World Englishes 2000: Resources for research and teaching. In L. Smith & M. Forman (Eds.), *World Englishes 2000* (pp. 209–251). Honolulu: University of Hawai'i Press.

Kachru, B. (1998). Raja Rao: *Madhyama* and *Mantra.* In R. Hardgrave (Ed.), *Word as mantra: The art of Raja Rao* (pp. 60–87). New Delhi: Katha.

Kachru, B. (2001). World Englishes and culture wars. In R. Goh et al. (Eds.), *Ariels-departures and returns* (pp. 391–414). Singapore: Oxford University Press.

Kachru, B. (2002). On nativizing *Mantra*: Identity construction in anglophone Englishes. In R. Ahrens, D. Parker, K. Stierstorfer & K-K Tam (Eds.), *Anglophone cultures in Southeast Asia: Appropriations, continuities, contexts* (pp. 55–72). Heidelberg, Germany: Heidelberg University Press.

Kachru, B. (in press). *Asian Englishes: Beyond the canon.* In K. Bolton (Series Ed.), *Asian Englishes today.* Hong Kong: Hong Kong University Press.

Kachru, B. (forthcoming). *World Englishes and culture wars.* Cambridge: Cambridge University Press.

Kachru, Y., & Nelson, C. L. (in press). *World Englishes in Asian contexts.* In K. Bolton (Series Ed.), *Asian Englishes today.* Hong Kong: Hong Kong University Press.

Kaplan, R. (Ed.). (2002). *The Oxford handbook of applied linguistics.* Oxford: Oxford University Press.

Labov, W. (1972). *Language in the inner city.* Philadelphia: University of Pennsylvania Press.

Lanehart, S. L. (Ed.). (2001). *Sociocultural and historical contexts of African American English.* In *Varieties of English around the world* (General Series No. 27). Amsterdam: John Benjamins.

Lippi-Green, R. (1997). *English with an accent.* New York: Routledge.

Lowenberg, P. H. (1992). Testing English as a world language: Issues in assessing non-native proficiency. In B. Kachru (Ed.), *The other tongue: English across cultures* (2nd rev. ed., pp. 108–121). Urbana: University of Illinois Press.

Lowenberg, P. H. (1993). Issues of validity in tests of English as a world language: Whose standards? *World Englishes, 12*(1), 95–106.

Marckwardt, A. H. (1942). *Introduction to the English language.* New York: Oxford University Press.

Matsuda, A. (2003). The ownership of English in Japanese secondary schools. *World Englishes, 22*(4), 483–496.

McArthur, T. (Ed.). (1992). *The Oxford companion to the English language.* Oxford: Oxford University Press.

McArthur, T. (1998). *The English languages.* Cambridge, UK: Cambridge University Press.

Melcher, G., & Shaw, P. (2003). *World Englishes: An introduction. The English language series.* London: Arnold.

Mencken, H. L. (1936). *The American language: An inquiry into the development of English in the United States* (4th ed.). New York: Knopf.

Modiano, M. (1996). The Americanization of Euro-English. *World Englishes, 15,* 207–215.

Mufwene, S., Rickford, J., Bailey, G., & Baugh, J. (Eds.). (1998). *African-American English: Structure, history and use.* New York: Routledge.

Nero, S. (2001). *Englishes in contact: Anglophone Caribbean students in an urban college.* Cresskill, NJ: Hampton Press.

Newbrook, M. (Ed.). (1999). *English is an Asian language: The Thai context.* Sydney, Australia: The Macquarie Library.

Ooi, V. B. Y. (Ed.). (2001). *Evolving identities: The English language in Singapore and Malaysia.* Singapore: Times Academic Press.

Pakir, A. (1993). *The English language in Singapore: Standards and norms.* Singapore: UniPress and Centre for the Arts, National University of Singapore.

Pandey, A. (2000a). TOEFL to the test: Are monodialectal AAL speakers similar to ESL students? *World Englishes, 19*(1), 89–106.

Pandey, A. (Ed.). (2000b). Symposium on the Ebonics debate and African American language. *World Englishes, 19*(1), 1–106.

Platt, J., Weber, H., & Ho, M. L. (1984). *The new Englishes.* London: Routledge & Kegan Paul.

Quirk, R. (1985). The English language in a global context. In R. Quirk & H. Widdowson (Eds.), *English in the world: Teaching and learning the language and literatures* (pp. 1–6). Cambridge: Cambridge University Press.

Quirk, R. (1988). The question of standards in the international use of English. In P. Lowenberg (Ed.), *Language spread and language policy: Issues, implications and case studies* (pp. 229–241). Washington, DC: Georgetown University Press.

Rahman, T. (1990). *Pakistani English: The linguistic description of a non-native variety of English* (NIPS Monograph Series 3). Islamabad: National Institute of Pakistan Studies.

Raslan, K. (2000). Writing fiction. In H. M. Said & K. S. Ng (Eds.), *English is an Asian language: The Malaysian context* (pp. 188–189). Kuala Lumpur: Persatuan Bahasa Moden Malaysia and the Macquarie Library.

Ricento, T. (Ed.). (2000). *Ideologies, politics and language policies: Focus on English.* Amsterdam: John Benjamins.

Said, H. M., & Ng, K. S. (Eds.). (2000). *English is an Asian language: The Malaysian context.* Kuala Lumpur: Persatuan Bahasa Moden Malaysia and The Macquarie Library.

Schneider, E. W. (Ed.). (1997a). *Englishes around the world 1. General studies, British Isles, North America: Studies in honour of Manfred Görlach.* Amsterdam: John Benjamins.

Schneider, E. W. (Ed.). (1997b). *Englishes around the world 2. Caribbean, Africa, Asia, Australasia: Studies in honour of Manfred Görlach.* Amsterdam: John Benjamins.

Seidlhofer, B. (1999). Double standards: Teacher education in the expanding circle. *World Englishes, 18*(2), 233–245.

Shim, R. J. (1999). Codified Korean English: Process, characteristics, and consequences. *World Englishes, 18*(2), 247–258.

Smith, L. E. (Ed.). (1981). *English for cross-cultural communication.* London: Macmillan.

Smith, L. E. (Ed.). (1987). *Discourse across cultures: Strategies in World Englishes.* New York: Prentice-Hall.

Smith, L. E., & Forman, M. (Eds.). (1997). *World Englishes 2000.* Honolulu: University of Hawai'i Press.

Smitherman, G. (1977). *Talkin and testifyin.* New York: Houghton Mifflin.

Stanlaw, J. (2003). *Japanese English: Language and culture contact.* In K. Bolton (Series Ed.), *Asian Englishes today.* Hong Kong: Hong Kong University Press.

Strevens, P. (1980). *Teaching English as an international language.* Oxford: Pergamon.

Stubbe, M., & Holmes, J. (1999). Talking Maori or Pakeha in English: Signaling identity in discourse. In A. Bell & K. Kuiper (Eds.), *New Zealand English* (pp. 249–278). *Varieties of English around the world* (Vol. 25). Amsterdam: John Benjamins.

Takeshita, Y. (2000). Japanese English as a variety of Asian Englishes and Japanese students of English. *Asian English Studies* (Monograph No. 1, pp. 1–10). (Also in *Language innovation and cultural change, 1,* 1–8)

Takeshita, Y. (2001). Japanese students' perception of the English language and its study—In search of a new direction. *Asian Englishes, 4*(2), 24–40.

Talib, I. S. (2002). *The language of postcolonial literatures: An introduction.* London: Routledge.

Tay, M. W. J. (Ed.). (1993). *The English language in Singapore: Issues and development.* Singapore: UniPress.

Thumboo, E. (Ed.). (2001). *The three circles of English.* Singapore: UniPress.

Tickoo, M. L. (1995a). Authenticity as a cultural concern: A view from the Asian English-language classroom. In M. L. Tickoo (Ed.), *Language and culture in multilingual societies: Viewpoints and visions* (Anthology Series 36). Singapore: SEAMEO Regional Language Center.

Tickoo, M. L. (Ed.). (1995b). *Language and culture in multilingual societies: Viewpoints and visions* (Anthology Series 36). Singapore: SEAMEO Regional Language Center.

Vavrus, F. (1991). When paradigms clash: The role of institutionalized varieties in language teacher education. *World Englishes, 10*(2), 181–195.

Widdowson, H. G. (1994). The ownership of English. *TESOL Quarterly, 28,* 377–392.

Zhang, H. (2003). *Chinese Englishes: History, contexts, and texts.* Unpublished doctoral dissertation. Urbana: University of Illinois.

Chapter 2

Keeping Creoles and Dialects Out of the Classroom: Is It Justified?

Jeff Siegel
University of New England (Australia)
and
University of Hawai'i

KEY POINTS

- Critical examination of barring Creoles and dialects from the class-room.
- Discussion of four categories of reasons for resisting vernacular use in the classroom: (1) beliefs about the nature of vernacular varieties, (2) misconceptions about the nature of educational programs using vernacular varieties, (3) concerns about the detrimental effects of using the vernacular in school, (4) scepticism about the value and practicality of alternative practices.
- Analyses of *instrumental, accommodation,* and *awareness* programs related to teaching speakers of nonstandard dialects of English.
- Reviews of studies on vernacular use.
- Benefits of using vernacular varieties in the classroom.

Nearly all teachers and educational administrators have the interests of their students at heart, and want to do what's best for them. They try to follow the well-known educational principle of moving from the known to the unknown, and they encourage their students to express themselves and to develop intellectually. Most teachers would never think of putting their students down because of their ethnicity or socioeconomic status. Yet, many teachers and administrators seem to abandon these principles and practices of nondiscrimination when their students speak vernacular varieties of English. Minority dialects (such as African American English [AAE]) and English-based creoles (such as those spoken in Hawai'i and the Caribbean) are generally kept out of the classroom. At worst, students' vernaculars are denigrated, and at best, teaching is done in standard English as if their vernaculars did not exist. In either case, students who speak minority dialects are not allowed to express themselves in the forms of speech they feel most comfortable with or hear the speech of their communities during the educational process. Why do these discriminatory linguistic practices exist, and why do parents and other speakers of minority language varieties generally support such practices?

Part of the answer is that the acquisition of standard English is considered to be one of the most important goals of formal education. What exactly standard English is, and why it is considered so important are other questions that we'll leave aside for the moment (see Lippi-Green, 1997). But the fact is that most people in English-speaking countries see a knowledge of standard English as the key to academic and economic success, and the vernacular as the greatest obstacle to the acquisition of this knowledge. Therefore, it seems logical to avoid the vernacular at all costs, especially when the language of the schools is standard English. But is this really logical? Couldn't we consider starting with the vernacular (the known) and gradually moving on to standard English (the unknown), and let students use it in the classroom until they feel comfortable with standard English? Why not treat the vernacular as a bridge to the standard, instead of an obstacle?

In this chapter, I will attempt to answer these complex questions by examining some of the reasons behind current practices and seeing whether they are justified according to research into alternative educational programs that do make use of the vernacular. These reasons fall into four categories:

- beliefs about the nature of vernacular varieties.
- misconceptions about the nature of educational programs using vernaculars.
- concerns that the use of vernaculars in schools will be detrimental to students' acquisition of standard English and to their overall success in life.
- scepticism about the value and practicality of alternative practices.

BELIEFS ABOUT THE NATURE OF VERNACULARS

Many teachers and administrators think of vernacular varieties as deviant forms of standard English, and many speakers themselves share this view. Terms such as *bad English, broken English* and *street language* are common. In the classroom, vernacular-speaking children are considered not as learners of a new variety, but as careless or lazy speakers of standard English. Some are even considered to have speech defects and are sent to special education classes (Pratt-Johnson, 1993; van Kuelen, Weddington & DeBose, 1998; Winer, 1993).

What is the reason for these attitudes? For one thing, since vernaculars and standard English share much of the same vocabulary, they are considered to be the same language. The average person does not learn about language diversity in school—but rather that there is one English language, and the form known as standard English is the correct or proper way of speaking and writing it. So when different words are used or the words are put together in patterns that differ from those of the standard, these are considered not as mere differences, but as inaccuracies or bad English.

It is interesting, however, that in the US such negative attitudes towards difference seem to be reserved for vernaculars such as creoles and AAE. The standard dialect of British English, for example, also has features that are unacceptable or incorrect in standard American English. It uses words such as *rubber* instead of *eraser*, and it has expressions such as *I haven't a book*. Just as those broken vernaculars leave out sounds in words and words in sentences—like saying *tol* instead of *told* and *He sick* instead of *He is sick*—British English has no *r* sound in words like *park* and leaves out words, as in *My father is in hospital* (instead of *in the hospital*). But in contrast to what many people say about vernaculars, they would not say that British people speak bad or incorrect English—just that they speak a different kind of English.

One reason for the negative attitudes toward vernaculars as opposed to other dialects is the misconception that they are haphazard—that there are no grammatical rules, and no correct or incorrect ways of speaking. However, since the 1960s, sociolinguists have been showing that vernaculars such as creoles and AAE are legitimate, rule-governed varieties of language which differ in systematic ways from the standard (e.g., Labov, 1969). For example, according to the grammatical rules of AAE, but not standard English, *be* is used to indicate a habitual action. This can cause miscommunication with standard speakers when they do not understand the rule, as shown in this example from Smitherman (2000, p. 25):

SCENE: First grade classroom, Detroit

Teacher: Where is Mary?

Student: She not here.

Teacher: (exasperatedly): She is *never* here!

Student: Yeah, she be here.

Teacher: Where? You just said she wasn't here.

When the student says *she be here*, it means *she is habitually here* (but just not today). But the teacher does not know this rule of AAE and interprets it according to the rules of standard English. Also according to the rules of AAE, habitual *be* can have an *-s* added on to it for third person, as in *He be(s) on my case*. Baugh (1992) reports that whites and standard English-speaking African Americans also add *-s* to the AAE completive marker *done*—e.g. *They dones blow them brothers away* (p. 322). But no native speaker of AAE would ever do this, so this is an example of a grammatical error in AAE.[1]

Another reason for negative attitudes towards vernaculars in comparison to a dialect such as British English is that British English is standardized and used in published texts and as the educational language in Britain. It also has a long historical tradition and a body of literature. On the other hand, vernaculars are either not standardized or only very recently standardized (as is the case with some creoles). They do not have a large body of literature and, of course, they are not used in education. Therefore, even if positive attitudes exist towards a vernacular as an important badge of social identity, or as language perfect for creating solidarity among family and friends, there is still the belief that vernaculars are fine for informal communication but that they have no place in the school, where the standard should be the norm. It should be noted, however, that five hundred years ago English itself was once an unstandardized language, and considered inappropriate for use in education. (At that time, Latin was the standard language of education.) Many other formerly unstandardized languages have become important vehicles of education, government and literature—for example, Bahasa Indonesia. Vernaculars are already being used in world class literature, such as AAE in the works of Toni Morrison, Sonia Sanchez and August Wilson. Thus, there is nothing intrinsically inferior about vernaculars. Like any other variety of language, they have their own grammatical rules and the potential to be standardized and used in education or any other domain. These facts are quite clear, and have been widely known for decades. Why, then, do many people still believe that vernaculars are just bad English?

One explanation may be that the facts have simply not trickled down to the general public. Another may be what Lippi-Green (1997, p. 64) calls the "Standard Language Ideology." This is the pervasive belief in the superiority of an abstracted and idealized form of language, based on the spoken language of the upper middle classes—the "standard" language. This bias towards one form of language is imposed and maintained by the dominant groups in society who speak this form of language. Those who believe in

---

[1]The grammatical rules of AAE and various creoles can be seen in many publications, some recent examples being Rickford & Rickford, 2000; Green, 2002; James & Youssef, 2002. (See also the Language Varieties website http://www.une.edu.au/langnet.)

Standard Language Ideology work to promote their own interests at the expense of marginalized, nondominant groups. One way that this bias is maintained is by perpetuation of beliefs about the superiority of the language of those in power, and the inferiority of the language of those not in power. This is done through the institutions controlled by those in power—the media and the education system.

We can see that vernacular varieties have a long history of being denigrated and marginalized in the media. For example, in publications starting from the 1920s, Hawai'i Creole was labelled with negative terms such as lazy, ungrammatical, faulty, sloppy, slothful and ugly (Da Pidgin Coup, 1999, pp. 6–8). Of course, this was before the many sociolinguistic studies over the last 40 years showing the legitimacy of vernaculars such as Hawai'i Creole. But vernaculars continue to get denigrated in the media, as was obvious during the public debate in the wake of the Oakland School Board's 1996 resolution to take AAE (or *Ebonics*) into account in the educational process. At that time, journalists gave this vernacular a variety of negative labels such as mutant English, fractured English, mumbo jumbo, slanguage and linguistic nightmare (Rickford & Rickford, 2000, p. 195).

The education system also perpetuates the Standard Language Ideology. Children who speak vernaculars are taught that the standard variety is superior in both structure and importance (e.g. for getting a good job). At the same time their own speech varieties are shown to be inferior if not by denigration, then by exclusion from the educational process.[2] By implication, their own social groups are being excluded from the institutions of power. But a large number of people in these marginalized social groups also accept this ideology, even though it disadvantages them, simply because this is what they have been taught by those in authority. Thus, belief in the inferiority of vernaculars is a major reason for the current educational practice of keeping them out of the classroom, and this practice helps to perpetuate the belief that these vernaculars are inferior.

Misconceptions About the Nature of Educational Programs Using Vernaculars

There are also widespread misconceptions about the nature of alternative education programs that do make use of vernaculars in the classroom. The most popular myth is that the vernacular will be taught to the students instead of standard English. For example, when the Oakland School Board proposed to make use of AAE (or Ebonics) in the classroom to help improve the educational performance of African American students, many

---

[2]This pertains not only to language but also to other aspects of marginalized groups' culture and history. (See, for example, Ogbu, 1978, p. 141.)

people thought that teachers would be teaching Ebonics itself rather than standard English—as Rickford & Rickford (2000) jokingly put it: "helping students therefore to master 'I be goin', you be goin', he/she/it be goin', and so on" (p. 172). This impression was reinforced by newspaper headlines such as "Oakland Schools OK Teaching of Black English" (Rickford & Rickford, 2000, p. 189). So, if the vernaculars are not being taught, how then are they being used in the classroom?

Three types of educational programs using vernacular varieties are in existence: *instrumental, accommodation* and *awareness*. Instrumental programs use a vernacular as a medium of instruction to teach initial literacy and sometimes content subjects such as mathematics, science and health. Such programs are useful mainly when the vernacular is markedly different from the standard language used in education—so different, in fact that the two varieties are not always mutually intelligible. Thus, instrumental programs are similar to bilingual programs in that the children's home language (the vernacular) is used at first while they are learning a second language or dialect (e.g. standard English). To date, such programs have been used only for speakers of creole languages—for example, in Australia, Papua New Guinea, the Seychelles, Haiti, and the Netherlands Antilles, and in the US with immigrants speaking Haitian Creole and Capeverdean (see Siegel, 1999a, 2002).

For minority dialects, which are usually much more similar to the standard than creoles are, more limited instrumental programs have been run only to teach students to read using materials prepared in their vernaculars, for example, in Sweden and Norway (Bull, 1990; Österberg, 1961). The closest thing to an instrumental program for AAE was a reading program using the "dialect readers" published as the *Bridge* series (Simpkins, Holt & Simpkins, 1977). However, even though the purpose of the program was to teach children to read, not to teach them AAE, it was not promoted because of negative reactions from parents and teachers (Labov, 1995).

In accommodation programs, students' vernacular varieties are not taught, but are accepted in the classroom. The standard remains the medium of instruction and the only subject of study. In the early years of school, students are allowed to use their home varieties of language for speaking and sometimes writing, and teachers may utilize their students' own interactional patterns and stories for teaching the standard variety. Individual accommodation programs of this type have existed in Hawai'i (see Boggs, 1985; Rynkofs, 1993). At the higher levels, literature and creative writing in a vernacular may be accommodated into the curriculum, as has been done in Trinidad and Tobago (Winer, 1990). Accommodation programs have also been run for speakers of AAE. For example, Campbell (1994) reports on one in an inner city senior high school that allowed freedom of expression in the students' home variety (AAE).

In awareness programs, the standard language remains the medium of instruction, but students' vernacular varieties are seen as a resource to be used for learning the standard—and for learning in general—rather than as an impediment. This approach has three components. First, students' vernacular varieties are accepted at times in the classroom, as just described (the accommodation component). Second, students learn about the many different varieties of language, such as dialects and creoles, and about the socio-historical processes that lead to a particular variety becoming accepted as the standard (the sociolinguistic component). Third, students are taught how to examine the linguistic characteristics of their own varieties and see how they differ from those of other students and from the standard (the contrastive component).

Awareness programs, or programs with awareness components, are found in many parts of the world. In Australia, for example, "Two-way English" (e.g. Malcolm et al., 1999) is a program for students in Western Australia who speak Aboriginal English. It recognizes and explores cultural and linguistic differences as a rich educational opportunity for both teachers and students. It is also "about a sharing of knowledge, and of the power linked in with that knowledge" (Malcolm, 1995, p. 39). In Los Angeles, California, the Academic English Mastery Program (LeMoine, 2001) trains teachers to build knowledge and understanding of various vernaculars and the students who use them, and then integrate this knowledge into instruction in standard English and other subjects. The handbook for this program, *English for Your Success* (Los Angeles Unified School District & LeMoine, 1999) outlines activities for contrasting AAE and standard English. Other current awareness programs include Fostering English Language in Kimberley Schools (FELIKS) in Australia (Berry & Hudson, 1997; Catholic Education Office, 1994), the Caribbean Academic Program (Fischer, 1992a), and the Bidialectal Communication Program (Harris-Wright, 1999) in the US. (For details about these programs, see Siegel, 1999a.)

Thus, programs using vernaculars in the classroom do not involve teaching the vernacular. At the most (in instrumental programs), the vernacular is used as a tool to help children adjust to school and learn basic skills, especially literacy, while at the same time learning the standard. As with bilingual programs, the belief that hardly any instruction is given in the standard is, in fact, a fallacy. However, in accommodation and awareness programs, the vernacular is not used as a medium of instruction, and these programs are part of a language arts curriculum which has the goal of teaching the standard language. But the overall objectives of these programs are to give students some opportunity to express themselves and read literature in a language they feel comfortable with, to make students aware of language diversity and the realities of the relationship between language and power, and at the same time to help students acquire the language of power by focusing on how it differs from their own varieties in both structure and use.

CONCERNS THAT THE USE OF VERNACULARS WILL BE DETRIMENTAL TO STUDENTS

Even though some teachers and administrators recognize vernaculars as rule-governed varieties of language and realize that using them in the classroom does not mean teaching them, many still have concerns about the possible effects that using vernaculars in education would have on their students—concerns that on the surface may seem quite legitimate. These concerns are of three types. The first is that paying attention to the vernacular will take away valuable time that could be devoted to learning standard English (the *waste of time* concern). The second concern is that the vernacular will get in the way or interfere with students' acquisition of the standard (the *interference* concern). Third is that using the vernacular will further disadvantage already disadvantaged vernacular-speaking students by not giving them an education equal to that of other students (the *ghettoization* concern). Let us look at each of these concerns in more detail.

Waste of Time

The *waste of time* concern seems at first glance to be plain common sense. If an important goal of formal education is to become proficient in standard English, then it seems logical that as much time as possible should be spent on learning standard English. Any time taken away from this—that is, time devoted to the vernacular—would appear, then, to be a waste of time. But behind this view are at least two underlying assumptions—both of which are problematic. The first is that the greater the amount of instruction time in standard English, the greater the achievement will be in standard English—the "time-on-task hypothesis" (Cummins, 1993, 2001). The second assumption is that the time used on the vernacular in the classroom would have absolutely no benefit for learning the standard, but rather would have a negative effect—the *no benefits* hypothesis. For example, with regard to the Caribbean, Elsasser and Irvine (1987) say that one of the reasons for the lack of use of the local creole vernacular is the assumption that "time devoted to writing in Creole detracts from students' ability to learn to write English" (p. 137).

A similar concern obtains in the US with regard to bilingual programs, and this has been reinforced by inaccurate media reports that children in bilingual programs do not do well in standard English. Propositions 227 in California and 203 in Arizona and other anti-bilingual education movements have also resulted in a lot of negative press. Most recently, there was a great deal of publicity about claims that drastic reduction of bilingual education in California due to Proposition 227 led to increased test scores in English. It was not reported, however, that test scores also increased for students still enrolled in bilingual programs. Further, there has been little mention of the fact that since Proposition 227 took effect on August 1998, more than two thirds of English learners remain limited in English proficiency (Crawford, 2002).

Unfortunately, the rigorous research conducted on the effect of bilingual education has not been reported. For example, comprehensive long-term studies in the US such as those of Ramirez (1992) and Thomas & Collier (1997, 2002) show that time taken away from the study of English and devoted to students' home language (in most cases, Spanish) did not detract from students' achievement in English. The studies clearly refute the *time on task* hypothesis. In fact, students who have studied in their mother tongue perform better in English (and mathematics) than comparable students who have studied only in English. This means that use of the mother tongue must provide some advantage as well, thus refuting the *no benefits* hypothesis. These studies have undergone much critical scrutiny, but even their strongest critics were unable to discredit their findings. (See also the review of research in Greene, 1998 and Cummins, 2001.)[3]

One might argue that the situation with regard to creoles and dialects is different from that of the bilingual programs, which use totally distinct languages. However, the research on some of the instrumental programs mentioned above shows similar results. Formal evaluations have been carried out on the use of at least three creoles in formal education: Kriol (a creole language spoken in northern Australia; Murtagh, 1982), Seselwa (the French Creole of the Seychelle Islands; Ravel & Thomas, 1985), and Tok Pisin (the expanded pidgin/creole of Papua New Guinea; Siegel, 1992, 1997). In each case, the results showed that students who were educated in both the creole and English achieved higher test scores in English and other subjects than students who were educated only in English.

Research was also conducted on the programs for regional dialect-speaking students in Sweden (Österberg, 1961) and Norway (Bull, 1990), mentioned previously. The findings in both studies were that students initially taught to read in their dialect and later in the standard had higher scores in reading speed and comprehension of the standard than students taught entirely in the standard. In the US, Leaverton (1973) found that the

---

[3]One important thing about these studies (and others done around the world) is that they are long term, following students' progress up through grades 5–6 and beyond. These contrast with short-term studies that test students' progress during or soon after bilingual programs. It is these short-term studies that show no advantages of using the mother tongue in education. And opponents of bilingual education generally refer only to these short-term studies.

reading performance of African American students increased when they used texts in AAE as well as in standard English. Simpkins & Simpkins (1981) reported that experimental groups of students using the AAE "dialect readers" in the *Bridge* series made significantly more progress in reading (as measured by the Iowa Test of Basic Skills in Reading Comprehension) than control groups who continued with the conventional reading instruction in standard English. (See further discussion in the section "No positive effects"). So with regard to vernaculars that are creoles or minority dialects, all these studies provide evidence against the *time on task* and *no benefit* hypotheses, at least with regard to instrumental programs. Therefore, the concern that use of the vernacular is a waste of time, detracting from the acquisition of the standard, is unjustified.

Interference

Interference, or *negative transfer*, can be defined as the inappropriate use of features of the first language (L1) or first dialect (D1) when speaking or writing the second language (L2) or dialect (D2)—in this context, standard English. There are many reports showing that fear of interference has kept vernaculars out of the classroom. For example, with regard to the Caribbean, Elsasser and Irvine (1987) say that one of the reasons for the lack of teaching literacy in the local creole vernacular is the assumption that "students' limited writing ability is due to linguistic interference" (p. 137). Similarly, Winer (1990) notes that "both educators and the public are concerned over the extent to which acceptance of the vernacular might negatively affect students' competence in standard English" (p. 241).

Such views do have some theoretical grounds. Although not as significant as once thought, transfer clearly does occur in second language and second dialect acquisition. Research over the last 25 years has concentrated on the factors that promote or inhibit transfer. (For a summary, see Ellis, 1994a). One of these is *language distance*, or the degree of typological similarity or difference between the L1 and the L2. It seems that the more similar varieties are, the more likely it is that transfer (and thus interference) will occur (e.g. Kellerman, 1979; Ringbom, 1987). Such is the case with minority dialects and creoles that are similar to the standard variety, at least superficially, in their lexicons and many grammatical rules. As Lin pointed out (1965): "The interference between two closely related dialects—such as a minority dialect and standard English—is far greater than between two completely different languages" (p. 8). Therefore, the fear of the vernacular interfering with the acquisition of the standard appears to be theoretically justified.

But the evidence that such interference occurs in the classroom is not so clear. For example, in a study of the writing of a group of tenth grade African American students in the US, Wolfram & Whiteman (1971) described several kinds of errors in standard English that they attribute to *dialect interference*. However, in a review of this and other studies, Hartwell (1980) pointed out that such errors occur randomly and only a small proportion of the time, and he presents evidence showing that problems in writing are due to general reading difficulties rather than interference. Conflicting evidence also exists with regard to the degree of interference of AAE in reading (Lucas & Borders, 1994; Scott, 1979; Wolfram, 1994). In the Caribbean, a study of the writing of first and final year secondary school students in Trinidad (Winer, 1989) revealed that interference from the local creole accounted wholly or partially for 65% of errors in standard English. In contrast, a study of the writing of children aged 9 to 11 in St Lucia (Winch & Gingell, 1994) found no significant indication of interference from the local creole.[4]

These studies show that despite the theoretical prediction of greater interference with closely related varieties of language, there is no clear evidence that it actually occurs. Furthermore, there is no evidence that using a vernacular in education will exacerbate the problem, since all the studies referred to above were done in situations where the vernacular was not being used in the classroom. Thus, we need to examine studies of programs where the vernacular was actually being used to see if this had a detrimental effect on students' achievement in the standard and general education as well.

Tables 2.1 and 2.2 list 13 evaluations of student achievement in programs with accommodation or awareness components. In addition, Table 2.3 lists four experimental studies that examined the use of a creole in teaching reading or AAE in contrastive activities. (See Siegel, 1999b, 2003 for a description of some of these studies). None of these evaluations or experimental studies show any negative effects resulting from the use of the vernacular in the classroom, clearly illustrating that the concern about interference is not justified. In fact, these evaluations and studies show positive effects in increased ability in standard English and general academic performance—further indicating that there are important benefits to using the vernacular in the classroom.

Ghettoization

The term ghettoization in this context is related to the belief that the use of language varieties other than standard English is a part of the disadvantage

---

[4]With regard to regional dialects, there are also differing viewpoints: Williams (1989) versus Williamson & Hardman (1997) in Britain; Stijnen & Vallen (1989) versus Giesbers, Kroon, & Liebrand (1988) in the Netherlands; and Rosenberg (1989) versus Barbour (1987) in Germany.

TABLE 2.1
Evaluations of Programs With an Accommodation Component

Variety	Study	Level
AAE	Cullinan, Jagger, & Strickland, 1974	K–grade 3
AAE	Piestrup, 1973	Grade 1
Hawai'i Creole	Day, 1989	K–grade 4
Hawai'i Creole	Rynkofs, 1993	Grade 2

TABLE 2.2
Evaluations of Programs With an Awareness Component

Variety	Study	Level
Hawai'i Creole (Project Holopono)	Actouka & Lai, 1989	Grades 4–6
Hawai'i Creole (Project Akamai)	Afaga & Lai, 1994	Grades 9–10
Caribbean Creole (Virgin Islands)	Elsasser & Irvine, 1987	College
Belize Creole	Decker, 2000	Grade 3
Caribbean English Creoles in US (Caribbean Academic Program)	Fischer, 1992b	High school
AAE	Hoover, 1991	College
AAE	Scherloh, 1991	Adult
AAE (Bidialectal Communication Program)	see Rickford, 2002	Grades 5–6
AAE and other vernaculars (Academic English Mastery Program)	Maddahian & Sandamela, 2000	Elementary

TABLE 2.3
Experimental Studies

Variety	Study	Level
Caribbean Creole (Carriacou)	Kephart, 1985, 1992a, b	Upper primary
AAE	Taylor, 1989	College
AAE	Fogel & Ehri, 2000	Grades 3–4
AAE	Pandey, 2000	Pre- and 1st year college

of marginalized groups, and a major factor that keeps them in urban ghettos. Thus, the concern here is closely related to the previous two: Devoting valuable class time to the vernacular deprives children of the instruction they need to learn standard English and in turn deprives them of the economic benefits that speakers of standard varieties have, thus ensuring that they remain in the ghetto (Snow, 1990). With regard to creoles, Shnukal (1992), for example, notes that in the Torres Strait (Australia) people are "reluctant to accept the use of creole as a formal medium of instruction in their schools, seeing it as a method of depriving them of instruction in the kind of English that white people use, and thus condemning them to permanent under-class status" (p. 4). A similar sentiment holds true for AAE where many observers thought that the Oakland School Board's Ebonics proposal was dangerously subversive (Rickford & Rickford, 2000, p. 197). There is another concern as well—that students in special programs using their vernaculars will be isolated, and not get the chance to interact with students who do speak varieties closer to the standard.

In examining this concern, we must first pose the question of whether a knowledge of standard English will actually give members of a marginalized group the economic benefits that speakers of the standard-speaking majority have. For example, Ogbu (1978) argues that equal opportunity in the US is a myth, and that because of "caste-like" barriers, members of disadvantaged groups such as African Americans cannot get certain high-level jobs, despite their qualifications or proficiency in standard English. Fordham & Ogbu (1986) comment that "black Americans have faced a job ceiling, so that even when they achieved in school in the past, i.e., had good educational credentials, they were not necessarily given access to jobs, wages, and other benefits commensurate with their academic achievements" (p. 179).

But even if one discounts these views and believes that there really is equal opportunity, a closer look at the facts should temper some of the fear of ghettoization. First of all, as we have just seen, the existing special programs for vernacular-speaking students help rather than hinder acquisition of the standard language of education. Such programs clearly do not result in students from disadvantaged groups being left behind. On the contrary, these programs give students the opportunity to catch up to and even go ahead of students who already speak varieties closer to the standard. Furthermore, in awareness programs, vernacular-speaking students do not have to be treated any differently from other students. All students can learn about different varieties of language, study literature written in different varieties, and examine the features of their own varieties in comparison to others. The same curriculum is used for all, and no one group is singled out. Consequently, all students can benefit from learning about the diversity of language and how their home language compares to those of other students and to the standard.

SCEPTICISM ABOUT THE VALUE AND PRACTICALITY OF ALTERNATIVE PRACTICES

The fourth reason for current educational practices is a general scepticism about the value and practicality of bringing vernaculars into the classroom. Here there are four main arguments against the use of vernaculars in formal education. The first is that the best way to acquire a new language variety is by immersion, not by making use of the first language or dialect (the *immersion* argument). The second argument is that the linguistic differ-

ences between some vernaculars and standard English are not that significant (the *similarity* argument). The third argument is that there are no
proven positive effects of using vernaculars in education (the *no positive effects* argument). Finally, it is considered too impractical to bring vernaculars
into formal education in terms of codification and materials production
(the *too hard* argument). We'll look at each of these individually.

Immersion

The first three arguments have been articulated by McWhorter (1998,
2000), the only respected linguist to come out strongly against the use of
AAE, and by implication other vernaculars, as a bridge to learning standard
English. First, he says (1998, p. 242) that "people learn speech varieties best
by immersion," and points to successful language learning by immigrants
who go to English-medium schools and to the French immersion programs
for English speakers in Canada. With regard to vernaculars, he refers to
places like Stuttgart, where students speaking the local dialect, Schwäbisch,
learn standard German through immersion in it, rather than through special programs using their vernacular.

However, there are several problems with these arguments. First of all,
the L2 immersion programs in Canada are actually bilingual programs.
Teachers are bilingual and the content in the L2 is modified to make it
more understandable to students. After the first few grades, there is a
strong emphasis on development of the L1 and instruction is in both languages (see García, 1997). This certainly does not happen for students
speaking AAE or other vernaculars, and McWhorter clearly does not have
this type of program in mind. Even if he did, it has been found that genuine
L2 immersion programs are effective only for learners from dominant, majority language groups, whose L1 is valued and supported at home and by
society in general (Auerbach, 1995, p. 25).

With regard to immigrants, the vast majority of so-called immersion programs are really submersion programs, and research has shown that such
programs have negative effects on many children (Cummins, 1988, p. 161).
Of course, it is this type of program that is generally the rule for speakers of
vernacular varieties, and many studies have shown such immersion (really
submersion) simply does not work with regard to AAE-speaking or Caribbean English Creole-speaking students acquiring standard English (Craig,
2001; Rickford & Rickford, 2000, p. 179). Finally, the teaching situation in
Stuttgart is quite different from what is normally found in the US or the
Caribbean. Children are allowed to speak in their vernacular dialect in
the classroom and never pushed to speak standard German (Fishman &

Lueders-Salmon, 1972). In other words, it is more like an accommodation program than a submersion program.

Similarity

McWhorter (1998, pp. 208–211) also argues that compared to other dialects—such as Schwäbisch, colloquial Finnish and Scottish English—AAE is a lot more similar to the respective standard variety. He asserts that if speakers of these dialects don't need special programs to help them learn the standard, why should speakers of AAE? In contrast, scholars such as Palacas (2001) have illustrated substantial typological differences between AAE and standard English, showing that "an unbridgeable chasm separates the grammatical systems of these two languages" (p. 344). He also notes: "The difficulty for student and teacher is not in a confusion that comes from the fact that the two language varieties are very similar, but a confusion from the fact that they are so very different yet *seem* so very similar" (Palacas, 2001, p. 349, emphasis in original). Also, in the study of AAE-speaking pre-college and first-year college students by Pandey (2000), mentioned above, their first-time performance on the Test of English as Foreign Language (TOEFL) was similar to that of low-level ESL/EFL students.

But even if we accept the view that AAE and standard English are very similar, that still is not a convincing argument against the use of the vernacular in the educational process. As we have seen above in the discussion of interference, when two varieties are similar, the subtle differences cause special learning difficulties. For example, Wolfram and Schilling-Estes observe (1998):

> When two systems are highly similar, with minor differences, it is sometimes difficult to keep the systems apart. . . . In some ways, it may be easier to work with language systems that are drastically different, since the temptation to merge overlapping structures and ignore relatively minor differences is not as great. (p. 287)

However, McWhorter (1998) disagrees with the idea that similarity may be a problem, saying that "we see hundreds of cases around the world where schoolchildren sail over just this type of narrow dialect gap" (p. 209). In support of this statement, he says that there is no problem for children speaking Canadian French learning standard French and similarly for rural Southern white children in the US learning standard English. However, in contrast to these assertions (which are not backed up by any evidence), there are many reports of cases where problems of similarity do exist for speakers of other vernaculars.

For example, Craig (1966, p. 58) noted that often when speakers of Jamaican Creole are being taught standard English, "the learner fails to perceive the new target element in the teaching situation" because of similarities between the varieties. Cheshire (1982) also mentioned problems caused by minority dialect-speaking children in British schools not being aware of specific differences between their speech and standard English: "They may simply recognise that school teachers and newsreaders, for example, do not speak in quite the same way as their family and friends" (p. 55). Similarly in the Netherlands, Van den Hoogen & Kuijper (1992, p. 223) indicated that speakers of regional dialects learning standard Dutch often cannot detect errors in their speech caused by linguistic differences between the varieties. It is this lack of awareness of differences that some scholars say may be one cause of the high degree of negative transfer (or interference) between similar varieties (e.g., Ellis, 1994b, p. 102; Van den Hoogen & Kuijper, 1992, p. 223).

Craig (1966, 1976, 1983) also pointed out that in situations where standard English is the target for speakers of vernaculars such as Caribbean creoles and AAE, learners already recognize and produce some aspects of it as part of their repertoires. As a result, in addition to the other problems of separation, speakers of vernacular varieties are often under the illusion that they already know the standard. This has also been pointed out by Fischer (1992a) and Nero (1997a, 1997b) with regard to Caribbean immigrants in the US. It seems, then, that it would be beneficial to have some kind of program with contrastive activities that would help students separate the vernacular from the standard, regardless of whether they are similar or different.

No Positive Effects

Finally, McWhorter (1998, 2000) claims that there is no conclusive evidence that children learn better when their vernacular is used in the educational process. This is part of his general argument that there is no reason to have special programs focusing on language for AAE-speaking students. Here, however, he concentrates on the use of the vernacular to teach reading (which he calls the *bridging approach*), rather than on other aspects, such as the contrastive component of the awareness approach.

McWhorter states that there are only seven publications on research studies that appear to present evidence for positive effects of the bridging approach (1998, pp. 218–220). We have already referred to six of these (and, of course, to others as well). The two Scandinavian studies using reading materials in the regional dialect (Bull, 1990; Österberg, 1961), he says, are not relevant because the dialects in question are much more different than AAE and standard English are (the similarity argument again). He dismisses the studies done by Piestrup (1973) and Taylor (1989),[5] saying that they are not concerned with the use of the bridging approach to teach initial literacy. That leaves three articles on the use of dialect readers for AAE-speaking students. One of these (which has not yet been mentioned here) is by Rickford and Rickford (1995). It presented results of some preliminary studies that McWhorter says were inconclusive. Another was the study by Leaverton (1973) that had methodological problems; both AAE and standard English reading materials were given to students. Only Simpkins & Simpkins (1981) showed very positive results from the use of the *Bridge* series readers, as mentioned previously.

In contrast to these studies, McWhorter refers to nine studies that he says test the use of AAE in teaching reading. He claims that these studies show that "dialect readers, and contrastive analysis had *no effect* on African American students' reading scores" (1998, p. 220, emphasis in original). Let us examine these studies. First of all, one general problem with all of them was that they were short-term experimental studies in contrast to Simpkins & Simpkins's (1981) longitudinal study. Second, in at least six of them (Marwit & Neumann, 1974; Mathewson, 1973; Nolen, 1972; Schaaf, 1971; Simons & Johnson, 1974; Sims, 1972), the children were already familiar with reading in standard English but not in AAE, and the results were most probably influenced by the factors of the novelty and apparent inappropriateness of the dialect materials to the students. In fact, the authors of four out of these six studies pointed this out themselves.[6] Two of these six studies (Schaaf, 1971; Sims, 1972) had methodological problems as well: a small sample size and failure to equate texts (mentioned by Simons & Johnson, 1974, p. 340).

The three remaining studies did not really address the question of the effectiveness of using the vernacular to teach reading. Melmed (1971) tested the assumption that AAE interferes with reading standard English. He found no difference in reading between African American and white

---

[5]The date for this work is incorrectly given as 1991 by McWhorter (1998) on p. 218, but correctly as 1989 in the list of references on p. 280.

[6]Mathewson (1973) noted: "If the children have learned to read in standard English, then they may lack the skills necessary to decode divergent syntax and phonology" (p. 115). Nolen (1972, pp. 1095–1096) mentioned "the novelty of the printed vernacular" and wrote that the results could have been different if children had been introduced to reading with "dialect primers." Simons and Johnson (1974, p. 355) also referred to the factor of previous exposure only to standard English texts and concluded: "If subjects had learned to read with dialect texts, they might read them better than standard texts" (p. 356). And Marwit & Neumann (1974) mentioned the factor of subjects' "distrust of nonstandard English in a setting where it was rarely, if ever, used and almost never rewarded" (p. 331). (See also Masland, 1979, p. 42 with regard to Sims, 1972, and other studies.)

groups, but used only standard English reading materials.[7] Torrey (1971) tested whether or not preliminary training in a feature of standard English helped to improve reading comprehension in the standard. Simons (1974) examined the hypothesis that African American children can read standard English words that are closer to their AAE pronunciation better than words that are further away—e.g. *coal* vs. *cold.* Thus, the evidence does not really lead to the conclusion that the use of AAE or any other vernacular in teaching reading is ineffective.

Too Hard

The final argument against the use of vernacular in education is that it is impractical because of two problems: The first problem is the lack of standardization in most creoles and all minority dialects. With both types of vernaculars, there is usually a continuum of varieties ranging from those that are quite different from the standard to those that are quite close to it. Therefore, it is difficult to select a norm to be used in education. Another impractical argument is that even if vernaculars could be standardized, the cost of developing written materials would be prohibitive. Thus, for example, linguists such as Todd (1990) advocate only the oral use of creoles in the classroom to facilitate communication in the early years, but not the written use.

The *too hard* arguments are countered, at least with regard to creoles, by the existence of viable educational programs that use these vernaculars as the languages of instruction and initial literacy in primary schools. One example is in Australia where the bilingual Krio/English program ran for more than 20 years at the Barunga Community Education Centre (Siegel, 1993). Another is in the Seychelles, mentioned above, where Seselwa has been the primary medium of instruction in all schools since 1981 (Bollée, 1993). Both programs have been successful despite some initial problems in standardization, and the Barunga program has illustrated how materials can be produced locally at a very low cost using modern desktop publishing technology (Northern Territory Department of Education, 1995).

However, the greatest scope for the use of vernaculars is not in instrumental programs such as these, but in accommodation and awareness pro-

---

[7]Two other factors also may have affected the results of this study. First, the content and subject matter for the reading tests were taken from stories written or told by children in the school district under study; therefore, the test items used, unlike reading materials normally found in the classroom, were "culturally realistic and environmentally relevant to the subjects" (Melmed, 1971, p. 71). Second, subjects in the study spoke standard English 70 per cent of the time (p. 75).

grams. In these kinds of programs, the problems of standardization and materials development are irrelevant because no special materials are necessary. In accommodation programs, students are sometimes given the opportunity to speak and write in their own vernaculars, but there is no need to use a standard form of the vernacular in such contexts. Also, literature using the vernacular may be studied—and this literature as well has been published despite the absence of standardization. These comments are true for the accommodation component of awareness programs as well. With regard to the contrastive component, since students come up with examples from their own vernaculars and describe them as they see fit, again there is also no need for any published teaching materials in the vernacular.

BENEFITS OF BRINGING VERNACULARS INTO THE CLASSROOM

So far in this chapter, I have shown that the various reasons for keeping vernaculars out of the classroom are not really justified if we look closely at the facts:

1. Vernaculars are legitimate, rule-governed forms of language.
2. When vernaculars are used in the educational process, they are not actually taught, but are used to help students in their educational development.
3. Using vernaculars in education does not interfere with the acquisition of the standard by being a waste of time or exacerbating interference, and therefore it does not further disadvantage students.
4. Submersion in the standard does not help vernacular-speaking students to acquire it, and scepticism about the effectiveness and practicality of programs making use of the vernacular is not supported by convincing evidence.

At the same time, the research on instrumental, accommodation and awareness programs described in this chapter has demonstrated some positive advantages from using vernaculars in the classroom. More specifically, the use of students' own varieties of language in long-term educational programs (not short-term experiments) has resulted in higher scores in tests measuring reading and writing skills in standard English and increases in overall academic achievement. The particular benefits of using vernaculars that account for these results appear to be related to one or more of five possible factors: easier acquisition of reading, greater cognitive development, more positive attitudes by teachers, increased motivation and self-esteem, and ability to separate codes and notice differences.

Easier Acquisition of Reading

It is well known that the acquisition of literacy is easier in a familiar variety of language and that these skills can then be transferred to another language (Collier, 1992; Snow, 1990). In the case of bilingual or instrumental programs, students were more easily able to acquire literacy in their vernacular and then apply these skills to literacy in the standard. On the more theoretical side, Cummins (1981, 1988, 2001) believes that specific knowledge and skills learned in the L1 or D1 have a positive effect on L2/D2 attainment. According to his "interdependency principle" or "common underlying proficiency generalization," the combination of linguistic knowledge and literacy skills necessary for academic work, which Cummins originally called *cognitive/academic language proficiency* (CALP), is common across languages and once acquired in one language or dialect can be transferred to another. Since CALP is easier to acquire in the L1/D1 than in the L2/D2, students in instrumental programs are more easily able to acquire these skills in their vernacular and then transfer them to general academic work in the standard.

Greater Cognitive Development

It is also well known that children's self-expression is facilitated in a familiar language, especially without fear of correction (see, for example, UNESCO, 1968, p. 690), and that children are clearly disadvantaged when they are not allowed to express themselves in their own variety of language (Thomas & Collier, 1997). This is because self-expression may be a prerequisite for cognitive development. For example, in a study of cognitive development and school achievement in a Hawai'i Creole–speaking community, Feldman, Stone, & Renderer (1990) found that students who do not perform well in high school have not developed *transfer ability*. Here *transfer* refers to the discovery or recognition by a learner that abstract reasoning processes learned with regard to materials in one context can be applied to different materials in a new context. For this to occur, new materials must be talked about, described, and encoded propositionally. The problem in Hawai'i is that some students do not feel comfortable expressing themselves in the language of formal education, standard English, and their own vernacular variety, Hawai'i Creole, is conventionally not used in school. Thus, one possible benefit of all three kinds of programs using the vernacular is that students are allowed to express themselves in their own varieties, thus better facilitating cognitive development.

More Positive Attitudes by Teachers

Many studies have shown that teachers, both African American and white, have less positive attitudes towards AAE-speaking students and lower expectations about their abilities and performance, and that this leads to lower results (e.g. Ogbu, 1978, 133–135). (For a good survey of these studies and a discussion of the self-fulfilling prophecies spawned by these attitudes, see Tauber, 1997.) But because of the nature of instrumental, accommodation or awareness programs, teachers themselves become aware of the legitimacy and complex rule-governed nature of their students' vernaculars. Therefore, they have more positive attitudes and higher expectations. It is also worth noting that educating teachers about language diversity and issues of language and power was the first step in most of the successful programs described above.

Increased Motivation and Self-Esteem

Most theories of second language acquisition (SLA) agree that the affective variables of learner motivation, attitudes, self-confidence, and anxiety have some effect on L2/D2 attainment. These factors are especially important with regard to speakers of vernaculars such as creoles and AAE, who often have a negative self-image because of the frequent denigration of their speech and culture in the schools. It may be that the use of the vernacular in formal education results in positive values to these variables with regard to learning the standard. Certainly, many of the studies referred to above describe increased participation and enthusiasm in the educational process. As Skutnabb-Kangas (1988, p. 29) points out, when the child's mother tongue is valued in the educational setting, it leads to low anxiety, high motivation and high self-confidence, three factors that are closely related to successful educational programs. Wolfram & Schilling-Estes (1998) also point out that "there is now some indication that students who feel more confident about their own vernacular dialect are more successful in learning the standard one" (p. 290).

Another related factor, although seemingly contradictory, is the vernacular's covert prestige as a marker of the socio-cultural group and a part of members' social identity. As Delpit (1990) observes, children often have the ability to speak standard English, but choose "to identify with their community rather than with the school" (p. 251). Also, because of the ideology of correctness attached to the standard, students may fear that learning it means abandoning their dialect and thus risking being ostracized from their social group. (See Fordham, 1999; Fordham & Ogbu, 1986). The use of the vernacular in the classroom would reduce some of this anxiety. According to Clément's (1980) Social Context Model, such use of the vernacular would be expected to reduce fear of assimilation and thus increase motivation to learn the L2/D2, here the standard.

Ability to Separate Codes and Notice Differences

We have seen that the similarities between the vernacular and the standard may make it difficult for learners to separate the two varieties. However, in the study of the Kriol/English bilingual program in Australia described previously, Murtagh (1982, p. 30) attributes the higher language proficiency of the bilingual program students to their "progressively greater success at separating the two languages" as a consequence of "the two languages being taught as separate entities in the classroom." (For a psycho-linguistic discussion of the notion of separation, see Siegel, 1999b, pp. 711–716).

A closely related possible benefit is that using the vernacular in educational programs may make learners aware of differences between it and the standard that they may not otherwise notice. Again we turn to SLA theory. According to Schmidt's "noticing hypothesis" (1990, 1993), attention to target language forms is necessary for acquisition; these forms will not be acquired unless they are noticed. As discussed above, because of the similarities between vernacular and the standard, learners often do not notice differences between the two varieties. However, it may be that looking at features of their own varieties in instrumental or awareness programs helps students to notice features of the standard that are different—the first step of acquisition.

In a study of errors made by Schwäbisch dialect speaking children learning standard German, Young-Scholten (1985, p. 11) observed: "[T]hose errors due to interference from a crucially similar first language will tend to persist if the learner's attention is not drawn to these errors." (See also, Politzer, 1993, p. 53). Winer (1989, p. 170) first suggested that "an overtly contrastive method" of comparing Caribbean Creole with standard English would help deal with interference, and similar methods of "contrastive analysis" have been suggested by Rickford (1999) for AAE. The contrastive component of awareness programs, then, serves to draw attention to potential errors that may be caused by lack of recognition of differences, thus leading to fewer interference errors in the standard.

CONCLUSION

We have seen that current educational practices generally do not allow students' creole or dialect vernaculars in the classroom. These practices may be well-intentioned and have the support of parents and the community. But a detailed examination of the reasons behind these practices shows that they are not justified, and that because of them, students are missing out on several potential benefits that would be gained from using their own vernaculars in the educational process.

The benefits of the alternative programs described in this chapter have been mainly in terms of test scores measuring the acquisition of the standard variety and academic achievement. But there are many other, more fundamental benefits as well—for example, the inclusion rather than exclusion of vernacular-speaking students and their culture into the education system. Such programs also have the potential to empower students and their communities by encouraging them to use their own voices and making them aware of the issues of language and power (see Delpit, 1988).

We can only hope that more teachers and educational administrators will look more closely at research in both linguistics and education, and base their classroom policies not on preconceptions, previous practices or current ideologies, but rather on the facts, no matter how radical or counter-intuitive they may seem. These educators can then take the lead and inform parents and communities about how alternative teaching programs that make use of vernaculars can benefit their children and their communities.

QUESTIONS FOR DISCUSSION AND REFLECTIVE WRITING

1. Siegel cites four categories of reasons for the resistance to the use of vernacular varieties in the classroom. Working with a partner, choose any two of these categories, and prepare a rebuttal to Siegel. Be sure to provide evidence for your arguments.

2. Imagine you wanted (or were asked) to implement one of the three types of programs (*instrumental, accommodation* or *awareness*) at your school. Which one would you choose, and why? How would you go about it? What factors would you need to take into account? What would be the benefits to the particular population served?

3. Examine the five specific benefits of using the vernacular as posited by Siegel, and discuss specific ways in which those benefits can affect a school environment.

REFERENCES

Actouka, M., & Lai, M. K. (1989). *Project Holopono, evaluation report, 1987–1988.* Honolulu: Curriculum Research and Development Group, College of Education, University of Hawai'i.

Afaga, L. B., & Lai, M. K. (1994). *Project Akamai, evaluation report, 1992–93, Year Four.* Honolulu: Curriculum Research and Development Group, College of Education, University of Hawai'i.

Auerbach, E. R. (1995). The politics of the ESL classroom: Issues of power in pedagogical choices. In J. W. Tollefson (Ed.), *Power and inequality in language education* (pp. 9–33). Cambridge: Cambridge University Press.

Barbour, S. (1987). Dialects and the teaching of standard language: Some West German work. *Language in Society, 16,* 227–244.

Baugh, J. (1992). Hypocorrection: Mistakes in production of vernacular African American English as a second dialect. *Language and Communication, 12,* 317–326.

Berry, R., & Hudson, J. (1997). *Making the jump: A resource book for teachers of Aboriginal students.* Broome: Catholic Education Office, Kimberley Region.

Boggs, S. T. (1985). *Speaking, relating, and learning: A study of Hawaiian children at home and at school.* Norwood, NJ: Ablex Publishing.

Bollée, A. (1993). Language policy in the Seychelles and its consequences. *International Journal of the Sociology of Language, 102,* 85–99.

Bull, T. (1990). Teaching school beginners to read and write in the vernacular. In E. H. Jahr & O. Lorentz (Eds.), *Tromsø linguistics in the eighties* (pp. 69–84). Oslo: Novus Press.

Campbell, E. D. (1994). *Empowerment through bidialectalism.* (ERIC Document Reproduction Service No. ED 386 034)

Catholic Education Office, Kimberley Region. (1994). *FELIKS: Fostering English language in Kimberley schools.* Broome: Catholic Education Commission of Western Australia.

Cheshire, J. (1982). Dialect features and linguistic conflict in schools. *Educational Review, 14,* 53–67.

Clément, R. (1980). Ethnicity, contact and communicative competence in a second language. In H. Giles, W. P. Robinson, & P. M. Smith (Eds.), *Language: Social psychological perspectives* (pp. 147–154). Oxford: Pergamon.

Collier, V. P. (1992). A synthesis of studies examining long-term language minority student data on academic achievement. *Bilingual Research Journal, 16*(1&2), 187–212.

Craig, D. R. (1966). Teaching English to Jamaican Creole speakers: A model of a multi-dialect situation. *Language Learning, 16*(1&2), 49–61.

Craig, D. R. (1976). Bidialectal education: Creole and standard in the West Indies. *International Journal of the Sociology of Language, 8,* 93–134.

Craig, D. R. (1983). Teaching standard English to nonstandard speakers: Some methodological issues. *Journal of Negro Education, 52*(1), 65–74.

Craig, D. R. (2001). Language education revisited in the Commonwealth Caribbean. In P. Christie (Ed.), *Due respect. Papers on English and English-related Creoles in the Caribbean in honour of Professor Robert Le Page* (pp. 61–76). Jamaica: University of the West Indies Press.

Crawford, J. (2002). *English learners in California.* Retrieved February 2, 2003, from http://ourworld.compuserve.com/homepages/JWCRAWFORD/castats.htm

Cullinan, B. E., Jagger, A. M., & Strickland, D. S. (1974). Language expansion for Black children in the primary grades: A research report. *Young Children, 24*(2), 98–112.

Cummins, J. (1981). The role of primary language development in promoting educational success for language minority students. In California State Department of Education (Ed.), *Schooling and language minority students: A theoretical framework* (pp. 3–49). Los Angeles: National Evaluation, Dissemination and Assessment Center.

Cummins, J. (1988). Second language acquisition within bilingual education programs. In L. M. Beebe (Ed.), *Issues in second language acquisition: Multiple perspectives* (pp. 145–166). New York: Newbury House.

Cummins, J. (1993). Bilingualism and second language learning. *Annual Review of Applied Linguistics, 13,* 51–70.

Cummins, J. (2001). *Language, power and pedagogy: Bilingual children in the crossfire.* Clevedon: Multilingual Matters.

Da Pidgin Coup. (1999). *Pidgin and education: A position paper.* University of Hawai'i. Retrieved February 12, 2003, from http://www.hawaii.edu/sls/pidgin.html

Day, R. R. (1989). The acquisition and maintenance of language by minority children. *Language Learning, 29*(2), 295–303.

Decker, K. (2000). *The use of Belize Kriol to improve English proficiency.* Paper presented at the 5th International Creole Workshop, Florida International University, Miami.

Delpit, L. D. (1988). The silenced dialogue: Power and pedagogy in educating other people's children. *Harvard Educational Review, 58*(3), 280–298.

Delpit, L. D. (1990). Language diversity and learning. In S. Hynds & D. L. Rubin (Eds.), *Perspectives on talk and learning* (pp. 247–266). Urbana, IL: National Council of Teachers of English.

Ellis, R. (1994a). *The study of second language acquisition.* Oxford: Oxford University Press.

Ellis, R. (1994b). A theory of instructed second language acquisition. In N. C. Ellis (Ed.), *Implicit and explicit learning of languages* (pp. 79–114). London: Academic Press.

Elsasser, N., & Irvine, P. (1987). English and Creole: The dialectics of choice in a college writing program. In I. Shor (Ed.), *Freire for the classroom: A sourcebook for literacy teaching* (pp. 129–149). Portsmouth, NH: Boynton/Cook.

Feldman, C. F., Stone, A., & Renderer, B. (1990). Stage, transfer, and academic achievement in dialect-speaking Hawaiian adolescents. *Child Development, 61*, 472–484.

Fischer, K. (1992a). Educating speakers of Caribbean English in the United States. In J. Siegel (Ed.), *Pidgins, creoles and nonstandard dialects in education* (Occasional Paper No. 12, pp. 99–123). Melbourne: Applied Linguistics Association of Australia.

Fischer, K. (1992b). Report. *Pidgins and Creoles in Education (PACE) Newsletter, 3*, 1.

Fishman, J. A., & Lueders-Salmon, E. (1972). What has the sociology of language to say to the teacher? On teaching the standard variety to speakers of dialectal or sociolectal varieties. In C. B. Cazden, V. P. John, & D. Hymes (Eds.), *Functions of language in the classroom* (pp. 67–83). New York: Teachers College, Columbia University.

Fogel, H., & Ehri, L. C. (2000). Teaching elementary students who speak Black English Vernacular to write in standard English: Effects of dialect transformation practice. *Contemporary Educational Psychology, 25*, 212–235.

Fordham, S. (1999). Dissin "the Standard": Ebonics as guerrilla warfare at Capital High. *Anthropology & Education Quarterly, 30*(3), 272–293.

Fordham, S., & Ogbu, J. C. (1986). Black students' school success: Coping with the "burden of acting white". *The Urban Review, 18*, 176–206.

García, O. (1997). Bilingual education. In F. Coulmas (Ed.), *The handbook of sociolinguistics* (pp. 405–420). Oxford: Blackwell.

Giesbers, H., Kroon, S., & Liebrand, R. (1988). Bidialectalism and primary school achievement in a Dutch dialect area. *Language and Education, 2*(2), 77–93.

Green, L. J. (2002). *African American English: A linguistic introduction.* Cambridge: Cambridge University Press.

Greene, J. P. (1998). *A meta-analysis of the effectiveness of bilingual education.* Claremont, CA: The Tomas Rivera Policy Institute.

Harris-Wright, K. (1999). Enhancing bidialectalism in urban African American students. In C. T. Adger, D. Christian, & O. Taylor (Eds.), *Making the connection: Language and academic achievement among African American students: Proceedings of a conference of the coalition on diversity in education* (pp. 30–53). McHenry, IL: Center for Applied Linguistics/Delta Systems.

Hartwell, P. (1980). Dialect interference in writing: A critical review. *Research in the Teaching of English, 14*(2), 101–118.

Hoover, M. R. (1991). Using the ethnography of African-American communication in teaching composition to bidialectal students. In M. E. McGroarty & C. J. Faltis (Eds.), *Languages in school and society: Policy and pedagogy* (pp. 465–485). Berlin: Mouton de Gruyter.

James, W., & Youssef, V. (2002). *The languages of Tobago: Genesis, structure and perspectives.* St Augustine, Trinidad & Tobago: The University of the West Indies School of Continuing Studies.

Kellerman, E. (1979). Transfer and non-transfer: Where are we now? *Studies in Second Language Acquisition, 2,* 37–57.

Kephart, R. F. (1985). *"It have more soft words": A study of Creole English and reading in Carriacou, Grenada.* Ann Arbor: University Microfilms.

Kephart, R. F. (1992a). Dissertation abstract. *Pidgins and Creoles in Education (PACE) Newsletter, 3,* 8.

Kephart, R. F. (1992b). Reading creole English does not destroy your brain cells! In J. Siegel (Ed.), *Pidgins, creoles and nonstandard dialects in education* (Occasional Paper No. 12, pp. 67–86). Melbourne: Applied Linguistics Association of Australia.

Labov, W. (1969). The logic of nonstandard English. In J. E. Alatis (Ed.), *Linguistics and the teaching of standard English* (pp. 1–24). Washington, DC: Georgetown University Press.

Labov, W. (1995). Can reading failure be reversed? A linguistic approach to the question. In V. L. Gadsden & D. A. Wagner (Eds.), *Literacy among African-American youth* (pp. 39–68). Cresskill, NJ: Hampton Press.

Leaverton, L. (1973). Dialectal readers: Rationale, use and value. In J. L. Laffey & R. W. Shuy (Eds.), *Language differences: Do they interfere?* (pp. 114–126). Newark, DE: International Reading Association.

LeMoine, N. (2001). Language variation and literacy acquisition in African American students. In J. L. Harris, A. G. Kamhi, & K. E. Pollock (Eds.), *Literacy in African American communities* (pp. 169–194). Mahwah, NJ: Lawrence Erlbaum Associates.

Lin, S. C. (1965). *Pattern practice in the teaching of standard English to students with a non-standard dialect.* New York: Teachers College, Columbia University.

Lippi-Green, R. (1997). *English with an accent.* New York: Routledge.

Los Angeles Unified School District, & LeMoine, N. (1999). *English for your success: Handbook of successful strategies for educators.* Maywood, NJ: Peoples Publishing.

Lucas, C., & Borders, D. G. (1994). *Language diversity and classroom discourse.* Norwood, NJ: Ablex.

Maddahian, E., & Sandamela, A. P. (2000). *Academic English Mastery Program: 1998 report* (Publication No. 781). Program Evaluation and Research Branch, Research and Evaluation Unit, Los Angeles Unified School District.

Malcolm, I. G. (1995). *Language and communication enhancement for two-way education: Report.* Perth: Edith Cowan University.

Malcolm, I., Haig, Y., Königsberg, P., Rochecouste, J., Collard, G., Hill, A., & Cahill, R. (1999). *Two-way English: Towards more user-friendly education for speakers of Aboriginal English.* East Perth, WA: Education Department of Western Australia.

Marwit, S. J., & Neumann, G. (1974). Black and white children's comprehension of standard and nonstandard English passages. *Journal of Educational Psychology, 66*(3), 329–332.

Masland, S. W. (1979). Black dialect and learning to read: What is the problem? *Journal of Teacher Education, 30*(2), 41–44.

Mathewson, G. C. (1973). *The effects of attitudes upon comprehension of dialect folktales.* Unpublished doctoral dissertation, University of California at Berkeley.

McWhorter, J. (1998). *The word on the street: Fact and fable about American English.* London: Plenum.

McWhorter, J. H. (2000). *Losing the race: Self-sabotage in Black America.* New York: Free Press.

Melmed, P. J. (1971). *Black phonology: The question of reading interference.* Berkeley: University of California.

Murtagh, E. J. (1982). Creole and English as languages of instruction in bilingual education with Aboriginal Australians: Some research findings. *International Journal of the Sociology of Language, 36,* 15–33.

Nero, S. J. (1997a). English is my native language . . . or so I believe. *TESOL Quarterly, 31,* 585–592.

Nero, S. J. (1997b). ESL or ESD? Teaching English to Caribbean English speakers. *TESOL Journal, 7*(2), 6–10.

Nolen, P. S. (1972). Reading nonstandard dialect materials: A study at grades two and four. *Child Development, 43,* 1092–1097.

Northern Territory Department of Education. (1995). *1994 Annual reports from specialist staff in bilingual programs in Northern Territory schools.* Darwin: Northern Territory Department of Education.

Ogbu, J. U. (1978). *Minority education and caste: The American system in cross-cultural perspective.* New York: Academic Press.

Österberg, T. (1961). *Bilingualism and the first school language: An educational problem illustrated by results from a Swedish language area.* Umeå: Västernbottens Tryckeri.

Palacas, A. (2001). Liberating American Ebonics from Euro-English. *College English, 63*(3), 326–352.

Pandey, A. (2000). TOEFL to the test: Are monodialectal AAL-speakers similar to ESL students? *World Englishes, 19*(1), 89–106.

Piestrup, A. M. (1973). *Black dialect interference and accommodation of reading instruction in first grade.* Berkeley: University of California.

Politzer, R. L. (1993). A researcher's reflections on bridging dialect and second language learning: Discussion of problems and solutions. In B. J. Merino, H. T. Trueba, & F. A. Samaniego (Eds.), *Language culture and learning: Teaching Spanish to native speakers of Spanish* (pp. 45–57). London: The Falmer Press.

Pratt-Johnson, Y. (1993). Curriculum for Jamaican Creole-speaking students in New York City. *World Englishes, 12*(2), 257–264.

Ramirez, J. D. (1992). Executive summary of the final report: Longitudinal study of structured English immersion strategy, early-exit and late-exit transitional bilingual education programs for language-minority children. *Bilingual Research Journal, 16*(1–2), 1–62.

Ravel, J.-L., & Thomas, P. (1985). *État de la réforme de l'enseignement aux Seychelles (1981–1985).* Paris: Ministère des Relations Extérieures, Coopération et Développement.

Rickford, J. R. (1999). *African American Vernacular English: Features, evolution, educational implications.* Oxford: Blackwell.

Rickford, J. R. (2002). Linguistics, education, and the Ebonics firestorm. In J. E. Alatis, H. E. Hamilton, & A-H. Tan (Eds.), *Linguistics, language and the professions (Georgetown University Round Table on Languages and Linguistics, 2000)* (pp. 25–45). Washington, DC: Georgetown University Press.

Rickford, J. R., & Rickford, A. E. (1995). Dialect readers revisited. *Linguistics and Education, 7,* 107–128.

Rickford, J. R., & Rickford, R. J. (2000). *Spoken soul: The story of Black English.* New York: Wiley.

Ringbom, H. (1987). *The role of the first language in foreign language learning.* Clevedon: Multilingual Matters.

Rosenberg, P. (1989). Dialect and education in West Germany. In J. Cheshire, V. Edwards, H. Münstermann, & B. Weltens (Eds.), *Dialect and education: Some European perspectives* (pp. 62–93). Clevedon: Multilingual Matters.

Rynkofs, J. T. (1993). *Culturally responsive talk between a second grade teacher and Hawaiian children during writing workshop.*

Schaaf, E. (1971). *A study of Black English syntax and reading comprehension.* Unpublished master's thesis, University of California, Berkeley.

Scherloh, J. M. (1991). Teaching standard English usage: A dialect-based approach. *Adult Learning, 2*(5), 20–22.

Schmidt, R. (1990). The role of consciousness in second language learning. *Applied Linguistics, 11,* 129–158.

Schmidt, R. (1993). Awareness and second language acquisition. *Annual Review of Applied Linguistics, 13,* 206–226.

Scott, J. (1979). Black dialect and reading: Which differences make a difference? In R. E. Shafer (Ed.), *Applied linguistics and reading* (pp. 51–62). Newark, DE: International Reading Association.

Shnukal, A. (1992). The case against a transfer bilingual program of Torres Strait Creole to English in Torres Strait schools. In J. Siegel (Ed.), *Pidgins, creoles and nonstandard dialects in education* (Occasional Paper No. 12, pp. 1–12). Melbourne: Applied Linguistics Association of Australia.

Siegel, J. (1992). Teaching initial literacy in a pidgin language: A preliminary evaluation. In J. Siegel (Ed.), *Pidgins, creoles and nonstandard dialects in education* (Occasional Paper No. 12, pp. 53–65). Melbourne: Applied Linguistics Association of Australia.

Siegel, J. (1993). Pidgins and creoles in education in Australia and the Southwest Pacific. In F. Byrne & J. Holm (Eds.), *Atlantic meets Pacific: A global view of pidginization and creolization* (pp. 299–308). Amsterdam: John Benjamins.

Siegel, J. (1997). Using a pidgin language in formal education: Help or hindrance? *Applied Linguistics, 18,* 86–100.

Siegel, J. (1999a). Creole and minority dialects in education: An overview. *Journal of Multilingual and Multicultural Development, 20*(6), 508–531.

Siegel, J. (1999b). Stigmatized and standardized varieties in the classroom: Interference or separation? *TESOL Quarterly, 33,* 701–728.

Siegel, J. (2002). Pidgins and Creoles. In R. Kaplan (Ed.), *Handbook of applied linguistics* (pp. 335–351). New York: Oxford University Press.

Siegel, J. (2003). Social context. In C. Doughty & M. H. Long (Eds.), *Handbook of second language acquisition* (pp. 178–223). Oxford: Blackwell.

Simons, H. D. (1974). Black dialect phonology and work recognition. *Journal of Educational Research, 68,* 67–70.

Simons, H. D., & Johnson, K. R. (1974). Black English syntax and reading interference. *Research in the Teaching of English, 8,* 339–358.

Simpkins, G. A., Holt, G., & Simpkins, C. (1977). *Bridge: A cross-cultural reading program.* Boston: Houghton Mifflin.

Simpkins, G., & Simpkins, C. (1981). Cross-cultural approach to curriculum development. In G. Smitherman (Ed.), *Black English and the education of black children and youth* (pp. 221–240). Detroit: Center for Black Studies, Wayne State University.

Sims, R. A. (1972). *A psycholinguistic description of miscues created by selected young readers during oral reading of texts in Black and standard English.* Unpublished doctoral dissertation, Wayne State University, Detroit, Michigan.

Skutnabb-Kangas, T. (1988). Multilingualism and the education of minority children. In T. Skutnabb-Kangas & J. Cummins (Eds.), *Minority education: From shame to struggle* (pp. 9–44). Clevedon: Multilingual Matters.

Smitherman, G. (2000). *Talkin that talk: Language, culture, and education in African America.* London: Routledge.

Snow, C. E. (1990). Rationales for native language instruction: Evidence from research. In A. M. Padilla, H. H. Fairchild, & C. M. Valdez (Eds.), *Bilingual education: Issues and strategies* (pp. 60–74). Newbury Park: Sage.

Stijnen, S., & Vallen, T. (1989). The Kerkrade Project: Background, main findings and an explanation. In J. Cheshire, V. Edwards, H. Münstermann, & B. Weltens (Eds.), *Dialect and education: Some European perspectives* (pp. 139–153). Clevedon: Multilingual Matters.

Tauber, R. T. (1997). *Self-fulfilling prophecy: A practical guide to its use in education.* Westport, CT: Praeger.

Taylor, H. (1989). *Standard English, Black English, and bidialectalism: A controversy.* New York: Peter Lang.

Thomas, W. P., & Collier, V. (1997). *School effectiveness for language minority students.* Washington, DC: National Clearinghouse for Bilingual Education.

Thomas, W. P., & Collier, V. P. (2002). *A national study of school effectiveness for language minority students' long-term academic achievement.* Santa Cruz: Center for Research on Education, Diversity & Excellence.

Todd, L. (1990). *Pidgins and creoles* (2nd ed.). London: Routledge.

Torrey, J. W. (1971). Teaching standard English to speakers of other dialects. In G. E. Perren & J. L. M. Trim (Eds.), *Applications of linguistics: Selected papers of the Second International Congress of Applied Linguistics, Cambridge 1969* (pp. 423–428). Cambridge: Cambridge University Press.

UNESCO. (1968). The use of vernacular languages in education: The report of the UNESCO meeting of specialists, 1951. In J. A. Fishman (Ed.), *Readings in the sociology of language* (pp. 688–716). The Hague: Mouton.

van den Hoogen, J., & Kuijper, H. (1992). The development phase of the Kerkrade Project. In J. Cheshire, V. Edwards, H. Münstermann, & B. Weltens (Eds.), *Dialect and education: Some European perspectives* (pp. 219–233). Clevedon: Multilingual Matters.

van Keulen, J. E., Weddington, G. T., & DeBose, C. E. (1998). *Speech, language, learning and the African American child.* Boston: Allyn & Bacon.

Williams, A. (1989). Dialect in school written work. In J. Cheshire, V. Edwards, H. Münstermann, & B. Weltens (Eds.), *Dialect and education: Some European perspectives* (pp. 182–199). Clevedon: Multilingual Matters.

Williamson, J., & Hardman, F. (1997). Those terrible marks of the beast: Non-standard dialect and children's writing. *Language and Education, 11*(4), 287–299.

Winch, C., & Gingell, J. (1994). Dialect interference and difficulties with writing: An investigation in St. Lucian primary schools. *Language and Education, 8*(3), 157–182.

Winer, L. (1989). Variation and transfer in English Creole–Standard English language learning. In M. R. Eisenstein (Ed.), *The dynamic interlanguage: Empirical studies in second language variation* (pp. 155–173). New York: Plennum Press.

Winer, L. (1990). Orthographic standardization for Trinidad and Tobago: Linguistic and sociopolitical considerations. *Language Problems and Language Planning, 14*(3), 237–268.

Winer, L. (1993). Teaching speakers of Caribbean English Creoles in North American classrooms. In A. W. Glowka & D. M. Lance (Eds.), *Language variation in North American English: Research and teaching* (pp. 191–198). New York: Modern Language Association of America.

Wolfram, W. (1994). Bidialectal literacy in the United States. In D. Spener (Ed.), *Adult biliteracy in the United States* (pp. 71–88). Washington, DC and McHenry, IL: Center for Applied Linguistics/Delta Systems.

Wolfram, W., & Schilling-Estes, N. (1998). *American English: Dialects and variation.* Malden, MA: Blackwell.

Wolfram, W., & Whiteman, M. (1971). The role of dialect interference in composition. *Florida FL Reporter, 9*(1&2), 34–38, 59.

Young-Scholten, M. (1985). Interference reconsidered: The role of similarity in second language acquisition. *Selecta, 6*, 6–12.

Part II

AFRICAN AMERICAN VERNACULAR ENGLISH (AAVE)/EBONICS

Chapter 3

Linguistics, Education, and the Ebonics Firestorm*

John R. Rickford
Stanford University

KEY POINTS

- Reasons for poor academic achievement among African American students.
- Reading achievement data for African American students in urban schools.
- English language proficiency and the Standard English Proficiency Program.
- Controversial 1996 Oakland School Board Resolution on Ebonics.
- Arguments for and against the Contrastive Analysis, bidialectal approach to language instruction.

INTRODUCTION

One profession with which linguistics has long been associated—at least through the research and activities of linguists in applied linguistics, sociolinguistics, and other subfields—is education. Applied linguistics has been primarily concerned with the teaching and learning of foreign languages, but it also includes the study of language disorders and mother tongue/bilingual education as well as other topics (Crystal, 1991, p. 22). Key journals in this area, among them *Applied Linguistics* and the *Annual Review of Applied Linguistics*, go back to the early 1980s and the late 1960s, respectively.

---

*Previously published in *Linguistics, language, and the professions: Education, journalism, law, medicine, and technology*, by J. Alatis, H. Hamilton, & A. H. Tan (Eds.), 2002. Copyright 2002 by the Georgetown University Press.

In the early 1960s, leading descriptive linguists like Leonard Bloomfield (Bloomfield & Barnhart, 1961) and Charles Fries (1962) contributed book-length works on the teaching of reading using a linguistics approach. More recently, Kenneth Goodman (1998) waded in to defend the *whole language* approach to the teaching of reading after the California legislature mandated that reading be taught through phonics and phonemic awareness. And Stephen Krashen (1999) and Kenji Hakuta (www.stanford.edu/~hakuta) were among the many linguists who rose to the defense of bilingual education, severely restricted in California since 1998 by Proposition 227, a state ballot initiative approved by 61% of the voting public.

The closing decade of the 20th century was an especially vigorous period for public debate about language in the United States and Canada (Heller, Rickford, LaForest, & Cyr, 1999), and, as the preceding examples suggest, nowhere was this truer than in California. In this chapter, I will sketch the outlines of the *other* big language and education controversy that exploded in California in this period—the Ebonics firestorm of 1996 and 1997—and discuss the role of linguistics and linguists in it. At the core of the conflagration were the resolutions approved by the Oakland School Board in December 1996, and I will therefore discuss what those meant, in pedagogical terms, and what the experimental evidence is in favor of and against such pedagogy. But the motivation for the Oakland resolutions was the limited academic progress and success that African American students experience(d) in elementary, junior, and high schools, particularly in curriculum-central, language arts areas like reading and writing, and it is with the evidence of this that we must properly begin.

How K–12 Schools Have Been Failing African American Students

The extent to which African American students were failing in Oakland schools—or, viewed another way, the extent to which such schools were failing African American students—was documented by Oakland Superintendent of Schools Carolyn Getridge in the *Monclarion* on December 31, 1996:[1]

> The findings on student achievement in Oakland are evidence that the current system is not working for most African-American children. While 53% of the students in the Oakland Unified School District (OUSD) are African-American, only 37% of the students enrolled in Gifted and Talented classes are African-American, and yet 71% of the students enrolled in Special Education are African-American.

----

[1] This article was reprinted in fall 1997 in *Rethinking Schools* (an urban education journal), 12, p. 27, and in the book-length version of that issue (Perry & Delpit, 1998).

The grade point average of African-American students is 1.80 [C–] compared to a district average of 2.40 [C+]. 64% of students who repeat the same grade are African-American; 67% of students classified as truant are African-American; 80% of all suspended students are African-American; and only 81% of the African-American students who make it to the 12th grade actually graduate.

It was statistics like these, which Getridge herself described as "mind-numbing and a cause for moral outrage" (as quoted in Perry & Delpit, 1998, p. 158) that prompted the OUSD to establish a Task Force on the Education of African American Students in June 1996; the school board's December resolutions were directly based on the task force's findings.

But the statistics that Superintendent Getridge presented, while indeed disturbing, were in one respect too general and in another too specific. They were too general insofar as they did not reveal how African American students were doing in subjects like reading and writing, justifying a specific response involving language. And they were too specific insofar as they failed to reveal that the situation was similar for African American students in virtually every urban school district across the country, making it not just Oakland's problem, but America's.

Consider, for instance, reading achievement data for students in several of the largest urban school districts (including Oakland, but also San Francisco, Los Angeles, New York, Atlanta, and fifty others)—districts that are part of a consortium called the Council of the Great City Schools. These statistics were presented by Michael Casserly, Executive Director of the Council of the Great City Schools, at a United States Senate Appropriations Subcommittee hearing on Ebonics chaired by Senator Arlen Specter on January 23, 1997.

Table 3.1 is a partial representation of Great City Schools results on standardized, norm-referenced reading achievement tests taken in 1992–93.[2] The achievement tests are normed so that 50% of the students who take them should score above the fiftieth percentile. The white students in fifty-five large United States urban school districts surpassed this norm at each school level, the percentage that did so increasing from 60.7 percent at the elementary level to 65.4 percent at the high school level. By contrast, only 31.3% of black elementary students scored above the fiftieth percentile, and this proportion declined to 26.6% by the high school level.

Reading proficiency data from the National Assessment of Educational Progress (NAEP)—also presented to the 1997 Senate Ebonics hearing by

---

[2]Casserly's tables also included results for Hispanic, Asian/Pacific Islander, and Alaskan/Native American/Other students. Of these other groups, the Hispanic students' reading scores were most comparable to those of African American students. Thirty-two percent of them scored above the fiftieth percentile at the K–6 grade level, 30.4% did so at the middle school level, and 24.2% did so at the high school level.

TABLE 3.1
Students Scoring Above the Fiftieth Percentile
on 1992–1993 Reading Achievement Tests

Ethnic group (%)	K–6th grade (%)	7th–8th grade (%)	9th–12th grade (%)
Blacks	31.3	26.9	26.6
Whites	60.7	63.4	65.4

TABLE 3.2
Difference in Average Proficiency of White
and Black Students in Reading

Year	9-year-olds (points)	13-year-olds (points)	17-year-olds (points)
1994	29	31	37
1984	32	26	31
1971	44	38	53

Michael Casserly—were similarly disconcerting. As Table 3.2 shows, the gap
between black and white reading scores is much less in 1994 than it was in
1971, but it is still considerable and shows signs of creeping up from 1984
levels. Moreover, the Table 3.1 pattern is repeated in Table 3.2, in the sense
that the performance of black students, relative to their white counterparts,
steadily declined as they got older. Nine-year-old black students had mean
scores 29 points (on a 500-point scale) behind those of their white counterparts; but thirteen-year-old black students were further behind their white
counterparts (31 points), and seventeen-year-old black students further still
(37 points behind).

Finally, lest it be imagined that the situation has improved since 1993
and 1994, Table 3.3 shows 1999 data from the Great City Schools (Michael
Casserly, personal communication, December 8, 2000). The data are similar to but not exactly comparable with those of Table 3.1, since they represent averages for one grade only (fourth, eighth, tenth) at the elementary,
middle, and senior high levels, rather than for all the grades at each level.
But they are just as devastating, if not more so. The percentage of blacks
scoring above the fiftieth percentile norm, which should be 50% if the population were reading on target, has sunk even further between 1993 and
1999, from 31% to 19% at the elementary level and from 27% to 10.5% at
the high school level. The fact that the relative gap between white *and* black
students is reduced in the tenth grade (they both show a precipitous decline from the eighth grade pass rates) is no cause for rejoicing, since the
percentage of black students who score above the fiftieth percentile is so
abysmally low (10.5%).

TABLE 3.3
Students Scoring Above the Fiftieth Percentile
on 1999 Reading Achievement Tests

Ethnic group	Grade 4 (%)	Grade 8 (%)	Grade 10 (%)
Blacks	19.4	21.5	10.5
Whites	55.5	61.2	36.4

It is statistics like these—largely ignored by the government, the media, and the general public in their amused and outraged reactions to the Oakland Ebonics resolutions—that prompted Oakland's African-American Task Force and the Oakland School Board to attempt to take corrective action in 1996. In the next section we'll consider the resolutions themselves, bearing in mind that most of Oakland's critics rarely did so.

Oakland's Ebonics Resolutions and Testimony Before the United States Senate Panel

In response to the educational malaise of black students in its district, Oakland's African-American Task Force in 1996 came up with nine recommendations, including full implementation of all existing educational programs, with new financial commitments to facilitate this. The Task Force also advocated reviewing the criteria for admitting students to Gifted and Talented Education and Special Education, mobilizing community involvement in partnership with the schools, and developing new procedures for the recruitment of teachers, counselors, and other staff. The number one recommendation, however, had to do with language:

> African American students shall develop English language proficiency as the foundation for their achievements in all core competency areas. (Oakland Unified School District, 1996)

In her statement before the United States Senate hearing on Ebonics on January 23, 1997,[3] Oakland School Superintendent Carolyn Getridge explained *why* the Task Force zeroed in on English language proficiency as a key element in improving student achievement:

> The Task Force's research identified the major role language development plays as the primary gatekeeper for academic success. Without English lan-

---

[3]More precisely, the hearing was before the United States Senate Subcommittee on Labor, Health and Human Services, and Education, chaired by Sen. Arlen Specter (R–Pa.).

guage proficiency students are unable to access or master advanced level course work in the areas of mathematics and science which have traditionally been viewed as the gatekeepers to enrollment in post-secondary institutions. (U.S. Senate, 1997, p. 1)

One could of course add that English language proficiency affects not only mathematics and science, but also social studies and every other subject in the curriculum. Going beyond the rationale for the language focus, Superintendent Carolyn Getridge said a little about *how* the OUSD would attempt to achieve increased competency in Standard American English—by building a bridge to it from the African American students' vernacular:

> Language development for African American students . . . will be enhanced with the recognition and understanding of the language structures unique to many African American students. . . . Our interest is in guaranteeing that conditions exist for high achievement and research indicates that an awareness of these language patterns by educators helps students build a bridge to Standard American English. A variety of strategies will be employed to support language development and achieve our goal of high academic performance for all students. (U.S. Senate, 1997, pp. 1–2)

Getridge's testimony added that such bridging would be achieved in part through increased implementation of the Standard English Proficiency program (SEP), a program authorized by state legislation since 1981 that she described briefly as follows:

> S.E.P. is a cultural–linguistic program that empowers African American students with knowledge and understanding of African American culture and languages. Classroom instruction demonstrates the differences in languages spoken in the student's home and standard English. The language students bring into the classroom is embraced and a bridge is constructed to standard English. (U.S. Senate, 1997, p. 13)

However, Getridge did not provide any experimental evidence in favor of this bridging or Contrastive Analysis (CA) approach. In this respect she failed to respond to the critique of California State Schools Superintendent Delaine Eastin that "We are not aware of any research which indicates that this kind of program will help address the language and achievement problems of African American students."[4] This is an issue that I'll address in the next subsection of this chapter. To lay the groundwork, first consider the OUSD's famous (or perhaps infamous) Ebonics Resolutions of December 18, 1996, and their revisions of January 17, 1997, both of which preceded

---

[4]Eastin's comment appeared in the *San Jose Mercury* newspaper, 20 December 1996, p. 1A, in an article by Frances Dinkelspiel titled, "Black Language Policy in Oakland: Talk of the Town."

the January 23, 1997 Senate hearing on Ebonics at which Superintendent Getridge testified.

For the sake of completeness, I will provide the full text of the resolutions, using the wording and format in Rickford & Rickford (2000, pp. 166–169). Each clause is numbered for easy reference (in both OUSD versions, the clauses were not numbered); underlining is added to highlight wording from the original December 18, 1996 version that was deleted in the revised version approved on January 17, 1997; and square brackets and boldface are used for replacement or new wording that was inserted on the latter date:

RESOLUTION (No. 9697-0063) OF THE BOARD OF EDUCATION ADOPTING THE REPORT AND RECOMMENDATIONS OF THE AFRICAN AMERICAN TASK FORCE; A POLICY STATEMENT, AND DIRECTING THE SUPERINTENDENT OF SCHOOLS TO DEVISE A PROGRAM TO IMPROVE THE ENGLISH LANGUAGE ACQUISITION AND APPLICATION SKILLS OF AFRICAN AMERICAN STUDENTS

1. WHEREAS, numerous validated scholarly studies demonstrate that African American students as a part of their culture and history as African people possess and utilize a language described in various scholarly approaches as "Ebonics" (literally "Black sounds") or "Pan African Communication Behaviors" or "African Language Systems"; and

2. WHEREAS, these studies have also demonstrated that African Language Systems are genetically based [**have origins in West and Niger-Congo languages**] and not a dialect of English [**are not merely dialects of English**]; and

3. WHEREAS, these studies demonstrate that such West and Niger-Congo African languages have been recognized and addressed in the educational community as worthy of study, understanding or [**and**] application of their principles, laws and structures for the benefit of African American students both in terms of positive appreciation of the language and these students' acquisition and mastery of English language skills; and

4. WHEREAS, such recognition by scholars has given rise over the past fifteen years to legislation passed by the State of California recognizing the unique language stature of descendants of slaves, with such legislation being prejudicially and unconstitutionally vetoed repeatedly by various California state governors; and

5. WHEREAS, judicial cases in states other than California have recognized the unique language stature of African American pupils, and

such recognition by courts has resulted in court-mandated educational programs which have substantially benefited African American children in the interest of vindicating their equal protection of the law rights under the Fourteenth Amendment to the United States Constitution; and

6. WHEREAS, the Federal Bilingual Education Act (20 U.S.C. 1402 et seq.) mandates that local educational agencies "build their capacities to establish, implement and sustain programs of instruction for children and youth of limited English proficiency"; and

7. WHEREAS, the interest of the Oakland Unified School District in providing equal opportunities for all its students dictate limited English proficient educational programs recognizing the English language acquisition and improvement skills of African American students are as fundamental as is application of bilingual education [**or second language learner**] principles for others whose primary languages are other than English [**Primary languages are the language patterns children bring to school**]; and

8. WHEREAS, the standardized tests and grade scores of African-American students in reading and language arts skills measuring their application of English skills are substantially below state and national norms and that such deficiencies will be remedied by application of a program featuring African Language Systems principles in instructing African American children both in their primary language and in English [**to move students from the language patterns they bring to school to English proficiency**]; and

9. WHEREAS, standardized tests and grade scores will be remedied by application of a program that teachers and aides [**instructional assistants**], who are certified in the methodology of featuring African Language Systems principles in instructing African American children both in their primary language and in English [**used to transition students from the language patterns they bring to school to English**]. The certified teachers of these students will be provided incentives including, but not limited to salary differentials;

10. NOW, THEREFORE, BE IT RESOLVED that the Board of Education officially recognizes the existence and the cultural and historic bases of West and Niger-Congo African Language Systems, and each language as the predominantly primary language of [**many**] African American students; and

11. BE IT FURTHER RESOLVED that the Board of Education hereby adopts the report, recommendations and attached Policy Statement of the District's African-American Task Force on language stature of African-American speech; and

12. BE IT FURTHER RESOLVED that the Superintendent in conjunc-
    tion with her staff shall immediately devise and implement the best
    possible academic program for imparting instruction to African
    American students in their primary language for the combined pur-
    poses of [**facilitating the acquisition and mastery of English language
    skills**] while maintaining [**respecting and embracing**] the legitimacy
    and richness of such language [**the language patterns**] whether it is
    [**they are**] known as "Ebonics," "African Language Systems," "Pan Af-
    rican Communication Behaviors," or other description, and to facili-
    tate their acquisition and mastery of English language skills; and

13. BE IT FURTHER RESOLVED that the Board of Education hereby
    commits to earmark District general and special funding as is rea-
    sonably necessary and appropriate to enable the Superintendent
    and her staff to accomplish the foregoing; and

14. BE IT FURTHER RESOLVED that the Superintendent and her staff
    shall utilize the input of the entire Oakland educational community
    as well as state and federal scholarly and educational input in devis-
    ing such a program; and

15. BE IT FURTHER RESOLVED that periodic reports on the progress
    of the creation and implementation of such an education program
    shall be made to the Board of Education at least once per month
    commencing at the Board meeting of December 18, 1996.

Many comments could be made about the various clauses of this resolution, considering, inter alia, the ones that were the source of public controversy about Ebonics as a separate Niger–Congo and genetically based language (clause 2, in its original wording), and whether the OUSD intended
to seek bilingual funding for its Ebonics speakers (clauses 6, 7, and 8).
These and related issues are discussed at length in other sources, including
McWhorter (1998, pp. 127–260), Baugh (2000, pp. 36–86), Rickford &
Rickford (2000, pp. 169–173), Smitherman (2000, pp. 150–162), and Crawford (2001).

What I want to focus on instead is the more fundamental issue of whether
the OUSD intended by these resolutions to teach African American students
Ebonics or in Ebonics, as most of the country and the world assumed, or to
use Ebonics partly as a springboard for helping them to master standard English.[5] The quotations from Superintendent Getridge's Senate testimony indi-

---

[5]In this paper, as in Rickford (1999c), I will use Ebonics and African-American Vernacular
English or Black English as essentially equivalent. Despite claims that they are different (see,
e.g., Smith, 2001), especially insofar as Ebonics is claimed to be an African variety and NOT a
dialect of English, the features cited as representative of these varieties are virtually identical,
as noted in Rickford (1999c).

cate that the latter rather than the former was the main goal. And the preamble (capitalized and unchanged in both versions) to the resolutions does refer explicitly to the goal of improving "the English language acquisition and application skills of African American students." It is true that the December 1996 wording of clauses 8, 9, and 12 does refer to instructing African American children "in their primary language" (as McWhorter, 2000, pp. 202–203 and others have pointed out). But, as noted by Rickford & Rickford (2000, p. 172), these could be legitimately interpreted as referring to technical instruction in features of the primary or source variety as part of the compare-and-contrast process used to develop mastery in the target variety (in this case, standard English). And while most Contrastive Analysis approaches are built on a philosophy of respect for the legitimacy of the source variety, which we certainly endorse, it is not necessary to try to develop verbal fluency in Ebonics among inner-city African American students: "tutoring them on Ebonics would be like giving a veteran angler a lesson on baiting hooks" (Rickford & Rickford, 2000, p. 172).

In any event, the revised resolution wording of January 1997 was clearly intended to remove ambiguities on this score, with clauses like "used to transition students from the language patterns they bring to school to English" replacing the earlier ambiguous wording. And to make the matter maximally explicit, the OUSD issued a press release shortly after the first version of the resolutions came out (and ran into a hornet's nest), emphasizing that:

1. The Oakland Unified School District is not replacing the teaching of Standard American English with any other language.
2. The District is not teaching Ebonics.
3. The District emphasizes teaching Standard American English and has set a high standard of excellence for all its students.

Given that the primary *goal* of the OUSD was to help its African American students master standard English (a goal that it ironically shared with its detractors!), the debate can be refocused (as it never was in the media) on the efficacy of the *means* (including CA) that Oakland wanted to use to achieve this end. To the extent that linguists specifically responded to this issue, the answer seemed to be that the approach was efficacious and advisable. But the relevant evidence was not always provided, and the endorsement was not completely unanimous, as we will see.

Arguments and Evidence FOR the Contrastive Analysis Approach that Oakland Intended to Use to Implement its Resolutions

The precise methods the OUSD intended to use in teaching its African American students standard English were never spelled out in detail, certainly not in its resolutions. The revised (January 17, 1997) resolution's closing clause (12) specified, in fact, that "the Superintendent in conjunction with her staff *shall immediately devise and implement* the best possible program for facilitating the acquisition and mastery of English language skills, while embracing the legitimacy and richness of the language patterns . . . known as Ebonics . . ." (emphasis added). The only methodological mandate in this was that the students' vernacular (Ebonics) was to be taken into account in the process. However, as noted above (see quotes at the beginning of section 2), Superintendent Getridge's Senate testimony on January 23, 1997, did indicate that the sixteen-year-old Standard English Proficiency (SEP) program, with its Contrastive Analysis and bridging strategies, was to be an important element in their approach.

The SEP program itself was already in use in some of Oakland's classrooms (the postresolution plan was to implement it more widely), and Oakland was a key SEP site in California, serving as host of its annual statewide conferences for several years. In the SEP handbook, a massive 340-page document,[6] the goal of helping vernacular-speaking African American students master standard English is spelled out quite explicitly (SEP handbook, n.d.):[7]

> This handbook is designed as a resource for school site administrators and classroom teachers in initiating, implementing and improving Standard English programs. The contributors to this handbook maintain that proficiency in Standard English is essential in providing students with those skills that will afford them the opportunity to experience optimum access to the social and economic mainstream.
>
> The handbook offers a theoretical and functional framework to operate an oral-based language program that is designed to assist speakers of Black Language [Black English or Ebonics] in becoming proficient in Standard English. (p. 5)

Moreover, while emphasizing that a positive attitude towards one's own language is the starting point for the program, the SEP handbook goes on

---

[6]The date of production of the handbook (which is not necessarily followed in all California schools that use the SEP approach) is unclear (in my copy at least), although it appears to be sometime in the 1980s. Its authors/contributors are listed in the acknowledgments (4) as: Sue Boston, Audrey Guess Knight, Yvonne Strozier, Rex Fortune, and Orlando Taylor. Taylor is a Howard University linguist and speech pathologist who has contributed to the study of Ebonics for decades, and who testified before the United States Senate panel on Ebonics in January 1997. He is also one of the coeditors of Adger, Christian, & Taylor (1999).

[7]In view of its explicit standard English orientation, it is especially ironic that California Senate Bill 205 was introduced in 1997 to kill the SEP program, on the argument that it was important for students to master standard English. Fortunately, the bill died in a state senate committee on April 7, 1997.

to specify that Contrastive Analysis, with its discrimination, identification, translation, and response drills (see Feigenbaum, 1970) is its basic methodology (SEP, n.d.):

> The approaches used in this study are drills which are variations of the contrastive analysis and the comparative analysis [techniques] in teaching Black children to use Standard English. . . . By comparing the Standard English structure to be taught and the equivalent or close nonstandard structure, the student can see how they differ. Many students have partial knowledge of standard English; that is, they can recognize and produce it but without accurate control. . . . For many students, this sorting out is the beginning of a series of steps from passive recognition to active production. (p. 27)

However, despite its twenty years of implementation and its reported use in over 300 schools, there is no publicly available empirical evidence of the SEP's effectiveness (as noted by Yarborough & Flores, 1997). So it is of little use in arguing for the approach the OUSD intended to take in implementing its resolutions or in defending it against its many critics. This is also true of the well-designed *Talkacross* program designed by Crowell and colleagues (1974), featuring Contrastive Analysis between *Black English* and Standard English in a 69-page teacher's manual and a 193-page activity book.

The Linguistics Society of America (LSA), the American Association for Applied Linguistics (AAAL), and Teachers of English to Speakers of Other Languages (TESOL) were among several language-related organizations that approved resolutions of their own in the wake of the Ebonics firestorm.[8] In general, these provided support for the principle of respecting the legitimacy of the linguistic systems students bring to school, recognized the systematic nature of Ebonics, and endorsed the value of taking it into account in teaching Standard English. But even when they made reference to the existence of evidence in favor of the latter approach, they did not specifically cite it. This was also the case with Parker & Crist (1995), who reported that they had used the bidialectal, Contrastive Analysis approach successfully with Ebonics speakers in Tennessee and Illinois, but provided no supporting empirical evidence.

Such evidence does exist, however, in at least three striking cases, and I will turn to them shortly. But it may be useful to enumerate some of the arguments that linguists and others make in favor of Contrastive Analysis specifically, or more generally, in favor of taking Ebonics and other vernacular varieties into account in developing reading, writing, and other language arts skills in standard English (see Rickford, 1999b).

---

[8]The LSA resolution, approved on January 3, 1997 is reprinted in Perry & Delpit (1998, pp. 160–161), Baugh (2000, pp. 117–118), and Crawford (2001, pp. 358–359). The AAAL resolution was approved on March 11, 1997, and the TESOL resolution on March 10, 1997.

One argument is that this approach proceeds from a position of strength: the students are already competent in a valid, systematic language variety (their vernacular), and this fluency can be used as a springboard for teaching about important qualities of language in general (metaphor and rhyme, logical argument, authentic dialogue, rhetorical strategy) and about differences between the vernacular and the standard or mainstream variety in particular. The general strategy is facilitated by the fact that Ebonics and other vernaculars are often used by award-winning writers (e.g., Langston Hughes, Toni Morrison, Sonia Sanchez, August Wilson; see Rickford & Rickford, 2000), several of whose works are already in use in American classrooms,[9] and by the fact that students encounter other fluent and effective vernacular users (e.g., preachers) regularly in their own communities (Rickford & Rickford, 2000). Another argument in relation to the specific contrastive strategy is that "this method allows for increased efficiency in the classroom, as teachers can concentrate on the systematic areas of contrast with SE [standard English] that cause difficulty for vernacular speakers rather than taking on the more daunting task of teaching all of English grammar" (Rickford, 1999a, p. 13).

Moreover, an approach like this, it might be argued, is likely to have positive effects on both teachers and their vernacular-speaking students. Teachers, like many members of the general public, often erroneously perceive students' vernaculars as illogical, unsystematic, and evidence of cognitive deficits or laziness (Labov, 1970; Van Keulen, Weddington, & DeBose, 1998, p. 232). These misperceptions irk linguists because they run counter to everything we know about human language. But what's worse, they can lead to lower teacher expectations and poorer student performance in a cycle of self-fulfilling prophecy that's now depressingly well-documented (Tauber, 1997). Students in turn are often relieved and delighted to learn that the vernacular they speak naturally is not the source of weakness that teachers often make it out to be, but a source of strength. Not only might their self-identity and motivation be enhanced by this,[10] but the resistance to standard English that's sometimes reported as an element in black students' limited success in school (cf., Fordham & Ogbu, 1986) is likely to be reduced in the process.

A third argument in favor of Contrastive Analysis and taking the vernacular into account is that the prevailing, status quo alternative of ignoring

---

[9]I received two requests in the winter of 2000 to speak to Palo Alto high school students studying August Wilson's *Fences* about the pervasive African-American vernacular in his plays.

[10]As Van Keulen, Weddington, & DeBose (1998, p. 243) note: "when teachers accept Black students' home language and use books, other materials, and activities that incorporate their culture, teachers signal their recognition of Black students' values and concern for their self-esteem. Self-esteem and confidence are very important to academic success because students with high self-esteem will have the confidence to take on new challenges in reading, writing, and other academic tasks."

and/or constantly correcting students' vernaculars in an ad hoc and disparaging fashion clearly does NOT seem to work. This is evident, not only from
the kinds of statistics reported in section 2, but also from reports in Piestrup
(1973) and elsewhere that the corrective, disparaging approach leads students to withdraw from participation, turn to disruptive behavior, and perform more poorly in school.

The fourth and perhaps most effective argument is that there are at least
three empirically validated studies of the effectiveness of taking the vernacular into account in teaching standard English using Contrastive Analysis.
The first is an experimental composition program conducted by Hanni
Taylor with African-American students at Aurora University, outside Chicago, in the 1980s. The second is a fifth- and sixth-grade program run by
Kelli Harris-Wright in DeKalb County, just outside Atlanta, in which home
speech and school speech are contrasted. The third is the Academic English Mastery Program (formerly the Language Development Program for
African American Students) in Los Angeles, run by Noma LeMoine. I'll say
some more about each of these before considering arguments and evidence against this approach.

In the Aurora University study (Taylor, 1989), African-American students from Chicago inner-city areas were divided into two groups. The experimental group was taught the differences between Black English and
standard English through Contrastive Analysis. The control group was
taught composition through conventional techniques, with no specific reference to the vernacular. After eleven weeks, Taylor found that the experimental group showed a dramatic *decrease* (−59%) in the use of ten targeted
Black English features in their standard English writing, whereas the control group in fact showed a slight *increase* (+8.5%) in their use of such features in their writing.

In the DeKalb County (Georgia) study, described by Harris-Wright
(1999), but without the specific results to be presented here, selected fifth
and sixth graders in the bidialectal group (primarily African American)
have for several years been taught English through a comparative approach
that does not involve "devaluing the skills that they learn at home" (Harris-
Wright, 1999, p. 55). By contrast, control groups are offered no explicit
comparison between their vernacular and standard English. As the results
in Table 3.4 show (Kelli Harris-Wright, personal communication), between
1995 and 1997, students in the bidialectal group made *bigger relative reading
composite gains* every year than students in the control group, who actually
showed slight losses in two of the three years.[11] More recent results (1998,

---

[11]Students in the bidialectal group generally had lower absolute scores (particularly in the
1996–97 year) than students in the control group, although it is striking that the bidialectal
group was able to surpass the control group in the posttest performance in 1995.

TABLE 3.4
Reading Composite Scores for Bidialectal and Control Groups

Group	1994–95	1995–96	1996–97
Bidialectal Posttest	42.39	41.16	34.26
Bidialectal Pretest	39.71	38.48	30.37
GAIN by bidialectal students	**+2.68**	**+2.68**	**+3.89**
Control Posttest	40.65	43.15	49.00
Control Pretest	41.02	41.15	49.05
GAIN by control students	**−0.37**	**+2.0**	**−0.05**

Note. Adapted from Kelli Harris-Wright, 1999, personal communication.

TABLE 3.5
Mean Scores and Gains for Experimental and Control
Writing Groups, Los Angeles Unified School District

Group Test	Mean Pretest score	Mean Posttest score	GAIN
Experimental Writing	10.80	13.30	2.5
Control Writing	9.06	10.74	**1.68**

Source. Maddahian and Sandamela 2000.

1999) for individual elementary schools in DeKalb County point in the same direction, with the experimental, bidialectal students showing greater gains between pretest and posttest than students in the control group.

Finally, we have results from the Academic English Mastery Program (AEMP) in the Los Angeles Unified School District, shown in Table 3.5.[12] Once again, students in the experimental group show greater gains (on tests taken in 1998–99) than students in the control group. Similar results obtain for the reading and language components of the SAT-9 test.[13]

Arguments and Evidence AGAINST the Contrastive Analysis, Bidialectal Approach

Many, many statements (sometimes diatribes) were broadcast in the media and voiced by the general public AGAINST the Contrastive Analysis vernac-

---

[12]The AEMP involves more than Contrastive Analysis, including language experience approaches, whole language, and an Afrocentric curriculum. But at the heart of it is respect for students' home languages and comparison of African-American language and standard American English structures. For more information, see LeMoine (2001).

[13]For instance, at the 109th Street school, African-American students in the experimental AEMP (n = 12) had mean scores of 21 and 24 on the reading and language components of the SAT-9, whereas a comparison group of African-American students who were not in the AEMP (n = 104) had lower mean scores of 16 and 20, respectively.

ular-respecting approach that Oakland proposed to use to implement its resolutions. However, since so many of these were uninformed about the OUSD resolutions and what they might mean in pedagogical terms, and about linguistics and its possible applications, they are of little utility in a reasoned discussion. By contrast, a number of linguists have, over the years, queried various aspects of the Contrastive Analysis, bidialectal approach, and at least one linguist has consistently opposed the Oakland resolutions and their implementation. It is their argumentation and evidence that we'll focus on in this section of the chapter.

One of the oldest positions, typified by Sledd (1972), is that the teaching of standard English under the guise of bidialectalism is both impossible and immoral. The impossibility claim hinged on the argument that "the necessary descriptions of standard and nonstandard dialects are non-existent, and materials and methods of teaching are dubious at best" (pp. 372–373). But the situation has changed dramatically in the intervening thirty years, especially in the last five years, in which we have seen a flood of books and articles about African-American Vernacular English, so this argument is no longer tenable. The immorality argument is that "forcing" students to learn standard English buys into the prejudices and corruption of the dominant society and ignores the fact that "in job hunting in America, pigmentation is more important than pronunciation" (p. 379). We should aim for higher ambitions and deeper values in educating students than kowtowing to the majority, and, if anything, we should work on changing the prejudices and increasing the receptive abilities of whites rather than the productive abilities of blacks. To the extent that this kind of argument takes the linguistic and moral high ground, it is attractive, but not entirely convincing. There does appear to be a relation between the ability to command standard English (whether or not one retains one's vernacular) and success in school and employment and mobility in a wide range of occupations. In addition, the parents of vernacular speakers are almost unanimous in wanting their children to master some variety of mainstream or standard English (Hoover, 1978).

The preceding argument is not really against Contrastive Analysis but against the explicit teaching of standard English. However, there does exist a cluster of arguments against Contrastive Analysis and bidialectalism as methodologies. One, summarized by Craig (1999), who in turn cites Jagger & Cullinan (1974), is that "such programmes were 'bi' in name only, because there was no structured use or development of cognitive/communicative capacity in the vernacular to match what was being attempted in English" (p. 38). Some programs (including the SEP) involve translation only into Standard English, and never into the vernacular. But, as I have noted in an earlier paper, "if translation is not carried out in both directions, the message . . . conveyed is that the vernacular variety has no integrity or validity" (Rickford, 1999a, p. 14). The boring, stultifying nature of the drills that some contrastive approaches depend on is also problematic. However, as I've observed elsewhere (Rickford, 1999a, p. 15): "these are not intrinsic weaknesses of contrastive analysis," and programs like the AEMP in Los Angeles that make extensive use of literature and other techniques, show that "drill and kill" can be minimized or eliminated.

A third methodological argument is that Contrastive Analysis and the interference hypothesis that undergirds it (Lado, 1957) no longer hold the theoretical sway they once did in the field of second language acquisition, where it was first developed, since they seem to account for only a limited portion of second language learner's errors (Ellis, 1994). However, the interference hypothesis does seem to account for a larger portion of errors when two dialects of a language are compared and contrasted, and while error analysis and other analytical strategies should also be pursued, we have no substantive evidence that Contrastive Analysis is unhelpful to dialect speakers seeking to add a second variety, and some strong evidence to the contrary (see the end of the section arguing for Contrastive Analysis).

We come now to more specific arguments raised by John McWhorter against the OUSD's "translation approach," as he calls it. I'll use the brief summary from his (1997) paper as my point of reference, but his (1998) book provides further details, especially in chapter 8 (pp. 201–261).

McWhorter's first argument is that "Black English is not different enough from standard English to be the cause of the alarming reading scores among black children" (1997, p. 2). However, the argument made by many linguists is that while there are indeed some major differences, it is precisely the many subtle differences between the two varieties that cause students difficulty in reading and especially in writing when they fail to recognize that they are switching between systems (Stewart, 1964; Taylor, 1989).

McWhorter dubs this latter position "Ebonics II"—especially to the extent that the subtle differences are negatively viewed and stigmatized by teachers—and he calls it a "thoroughly reasonable position." However, he still feels that the concerns could be better addressed by having students learn standard English via immersion. But immersion is already the method used in most urban school districts; and the results, as noted above, are not encouraging. Moreover, in the homes and communities where the students spend most of their time when not in school, Ebonics is widely heard and spoken, so immersion in standard English on the model of students who go to another country for immersion in the language of that country is quite impractical.

McWhorter's other concerns include the claim that students speaking other dialects (e.g., Brooklyn, Appalachian, or rural Southern white English) "are not taught standard English as a foreign language, even though the latter is extremely similar to Black English. To impose translation exercises on black children implies that they are not as intelligent as white children" (1997, p. 2). To which I would retort that students from these other dialect areas often do have language arts and other educational problems that may well relate to their language differences. To the extent that this is so, I would rather give them the same benefit of linguistically informed bidialectal methods than deny the latter to everyone. Moreover, I am not convinced by the intelligence insulting argument. Nothing is more stultifying than the devastating rates of school failure with existing methods shown in section 2. If Contrastive Analysis and bidialectal education help to alleviate and even reverse the situation, as the evidence suggests, they are worth the effort.

McWhorter (1997) also argues that "the reason African American children fail disproportionately in school is due to declining school quality and the pathologies of the inner city" (p. 2). I would agree that the (primarily) urban schools in which African Americans receive their education are indeed worse off than the ones in which whites do, in general terms (see Rickford, 1999a, pp. 5–8), but I would still argue that, other things being equal, an approach that took students' language into account, as the Contrastive Analysis approach does, is still more likely to succeed than one that does not.

McWhorter's biggest argument is that there are at least nine studies, including Melmed (1971), Nolen (1972), Marwit & Neumann (1974), and Simons & Johnson (1974), that show that "dialect readers have no effect whatsoever on African American students' reading scores" (Rickford, 1999a, p. 2). But notwithstanding the fact that these are all nonlongitudinal, one-time studies, and that the only longitudinal dialect reader study involving African American students (Simpkins & Simpkins, 1981) shows very positive results, the crucial point to be noted is that Oakland never proposed using dialect readers in their language arts programs. The SEP program that was to be their primary implementation vehicle used Contrastive Analysis rather than dialect readers as their method of choice. McWhorter does not cite one empirical study that provides evidence against the efficacy of the Contrastive Analysis, bidialectal approach, and we have already seen several arguments and significant experimental evidence in its favor.

Summary and Conclusion

My goal in this chapter has been to sketch the outlines of a recent major public debate involving language and education—the Oakland school district's resolutions about taking Ebonics into account in teaching standard English and the language arts—and to summarize the linguistic and pedagogical arguments in favor of and against Contrastive Analysis, the major strategy that they planned to implement. My own preference for the kind of innovative methods the OUSD proposed is probably obvious. I am led to this both because of the obvious failures of existing methods that make no reference to the vernacular, and show no concern for bidialectalism, and by the arguments in favor of Contrastive Analysis approaches, especially the empirical evidence of their success where they have been given time to succeed.

But I am not wedded to this method, and I even tend to feel, with respect to writing at the secondary school level, for instance, that we do have to tackle larger conceptual and organizational problems rather than getting bogged down in grammatical minutiae. Some recent high school writing samples I have seen do indeed have several intrusions from the vernacular into what was supposed/expected to be a standard English text. But if all those were converted to standard English immediately, the writing would be no less poor, and we can't fix the minor mechanical issues and ignore the larger conceptual ones. I think the kinds of Contrastive Analysis methods that the OUSD proposed to follow will be most useful and effective at the elementary and middle school levels, and I think that given the myriad problems with existing approaches, the OUSD deserved to be free to experiment with other alternatives.

Regrettably, it must be reported that in early 2001, four years after the OUSD took America and the world by storm with its Ebonics proposals, much of the vigor of that early drive has gone. Key personnel such as Superintendent Carolyn Getridge and School Board Member Toni Cook are no longer in those positions, and the SEP, while still practiced by a valiant few, is no longer a favored district-wide strategy. It is true that personnel from the OUSD partnered with William Labov and others from the University of Pennsylvania in a million dollar study of "African American Literacy and Culture," but the OUSD component was mostly focused on cultural and general pedagogical strategies rather than specific language-related ones. The SEP itself is very much on the ropes in California with funding for the annual conference and oversight by personnel in the state superintendent's office no longer available.

At the same time, linguistically aware and committed personnel such as Folasade Oladele remain in the district, and they have been trying, through teacher education sessions, to sensitize teachers to the regularities of African-American vernacular and the value of taking it into account in teaching standard English. The prospects for larger-scale efforts involving linguists are promising.

QUESTIONS FOR DISCUSSION AND REFLECTIVE WRITING

1. Look at the various tables comparing reading achievement between black and white students. What are the most striking findings? In what ways might these statistics inform classroom practice?

2. Work in a group. Do a close reading of the Oakland School Board Resolution. Discuss which clauses are the most controversial. Why? What questions/issues does this Resolution raise for you?

3. Examine the arguments for and against the Contrastive Analysis (CA)/bidialectal approach. In your journal, write about what you see as the benefits and disadvantages of CA and give reasons.

REFERENCES

Adger, C. T., Christian, D., & Taylor, O. (Eds.). (1999). *Making the connection: Language and academic achievement among African American students.* McHenry, IL: Delta Systems and Washington DC: Center for Applied Linguistics.

Baugh, J. (2000). *Beyond Ebonics: Linguistic pride and racial prejudice.* New York: Oxford University Press.

Bloomfield, L., & Barnhart, C. L. (1961). *Let's read, a linguistic approach.* Detroit: Wayne State University Press.

Craig, D. R. (1999). *Teaching language and literacy: Policies and procedures for vernacular situations.* Georgetown, Guyana: Education and Development Services.

Crawford, C. (Ed.). (2001). *Ebonics and language education.* New York: Sankofa World Publishers.

Crowell, S., Kolba, E., Stewart, W., & Johnson, K. (1974). *Talkacross: Materials for teaching English as a second dialect.* (Teacher's handbook and student activity book). Montclair, NJ: Caribou Associated.

Crystal, D. (1991). *A dictionary of linguistics and phonetics* (3rd ed.). Oxford: Blackwell.

Ellis, R. (1994). *The study of second language acquisition.* Oxford: Oxford University Press.

Feigenbaum, I. (1970). The use of nonstandard English in teaching standard: Contrast and comparison. In R. W. Fasold & R. W. Shuy (Eds.), *Teaching English in the inner city* (pp. 87–107). Washington, DC: Center for Applied Linguistics.

Fordham, S., & Ogbu, J. (1986). Black students' school success: Coping with the burden of "acting white." *The Urban Review, 18*(3), 176–206.

Fries, C. (1962). *Linguistics and reading.* New York: Holt, Rinehart and Winston.

Goodman, K. (Ed.). (1998). *In defense of good teaching: What teachers need to know about the "reading wars."* York, Maine: Stenhouse Publishers.

Harris-Wright, K. (1999). Enhancing bidialectalism in urban African American students. In C. T. Adger, D. Christian, & O. Taylor (Eds.), *Making the connection: Language and academic achievement among African American students* (pp. 53–60). McHenry, IL: Delta Systems, and Washington, DC: Center for Applied Linguistics.

Heller, M., Rickford, J., LaForest, M., & Cyr, D. (1999). Sociolinguistics and debate. *Journal of Sociolinguistics, 3*(2), 260–288.

Hoover, M. (1978). Community attitudes toward Black English. *Language in Society, 7,* 65–87.

Jagger, A., & Cullinan, B. (1974). Teaching Standard English to achieve bidialectalism: Problems with current practices. In A. Aarons (Ed.), *The Florida FL Reporter: Issues in the Teaching of Standard English,* (spring/fall), 63–70.

Krashen, S. (1999). *Condemned without a trial: Bogus arguments against bilingual education.* Portsmouth, NH: Heinemann.

Labov, W. (1970). The logic of nonstandard English. In J. Alatis (Ed.), *Twentieth annual round table: Linguistics and the teaching of Standard English to speakers of other languages or dialects* (pp. 1–44). Washington, DC: Georgetown University Press.

Lado, R. (1957). *Linguistics across cultures: Applied linguistics for language teachers.* Ann Arbor: University of Michigan Press.

LeMoine, N. (2001). Language variation and literacy acquisition in African American students. In J. Harris, A. Kamhi, & K. Pollock (Eds.), *Literacy in African American communities* (pp. 169–194). Mahwah, NJ: Lawrence Erlbaum Associates.

Maddahian, E., & Sandamela, A. P. (2000). *Academic English Mastery Program: 1998 evaluation report* (Publication No. 781). Program Evaluation and Research Branch, Research and Evaluation Unit, Los Angeles Unified School District.

Marwit, S., & Neumann, G. (1974). Black and white children's comprehension of standard and nonstandard English passages. *Journal of Educational Psychology, 66*(3), 329–332.

McWhorter, J. (1997). Wasting energy on an illusion: Six months later. *The Black Scholar, 27*(2), 2–5.

McWhorter, J. (1998). *The word on the street: Fact and fable about American English.* New York: Plenum.

McWhorter, J. (2000). *Losing the race: Self-sabotage in Black America.* New York: The Free Press.

Melmed, P. (1971). *Black English phonology: The question of reading interference.* (Monographs of the Language Behavior Research Laboratory, No. 1). Berkeley: University of California.

Nolen, P. (1972). Reading nonstandard dialect materials: A study of grades two and four. *Child Development, 43*, 1092–1097.

Oakland Unified School District. (1996). Overview of recommendations. In *Synopsis of the adopted policy on Standard English language development.* Retrieved December, from www.west.net/~joyland/oakland.htm

Parker, H., & Crist, M. (1995). *Teaching minorities to play the corporate language game.* Columbia: University of South Carolina, Resource Center for the Freshman Year Experience and Students in Transition.

Perry, T., & Delpit, L. (Eds.). (1998). *The real Ebonics debate: Power, language, and the education of African-American children.* Boston: Beacon Press.

Piestrup, A. (1973). *Black dialect interference and accommodation of reading instruction in the first grade.* (Monographs of the Language Behavior Research Laboratory, No. 4). Berkeley: University of California.

Rickford, J. R. (1999a). Language diversity and academic achievement in the education of African American students—an overview of the issues. In C. T. Adger, D. Christian, & O. Taylor (Eds.), *Making the connection: Language and academic achievement among African American students* (pp. 1–20). McHenry, IL: Delta Systems, and Washington, DC: Center for Applied Linguistics.

Rickford, J. R. (1999b). Using the vernacular to teach the standard. In J. D. Ramirez, T. Wiley, G. de Klerk, & E. Lee (Eds.), *Ebonics in the urban education debate* (pp. 23–41). Long Beach: Center for Language Minority Education and Research, California Research, California State University. Also in J. Rickford, *African American Vernacular English: Features, evolution, educational implications* (pp. 329–347). Oxford, UK: Blackwell.

Rickford, J. R. (1999c). *African American Vernacular English: Features, evolution educational implications.* Oxford: Blackwell.

Rickford, J. R., & Rickford, R. J. (2000). *Spoken soul: The story of Black English.* New York: Wiley.

Simons, H., & Johnson, K. (1974). Black English syntax and reading interference. *Research in the Teaching of English, 8*, 339–358.

Simpkins, G., & Simpkins, C. (1981). Cross cultural approach to curriculum development. In G. Smitherman (Ed.), *Black English and the education of Black children and youth: Proceedings of the national invitational symposium on the King decision* (pp. 221–240). Detroit: Center for Black Studies, Wayne State University.

Sledd, J. (1972). Doublespeak: Dialectology in the service of big brother. *College English, 33,* 439–456.

Smith, E. (2001). Ebonics and bilingual education of the African American child. In C. Crawford (Ed.), *Ebonics and language education* (pp. 123–163). New York: Sankofa World Publishers.

Smitherman, G. (2000). *Talkin that talk: Language, culture, and education in African America.* London: Routledge.

Stewart, W. (1964). *Foreign language teaching methods in quasi-foreign language situations: Non-standard speech and the teaching of English.* Washington, DC: Center for Applied Linguistics.

Tauber, R. T. (1997). *Self-fulfilling prophecy: A practical guide to its use in education.* Westport, CT: Praeger.

Taylor, H. (1989). *Standard English, Black English, and bidialectalism.* New York: Peter Lang.

U.S. Senate. (1997). Subcommittee on Labor, Health and Human Services, and Education Appropriations. *Ebonics Hearings.* 105th Cong., 2d sess., 23 January.

Van Keulen, J., Weddington, G., & DeBose, C. (1998). *Speech, language, learning, and the African American child.* Boston: Allyn and Bacon.

Yarborough, S., & Flores, L. (1997). Using Ebonics to teach Standard English. In *Long Beach Press Telegram,* 30 April 1997, p. A1.

Chapter 4

What Should Teachers Do?
Ebonics and Culturally
Responsive Instruction*

Lisa Delpit
Florida International University

KEY POINTS

- Educators' dual desire to affirm students' language and teach standard English.
- Group identity and its effect on language use.
- Strategies for integrating language diversity into the curriculum.
- Negative attitudes towards Black children's language.
- Ebonics, reading ability, and reading instruction.

The Ebonics Debate has created much more heat than light for most of the country. For teachers trying to determine what implications there might be for classroom practice, enlightenment has been a completely nonexistent commodity. I have been asked often enough recently, "What do you think about Ebonics? Are you for it or against it?" My answer must be neither. I can be neither for Ebonics or against Ebonics any more than I can be for or against air. It exists. It is the language spoken by many of our African-American children. It is the language they heard as their mothers nursed them and changed their diapers and played peek-a-boo with them. It is the language through which they first encountered love, nurturance, and joy.

On the other hand, most teachers of those African-American children who have been least well-served by educational systems believe that their

---

*Previously published in *The Real Ebonics Debate*, by T. Perry & L. Delpit (Eds.), 1998. Copyright 1998 by the Beacon Press.

students' life chances will be further hampered if they do not learn standard English. In the stratified society in which we live, they are absolutely correct. Having access to the politically mandated language form will not, by any means, guarantee economic success (witness the growing number of unemployed African Americans holding doctorates), but not having access will almost certainly guarantee failure.

So what must teachers do? Should they spend their time relentlessly "correcting" their Ebonics-speaking children's language so that it might conform to what we have learned to refer to as standard English? Despite good intentions, constant correction seldom has the desired effect. Such correction increases cognitive monitoring of speech, thereby making talking difficult. To illustrate, I have frequently taught a relatively simple new "dialect" to classes of preservice teachers. In this dialect, the phonetic element *iz* is added after the first consonant or consonant cluster in each syllable of a word. (*Maybe* becomes miz-ay-biz-ee and *apple*, iz-ap-piz-le). After a bit of drill and practice, the students are asked to tell a partner in "iz" language why they decided to become teachers. Most only haltingly attempt a few words before lapsing into either silence or into standard English. During a follow-up discussion, all students invariably speak of the impossibility of attempting to apply rules while trying to formulate and express a thought. Forcing speakers to monitor their language typically produces silence.

Correction may also affect students' attitudes toward their teachers. In a recent research project, middle school, inner-city students were interviewed about their attitudes toward their teachers and school. One young woman complained bitterly, "Mrs. _____ always be interrupting to make you 'talk correct' and stuff. She be butting into your conversations when you not even talking to her! She need to mind her own business." Clearly this student will be unlikely to either follow the teacher's directives or want to imitate her speech style.

GROUP IDENTITY

Issues of group identity may also affect students' oral production of a different dialect. Researcher Sharon Nelson-Barber (1982), in a study of phonologic aspects of Pima Indian language, found that, in grades 1–3, the children's English most approximated the standard dialect of their teachers. But surprisingly, by fourth grade, when one might assume growing competence in standard forms, their language moved significantly toward the local dialect. These fourth graders had the *competence* to express themselves in a more standard form but chose, consciously or unconsciously, to use the language of those in their local environments. The researcher believes that, by ages eight to nine, these children became aware of their group membership and its importance to their well-being, and this realization was reflected in their language. They may also have become increasingly aware of the school's negative attitude toward their community and found it necessary—through choice of linguistic form—to decide with which camp to identify.

What should teachers do about helping students acquire an additional oral form? First, they should recognize that the linguistic form a student brings to school is intimately connected with loved ones, community, and personal identity. To suggest that this form is wrong or, even worse, ignorant, is to suggest that something is wrong with the student and his or her family. To denigrate your language is, then, in African-American terms, to "talk about your mama." Anyone who knows anything about African-American culture knows the consequences of that speech act!

On the other hand, it is equally important to understand that students who do not have access to the politically popular dialect in this country are less likely to succeed economically than their peers who do. How can both realities be embraced in classroom instruction?

It is possible and desirable to make the actual study of language diversity a part of the curriculum for all students. For younger children, discussions about the differences in the ways TV characters from different cultural groups speak can provide a starting point. A collection of the many children's books written in the dialects of various cultural groups can also provide a wonderful basis for learning about linguistic diversity,[1] as can audiotaped stories narrated by individuals from different cultures, including taped books read by members of the children's home communities. Mrs. Pat, a teacher chronicled by Stanford University researcher Shirley Brice Heath (1983), had her students become language detectives, interviewing a variety of individuals and listening to the radio and TV to discover the differences and similarities in the ways people talked. Children can learn that there are many ways of saying the same thing, and that certain contexts suggest particular kinds of linguistic performances.

Some teachers have groups of students create bilingual dictionaries of their own language form and standard English. Both the students and the teacher become engaged in identifying terms and deciding upon the best translations. This can be done as generational dictionaries, too, given the proliferation of "youth culture" terms growing out of the Ebonics-influenced tendency for the continual regeneration of vocabulary. Contrastive

---

[1] Some of these books include Lucille Clifton, *All Us Come 'Cross the Water* (New York: Holt, Rinehart, and Winston, 1973); Paul Green (aided by Abbe Abbott), *I Am Eskimo—Aknik My Name* (Juneau: Alaska Northwest Publishing, 1959); Howard Jacobs and Jim Rice, *Once upon a Bayou* (New Orleans: Phideaux Publications, 1983); Tim Elder, *Santa's Cajun Christmas Adventure* (Baton Rouge: Little Cajun Books, 1981); and a series of biographies produced by Yukon-Koyukkuk School District of Alaska and published by Hancock House Publishers in North Vancouver, British Columbia, Canada.

grammatical structures can be studied similarly, but, of course, as the Oakland policy suggests, teachers must be aware of the grammatical structure of Ebonics before they can launch into this complex study.

Other teachers have had students become involved with standard forms through various kinds of role play. For example, memorizing parts for drama productions allows students to practice and "get the feel" of speaking standard English while not under the threat of correction. A master teacher of African American children in Oakland, Carrie Secret, uses this technique and extends it so that students videotape their practice performances and self-critique them as to the appropriate use of standard English. (But I must add that Carrie's use of drama and oration goes much beyond acquiring standard English. She inspires pride and community connections that are truly wondrous to behold). The use of self-critique of recorded forms may prove even more useful than I initially realized. California State University–Hayward professor Etta Hollins has reported that just by leaving a tape recorder on during an informal class period and playing it back with no comment, students began to code-switch—moving between standard English and Ebonics—more effectively. It appears that they may have not realized which language form they were using until they heard themselves speak on tape.

Young students can create puppet shows or role play cartoon characters. Many superheroes speak almost hypercorrect Standard English! Playing a role eliminates the possibility of implying that the child's language is inadequate and suggests, instead, that different language forms are appropriate in different contexts. Some other teachers in New York City have had their students produce a news show every day for the rest of the school. The students take on the personae of famous newscasters, keeping in character as they develop and read their news reports. Discussions ensue about whether Tom Brokaw would have said it that way, again taking the focus off the child's speech.

Although most educators think of Black Language as primarily differing in grammar and syntax, there are other differences in oral language of which teachers should be aware in a multicultural context, particularly in discourse style and language use. Harvard University researcher Sarah Michaels and other researchers identified differences in children's narratives at sharing time (Michaels & Cazden, 1986). They found that there was a tendency among young white children to tell "topic-centered" narratives—stories focused on one event—and a tendency among Black youngsters, especially girls, to tell "episodic" narratives—stories that include shifting scenes and are typically longer. Although these differences are interesting in themselves, what is of greater significance is adults' responses to the differences. C. B. Cazden (1988) reports on a subsequent project in which a white adult was taped reading the oral narratives of Black and white first graders, with all syntax dialectal markers removed. Adults were asked to listen to the stories and comment about the children's likelihood of success in school. The researchers were surprised by the differential responses given by Black and white adults.

VARYING REACTIONS

In responding to the retelling of a Black child's story, the white adults were uniformly negative, making such comments as "terrible story, incoherent" and "[n]ot a story at all in the sense of describing something that happened." Asked to judge this child's academic competence, all of the white adults rated her below the children who told topic-centered stories. Most of these adults also predicted difficulties for this child's future school career, such as "This child might have trouble reading," that she exhibited "language problems that affect school achievement," and that "family problems" or "emotional problems" might hamper her academic progress.

The Black adults had very different reactions. They found this child's story "well formed, easy to understand, and interesting, with lots of detail and description." Even though all five of these adults mentioned the "shifts" and "associations" or "nonlinear" quality of the story, they did not find these features distracting. Three of the Black adults selected the story as the best of the five they had heard, and all but one judged the child as exceptionally bright, highly verbal, and successful in school (Cazden, 1988).

This is not a story about racism, but one about cultural familiarity. However, when differences in narrative style produce differences in interpretation of competence, the pedagogical implications are evident. If children who produce stories based on differing discourse styles are expected to have trouble reading and viewed as having language, family, or emotional problems, as was the case with the informants quoted by Cazden, they are unlikely to be viewed as ready for the same challenging instruction awarded students whose language patterns more closely parallel the teacher's.

Most teachers are particularly concerned about how speaking Ebonics might affect learning to read. There is little evidence that speaking another mutually intelligible language form, per se, negatively affects one's ability to learn to read (Sims, 1982). For commonsensical proof, one need only reflect on nonstandard English-speaking Africans who, though enslaved, not only taught themselves to read English, but did so under the threat of severe punishment or death. But children who speak Ebonics do have a more difficult time becoming proficient readers. Why? In part, appropriate instructional methodologies are frequently not adopted. There is ample evidence that children who do not come to school with knowledge about letters, sounds, and symbols need to experience some explicit instruction in these areas in order to become independent readers. Another explanation is that, where teachers' assessments of competence are influenced by the language children speak, teachers may develop low expectations for certain students and subsequently teach them less (Sims, 1982). A third explanation rests in teachers' confusing the teaching of reading with the teaching of a new language form.

Reading researcher Patricia Cunningham (1976–1977) found that teachers across the United States were more likely to correct reading miscues that were dialect-related ("Here go a table" for "Here is a table") than those that were nondialect-related ("Here is a dog" for "There is a dog"). Seventy-eight percent of the former types of miscues were corrected, compared with only 27% of the latter. She concludes that the teachers were acting out of ignorance, not realizing that "here go" and "here is" represent the same meaning in some Black children's language.

In my observations of many classrooms, however, I have come to conclude that even when teachers recognize the similarity of meaning, they are likely to correct Ebonics-related miscues. Consider a typical example:

Text: Yesterday I washed my brother's clothes.

Student's rendition: Yesterday I wash my bruvver close.

The subsequent exchange between student and teacher sounds something like this:

T: Wait, let's go back. What's that word again? [Points at *washed*.]
S: Wash
T: No. Look at it again. What letters do you see at the end? You see *e-d*. Do you remember what we say when we see those letters on the end of the word?
S: *ed.*
T: OK, but in this case we say washed. Can you say that?
S: Wash*ed.*
T: Good. Now read it again.
S: Yesterday, I wash*ed* my bruvver . . .
T: Wait a minute, what's that word again? [Points to *brother.*]
S: Bruvver.
T: No. Look at these letters in the middle. [Points to brother.] Remember to read what you see. Do you remember how we say that sound? Put your tongue between your teeth and say /th/ . . .

The lesson continues in such a fashion, the teacher proceeding to correct the student's Ebonics-influenced pronunciations and grammar while ignoring the fact that the student had to have comprehended the sentence in order to translate it into her own language. Such instruction occurs daily and blocks reading development in a number of ways. First, because children become better readers by having the opportunity to read, the overcorrection exhibited in this lesson means that this child will be less likely to become a fluent reader than other children that are not interrupted so consistently. Second, a complete focus on code and pronunciation blocks children's understanding that reading is essentially a meaning-making process. This child, who understands the text, is led to believe that she is doing something wrong. She is encouraged to think of reading not as something you do to get a message, but something you pronounce. Third, constant corrections by the teacher are likely to cause this student and others like her to resist reading and to resent the teacher.

Language researcher Robert Berdan (1980) reports that, after observing the kind of teaching routine described above in a number of settings, he incorporated the teacher behaviors into a reading instruction exercise that he used with students in a college class. He put together sundry rules from a number of American social and regional dialects to create what he called the "language of Atlantis." Students were then called upon to read aloud in this dialect they did not know. When they made errors he interrupted them, using some of the same statements and comments he had heard elementary school teachers routinely make to their students. He concludes:

> The results were rather shocking. By the time these Ph.D. candidates in English or linguistics had read 10–20 words, I could make them sound totally illiterate. . . . The first thing that goes is sentence intonation: they sound like they are reading a list from the telephone book. Comment on their pronunciation a bit more, and they begin to subvocalize, rehearsing pronunciations for themselves before they dare to say them out loud. They begin to guess at pronunciations. . . . They switch letters around for no reason. They stumble; they repeat. In short, when I attack them for their failure to conform to my demands for Atlantis English pronunciations, they sound very much like the worst of the second graders in any of the classrooms I have observed. They also begin to fidget. They wad up their papers, bite their fingernails, whisper, and some finally refuse to continue. They do all the things that children do while they are busily failing to learn to read.

The moral of this story is not to confuse learning a new language form with reading comprehension. To do so will only confuse the child, leading her away from those intuitive understandings about language that will promote reading development, and toward a school career of resistance and a lifetime of avoiding reading.

Unlike unplanned oral language or public reading, writing lends itself to editing. Although conversational talk is spontaneous and must be responsive to an immediate context, writing is a mediated process that may be written and rewritten any number of times before being introduced to public scrutiny. Consequently, writing is more amenable to rule application. One may first write freely to get one's thoughts down, and then edit to hone the message and apply specific spelling, syntactical, or punctuation rules. My college students who had such difficulty in the "iz" dialect found writing it, with the rules displayed before them, a relatively easy task.

To conclude, the teacher's job is to provide access to the national standard as well as to understand the language the children speak sufficiently to celebrate its beauty. The verbal adroitness, the cogent and quick wit, the brilliant use of metaphor, the facility in rhythm and rhyme, evident in the language of Jesse Jackson, Whoopi Goldberg, Toni Morrison, Henry Louis Gates, Jr., Tupac Shakur, and Maya Angelou, as well as in that of many inner-city Black students, may all be drawn upon to facilitate school learning. The teacher must know how to effectively teach reading and writing to students whose culture and language differ from that of the school, and must understand how and why students decide to add another language form to their repertoire. All we can do is provide students with access to additional language forms. Inevitably, each speaker will make his or her own decision about what to say in any context.

But I must end with a caveat that we keep in mind a simple truth: Despite our necessary efforts to provide access to standard English, such access will not make any of our students more intelligent. It will not teach them math or science or geography—or, for that matter, compassion, courage, or responsibility. Let us not become so overly concerned with the language form that we ignore academic and moral content. Access to the standard language may be necessary, but it is definitely not sufficient to produce intelligent, competent caretakers of the future.

QUESTIONS FOR DISCUSSION AND REFLECTIVE WRITING

1. Delpit articulates teachers' dual desire to affirm their students' language and teach them standard English. What types of attitudes and resources are necessary to achieve this goal? Describe your own attitudes on this subject.

2. Discuss Delpit's view on correcting Ebonics-speaking children's language. Do you agree/disagree with her? Give reasons. Can you suggest other ways that the response to the student's reading of the text, "Yesterday I washed my brother's clothes" could have been handled?

3. Delpit describes the relationship between group identity and language. How can this relationship play out in the classroom?

REFERENCES

Berdan, R. (1980). Knowledge into practice: Delivering research to teachers. In M. F. Whiteman (Ed.), *Reactions to Ann Arbor: Vernacular Black English and education.* Arlington, VA: Center for Applied Linguistics.

Brice Heath, S. (1983). *Ways with words.* Cambridge: Cambridge University Press.

Cazden, C. B. (1988). *Classroom discourse.* Portsmouth, NH: Heinemann.

Cunningham, P. M. (1976–1977). Teachers' correction responses to Black-Dialect miscues which are nonmeaning-changing. *Reading Research Quarterly, 12.*

Michaels, S., & Cazden, C. B. (1986). Teacher-child collaboration on oral preparation for literacy. In B. Scheiffer (Ed.), *Acquisition of literacy: Ethnographic perspectives.* Norwood, NJ: Ablex.

Nelson-Barber, S. (1982). Phonologic variations in Pima English. In R. St. Clair & W. Leap (Eds.), *Language renewal among American Indian tribes: Issues, problems and prospects.* Rosslyn, VA: National Clearinghouse for Bilingual Education.

Sims, R. (1982). Dialect and reading: Toward redefining the issues. In J. Langer & M. T. Smith-Burke (Eds.), *Reader meets author/Bridging the gap.* Newark, DE: International Reading Association.

Part III

CARIBBEAN CREOLE ENGLISH

Teaching English to Caribbean English Creole–Speaking Students in the Caribbean and North America

Lise Winer
McGill University
Montréal, Canada

KEY POINTS

- Attitudes toward the vernacular and standard English among Caribbean natives.
- Language awareness approaches and resources used in the Caribbean.
- Social and psychological adjustments facing Caribbean immigrants in North America.
- Placement/assessment issues and language programs geared for Caribbean immigrants.
- Recommended principles of best practice for teaching Caribbean students.

Over the last three decades, perceptions and treatment of Caribbean English Creole (CEC)–speaking students have undergone some overall positive changes, while still maintaining a discouraging lack of progress. Though many linguists and policymakers have encouraged the simultaneous acceptance of CEC and the better teaching of standard English, the implementation of informed practice by teachers and support by parents has often lagged far behind. The reasons for this are to some extent linguistic, but primarily, as in most educational situations, social and political. This chapter summarizes current issues and practices pertinent to both the Caribbean and to North America (Canada and the United States).[1] In the final part of this chapter, a summary of best practice principles is provided.

ENGLISH AND ENGLISH CREOLE WITHIN THE CARIBBEAN

The early 1960s saw the beginning of political independence for the British colonies of the Caribbean. Along with formal independence arose nationalism identified by and through culture and language. Vernacular language forms that had long been castigated and scorned as substandard and broken, even by their own speakers, became a "badge of Antillean identity and consequently a positive force" (Carrington, 1979, p. 103) to be valued, not denigrated. Linguists working in the Caribbean pushed for recognition of creoles as legitimate language systems. This resulted in several advances. One has been the production of crucial reference works such as the *Dictionary of Jamaican English* (Cassidy & Le Page, 1967, 1980)[2] and more recently, Allsopp's (1996) *Dictionary of Caribbean English Usage.*[3]

Another crucial development has been the formulation of language policies, such as that first put forward by the Trinidad & Tobago Ministry of Education in 1975 that not only recognized creole language as the first language of most school-age children, but also laid the groundwork for increasingly progressive measures, including: (a) the development of Caribbean standardized secondary-school-leaving examinations to replace the Cambridge O Levels, and (b) official curriculum guidelines that included Caribbean English works of fiction with creole language as set texts.

Though the mainstream and popular cultures of the English Caribbean are commonly and no doubt properly referred to as oral cultures, there is nonetheless a long tradition of written creole language in the region (Buzelin & Winer, in press). And, although a small elite have been fluent in standard English—whether considered British or Caribbean standard—from the mid-twentieth century onward there has also been increased access to formal education and mass media, such that many people through-

---

[1]Many of these issues are virtually identical in the U.K., as are some of the approaches, such as the multilingual language awareness materials of the now-disbanded Inner London Education Authority, and the Education Service's resource for teachers and other education professionals, *Meeting the Needs of New Arrivals from Jamaica: Information and Advice for Schools.*

[2]It is not unimportant that the original version of this book, published by Cambridge University Press, though remaining generally in print, was available only in a hard cover edition, for over $60 U.S. It has recently been republished by the University of the West Indies Press in a more affordable paperback.

[3]Though not entirely reliable, this work constitutes an indispensably useful resource for students and teachers dealing with any of the CEC varieties.

out the region have developed high degrees of oral and written competence in English. This competence in English is still greatly uneven, with location (both country and rural–urban) and socioeconomic class playing considerable roles in educational results. This variation in levels of English proves especially confusing when school systems in North America try to deal with Caribbean students (this issue will be taken up later).

During the 1960s and 1970s, it was assumed by most Caribbean educators and the general public that the road to educational, and therefore political and economic, success of an individual was very much tied to that person's ability to command a high level of formal standard English. During the subsequent period of relative economic prosperity, however, it became evident that being a monolingual English-Creole speaker, perhaps with heavily Creole-influenced English as well, was not a bar to economic success outside some professions. Justification for trying to ensure greater student success levels in schools then became closely linked to the arguments that achievement and success, even locally, were dependent on the understanding of written texts and information from, as well as opportunities for education in and business dealings with, contexts outside the region. Educators in the Caribbean have by and large accepted that *bidialectalism*, in local English Creole and local standard English, is an important goal in the school system. Overall, however, educators are greatly concerned about low levels of academic competence, especially in written English and particularly at the post-secondary level.

Siegel (1999) has categorized programs specifically designed to respond to teaching creole speakers within such linguistic situations. In *instrumental* programs, the vernacular is used only as a medium of instruction to teach initial literacy and to transition into standard English. In *accommodation* programs, the vernacular is accepted for use in the classroom but not used as a medium of instruction nor as a goal of literacy competence. In language *awareness* programs, the vernacular is a specific area of study, usually within a larger context of understanding language diversity.

By and large, progressive Caribbean educators are increasingly using the language awareness approach, although the degree to which first language literacy is a stated goal varies tremendously. Two recent studies, both carried out in Jamaica, have examined programs that emphasize overt awareness of language, in particular the differences between Creole and English, as a useful way to increase students' linguistic competence and self-confidence. Bryan's "Making Language Visible: Language Awareness in a Creole-Speaking Environment" (2000) and Kouwenberg's "Bringing Language Awareness into the High School Curriculum: The Opportunities Offered by CAPE Communication Studies" (2000) both include highly focused analysis of areas of difference such as pluralization, tense marking, and pronunciation, but within an overall framework of discussion of "language in society."

In terms of teacher resources that are not linked to a particular school curriculum, a very helpful work applicable to a variety of situations is Craig's *Teaching Language and Literacy: Policies and Procedures for Vernacular Situations* (1999), which focuses on CEC in the Caribbean as well as African American Vernacular English (AAVE)/Black English (BE) in the United States. It addresses both primary and secondary school levels, and includes a review of various past and present approaches, as well as practical suggestions for classroom teaching that will be referred to in more detail later. Similarly, some textbooks aimed at secondary or post-secondary students, such as *Writing in English: A Course Book for Caribbean Students* (Simmons-McDonald, Fields, & Roberts, 1997), are also grounded in a language awareness approach. This book addresses formal (academic) written English as a specific variety in itself; the principles and points of their approach to discourse are the same as those in British or North American textbooks of this type, the main differences being the explanation of language variety from within a Caribbean context, and the use of some Caribbean topics and written texts.

CARIBBEAN STUDENTS IN NORTH AMERICA

Although the general level of migration from the English Caribbean to North America has declined somewhat in recent years, it is still quite substantial, particularly in large urban areas such as Toronto, New York, and Chicago.[4] There are vast differences, both social and educational, in the backgrounds of Caribbean students who immigrate to North America. In the social realm, as discussed thoroughly in *Caribbean Students in Canadian Schools, Book 1* (Coelho, 1988), patterns of migration often lead to long periods of parent–child separation, with children often coming to join the immigrant parent(s) as older children or young adolescents. Furthermore, their introduction to living in North America is usually their first experience with extensive racism, not just at the personal level, but systematically in, for example, the absence of the non-white role models at every level of the society as they were accustomed to previously.

Although some teachers in Caribbean schools still criticize or even punish use of Creole in the classroom, the Creole-speaking child in a Caribbean school nonetheless expects to be and is understood by the teacher. In a North American context, teachers routinely misunderstand students, lead-

---

[4]For purposes of this paper, the province of Québec in Canada is not considered. Here all children without eligibility, that is, having one parent who attended most of primary school in English within Canada, go to French primary and secondary schools. For an overview of the English Caribbean presence in New York, see Winer & Jack (1997).

ing to seriously strained classroom relationships. This is exacerbated, perhaps even primarily caused, by the fact that the teachers—as well as many of the students themselves—regard this speech as bad English, and thus do not assume that there may be some other meaning or rationale for the students' speech and behavior.[5] At a more global level of school culture, the authoritarian tyrants so vividly depicted by Merle Hodge (1970) are still to be found here and there, but the region has certainly moved beyond "rote and rod" as the basis of pedagogy. On the other hand, a recently arrived student from the Caribbean, faced with a typical North American classroom, might well be excused for interpreting the more open classroom as chaos.

The immigrant student from the Caribbean who arrives at a school in North America faces a number of possible ways of being treated (i.e. assessed, placed, and taught) although there may or may not be many options in any individual situation. What determines the presence of such options depends on population demographics, educator/school awareness, and funding.

In terms of the language-focus program types described above, the reaction to CEC has not generally been supportive of either instrumental or accommodation programs, except in a kind of default, given that almost all the teachers of CEC-speaking students will not be able to use CEC in these fashions. In terms of language awareness, historically there have been several excellent programs developed, notably in Toronto (Coelho, 1991), Chicago (Fischer, 1992), and New York (Pollard, 1993), but many of the excellent aspects of teacher training, materials development, and general interest in this area have dwindled rather than blossomed. This is overall due to a lack of political commitment to deal with these children in an educationally sound way, and justified by reference to lack of economic resources, particularly within the current atmosphere that does not support much that is good in educational practice for these as well as other students. Often, CEC speakers do not fit neatly into any of the typically available models or programs for students requiring extra help with language issues.

The most common traditional ways of dealing with immigrant children from the English Caribbean, have been the *mainstream* ("sink or swim") model, special education, or ESL programs. In cases where the CEC child is the sole such individual in a school, or one of what the school system per-

---

[5]A classic example of such misunderstanding was presented by a teacher in a New York suburb who asked why there was such a high rate of deafness amongst children from Guyana (which, incidentally, he mispronounced despite correction). It turned out he had based this judgment on the fact that these children never looked directly at him when he asked them questions, or asked for explanations. The children were simply demonstrating traditional Caribbean good manners of not rudely confronting an adult.

ceives to be an unworkably small number of students,[6] schools still have the choice of treating even individual students with one of these approaches.

The mainstream model, also used for all kinds of other students for whom special resources are not made available, too often depends for its success on the chance individual background of teachers. CEC speakers perceived as persistent bad English speakers are generally not given appropriate recognition and explanations or examples.

The categorization of CEC speakers into remedial, let alone special education programs sends a clear message to both students and parents that their language is deemed to reflect underlying cognitive deficiencies.[7] Similarly, the referral of CEC speakers to speech therapists implies that linguistic differences are an individual's pathology. This is, of course, not to say that such children may not indeed have learning, hearing or speech disorders, but simply that such diagnosis must be carried out by people qualified to recognize the difference between a speech variety and a speech impediment.

Most CEC-speaking students who are deliberately placed into language-oriented classrooms have been placed in ESL classes. This is on the one hand a result of educators' recognizing that the students' language is systematic and legitimate; on the other hand, it is often the result of funding structures in which only students whose first language is not English are entitled to additional support. The difficulties of such placement have been well documented (Coard, 1971; Coelho 1988, 1991). The most obvious difference is that incoming students already perceive themselves as English speakers (in some cases, as bilingual Creole/English). They are astonished and resentful at being treated in this fashion. At beginner and intermediate class levels especially, CEC-speaking students have a much greater knowledge—especially receptive—of English than "real" ESL students. Nonetheless, CEC students may end up being eventually outperformed by ESL students who have started with less English, because of persistent errors. Continued problems involve both transfer from CEC and subsequent direct or approximative forms in English, as well as problems common to any student learning formal written English (see Nero, 2001).

Apart from the students' resentment at being classified as "non-English" speakers, there are two main additional features of the inappropriateness

---

[6]Such judgment varies enormously. In one school region of Toronto, for example, isolated CEC students were routinely gathered together for special classes several times a week. In another region, school officials claimed that the *percentage* of such students in the overall enrollment was too low to warrant special treatment, even though the actual *number* of students was in the hundreds.

[7]The disproportionate placement of black children into such programs, out of all relation to legitimate expectations, reflects not only a linguistic bias but systemic racial and class prejudice. Protests from parents and communities have to a great extent mitigated this phenomenon among both CEC and AAVE students.

of ESL classes for CEC students. The first is the difficulty that many teachers have in analyzing errors and devising strategies for them. It is nothing short of perplexing that a well-trained ESL teacher can deal effectively with a class of 28 students with 28 first languages, none of which is known by the teacher, but that same teacher cannot apply the same processes of analysis to the language produced by CEC speakers. To a great extent such difficulty is based on the misleadingly large amount of English these students know compared to regular ESL students. A consistent approach of *suspect* (that students are using rational strategies) and *respect* (their language and their processes) regarding any student whose language is different (or wrong in regard to a particular target) is a good policy.

The second problem is the difficulty that some teachers have in dealing with "non-white" students—either in terms of the usual forms of institutionalized racism, or by lumping them together with speakers of AAVE, who are faced with a huge array of stereotypes and historical backlashes (discussed elsewhere in this volume). (One notable point is that by no means all "non-white" Caribbean students are "black"—many, especially from Guyana and Trinidad, are of (East) Indian descent and many are mixed-race.) Although some linguists have argued that, essentially, AAVE is structurally the same as CEC, the social contexts of the two general language varieties are very different. However, within the Caribbean, few local people truly do not use and understand some level or variety of the local creole language, whereas the same is not true of AAVE in North America.[8] Moreover, CEC and AAVE speakers are often inclined to mutual distancing in order to avoid concomitant stereotyping (Winer & Jack, 1997). In terms of educational implications, not only are many of the linguistic features and patterns of language usage significantly different, but the mainstream view of the groups also differs.

STANDARD ENGLISH AS A SECOND DIALECT

In an attempt to address the linguistic needs of Caribbean students, classes termed *Standard English as a Second Dialect* (SESD) began in the late 1960s in England, and were well developed in areas including Toronto and Hartford during the 1970s and 80s. However, cuts to educational funding have managed to terminate most of these special programs except in cases where "numbers warrant" and where educators are both aware of this approach and able to carry it out. Successful continuing programs (Fischer, 1992)

---

[8]One intriguing similarity, noted by many researchers in code-switching for example, is the covert prestige awarded to Jamaican EC, AAVE and British Black English (Jamaican) in the lyrics to rap and hip-hop music of the youth culture (Leung, Harris & Rampton, 1997).

have been able to show direct benefits to the school system by having students in such (part-time or complementary) programs improving at greater than expected achievement rates in regular classes. This approach is based on intense language awareness work and a strongly contrastive approach, focusing on those elements of the differences between CEC and English that are held to most strongly penalize CEC student performance (e.g. verb tense marking, pluralization); they also focus on recognition of and pride in CEC as a legitimate and cultured language variety that has much to offer anyone.

Language awareness programs are a good idea for any classroom; specific emphasis can be shifted depending on the make-up of the class and available resources. The work carried out by Wolfram in the southern U.S. (see Wolfram, Adger & Christian, 1999) is a model of how to develop children's analytical and reflective skills in any situation where their own speech is considered to differ (i.e. negatively) from that of the mainstream.

Generally speaking, teachers who are themselves of Caribbean origin or background can be excellent resources for schools and students. They can provide a bridge that is both cultural and linguistic. On the other hand, some of these teachers may not have kept up with more progressive developments in awareness of language variety in the Caribbean, may not have an overt or explicit understanding of linguistic features, or may not be familiar with the current school situations that Caribbean children are now experiencing. Like many North Americans, they may be overly invested in a romantic image of the Caribbean frozen in time.

Most materials developed specifically for Caribbean students in North American schools have tended to focus on grammar from a contrastive perspective, and to focus on those points of grammar that are persistent and difficult to keep separated—pluralization, subject–verb agreement, relativization, pronoun usage, etc. The most interesting and promising approaches are developed from within a framework of literature and discourse styles (e.g. Coelho, 1991; Pollard, 1993; Winer, 1990), and focus on developing competence in both standard English and Creole.

THE CONTEMPORARY CARIBBEAN STUDENT

Although many North Americans regard the Caribbean as a vacation paradise of lovely beaches, sleepy villages and isolated islanders, the Caribbean countries contain a very wide range of social, cultural, historical, linguistic, economic, political and educational situations. More educational options are available now for some students in the Caribbean than previously, but the range in quality of schooling is considerable. The amount and type of language training that students have now also varies depending on the regional, national and local situation. Thus, it is important not to make assumptions about the extent or nature of students' linguistic abilities or social proclivities.

The general (and police) perception of (black) immigrants from the Caribbean as increasingly associated with criminal elements such as drug posses is a dangerous stereotype. Attitudes toward school and schooling amongst Caribbean-background students vary, just as they do within the rest of the population. Questions about the value and relevance of educational structures should be examined openly within schools and classrooms. A classroom that allows discrimination against language—whether by tests or peer ridicule—is not good for anyone. A classroom that values diversity in language as well as other areas is good for everyone. Awareness of variation in language should be based on the linguistic dexterity that students already have, and should develop to include better understanding of both standard and creole language. Bilingualism or bidialectalism does not need to be equal in all domains, though creole should not be limited only to the functions of amusement.

PRINCIPLES OF BEST PRACTICE

Given the foregoing discussion, it is impossible to predict every single eventuality or uncertainty or conflict in any classroom; neither is it possible to predict every utterance that will be made or strategy that will be used by Caribbean students or language learners in general. Nonetheless, general guiding principles can help frame considerations and actions of educators, in a wide variety of situations with a wide variety of individuals. The following eight principles of best practice are particularly applicable for assessment specialists and classroom teachers. These principles are based on research and practice in a number of classrooms and school boards which have actively attempted to treat Caribbean background students in a positive and productive manner.[9] They are meant to serve as starting or reference points within any specific situation.

---

[9]For research and teaching practice within the Caribbean, see Bryan (2000), Kouwenberg (2000) on language awareness, and Pollard (1993, 2000), Simmons-McDonald, Fields & Roberts (1997) for textbooks. For teaching practice and social environment in North American schools, see Coelho (1988, 1991), Fischer (1992), Nero (2000), and Winer (1990, 1993). For general treatments of language variation in educational contexts, see Craig (1999), Gass & Lefkowitz (1995), Siegel (1999) and Wolfram, Adger, & Christian (1999).

Principle 1: Use Appropriate Language Proficiency Testing

- As with all students, a native language assessment should be carried out, by someone native or fluent in the student's language.
- Assess proficiency in both Creole and standard English. English-only assessments must be designed and interpreted with great caution.
- Do not confuse oral reading with reading comprehension.
- Ensure that reading texts—oral or written—do not contain culturally unfamiliar or infrequent topics, vocabulary, etc.
- Make sure students are familiar with the test question format.
- Ensure that the content of (simplified) texts is age-appropriate; rewrite test passages to adapt content if necessary.
- In test writing—if student has demonstrated some competence in reading—a narrative may be enough, or you may want to use a cloze passage to focus on particular target areas.

Principle 2: Make Appropriate Classroom Placement

- If possible, students should be placed in a *Standard English as a Second Dialect* type of class for part of the day.
- In ESL placements, students will know much more English than beginner ESL students, but will have more persistent errors in English than advanced ESL students.
- Mainstream class placement can be good if there is a program of language awareness for the class, and if a variety of readings are used, including ones from all students' backgrounds.

Principle 3: Address the Immigrant Child's Social and Psychological Needs

- Do not make assumptions about the child's family situation.
- Do not make assumptions about the child's cultural background or affinities, e.g. that all Jamaicans are drug dealers.
- Involve parents or guardians in the school process—this may mean unconventional hours or places for conferences.
- Address problems of racism within the classroom and school community.

Principle 4: Make Classroom and School Rules Explicit

- Organize a formal orientation to school practices, including rules and disciplinary procedures. (Make sure the guidelines reflect school reality.) It is helpful to provide this in writing as well, but make sure that students understand orally.

- Organize buddy systems for newcomer students. A buddy is usually someone from the same cultural and linguistic background, who has previously followed a path similar to the newcomer's.
- Support peer mediation processes throughout the school.

Principle 5: Get and Use Appropriate Resource Materials

- Get beyond the "sun and fun" view of the Caribbean yourself. Provide background reading in both fiction and nonfiction for teachers and school personnel.
- Provide classrooms with appropriate reference resources, such as Caribbean dictionaries.
- Use Caribbean oral and written literature as part of the texts of English classes. Include content from the Caribbean outside literary topics (e.g. Winer, 1983).

Principle 6: Use a Language Awareness Approach

- Make language variation a part of the school language arts curriculum, including regional and class dialects.
- Give Caribbean students' language particular support in terms of legitimacy and variation.
- Emphasize the appropriateness of different language varieties for different situations.

Principle 7: Respect the Logic of a Student's Language

- Always suspect that a student is applying a rule, consciously or unconsciously, in the production of language.
- Become aware of common *false friends*, and have reference sheets or posters for student reference. For example, "Mind you bring your book on Monday" might well mean, to a Jamaican student, that she should *not* bring her book then. If a Trinidadian child asks to meet with a teacher in the "evening," this can refer to 3:00 p.m.
- Focus on different aspects of language on different assignments; make it clear what that focus is.

Principle 8: Embed Linguistic Targets in Situational Discourse, Especially Literature

- Discuss language variation in literature, particularly in dialogue.

- Use a focused contrastive approach to common errors resulting from transfer between Creole and English.
- Use good Caribbean literature for all students as an opportunity to examine language usage, as well as discuss literary themes and styles.

These principles of best practice can be useful in any classroom, even when language variation per se is not on the course syllabus, since we all vary our language, most commonly by what we consider appropriate to a particular situation (register). Looking at the relationship between orality and literature, the representation of speech, the differences and similarities among language varieties, should be an integral part of any language arts program.

Why should we, then, pay special attention to the role of teachers in teaching learners of English who are speakers of Caribbean varieties of English and English Creole? As discussed above, the main reasons are the misunderstandings caused by misperceptions of the similarities and differences between two closely related language systems: we think we understand when we may not, and we do not understand when we might. Awareness, and "awareness of awareness" is even more important in this situation, compared, for example, to a recognizably two-language system used by a speaker of Chinese. Finally, because the societies in which these language varieties are used, and thus the languages themselves, have traditionally been devalued, stigmatized, misunderstood and viewed negatively, both within and outside those societies, and because these languages cut across ethnic and racial boundaries, it is important to value, and be seen to value, these particular speakers, and hence their languages.

QUESTIONS FOR DISCUSSION AND REFLECTIVE WRITING

1. In addition to language, Winer highlights some of the social/psychological challenges facing Caribbean students in North America (e.g., racism, parent–child separation, and so forth). How might these issues affect the school performance of Caribbean students, and what responses would you propose in this regard?
2. What are the implications of the categorization quandary of Caribbean Creole English speakers (remedial, special education, ESL) as discussed by Winer?
3. In pairs or groups, discuss ways in which you would implement Winer's principles of best practice in your own classroom. You can also add principles of your own and justify them.

REFERENCES

Allsopp, R. (1996). *Dictionary of Caribbean English usage.* New York: Oxford University Press.

Bryan, B. (2000, August). *Making language visible: Language awareness in a Creole-speaking environment.* Paper presented at the Conference of the Society for Caribbean Linguistics, Trinidad.

Buzelin, H., & Winer, L. (in press). Literary representations of creole languages: Cross-linguistic perspectives from the Caribbean. In J. V. Singler & S. Kouwenberg (Eds.), *Handbook of pidgin and creole linguistics.* Oxford: Blackwell.

Carrington, L. D. (1979, July). *Linguistic conflict in Caribbean education.* Paper presented at the International Congress of Psychology of the Child, Paris, France.

Cassidy, F., & Le Page, R. (1967/1980). *Dictionary of Jamaican English.* Cambridge: Cambridge University Press.

Coard, B. (1971). *How the West Indian child is made educationally sub-normal in the British school system.* London: New Beacon Books.

Coelho, El. (1988). *Caribbean students in Canadian schools, Book 1.* Toronto: Carib-Can Publishers [Pippin Publishing].

Coelho, E. (1991). *Caribbean students in Canadian schools, Book 2.* Markham, Ontario: Pippin Publishing.

Craig, D. (1999). *Teaching language and literacy: Policies and procedures for vernacular situations.* Georgetown, Guyana: Education and Development Services.

Fischer, K. (1992). Educating speakers of Caribbean English in the United States. In J. Siegel (Ed.), *Pidgins, creoles, and nonstandard dialects in education* (pp. 99–123). Melbourne: Applied Linguistics Association of Australia.

Gass, S., & Lefkowitz, N. (1995). *Varieties of English.* Ann Arbor: University of Michigan Press.

Hodge, M. (1970). *Crick crack monkey.* London: Heinemann.

Kouwenberg, S. (2000, August). *Bringing language awareness into the high school curriculum: The opportunities offered by CAPE communication studies.* Paper presented at the Conference of the Society for Caribbean Linguistics, Trinidad.

Leung, C., Harris, R., & Rampton, B. (1997). The idealized native speaker, reified ethnicities, and classroom realities. *TESOL Quarterly, 31*(3), 543–559.

Nero, S. (2000). The changing faces of English: A Caribbean perspective. *TESOL Quarterly, 34*(3), 483–510.

Nero, S. (2001). *Englishes in contact: Anglophone Caribbean students in an urban college.* Cresskill, NJ: Hampton Press.

Pollard, V. (1993). *From Jamaican Creole to Standard English: A handbook for teachers.* Brooklyn, NY: Caribbean Research Center, Medgar Evers College (CUNY).

Pollard, V. (2000). *The role of Jamaican Creole in language education* (Popular Series Paper No. 2). Society for Caribbean Linguistics.

Siegel, J. (1999). Stigmatized and standardized varieties in the classroom: Interference or separation? *TESOL Quarterly, 33,* 701–728.

Simmons-McDonald, H., Fields, L., & Roberts, P. (1997). *Writing in English: A course book for Caribbean students.* Kingston, Jamaica: Ian Randle Publishers.

Winer, L. (1983). *Animal mysteries.* New York: Regents.

Winer, L. (1990). *Caribbean voices: The North York anthology* (Teacher's Guide). Toronto: North York Board of Education, Toronto.

Winer, L. (1993). Teaching speakers of Caribbean English Creoles in North American classrooms. In A. W. Glowka & D. Lance (Eds.), *Language variation in North American English* (pp. 191–198). New York: Modern Language Association.

Winer, L., & Jack, L. (1997). Caribbean English Creole in New York City. In O. García & J. A. Fishman (Eds.), *The multilingual apple: Language in New York City* (pp. 301–337). Berlin: Mouton de Gruyter.

Wolfram, W., Adger, C. T., & Christian, D. (1999). *Dialects in schools and communities.* Mahwah, NJ: Lawrence Erlbaum Associates.

Chapter 6

Teaching Jamaican Creole–Speaking Students

Yvonne Pratt-Johnson
St. John's University

KEY POINTS

- Differences among Caribbean students.
- Common features of Caribbean English Creoles, particularly Jamaican Creole.
- Strategies for teaching Caribbean students.
- Fostering cultural/linguistic sensitivity.
- Developing culturally relevant curricula and materials.

INTRODUCTION

The past several decades have seen a continued increase in the number of English-speaking people from the Caribbean[1] who have migrated to the United States, especially from Jamaica, Guyana, Trinidad and Tobago and

---

[1]The English-speaking Caribbean includes Jamaica, Trinidad and Tobago, Barbados, The Bahamas, Grenada, Dominica, St. Lucia, St. Vincent and the Grenadines, Antigua and Barbuda, St. Kitts and Nevis, Guyana and Belize. Guyana and Belize are not geographically in the Caribbean but are linked to the region culturally and historically by a shared background with the other Caribbean nations. Each of these nations has its own separate and well defined identity, but there are still similar historical experiences that link them together: slavery, colonial rule, and national independence. Language is yet another factor that connects these nations, English being the official language in each of these territories.

119

Barbados.[2] The great majority settle in the large cities and their surrounding suburbs with the largest concentrations found in and around Baltimore, Chicago, Detroit, Hartford, Miami, New York City, Philadelphia, and Washington, D.C. (Sunshine & Warner, 1998). In Miami, for example, the English-speaking Caribbean population is presently 48% of the city's black community and is expected, within eight years, to even surpass the native-born African American population (Perry & Mackun, 2001). In New York City, Jamaicans represent the second largest immigrant population in the school system of over one million students (Pratt-Johnson & Richards, 1995).

When these immigrants from the English-speaking Caribbean arrive in the United States, they often enroll their school-aged children in the nearby public school systems. They have high hopes and expectations that their children will succeed in American schools, and many of them do succeed because, unlike other immigrant children whose native language is not English, they come into the classroom with a knowledge and mastery of the English language. Not only does their competence in English increase their chances for success in American schools, but the formal education and the academic preparedness they have received in their home countries also enable them to perform at or above grade levels (West-White, 2003). Therefore, they are able to take advantage of the educational challenges and opportunities that await them, and they are more easily able to adjust to and integrate into American schools and society.

Another group of students, however, who enter American schools from the English-speaking Caribbean, are not proficient speakers of English but rather of their native *English Creole*, and, in general, have received little or no formal education in their home countries. These are the students who usually struggle in American schools and, without appropriate intervention, will flounder and fail (Pratt-Johnson & Richards, 1995). They have difficulty in school because, among other reasons, the language used in American schools differs from the language they use in their homes and communities. It is this group of students and, in particular, Jamaican students, for whom the data in this paper have been collected and presented and who will be the focus of this discussion hereafter. However, the issues explored in the following pages are equally relevant and applicable to other English-speaking Caribbeans as well.

ENGLISH CREOLES OF THE CARIBBEAN

The Creole Continuum (DeCamp, 1971), a continuum of varieties between the creole language and the standard variety, is often used to describe the lin-

---

[2]US Immigration and Naturalization Services Statistical Yearbook of the Immigration and Naturalization Service, 1999.

guistic situation in the English-speaking Caribbean. At one end of the continuum is the standard English variety, the *acrolect,* the most prestigious variety spoken. At the other end of the continuum is the *basilect,* the language variety furthest away from the acrolect. Between the acrolect and the basilect is the *mesolect.* Many people in the English-speaking Caribbean function at the mesolectal level or freely go back and forth along the continuum.

None of the Caribbean English Creoles has a standardized orthographic system; they are almost exclusively spoken forms. While poets, writers and lyricists have made attempts at capturing the authenticity and beauty of the Caribbean Creoles through written forms, these attempts have not led to standardization either of the spoken or written form. Therefore, it is not uncommon to see a single word, e.g. *little,* spelled in a variety of ways: *lickle, likkle, licle, likle* in the works of Caribbean writers.

All Caribbeans may understand and speak their native Creole to a certain degree; however, not all Caribbeans are fluent speakers of it. Such factors as education, home environment, socioeconomic status, rural versus urban provenance, and perceptions of Creole seem to determine to what extent Caribbeans become proficient in their Creole. Language proficiency ranges from those who are proficient in English and less proficient in their native Creole, to some who are native speakers of their Creole and less proficient in the standard English variety, to others who are completely bilingual, equally proficient in both varieties.

An English Creole is a language variety that differs from the standard variety of English in grammatical structure, word order, pronunciation, and, in some cases, even vocabulary—although most of its vocabulary comes from English. There are some similarities among the English Creoles of the Caribbean, but there are also some marked differences (Allsopp, 1996; Holm, 2000; Winford, 2001), and it is through some of these differences that one can generally know in which part of the English-speaking Caribbean a person was born and/or raised.

It would be impossible to provide detailed accounts of all of the Caribbean English Creoles in this chapter. However, for the purposes of this discussion, Jamaican Creole will be highlighted since Jamaican students, more than any other Caribbean group, are in the United States in far greater numbers, and teachers are therefore more likely to encounter them in their classrooms.[3]

A brief description of a few of the specific features of Jamaican Creole (sometimes called *patois/patwa*) is given below. Some of these characteristics may or may not be present in all of the other Creoles. The following example sentences, taken from Jamaican students' written works at the ele-

---

[3]US Immigration and Naturalization Services Statistical Yearbook of the Immigration and Naturalization Service, 1999.

mentary, middle, and high school levels, were compiled by teachers as well as the researcher in New York City. They reflect the ways that the standard variety of American English differs from Jamaican Creole.

Features of Jamaican Creole

Grammar:

1. The deletion of the <u>BE</u> copula.
   a. *The house have to clean.* (The house has to be cleaned.)
   b. *The school in Brooklyn.* (The school is in Brooklyn.)
2. The flexible use of pronouns in subject/object position.
   a. *Him don't seem to understand I.* (He doesn't seem to understand me.)
   b. *Them (Dem) go straight home after school.* (They go straight home after school.)
3. The use of *done* to mark or indicate a completed action.
   a. *Mi done forget about it.* (I forgot about it.)
   b. *Mi done cooked dinner.* (I have finished cooking dinner.)

Word Order:

1. Order of words in Jamaican Creole may differ from that in the standard variety.
   a. *Gimi dem.* (Give them to me.)
   b. *Turn the lights on back.* (Turn the lights back on.)
   c. *She did wear a new brand dress.* (She wore a brand new dress.)
2. The use of *so* to express emphasis.
   a. *Is here so mi live.* (I live right here.)
   b. *Stay here so.* (Just stay right here.)
   c. *Gime doze over dere so.* (Give me those over there.)
3. The formation of interrogation may take on a different word order.
   a. *How much you want?* (How much do you want?)
   b. *Who tell you that?* (Who told you that?)
   c. *How much o'clock now?* (What time is it now?)
   d. *Is where you going?* (Where are you going?)

Pronunciation:

1. The addition of /h/ before vowels.
   a. *The bottle hempty still.* (The bottle is still empty.)
   b. *Now dis horgan ere sound good.* (Now this organ here sounds good.)
2. The deletion of /h/.
   a. *Im a oly man.* (He is a holy man.)
   b. *A did need mi at right away.* (I needed my hat right away.)
3. The / th / ——————— /D/ in initial position in such words as <u>the</u>, <u>there</u>, <u>this</u>, <u>that</u>, <u>them</u> and <u>then</u>.
   a. *Dere is nobody nowhere in sight.* (There is nobody anywhere in sight.)
   b. *De pen dem don't work.* (The pens don't work.)

Vocabulary:

A. *Translations*

Jamaican Creole	Standard English
sinting	*something*
pickney	*child*
duppy	*ghost*
bickle	*food*
facety	*rude*
mawga	*thin, skinny*
nuff	*plenty*
smaddy	*somebody*
irie	*cool, good, nice*
ginnal	*trickster*
craven	*greedy*
to labrish	*to gossip*
to nyam	*to eat*
to grudge	*to envy*

B. *Standard English Words Carrying Creole Meanings:*

Standard English	Special Creole Meanings
so	to express emphasis
yard	Jamaica (home)
foot	leg
hand	arm
sweetie	candy

waiter	tray
mean	stingy
hush	Excuse me; I'm sorry
to fast	to be nosey
to box	to hit
to look for	to visit
good night[4]	good evening

ADDRESSING THE SPECIFIC NEEDS OF CREOLE-SPEAKING STUDENTS

Teaching Creole-speaking students has often brought several challenges to teachers in the U.S., and has raised implications for teacher–student and student–student interaction in the classroom.

Communication in the Classroom

Miscommunication in the classroom is the primary concern that teachers raise when teaching Creole-speaking students (Pratt-Johnson, 1993). Because the Caribbean English Creoles differ significantly from the standard variety of English in their structure, pronunciation and, in some cases, vocabulary, communication difficulties may arise. Creole speakers find it difficult to communicate in the school language, and teachers and students find it just as difficult to understand them. Teachers are encouraged to be patient. As they become familiar with the linguistic patterns of the Creoles and the cultures of their students, they will feel more comfortable.

To enhance communication in the classroom, teachers may employ various techniques. One such technique is for teachers to rephrase their questions and the questions and answers of the students. This may be helpful for the Creole-speaking students, especially those who are recently arrived and may find it difficult to understand the speech patterns, including intonation, pace and general flow of the school language. If teachers do not understand the Creoles of their students, they may ask them to repeat what they have said: "Would you mind repeating what you have just said? I did not quite understand." Sometimes by focusing on a particular sound or word or a part of the sentence, teachers may be able to understand what their students have said. Alternatively, a teacher may repeat

---

[4]A teacher at a workshop shared the following story: "I called a parent of one of my Jamaican students to tell her about her son's progress; he wasn't doing well at all. I introduced myself as his teacher and stated the reason for my call. She, in turn, responded by telling me 'Good night!' Imagine how offended I was! I wanted to end the conversation immediately since she obviously showed no interest. At that time, I didn't know that 'good night' in Jamaican patois meant 'good evening' in Standard American English."

what a student has said until the part that was unclear: "So, you believe that women should . . ." The pause indicates to the student that their response was not completely understood. This may encourage a student to find another way to express their response. Still another strategy used by teachers is to solicit the help of other Caribbean students in the class to serve as resource people: "Linsford, would you rephrase Mary's response in your own words?" This technique can be effective provided that there are other students in the class who are familiar with the Creole. These resource people often feel a sense of pride and usefulness in the classroom (Suarez-Orozco, 2001).

Student Participation and Collaborative Work in the Classroom

Creole-speaking students may not always feel comfortable volunteering information or participating in class discussions if they feel they have not mastered the standard variety of English preferred in school (Pratt-Johnson, 1993). It is important that teachers create a safe environment, where students are comfortable to be themselves and where they feel free to speak—at whatever level of language proficiency they are. They must be encouraged to experiment with the school language while teachers must listen carefully to their Creoles, make a genuine effort to understand them, and validate their Creoles and their efforts.

It should also be noted that despite the best efforts of instructors to promote an atmosphere that is engaging and conducive to learning, instructors will occasionally encounter some students who may be less than sensitive to cultural/linguistic differences or perhaps even openly hostile to those that they perceive to be different. The ability to be perceptive to these prejudicial attitudes and to constructively confront and challenge these notions is an important responsibility of teachers. These are moments for teachers to urge students to be culturally sensitive, pointing out the destructive nature of cultural/linguistic discrimination. One Jamaican tenth-grade student in a New York City high school shares her own experience of linguistic discrimination in an interview:

> The second day in my social studies class in my new school, I was asked to read from my text. My accent was thick at that time I have to admit. Two American students sitting next to each other laughed at me when I was reading. But right away my teacher yelled at them real bad. He told them that kind of behavior would not be allowed in this class. He was angry and very serious. They never did that again. And no one else either. That's one reason why I could deal with my new school life in New York. I felt equal with everybody else in that class—even if I did have an accent. (March, 2001)

Here the student recalls her initial high school experience in one of her classes, where her classmates ridiculed her because of her "thick" Jamaican accent. Had it not been for her teacher's decisive action, this student's experience might not have been as propitious. The very direct and confrontational approach taken by this instructor had its desired effect, and from the student's perspective, it doubtlessly conveyed to her, and her classmates, that she was a valued member of the class and, as such, she was to be respected, not an object of ridicule. For this student, this was a supportive and affirming environment that favorably impacted her experience in this class.

Initially, Creole-speaking students may seem reluctant to participate in collaborative classroom activities, and there may be a combination of reasons for their reticence. First, they may experience fear, nervousness, and discomfort about their perceived or actual inability to speak the school language proficiently and therefore may choose to remain silent (Henry, 2001; Pratt-Johnson & Richards, 1995). In addition, these students may have reservations because, in many cases, collaborative learning may be a completely new experience for them. The classrooms in the Caribbean are traditionally teacher-centered and based on an authoritarian teaching style; students sit still, listen, and remain silent while their teachers lecture (Henry, 2001; Kuboni, 2003; Manswell Butty, 2003). It takes time, then, for students to approach and adapt to this new type of activity, to feel comfortable to communicate in a language different from their Creole, and become a viable, contributing member of the collaborative process. Therefore, at the beginning, students will do well just being permitted to sit in on collaborative classroom assignments to observe and listen. However, during this time, to ensure that these students are actively listening and observing, teachers are encouraged to consistently monitor their progress. For example, at the end of a collaborative activity, a questionnaire might be disseminated on which students respond to a few teacher-constructed questions about the activity, or students may keep a journal in which they write down what they learned after each collaborative activity, what they observed and/ or what might have been confusing to them. Through such monitoring, teachers not only learn about their students, but they can also determine how they might improve and/or modify their teaching approaches, strategies and techniques. It is also suggested that they be placed with sensitive students who understand and appreciate cultural and linguistic diversity and who are willing to help their new classmates gradually take risks and reach a level of comfort to participate.

Error Correction

Many teachers who teach Creole-speaking students have raised questions about error corrections. They often admit that they are unclear as to how and when student errors in the classroom should be handled. Most of the errors to which they refer are found in their students' speaking and writing, often resulting from the students' unconscious translating from their native Creole. How do teachers provide meaningful feedback for their Creole-speaking students? Teacher feedback should always be constructive and encouraging, not punitive and demeaning. This is especially true for Creole-speaking students, who may already experience feelings of inferiority and inadequacy about the Creoles they speak and about themselves as students.

Diligent and conscientious teachers may attempt to correct all of their students' errors. However, there are a few drawbacks in making such an attempt. First of all, correcting errors can be a time consuming activity. Pointing out and commenting on every single error that their students make in communicating in a language different from their native Creole can prove taxing and tedious for teachers. In addition, it usually takes an enormous amount of time for students to absorb and internalize the corrections and then apply the new linguistic information provided by their teachers to all appropriate contexts thereafter. Only when students produce the identical errors in subsequent speaking and writing will teachers realize the futility in attempting to correct every error their students make. Neither does correcting all of a student's errors hasten the learning process. Time, repetition, and practice do. Moreover, correcting every error, be it in speaking or writing, can be devastating for Creole-speaking students. At times it may cause them to withdraw, to refrain from experimenting and taking further risks in the classroom. Therefore, it is important that teachers understand that not all errors need be corrected. In fact, some researchers have offered the language teacher ways of ordering or prioritizing errors (Cross, 1992; Harris & Silva, 1993; Rudder, 1999).

In offering Creole-speakers feedback, teachers are encouraged to give priority to communication errors. These are considered more serious errors since they are the ones that may impede communication. When a Creole-speaking student is speaking or writing in class, he should be able to convey meaning to his listener despite linguistic differences. Form errors, on the other hand, are those which deal with the accuracy of what a student says or writes, yet they do not interfere with communication. Consider the following student-written sentence from a New York City eleventh grader (October, 2002):

The boy nyam him lunch hat one.
    (1)   (2)   (3)

[The boy eats his lunch at one.]

Which error(s) should be corrected? There are three errors found in the sentence. First, we consider which error(s) causes(cause) problems in comprehension. Some teachers believe that Errors 1 and 3 should be treated first as they present difficulties in comprehension. Although Error 2 is distracting and inaccurate and violates a rule of standard English, teachers may choose instead to tolerate this error initially and not to correct it since it does not hinder communication. It can be dealt with on a subsequent occasion. Teachers may also feel free to make corrections of work already presented and practiced in class. For example, if a teacher has discussed possessive adjectives prior to this student's producing the sentence above, he or she may point out Error 2 to the student.

One important suggestion for teachers in terms of dealing with error is to become familiar with their students' particular error patterns. Individual students may exhibit their unique error patterns in speaking and writing; however, teachers will also notice that there are more global, more general characteristics of students who speak English Creoles. For example, in studying linguistic differences between the English standard variety (the school language) and the English Creoles of the Caribbean (the home languages), attentive teachers will observe that their English creole-speaking students in speaking and writing are likely to produce language errors with regard to: subject–verb agreement, use of prepositions, inflections in nouns, pronouns, verbs, spelling and pronunciation (West-White, 2003). Any of these errors may also be observed in the speech and writing of weak students in general, but English creole-speaking students are likely to manifest these error patterns, not because of weakness but rather because of the ongoing interaction between their native creoles and standard English along the creole continuum. In this sense, the students may not readily discern the difference between their spoken language and the standard variety. In addition, while attempting to use the school language, English creole-speaking students may also produce special errors in syntax (*She did wear a new brand dress.* [She wore a brand new dress.]); use vocabulary from their native creoles (*pickney, nyam*); or add and delete the letter _h_ in front of vowels (**orse* [_h_orse], **hairplane* [airplane]. These are error patterns characteristic of many Jamaican creole-speaking students.

Below are some priority areas that may hinder comprehension/communication in the classroom. Teachers may choose to work with their Creole-speaking students on these specific points first as they begin their journey toward mastering the school language:

Pronunciation: /h/ in initial position
                    /th/ in initial, mid and end positions
                    /thr/ in initial position

In Jamaican Creole, the following word pairs are homonyms:

	at	hat
/H/	*own*	hone
	it	hit
	owe	hoe
	and	hand
/TH/	*thin*	tin
	though	dough
	three	tree
	breathe	breed
	faith	fate
	through	true

The *H*, *TH* and *TH* clusters (i.e., *THR*) may present difficulty for the Creole-speaking student and when pronounced or written, communication errors may result between the teacher and student. Other areas include:

Grammar:	pronouns
	verb and noun inflections
	plural markers
	prepositions
	possessive markers
Word Order:	formation of interrogative sentences

Assessment in the Classroom

To assess what students have mastered and to measure ongoing growth and development of Creole speakers, teachers are encouraged to use *varied* forms of assessment in the classroom. Traditional written tests do not always reveal a student's ability or knowledge accurately. This is not to say that written tests have no place in the classroom. However, they should not be the sole means of evaluating these students, for such assessment may not adequately reflect their strengths. Recent research continues to show not all students learn the same way or demonstrate mastery of material in the same way (Gardner, 1993). Moreover, research supports the notion that alternate forms of assessment can be both valid and effective approaches in monitoring and measuring a student's progress (Nero, 2000, 2001; Pierce, Swain, & Hart, 1993; Suarez-Orozco, 2001).

Since many Creole speakers, especially those who are newly arrived, may not be proficient in the school language, using alternate forms of assessment may be a better approach in assessing their knowledge and skills, which might not otherwise be disclosed with paper and pencil tests. Drawing, labeling, making oral presentations, keeping journals, creating portfolios, performing, problem solving, designing a science project, researching, using an online database to retrieve information, and creating a computer project, for example, are all valid and alternate methods of assessment as well. Through these alternative forms of assessment, teachers of Caribbean creole-speakers will have a greater array of data on which to substantiate and evaluate their students' progress and growth, and students can receive appropriate and focused feedback.

INSTRUCTIONAL APPROACHES AND STRATEGIES

Academic Language

Many Caribbean Creole-speaking students come to the classroom lacking academic language: the language of mathematics, science, history and other content areas. Some enter the school systems with interruptions in their education, attendance at school in their home countries having been irregular and spotty. Nevertheless, it is essential that these students be exposed to and learn academic language. This language is abstract and cognitively demanding, but when students do not possess knowledge of that language, it impedes learning and success (Cummins, 1980, 1981).

When teaching Creole-speaking students, a teacher may believe that these students are not capable of learning academic language. Such thinking may lead teachers to employ dull, repetitive drills and exercises and overlook or neglect the wide range of effective strategies and approaches at their disposal. Or, they may serve these students a modified version of the curriculum. However, when Creole speakers are presented with challenging and meaningful tasks, they can become motivated and successful learners in any school system.

Since these students eventually need to master the academic language taught in the various subject areas and must also demonstrate evidence that indicates they are able to produce work that is appropriate for their grade levels on mandated citywide and state assessments, teachers must provide numerous opportunities for them to both become familiar with and use academic language. In the classroom teachers can help to ensure that their Creole-speakers acquire academic language through such strategies as: integrating language and content areas, providing a variety of learning tasks with different formats, incorporating peer interaction and cooperative learning, encouraging students to use language productively in oral tasks, relating new learning to students' previous experiences, and bridging materials that are interesting and stimulating to content areas and to students' real life experiences (Brisk & Harrington, 2000; Daniels, 2002; Lewis-Smikle, 2003; Padron, Waxman, & Rivera, 2002).

In addition, teachers may incorporate specific assignments both in and out of the classroom as ways to increase academic language among creole-speaking students. Such assignments may include having students:

- *Make predictions* about what will happen or what might happen in the future (using current events topics from newspapers articles or graphs).
- *Analyze* two or three views on a single issue and then ask them to *argue* the view they support (debates, argumentative essays, editorials, letter writing).
- *Apply* their knowledge to new situations.
- *Create* or *invent* something that is new, different, and/or unique (advertisements, diorama, drawing).
- *Compare* two or more people or places (discussions, maps, surveys)
- *Set up an experiment* to which they must *test an hypothesis* (science projects, science lab demonstrations).

Teaching What Is Familiar

Students identify with what is familiar to them (Ladson-Billings, 1995; Padron, Waxman, & Rivera, 2002), and they learn about themselves and the world around them through the context of culture (Northeast and Islands Regional Educational Laboratory at Brown University, 2002). Students' cultural and linguistic backgrounds are strengths which teachers can utilize. Curricula should incorporate topics that relate to students' backgrounds, experiences and their needs (Hollins, 1996; Wilson & Carrington, 1999). Particularly in reading, research shows that reading is more likely to be successful when the curriculum and goals are culturally meaningful to students (Brokop, 1999; Wilson & Carrington, 1999). Therefore, it makes sense for teachers to start where their students are by building upon their students' prior knowledge and experiences in teaching new concepts and other materials. Once students' background knowledge is activated, it can be further developed. New information presented to students in class becomes meaningful and functional to them, and as a consequence, the tendency to retain what they have read or heard in class is greatly enhanced. Additionally, familiarity in the classroom fosters students' confidence, enhances pride, and creates positive attitudes towards learning. Moreover, introducing Caribbean culture in the classroom, when and wherever possible, promotes respect for the culture and traditions, and provides a balanced and equal recognition to both American and Caribbean cultures. Both non-Caribbean and Caribbean students learn about and from each other.

In light of this, knowledge of students' culture is helpful and can serve as a bridge between past experiences and new experiences, between what has been learned and what is to be learned. Further, having a grasp of students' culture helps teachers to understand their world, to be empathetic, and to heighten their awareness of cross-cultural differences.

Since most teachers do not have the time to thoroughly research the culture of all of their Caribbean students, they can be asked to complete a teacher-designed questionnaire or information form similar to the one in the appendix used by teachers at a high school in New York City. Such a list may provide teachers with some important aspects of Caribbean culture—in order that they might creatively incorporate and integrate these cultural facts into their classroom lessons for instructional purposes. Once these lists are completed by students and/or with the help of their parents, they may be compiled by teachers and used repeatedly since the information is unlikely to change often. Although several students in a class may be from one cultural background (e.g., Trinidad), every student is encouraged to complete a form. A more complete and accurate picture of each student's country will undoubtedly emerge.

CONCLUSION

Creole-speaking immigrant children from the English speaking Caribbean comprise a large number in the public school systems throughout parts of the United States. Therefore, it is likely that many teachers in these areas will encounter them in their classrooms at all levels (K–12) and in all subject areas. Educators teaching these students will also be faced with new curricular and procedural challenges in the classroom. However, they may be better prepared to meet these demands by:

- Learning about Caribbean English Creoles and the cultures of the students they teach.
- Holding high expectations for students.
- Developing curricula and materials for Creole-speaking students designed to help them learn and succeed in schools.
- Designing curricular content so that it reflects the concerns, cultures, and linguistic backgrounds of the students.
- Exploring and discovering alternate forms of classroom assessment.

QUESTIONS FOR DISCUSSION AND REFLECTIVE WRITING

1. How can teachers promote a classroom environment that is sensitive to the language of Caribbean Creole-speaking students and to all forms of cultural/linguistic differences?

2. What challenges might teachers encounter in developing culturally relevant curricular content and materials for Caribbean and other linguistically diverse students? How might these be addressed?
3. In what ways are the linguistic and educational issues surrounding Caribbean Creole English speakers similar to and different from African American Vernacular English speakers?

APPENDIX

Student Information Form

Name of Student _____

Country of Birth _____

Directions: This form asks you to supply information about your country and its culture. Please fill out this form as completely as you can.

The Arts

The Capital City of Country

Food

Music

National Anthem

National Bird

National Dish

National Flower

National Heroes

National Holidays

National Motto

National Political Parties

People

Places

Sports

Symbols and Images

Words and Phrases

An information form completed by a Jamaican high school student was completed this way:

Student Information Form

Name of Student Wrenford Kerr

Country of Birth Jamaica

Directions: This form asks you to supply information about your country and its culture. Please fill out this form as completely as you can.

The Arts Pantomime, The National Dance Theatre Company

The Capital City of Country Kingston

Food curry (curried) goat; breadfruit; yam, cho

Music reggae

National Anthem Jamaica Land We Love

National Bird the doctor bird

National Dish ackee and saltfish

National Flower Lignum Viate

National Heroes Manley, Bustamante, Bogle, Nanny, Garvey

National Holidays National Heroes Day (October?) Abolition Day

National Motto Out of many one people

National Political Parties Peoples National Party (PNP) Jamaica Labor Party (JLP)

People Louise Bennett (comme dienne); Bob Marley (musician)

Places Jamaica House, Devon House, Vale Royal

Sports cricket, soccer, basketball

Symbols and Images Anancy (a spider that teach. children moral lessons)

Words and Phrases

Cuyah — Look at this!
Irie — Everything is okay
Yard — Jamaica
No problem

REFERENCES

Allsopp, R. (1996). *Dictionary of Caribbean English usage*. Oxford: Oxford University Press.

Brisk, M., & Harrington, M. (2000). *Literacy and bilingualism: A handbook for all teachers*. Mahwah, NJ: Lawrence Erlbaum Associates.

Brokop, F. (1999). Literacy and ESL Learners. *Literacy partners of Manitoba*. Retrieved June 2, 2004, from http://www.mb.literacy.ca/Newslet/nwriteon/dec99/page13.htm

Cross, D. (1992). *A practical handbook of language teaching*. London: Prentice Hall.

Cummins, J. (1980). The entry and exit fallacy in bilingual education. *NABE Journal, 4*(3), 25–59.

Cummins, J. (1981). Four misconceptions about language proficiency in bilingual education. *NABE Journal, 5*(3), 31–45.

Daniels, H. (2002). *Literature circles: Voice and choice in book clubs and reading*. Portland: Stenhouse.

DeCamp, D. (1971). Towards a generative analysis of a post-Creole speech continuum. In D. Hymes (Ed.), *Pidginization and creolization of languages* (pp. 349–370). Cambridge: Cambridge University Press.

Gardner, H. (1993). *Multiple intelligences: The theory in practice*. New York: Basic Books.

Harris, M., & Silva, T. (1993). Tutoring ESL students: Issues and options. *College Composition and Communication, 44*, 525–537.

Henry, A. (2001). The politics of unpredictability in a reading/writing/discussion group with girls from the Caribbean. *Theory into Practice, 40*, 184–189.

Hollins, E. (1996). *Culture in school learning: Revealing the deep meaning*. Mahwah, NJ: Lawrence Erlbaum Associates.

Holm, J. (2000). The creole verb: A comparative study of stativity and tense reference. In J. McWhorter (Ed.), *Language change and language contact in pidgins and creoles* (pp. 133–161). Amsterdam: John Benjamins.

Kuboni, O. (2003). Collaborative learning in Caribbean higher education: Examining the prospects. In T. Bastick & A. Ezenne (Eds.), *Researching change in Caribbean education: Curriculum, teaching and administration* (pp. 217–250). Kingston: Department of Educational Studies, University of the West Indies.

Ladson-Billings, G. (1995). But that's just good teaching! The case for culturally relevant pedagogy. *Theory into Practice, 34*(3), 159–165.

Lewis-Smikle, J. (2003). Reading comprehension, attitudes to reading and locus of control beliefs of Jamaican students in primary and secondary schools. In T. Bastick & A. Ezenne (Eds.), *Teaching Caribbean students: Research on social issues in the Caribbean and abroad* (pp. 403–432). Kingston: Department of educational Studies, University of the West Indies.

Manswell Butty, J. (2003). Caribbean teachers in U.S. urban schools. In T. Bastick & A. Ezenne (Eds.), *Researching change in Caribbean education: Curriculum, teaching and administration* (pp. 165–194). Kingston: Department of Educational Studies, University of the West Indies.

Nero, S. (2000). The changing faces of English: A Caribbean perspective. *TESOL Quarterly, 34*(3), 483–510.

Nero, S. (2001). *Englishes in contact: Anglophone Caribbean students in an urban college*. Cresskill, NJ: Hampton Press.

Northeast and Islands Regional Educational Laboratory at Brown University. (2002). *The diversity skit: An introductory resource for social change in education*. Providence: Brown University.

Padron, Y. N., Waxman, H. C., & Rivera, H. H. (2002). *Educating Hispanic students: Effective instructional practices* (Practitioner Brief #5). Retrieved June 2, 2005, from http://www.cal.org/crede/Pubs/PracBrief5.htm

Perry, M. J., & Mackun, P. J. (2001). *Population change and distribution 1990 to 2000: Census 2000 brief* (Report No. C2KBR/01-2). Washington, DC: US Census Bureau.

Pierce, B. N., Swain, M., & Hart, D. (1993). Self-assessment in two French immersion programs. *Applied Linguistics, 14,* 25–42.

Pratt-Johnson, Y. (1993). Curriculum for Jamaican creole-speaking students in New York City. *World Englishes, 12*(2), 257–264.

Pratt-Johnson, Y., & Richards, C. (1995). The use of Jamaican Creole in the classroom and educational implications for the New York City public school and CUNY systems. In J. A. G. Irish (Ed.), *Caribbean students in New York* (pp. 59–71). New York: Caribbean Diaspora Press.

Rudder, M. (1999). Eliciting Student-Talk. *Forum, 37*(2), 24–27.

Suarez-Orozco, C. (2001). Afterword: Understanding and serving the children of immigrants. *Harvard Educational Review, 71,* 579–589.

Sunshine, C. A., & Warner, K. Q. (Eds.). (1998). *Caribbean connections: Moving north.* Washington, DC: Network of Educators on the Americas.

West-White, C. (2003). Caribbean student speakers' education and experiences in American schools. In T. Bastick & A. Ezenne (Eds.), *Teaching Caribbean students: Research on social issues in the Caribbean and abroad* (pp. 215–248). Kingston: Department of Educational Studies, University of the West Indies.

Wilson, D., & Carrington, L. (1999). *Report of the workshop: Creole speakers and language education in schools.* The International Federation for the Teaching of English. Retrieved August 10, 2003, from http://www.nyu.edu/education/teach/learn/ifte/creole.htm

Winford, D. (2001). A comparison of tense/aspect systems in Caribbean English creoles. In P. Christie (Ed.), *Due respect: Essays on English and English-related creoles in the Caribbean* (pp. 155–183). Kingston: University of the West Indies.

Part IV

HAWAI'I CREOLE ENGLISH (HCE)/PIDGIN

VI

Chapter 7

Pidgin, Local Identity, and Schooling in Hawai'i

Diana Eades
University of New England, Australia

Suzie Jacobs
*Formerly Professor of English, University of Hawai'i at Manoa
presently International Community School, Decatur, Georgia*

Ermile Hargrove
Educational Consultant

Terri Menacker
University of Hawai'i at Manoa

KEY POINTS

Part I

- The appropriateness approach and standard language ideology in relation to Hawai'i Creole English/Pidgin.
- The role of Pidgin in group identity and appropriateness judgments.
- Testing the boundaries of appropriateness in various contexts and movements.

Part II

- English Standard Schools and segregationist language practices in Hawai'i.
- Effects of the attempted ban of Pidgin from the classroom.
- Review of programs that address Pidgin speakers in school.

This chapter has two parts. The first focuses on the use of Pidgin (or Hawai'i Creole English) in Hawai'i, examining the way in which appropriateness interacts with the role of this language variety in local identity. The second part addresses Pidgin in Hawai'i schools.

PART I: PUSHING THE BOUNDARIES OF
"APPROPRIATENESS": PIDGIN AND LOCAL IDENTITY

The Appropriateness Question

Teachers of English and Language Arts often teach their students to ask themselves the *appropriateness* question: "Is my choice of language appropriate?" Students are taught that the word means suited to the context and that their choice of language at any particular moment should take context into account. When students live in a multilingual or multidialectal society, then context will often dictate a decision about which language or dialect to choose. Though students are seldom given the choice about which language variety to use inside classrooms, the basis for making the choice outside of school seems clear enough. They should use good sense about when and where they use each of their languages or dialects.

We take the view that the appropriateness argument is far more complex than it is presented above. Students sitting in today's classroom may have learned from parents and grandparents, not to mention peers, that appropriate means sanctioned or approved by a higher authority. Rather than an emphasis on differing contexts and the values of flexibility, the word suggests, more or less firmly, "Let's do it this way."

For linguists, especially sociolinguists, and those who study other non-standard language varieties in school contexts (e.g., Berry & Hudson, 1997; Eades, 1995; Wolfram & Christian, 1989), the notion of *appropriate to context* is in line with the intent to be descriptive rather than prescriptive—that is, to observe how language is actually spoken or used rather than how it should be used. In this sense, appropriateness is intended to be a term to describe the viewpoint of society or segments of society, not that of the linguist. But this approach, combined with the cultural relativism that has dominated modern sociolinguistics, has led scholars and educators to draw such conclusions as the following: Standard English is the language most commonly and successfully used in job interviews in the US, and some varieties of English are highly stigmatized, therefore they are not appropriate in job interviews. But, as Fairclough (1992) points out, close attention to actual language use shows that people are misled by so-called appropriate contexts, since these tend to be based on overgeneralized observations. Further, recent critical sociolinguistic scholars (e.g., Fairclough, 1992; Lippi-Green, 1997) argue that this appropriateness approach, which has been so influential in educational settings, serves to reproduce unequal power relations and reinforce standard language ideology.[1]

---

[1]Lippi-Green defines standard language ideology as "a bias toward an abstract, idealized homogeneous spoken language which is imposed and maintained by dominant bloc institutions and which names as its model the written language, but which is drawn primarily from the spoken language of the upper middle class" (Lippi-Green, 1997, p. 64).

Critics of this notion argue instead that speakers should have the right to choose where and when to use their language variety. Hargrove and Sakoda make the point, in dealing with the issue of where and when to use Pidgin in Hawai'i: "[Pidgin speakers] should not be condemned to disadvantage and marginalization—the final choice should be theirs to make" (1999, p. 61).

In this chapter, we suggest that within the framework of unequal power relations, group identity plays an important role in the way appropriateness judgments are made. We will demonstrate that, in some instances in Hawai'i, these judgments have been changed by the efforts of active groups or communities and may continue to change in the future.

Pidgin's Origins and Its Role in Local Identity

Immigration has brought people from all over the world to Hawai'i. Sato (1985, 1991) provides a compact history of the way that the state's diversity has largely resulted from "massive labor importation, triggered by the development of sugar plantations by North Americans during the late nineteenth and early twentieth centuries" (1991, p. 647). Reinecke (1969) details the numbers of immigrants in that boom period; this resulted in a truly multilingual society in Hawai'i beginning some hundred years ago (see also Siegel, 2000).

Immigration continues to bring people from all over the world to Hawai'i, a state of many languages. Two of these languages are unique to Hawai'i. The first, a co-official language with English, is Hawaiian, the indigenous language and a member of the Austronesian language family. By the mid 1960s, Hawaiian was in the process of language death, and it now has only a small number of native speakers. But a strong language revival movement, centered on more than 10 language immersion schools (Warner, 1999), has increased its vitality and particularly its role in the identity of native Hawaiians. The other language unique to Hawai'i is much more widely spoken. This language, called *Pidgin* by its speakers, is defined as a creole language by linguists, who often use the name Hawai'i Creole English (HCE) to refer to it, and Hawai'i Pidgin English (or HPE) to refer to its predecessor, a pidgin language.

It developed on the sugar plantations at the end of the nineteenth century as immigrant workers adapted English for intercultural communication. The early version of the language was "rather unstable and highly variable" (Sato, 1991, p. 648) and was used by the immigrant plantation workers as a second language. The workers primarily lived in a multilingual society, speaking the languages from their home countries (China, Japan, Portugal, the Philippines, and others) as well as Hawaiian, so the pidgin in those days was nobody's first language. But, as documented by linguists, this early version expanded, stabilized and became the first language of the plantation children, starting around the early part of the 20th century (Siegel, 2000). From that point, it was technically no longer a pidgin language, but a creole, although its speakers in Hawai'i still call it Pidgin, the name we use throughout the paper.[2]

Currently, a range of Pidgin varieties is found throughout the Hawaiian islands, with a particular concentration of acrolectal varieties in Honolulu, and basilectal varieties in rural Oahu and the neighbor islands. There are clearly recognizable features of basilectal Pidgin—such as *wen* past tense marker, *neva* past tense negator, *wan* as indefinite article. In the acrolectal varieties, in which there are many overlaps with general Hawai'i English, these features may occur only rarely.[3] But arguably, intonation and certain key lexical items (such as *bambai* for English "later," *bambucha* for English "huge") persist in even the most acrolectal varieties of Pidgin.[4]

The fact of variation does not indicate that Pidgin is presently converging with English, as some have suggested. Siegel (2000) notes that Pidgin in Hawai'i has been characterized by variation since its beginnings. Roberts (2002) shows that rather than converging towards American Standard English at this early time, Pidgin (or HCE) actually diverged from it. Sato (1991) examined the way that individuals' speech might have converged with Hawai'i Standard English over time—but found the evidence inconclusive. Some features were found to be decreolizing while others were not. While variation and change characterize the language, it is clearly not a disappearing language.

There has never been a census question or similar survey regarding the number of Pidgin speakers. As long as it continues to be widely regarded as bad English or slang, asking people if they speak Pidgin will not yield reliable statistics. Romaine's (1994) guesstimate is that "somewhat less than half the state's population of just over one million" speaks Pidgin (p. 527), but this is considered by some to be rather conservative. Certainly, Pidgin can be heard on all of the islands in the state, in a wide range of localities and social settings.

---

[2]It should be pointed out that the pidgin variety (HPE) continued for some time after the creole (HCE) was established, although there appear to be no longer any speakers of the pidgin variety.

[3]An example of basilectal Pidgin from Lum (1990, p. 71) *Da Bag Man neva know what for do* ("The homeless man didn't know what to do"). Also, an example of acrolectal Pidgin from Tonouchi (2001a, p. 23) *"So wot you tot,"* I axed (" 'So, what did you think?' I asked").

[4]There has never been a comprehensive description of the features of Pidgin, but Kent Sakoda of the Department of Second Language Studies and Jeff Siegel of the Sato Center for Pidgin, Creole and Dialect Studies, both at the University of Hawai'i, are working on a linguistic description of variation in contemporary Pidgin, as well as a teachers' guide to features of the language.

As with many creole speakers around the world, Pidgin's present-day speakers are ethnically diverse. Hawai'i still has large populations which are neither Hawaiian nor Caucasian. The 2000 census (Hawai'i, 2000) reports that the largest ethnic groups are Hawaiian/Part Hawaiian (22.1%), Caucasian (20.5%), Japanese (18.3%), Filipino (12.3%), and Chinese (4.1%).

Since its birth as a language of intercultural communication in multilingual plantation environments, Pidgin has played an important role in the identity of its speakers (Kawamoto, 1993; Sato, 1991; Watson-Gegeo, 1994). Detailed historical sociolinguistic research by Roberts (2002) has found that at the time of creole formation in the early 1900s, Pidgin was central to a double sociopolitical process, distinguishing its speakers from white Americans speaking American Standard English, on the one hand, and from foreign-born immigrants speaking their ancestral languages, on the other.

Kawamoto (1993) stressed the role of Pidgin in "forming a *single* identity among the immigrant groups which cut across ethnic lines" (pp. 200–201, emphasis in original). So, Pidgin was at the same time a powerful force both separating its speakers from white Americans and immigrants, and uniting descendants of the immigrants. As Kawamoto puts it, Pidgin, and its predecessor HPE, were the "glue which bonded the descendants of the immigrants" (p. 201). The combined separating and uniting power of Pidgin is still seen today. Its use continues to be central to the construction of local identity.

Being *local*, in its narrowest usage, means that a person is either Hawaiian or a descendant of the plantation workers. It is most frequently contrasted with *haole*, a word from the Hawaiian language that originally meant foreigner, but has come to refer to Caucasians, typically white Americans. (Interestingly, *haole* does not refer to those of Portuguese descent). The term local is now also frequently extended beyond its meaning of descendants of plantation workers to include more recent immigrants, primarily from Asian countries, who have become residents and share in local culture. Lum (1997) discusses local cultural values, pointing to the way they are captured in common Pidgin expressions, such as:

Expressions	*Values*
What school you went?	community and the primacy of relationships and genealogy
Talk story:	the importance of oral tradition, narrative and multivocality

Many, perhaps most, Pidgin speakers are also speakers of English and, like bilingual people the world over, make the choice about which language to use in a particular situation depending on a range of contextual factors. Lum's (1997) description of a local party shows family and friends sitting on coolers, chatting in Pidgin. "What school you went?" they ask the newcomer, by way of establishing the newcomer's connection to the group. This is a pattern in which self-identity in an in-group plays a role in the choice of language. In line with this pattern, the nonstandard variety is used for solidarity with friends and family (or the in-group), and the standard variety is more likely to be used in the mainstream or out-group setting (De Bose, 1992; Leong, 2000).

Underlying the "Appropriateness" Question:
A History of Stigma

Despite its ongoing importance in the construction of local identity and its covert prestige among speakers, Pidgin has a history of stigma and denigration in many contexts, both by speakers and non-speakers. There is still considerable public discourse both in support of Pidgin as a valued part of local culture and identity, and against Pidgin, usually because of the negative role it is believed to play in the educational and employment opportunities and achievements of its speakers. From the 1930s and 40s up to the present, island newspapers have recorded the tension between the positive and the negative views, even contributing to that tension in some instances.

The negative views have not disappeared over time. A 1996 study found (as letters to the editors of the local newspapers demonstrate), that people link Pidgin with poor job prospects (Tomita & Sawyer, 1996). Some continue to describe it as bad English. As recently as the last few years, people have written to local newspapers that Pidgin is "not a language," and that it is "inferior to modern English" (*HSB*, 12/10/99).[5] One wrote that:

> Hawaiian Creole is a kind of shadow language, without a fully developed grammar and vocabulary, that seductively undermines and corrupts the study of Standard English. (*HA*, 4/25/01)

But nowadays, with few exceptions, negative views of Pidgin are phrased more carefully than they used to be, especially by public figures. The critique has been muted, as we shall see.

In the 60s, the 50s, and earlier decades, the stance of public figures was confrontational. Pidgin was the "plain misuse of English" (Lowell Jackson, Superintendent of Public Instruction, *HSB*, 8/10/66), it was "abominable English" (Manuel Kwon, school principal, *HSB*, 11/29/59), and "the most

---

[5]*HSB* refers to the *Honolulu Star Bulletin*, and *HA* refers to the *Honolulu Advertiser*, both daily newspapers.

execrable language in the world" (Bill Ewing, editor of the *HSB*, speaking at the annual Pacific Speech Association meeting, *HSB*, 2/11/62). It is no coincidence that some of the strongest criticism of Pidgin came from educators, or in relation to educational issues (see Hargrove and Menacker, part II of this chapter).

In the mid 60s, journalists writing news reports (as opposed to opinion pieces) frequently characterized Pidgin as a problem, as in: ". . . a statewide attack on one of Hawai'i's biggest language problems: pidgin" (*HSB*, 8/4/65) and "Pidgin problems are probably most acute in the Kalihi area" (*HSB*, *HA* 1/30/66). Headlines put the word "problem" in big print:

> Pidgin English still big problem here (*HSB*, *HA* 1/30/66)
> Speech center proposed for problems of Pidgin (*HSB*, 2/11/66)
> The problems of Pidgin English (*HA*, 7/5/66)

Occasionally, an intrepid citizen chose to challenge the characterization, as in "I say, there is no problem. Let 'Hawai'i's Dialect' continue and bring the joy and pleasure to all who use it" (*HSB*, 8/27/64). But the press was generally negative.

A more middle-of-the-road approach to Pidgin in those days, especially in the mid 60s, was to address Pidgin issues in terms of language improvement. Whatever the intentions of the teachers and institutions that offered the programs intended to improve islanders' English, newspapers almost always portrayed these programs as getting rid of Pidgin. "Good English" was almost always a code phrase for Pidgin avoidance.

In those years the newspapers hardly mentioned Pidgin as a product of community interaction. There was little or no reporting of the language in any cultural context. Language use was good or bad, right or wrong, correct or incorrect. Pidgin was no longer referred to as impure, as it had been in the 1920s, when educational authorities described it as though it were related to racial impurity (e.g., Anon, 1921, p. 10). But neither was there reference to the community's use of the language. When university academics referred to the language's social function—and the newspapers occasionally reported a sociologist's remark in this regard—they apparently went unheard.[6] A columnist for a leading newspaper wrote that there was nothing "to justify [Pidgin] as part of Hawai'i's cultural heritage, to be preserved along with poi pounders and bone fishhooks" (*HSB*, 11/11/67).

When islanders were heard speaking a form of standard English with one group and Pidgin with another, figures in authority looked at them balefully. In speaking Pidgin, these speakers had relapsed (Beck, 1940, p.

---

[6]For example the sociologist Andrew Lind, *HA*, 7/8/60, and a visiting sociologist Bernhard Hormann, *HSB* 3/28/58.

262) or regressed.[7] There was little awareness of switching by people skillful in more than one language or dialect. Elizabeth Carr, a speech professor who repeatedly urged the public to view both Pidgin and standard English as dialects, was not listened to. She described the concepts of bilingualism and bi-dialectalism, recommending that "we leave 'good' and 'bad' out of the question and think of the forms of the language as the results of circumstance and environment" (*HSB*, 6/22/66). Said Superintendent Jackson a few months later: "I don't buy this dialect business" (*HSB*, 8/10/66).

By the late 1970s, the connection between language and identity—between speaking Pidgin and being local—had scarcely been considered. But still, the cultural point had been raised. Hawai'i's plantation culture was now publicly valued, especially by those now of middle class status whose parents and grandparents had once worked in the fields.

In 1978, there was a turning point in the recognition of the culture's rich verbal tradition—a Talk Story[8] conference held on the campus of the state's major university. With the joint participation of linguists, writers, and the public at large, the conference articulated the link between cultural experience, stories that communicated that experience, and the Pidgin language in which the stories were told. The newspapers got the message out, putting Pidgin—at last—into a cultural context.

A New and "Appropriate" Context for Pidgin Use

The Talk Story Conference was significant for a second reason as well. It launched a literary movement by local writers that went well beyond earlier attempts to use the island idiom in print. Now, more than twenty years after the literary move was initiated, Pidgin in literary contexts enjoys a measure of prestige. Newspapers, even when they continue to attack Pidgin as a cause of this or that island failure, now feel compelled to acknowledge the language's literary value. In one negative editorial (where, once more, the schools are exhorted to keep Pidgin out of their classrooms), the writer for *HA*, before launching into his main theme, begins by conceding the success of the literary movement: "Pidgin is now in the mainstream in literature and the arts in Hawai'i" (*HA*, 8/15/95). Again, in 1999, making the same negative argument, another writer feels compelled to begin in the same positive way:

---

[7]See, for example, the remarks attributed to Hubert Everly, Dean of the College of Education (*HSB* 8/10/66). It is, however, unclear whether this word was used by the dean or the reporter who paraphrased his remarks.

[8]*Talk story* refers to a central activity in local culture, involving the building of shared feelings by "a variety of verbal routines, which include recalled events, either personal or folktales, verbal play, joking, and conversing" (Boggs, 1985, p. 7).

> This is not a slap at pidgin, which is rapidly developing its own body of work in
> art and literature and is a core component of the unique Island experience.
> (*HA*, 9/30/99)

In sum, Pidgin is now appropriate when used in a literary context. Editorial
writers have made it a point to say so.

How did this happen? Not quickly and not easily. The history of the
move over the years since 1978 points to three factors: first, the maintenance and development of a writing community through the work of a
small publisher; second, the support of the public; and third, the literary
quality of much of the work.

The small publisher was the Bamboo Ridge Press, established by Eric
Chock and Darrell Lum, with other members of the writing community
soon after the 1978 Talk Story conference. Mainly these were writers who
had run the state's Poets in the Schools program, which at that time was losing its funding. They held public readings in classrooms, coffee shops, and
bookstores. They encouraged re-writing, until eventually several writers had
learned to convey the island voice in a written form that seemed to listeners
much like the genuine *talk story* tradition they had grown up with. Not all
wrote in Pidgin, but many did, experimenting with the language to convey
the feelings of characters with wit, economy, and intensity. Some only put
Pidgin into dialogue. Others used it for the narrator's voice. In the early
days of this local literature movement, the act of putting Pidgin on paper
felt strange. Said Maxine Hong Kingston, who was living and writing in
Honolulu during these years:

> We are still experimenting with how to render pidgin—the language used at
> home, the language of childhood and the sub-conscious, the language used
> in emotion—into writing, figuring out its spellings and phonics. (Chock et al.,
> 1978, p. 6)

Local writers have still not agreed on a conventional spelling system for Pidgin phrases, but this seems not to have deterred either their publishing, or
their Pidgin readers' enjoyment. Bamboo Ridge has continued to publish
for over twenty years, keeping the community of writers alive by providing
an avenue of publication.

A second factor in making Pidgin an appropriate language for print has
been enthusiastic public support. In a state whose entire population could
fit into San Diego, the Bamboo Ridge Press sells about 12,000 books a year
as well as its journal and estimates its readership at 18,000 annually. Since
1980, the local literature shelves of the state's bookstores have grown remarkably in number. Several writers have drawn sizable crowds in university

auditoriums and bookstores, and productions of local plays are now a fixture in the intimate downtown theatre, Kumu Kahua.

Finally, written Pidgin became appropriate in the eyes of local standard setters because of literary quality. Local writers earned accolades that could hardly be ignored. A number of Bamboo Ridge writers have won national awards,[9] and several, such as Lois Ann Yamanaka and Kathleen Tyau have been reviewed in the New York Times and are now on contract with publishers in New York and Boston. A few works, now classics, have become required reading in Hawai'i's college level American literature courses.

New Boundaries of Pidgin's "Appropriateness"

At the same time that the literary movement made it increasingly appropriate to write in Pidgin, pushing outward the boundaries of use, it also opened the doors to new and more open expression of questions of a Pidgin speaker's identity. What does it mean to be a Pidgin speaker? How does it feel? The answers, heard in Pidgin by island audiences, are often simultaneously funny and painful.

> *I no can open my mouth.*
> *My words,*
> *My sentences,*
> *Not going make sense.*
> *Too much pidgin.*
> *Pudgy, pilipino, pidgin speaking pygmy.*
> *I no like make shame.*
> (from "Shame and the First Day of College," by Darlene Javar, 1998, p. 293)

(I can't open my mouth. My words, my sentences, won't make sense. There's too much Pidgin. Pudgy, Filipino, Pidgin-speaking pygmy. I don't want to make a fool of myself.)

The local literature movement has also shown how difficult the relationship of Pidgin language and Pidgin identity can be. Let us suppose that I consider my language bad, as important voices in the newspaper have suggested. If my language is bad, and I am identified with my language, what does that make me? I am left with several choices, none of them good or

---

[9]Four National Endowment for the Arts Creative Writing Fellowships, two Before Columbus Foundation American Book Awards, six Pushcart Prizes and one O. Henry Award for works published in *Bamboo Ridge*, four Association for Asian American Studies National Book Awards, a 1991 James Clavell Award for Fiction, 1998 Small Press Book Award for Poetry, 1998–2000 Artists Embassy International Literacy/Cultural Award, eight Elliot Cades Awards, and seven Ka Palapala Po'okela Awards from the Hawai'i Book Publishers Association. (Information provided by the office of Bamboo Ridge Press.)

easy. I can repudiate my language. That's one solution, but it usually requires me to lie, both to others and to myself, by denying that I speak it. Of course, I can accept it, and my inferior status. Or, I can even defend it.

But in the experience of many, defending Pidgin is extremely difficult, given the dominant standard language ideology and people's desire to fit in with prevailing values, especially those dominating educational contexts. It has been observed in classrooms that when Pidgin speaking students are asked to comment, they often have what Hargrove and Sakoda (1999) term "a schizophrenic attitude"—a kind of "yes, I love my culture and language, and yes my language is terrible" (p. 63).

Limits of "Appropriateness"

In spite of the consciousness of local identity, there is an equally strong sense in Hawai'i of occasions and contexts where Pidgin is not appropriate. Even local writers using Pidgin have observed rather strict boundaries of use. As Romaine (1994) has pointed out, writers have used Pidgin for characters' voices but not for informed or knowledgeable narration. They use Pidgin in a variety of forms—as dialogue in quotes, as monologue without quotes, or as straight narrative from a character's vantage point, also without quotes—but authors avoid Pidgin if they speak as themselves. (We will come to an exception later.)

Some local advocates of Pidgin who have lived with the public debate on the language for many years understand the appropriateness point to be nothing more than another put-down (Hargrove & Sakoda, 1999; Wong, 1999). What is really meant, they contend, is negative and prescriptive. The tone of the appropriateness point is said to be cautionary, as in "Be careful. Don't go here, and don't go there." Specifically, don't use Pidgin outside of light hearted conversational settings, as in comedy routines. Don't use it in literature, except to represent the voices of children, rural people, or working people—mainly in dialogue. Don't use Pidgin for serious or formal contexts. Says Wong (1999): "The Pidgin voice has been effectively silenced in certain domains where its use is viewed as inappropriate" (p. 207).

Clearly, the appropriateness approach is powerful in confining Pidgin within its prescribed boundaries of use. Unlike Haiti, for example, Hawai'i has no news or weather broadcast in Pidgin, on either radio or TV. Indeed, a famous 1987 language discrimination case showed that reading the weather on TV with a Pidgin accent can be judged as unacceptable (see Sato, 1991). There is no Pidgin in print for the purpose of news reporting, nor is there an accepted standard orthography that serious newswriters might use. The Odo orthography, which uses spelling conventions like those in Hawaiian, is used in limited scholarly contexts by some linguists but not by members of the public. There is likewise no attempt to provide

Pidgin translations of bureaucratic documents such as welfare guidelines, tax instructions, or directions for drivers' tests, though bureaucrats on the job may speak to their clients in Pidgin, depending—it seems—on their inclination, and communicative needs. Most times, in spite of people's needs and the demonstrated power of Pidgin in the political and literary arenas, Pidgin used for any formal or serious purpose in the public domain is deemed to be out of line. In two key institutional contexts—education and law—Pidgin is generally considered inappropriate (although some lawyers, judges, and teachers use it).

Pushing the Boundaries: New Contexts of Pidgin Use

It is clear that the future boundaries of appropriate use of Pidgin depend on whether or not today's users of Pidgin make a reasonable and persuasive case for expanding the number of occasions or contexts for use, and whether others, in fact, decide to follow the leader. It is impossible to know at this stage the extent to which voices of authority from the past and present will be echoed by those in the future, and whether the innovations of the current literary movement will stay within the boundaries so far observed. Language situations are always changeable. Indeed, change in language use and in opinions about appropriate contexts is often precipitated by speakers who make such choices in ways that initially seem inappropriate or even radical. Worshippers learned to accept the Catholic Mass in the vernacular rather than Latin. Likewise, readers in various cultures have become accustomed to new alphabetic conventions. In such ways, the boundaries of so-called appropriate contexts can shift. The following are recent examples of this shift in the contexts of Pidgin use.

The first example of pushing the boundaries was at a 1999 University of Hawai'i conference on Pidgin (entitled "*Wat, bada yu? Voices heard and voices unheard: Pidgin, local identities and multicultural learning*") where there were heated discussions about appropriate context. The members of the audience had already, at this point in the conference, engaged seriously on a number of topics related to Pidgin use: Pidgin in schools, language discrimination, and writing in Pidgin. Nearly everyone there was an advocate. Many spoke the language at home, and they were comfortable with standard English in the academic environment. At this point, some asked why conference presenters were using English instead of Pidgin. Did it matter that standard English was the ordinary language of academia? Was this conference not an occasion better suited to Pidgin than to English? The point, forcefully made, was that the academic English-only convention had overridden the important concern of the conference, which after all was language as empowerment.

A second heated controversy at this conference concerned the Odo orthography, the Pidgin spelling system mentioned earlier that shares some of the orthographic principles of the system for spelling Hawaiian. Some members of the audience could read Hawaiian but had never practiced using these spelling conventions for Pidgin. (The orthography spells 'like', for example as *laik*, 'cat' as *kaet* and the commonly used past tense negator 'never' as *neva*.) The 14-page conference program had been written in the orthography, by Kent Sakoda, a Pidgin speaker, teacher, and expert from the university's Department of Second Language Studies.[10] But a very general audience reaction was negative. They wanted to continue to spell Pidgin in ways more familiar to them, which is to say more like English. They complained that the strange orthography made their own language inaccessible to them, and others complained that it made Pidgin accessible to outsiders in a way that it had not otherwise been.

In fact, we have noted in our conversations with members of the non-linguistics community (such as the creative writers) a strongly felt belief that Pidgin use is incompatible with rules of any kind. There should be no spelling rules, no set guidelines of use, and no policy statements. Other languages are dominated by people who have made rules for their use. Pidgin has never been ruled over in this way and should not begin imposing rules now, not with an orthography and not with guidelines for when and where Pidgin is acceptable (whether recommendations, suggestions, or rules by any other name). This attitude, if widely held among influential Pidgin speakers, may work for the maintenance of the status quo. That is, Pidgin would continue to have an important solidarity function in the construction and expression of local, island identity, but it would likely never be used in contexts that are official in style (in written minutes of meetings, for example, or in a manual for drivers).

A second example of pushing the boundaries was taken in 1997 when the Wycliffe Bible Translators published a Pidgin translation of the *New Testament Book of Matthew*, titled *Matthew Tell Bout Jesus*. This was followed in 2000 by the full New Testament in Pidgin, titled *Da Jesus Book*, and in 2002 by the first in a series of audio CD versions, titled *Da Jesus Story*.

The other case of stepping across the boundaries of appropriate context is the one-man campaign to legitimize Pidgin now being carried out by a lo-

---

[10]An example from the conference program: *Wen yu tawk Pijin wea yu wrk o in skul, yu goin get pilikia o wat? Da kawt sistom in da west, de kea or de no kea hau yu tawk laidaet? Da paenol goin tawk about sam keises wea wen get sam pipol laik imigrent kain, aen neitiv kain, aen da kain daet tawk pijin wen get diskrimineishen bikawz de no tawk Gud Ingglish.*

Translation: When you speak Pidgin in the workplace or in school, will you be in trouble? What is the reaction of the western legal system to the use of Pidgin in these settings? The panel will discuss some cases involving immigrants, native peoples and Pidgin speakers, who have been discriminated [*sic*] because they don't speak standard English.

cal writer turned teacher and public speaker. Lee Tonouchi, who often refers to himself as *Da Pidgin Guerilla*, has crossed all the appropriateness
boundaries mentioned earlier. Not only do his child characters and unreli-
able narrators use Pidgin; so do the grown-up and thoughtful ones (2001).
Even when he writes in his own authorial voice as opposed to creating a narrator voice, he writes in Pidgin (2002). Then, breaking through a final bar-
rier, he claimed that standard English was unnecessary for schooling, for
passing exams, for getting an interview and a job. He himself had done all
of these things, even writing a successful job application in Pidgin for a faculty position at a community college (which he now holds).

Summary

In Hawai'i, where at least half of the population speak a creole that most
people call Pidgin, it is now widely (though not universally) recognized that
Pidgin is inseparable from local identity. This is a relatively recent public attitude. In earlier years, Pidgin was publicly derided, even by persons of importance and education. Though there is still evidence that Pidgin speakers
may be disadvantaged in the employment market and in the courts, in the
last twenty years public discourse about Pidgin has matured. Apparently
tempered by a dynamic and successful movement of local creative writers,
the talk about Pidgin has turned toward a discussion of "who we are." Local
identity—and those values associated with local identity such as loyalty,
connectedness, hard work, and caring—is now linked in the minds of many
with the Pidgin language.

But even while Pidgin, especially among those who read literary works, is
enjoying a respect for its contribution to Hawai'i's rainbow of cultures, a
cautionary attitude may also be gaining adherents. This is the attitude, now
frequently expressed in educational circles, that Pidgin should be used in
appropriate contexts. This part of our chapter has explored the notion of
fixed boundaries of Pidgin use, the apparent force of the appropriateness
approach in keeping Pidgin within those boundaries, and the question of
whether or not the efforts of individuals to cross over those boundaries will
lead others to follow their example.

Further study will be necessary to reveal how the appropriateness notion
is actually perceived. Possibly it is heard as an invitation to use Pidgin, as
creative writers have used it, in stories and poems. On the other hand, the
perception that appropriate use really means "little use" or "use only in
jokes with your friends" may be widespread. We are concerned that the
phrase may become a formulaic answer to hard questions of how teachers
should deal with Pidgin in school. Too easily appropriateness can become
another way of perpetuating a standard English ideology. In Hawai'i, it may

even be the case, that the appropriateness approach works as a backlash against the literary movement, a kind of "Yes, BUT."

We believe that schooling is most successful when it starts with respect for the home language of the school community and the cultural identity associated with that language. This is not to deny the importance of standard English. Like a number of educators and scholars we support the goal of "additive bilingualism," following Sato (1989). The challenge facing the education system is to facilitate additive bilingualism, building on the strong connection between Pidgin and local identity, teaching students to be aware of the consequences of language choice, and not limiting their agency as bilingual speakers through the notions of appropriateness fostered by the power structure. The next section focuses on these and related issues concerning Pidgin and education.

PART II: PIDGIN AND EDUCATION IN HAWAI'I

Historical records show that by the early 20th century the descendants of the missionaries and plantation owners in Hawai'i were attending their own school (Punahou). Kamehameha Schools were addressing the needs of Hawaiian children, and the public schools were available to other children. Whereas previous instruction had been in Hawaiian, schooling now was completely in English. For many children, the public school teacher was the sole source of the English language, and for many teachers English was a second language (Dotts & Sikkema, 1994).

The English Standard School Period

Today, nearly one in five of Hawai'i's school-age students attends private schools, one of the highest percentages in the U.S. (Rogers, 2002). The private school movement arose early in Hawai'i as a way for American and European parents to provide the kind of education they wanted for their children as well as to isolate their children from the assumed negative effects of contact with local children. The schools called "English Standard Schools" were first established in the 1920s (with the last class graduating in the 1960s) by the Hawai'i Department of Public Instruction primarily to provide the segregation desired by those Americans and Europeans who couldn't afford private schools. In order not to be unconstitutional, these schools based their segregation on "language usage, not race" and claimed "that a model American standard school system was essential to the Americanization process" (Stueber, 1991, p. 28). Potential students were required to demonstrate their command of standard English as illustrated by the following excerpt from a story by Marie Hara (1998):

By the time we were back in the office for the part called The Interview, which was really a test to see if I could speak perfect Standard English, I knew something was funny . . . The woman tester kept after me to say the printed words on the picture cards that she, now unsmiling, held before my eyes . . .

. . . She shook her head. "Again"

"Da BO-LO-CA-NO," I repeated loudly. Maybe like O-Jiji with the stink ear on his left side, she couldn't hear: "we we' go'n see da bolocano," I explained confidentially to her . . .

"It's the vol-cano," she enunciated clearly, forcing me to watch her mouth move aggressively. She continued with downcast eyes. "We went to see the vol-cano.' You can go and wait outside, okay?"

. . . Mama shrugged it off as we trudged home.

"Neva' mind. Get too many stuck shet ladies ova dea. People no need act, Lei. You wait. You gon 'get one good education, not like me." (pp. 32–33)

The English standard schools protected both the speech habits and the preferred position in the Islands' stratified society of those who spoke English as their first language (Stueber, 1991, p. 29). Ironically, these schools may have played a key role in the establishment of Pidgin as a vernacular of Hawai'i since they restricted the extended interaction of locals with native English speakers that might have led to second language acquisition rather than the formation of a creole (Sato, 1989).

English Standard schools were the embodiment of the belief that standard English was the key to education and opportunity prompting parents to send their children to special tutoring schools so that they could pass the English entry examination. By the time the last class was admitted in 1947, the segregative purpose of the schools had lost its impetus and the white students had become a minority comprising less than 25% of the school population (Rogers, 2002).

Outside of the English Standard schools, children of the early plantation workers were told their English was poor or that they spoke broken English. In fact, these children spoke Pidgin and were learning English as a second language through submersion. Because the children were separated from monolingual English speaking children until well into the 1940s, they were not likely to become proficient English speakers. They did not receive any special English language instruction to bridge the gap between home and school but had traditional grammar lessons and spelling tests. As they gained greater access to English speakers, their proficiency rose but was often still not at the level of a monolingual English speaker (Tamura, 1994).

Because of the lexical similarities between Pidgin and English, the submersion process went unrecognized and it is only recently that this tangle of misinformation has become unraveled and teachers are learning that Pidgin is a language, similar to, but separate from, English. In fact, when teachers are presented with evidence of the structures of Pidgin (e.g., the construction of negation in Pidgin), they often appear skeptical. The treatment of Pidgin as an English has left a legacy of negative self-image for those corrected in school for their bad English or for not speaking proper English. Even as adults, some still suffer from feelings of linguistic ineptness and a reticence to speak publicly.

Attitudes that equated being educated with speaking standard English rather than Pidgin became institutionalized at the University. Between 1969 and 1974, University of Hawai'i students' speech was rated and they were sent to speech classes until they had "a generally intelligible and acceptable form of spoken English." Anecdotal reports include stories of future teachers being sent to these classes until they said "STRAWberry" rather than the local Pidgin-influenced variant "shtrawBERRY".

Attempted Ban of Pidgin in the Classroom

In 1987, the Curriculum Committee of the Hawai'i Board of Education (that directs public education for the entire state) put forward a proposal mandating that only standard English be used in the classroom (effectively banning Pidgin). They were surprised by the strong response against the proposal by academics, parents, teachers and Hawaiian rights activists (Sato, 1989). Eventually a much softer statement which "encouraged" the modeling of standard English by teachers and staff was adopted. Despite the vocal opposition to a ban on Pidgin at school, an August, 1995 *Honolulu Advertiser* poll found that "two thirds of Hawai'i's residents say standard English should be the only language used to teach in the classroom" (Rogers, 2002).

The banning of Pidgin in the classroom can have a number of negative effects. Hargrove & Sakoda (1999) point out that when children say something in Pidgin in the classroom and it is corrected as though the child were trying to speak English, the result is often confusion about the boundaries between the two languages. A surface level Pidgin word might be replaced by an English word with a similar surface form but different nuances, meanings or uses. This is particularly easy to do for teachers with little knowledge of Pidgin. In contrast, when language difference is explicitly dealt with, as in Language Awareness approaches, features of closely related languages or dialects are clarified and disambiguated. This helps learners control and separate the languages in their repertoire and function effectively in a variety of sociolinguistic settings. Critical Language Awareness approaches go a step further by examining issues of power and choice in language use.

In a study of writing conferencing in a third-grade class of a Hawai'i school, Rynkofs (1993) found that teachers and students used both Pidgin and English in the classroom but that the teacher gradually steered children in the direction of standard English writing without overtly making an issue of their Pidgin use. Similarly Menacker (2004), in examining language use at another Hawai'i elementary school, found that when language use wasn't made an issue of, children naturally shifted to use of English at school for most school functions, particularly writing. Pidgin was heard from teachers or students at various points during the day, in the way that bilinguals will switch languages for a particular effect.

The situations described above contrast with Fordham's (1999) finding that when language choice is made an issue or a point of struggle, the resulting situation becomes counter-productive to educators' goals, setting up a situation in which standard English use becomes highly symbolic of identity choices and affiliations. As noted in Da Pidgin Coup's 1999 Position Paper, one common result of a ban on student's home language is that the student simply remains silent. Classrooms where Pidgin is not made an issue of, what Siegel (1992) refers to as accommodation, are not as problematic as classes where the home language is banned but fall short of the mark of language awareness or bilingual approaches that celebrate the students' home language as a valuable resource and seek to expand and add to students' language repertoires rather than subtract from them (see Sato, 1989).

Despite the wide-spread attention that the controversy over the attempted ban of Pidgin drew—during September, 1987, eight articles about Pidgin in the front pages of Hawai'i's two major daily newspapers (DOE, 1988)—no educational plan for working with Pidgin speaking students in Hawai'i emerged. Currently, public school teachers are required to have six credits of coursework related to the teaching of English as a Second Language but this may or may not include any time spent related to the needs of Pidgin-speaking children depending on the discretion of individual instructors.

Special Programs

No system-wide plans or programs have been established for dealing with the needs of Pidgin speakers, but there have been small, experimental programs in various schools and districts. One of the earliest programs to attempt educational intervention for Pidgin speakers was a federally-funded project initiated by a team of local educators and Peace Corps trainers and set in a Hilo elementary school (DOE, 1988; Rogers, 2002). The program used the audio-lingual method of drilling and pattern practice that was in favor at the time for teachers of English as a second language. This approach improved students' surface level ability to produce oral English but did not transfer to greater success in academic language arts or reading. The project was not renewed after the initial four-year funding period.

Hawai'i is unique in having secured Title VII Bilingual Education Federal Funds for teaching English to speakers of Pidgin. Of twenty-eight Title

VII Bilingual Education projects funded in the state between 1978 and 2000, five have native speakers of Pidgin listed as amongst the population of "limited English proficient" students (and sometimes parents) being serviced. One of these, Project Akamai, was designed specifically for Pidgin speakers.

These programs have had two important limitations. The first is that they tend to exist for the three to five year period during which federal funding is available and then disappear, even if they were found to be successful, due to lack of state resources (or a commitment to make such programs a priority). The second important limitation of these programs, from the perspective of those interested in Pidgin speakers, is that they are grouping Pidgin speakers together with immigrant speakers of languages such as Tagalog and Samoan rather than recognizing their unique educational needs. Even Project Akamai, set-up specifically to serve Pidgin speakers, "focused on the use of ESL approaches (i.e. Sheltered English Instruction, Natural Approach; Pablo, Ongteco, & Koki, 2000). Someone who grows up in Hawai'i speaking Pidgin has very different educational needs from, for example, a recent immigrant from China. Despite the limitations of these federally-funded programs, they are to be commended for recognizing that the large number of Pidgin speakers in Hawai'i come to school with educational needs that must be addressed.

Although Pidgin advocates in Hawai'i consider it important to acknowledge Pidgin as a separate language rather than a dialect or nonstandard variety of English (so that it is not thought of as broken English), programs that have been developed for speakers of English as a second dialect rather than English as a second language are most appropriate for and helpful to Pidgin speakers in Hawai'i. As noted earlier, these programs emphasize a *language awareness* approach (see Siegel, chap. 2, this volume).

Hawai'i English Program

Another program in Hawai'i that made efforts to address these needs is the Hawai'i English Program (HEP). This long-running program (1968–1983) had many of the features of a sound educational approach for Pidgin speakers: an attitude of respect towards Pidgin; explanations and discussions of dialect and language choice; a focus on the features of Pidgin; exercises that helped children discriminate between features of Pidgin and features of English; Pidgin literature; and engaging materials such as a board game in which students identified the occasion and location of taped speech samples (ranging from stage pidgin to standard English) and comic book stories that students translated from English into Pidgin or Pidgin into English (Rogers, 1996). This program was followed by the Secondary English Program that made use of increasingly available local literature.

Literature and creative writing are the areas in which educators tend to be more accepting of the use of Pidgin at school (as noted in the earlier discussion on appropriateness). Tonouchi (2002) reports that as early as 1979, writers in the Poets-in-the-Schools program were using Pidgin as a "helpful tool for . . . getting Local kids all excited about language" (p. 3). Volumes of writings of children have been produced—*Born Pidgin: Pidgin Poetry by Children of Hawai'i 1978–1989*. Other collections of student writings such as *Small Kid Time* are a mixture of Pidgin and English. In general, though, the Poets-in-the-Schools were careful to emphasize that they strove for expression and authentic voice in writing, not necessarily the use of Pidgin.

The availability of Pidgin literature has grown tremendously in recent years, but yet there are no policies requiring or encouraging its use. The number of teachers who make use of this literature in schools seems to be relatively small, with most students encountering it for the first time at college. Efforts to encourage the use of local literature at school include a volume entitled "Growing Up Local" (Chock et al., 1998), a collection of prose and poetry of local authors specifically chosen for secondary school students. Teachers' guides have been written to go along with it.

The Pidgin component of the Hawai'i English Program was only one part of the overall language arts curriculum approach in HEP and SEP and, unfortunately, teachers often ignored and passed over these parts due to time constraints, lack of comfort with the materials, negative attitudes about Pidgin's place in the educational system or feelings that exercises such as distinguishing between Pidgin and English features were so obvious or trivial as to be unnecessary. Similar results have been found in other school systems where teachers have been given curriculum materials or been mandated to make use of the home language variety in instruction. Without attitudes in alignment with program goals, accompanied by appropriate training, teachers are not willing or able to carry out the visions of policy makers and program developers. This is the reason why significant efforts have been put forward in Hawai'i to educate about Pidgin, and this challenges long-held negative beliefs and attitudes (see recent developments discussed below).

Kamehameha Schools and Kamehameha Early Education Program (KEEP)

Some of the most often cited language and education research to come out of Hawai'i schools comes from the KEEP program of Kamehameha Schools, private K–12 schools established to support the education of Hawaiian and part-Hawaiian children. The KEEP researchers, who had set out to improve students' reading scores, found that the students (most of whom were Pidgin speakers) did better in their reading work when modifications were made to the school discourse pattern so that it was closer to that of the home and community. Previously, the classroom pattern followed the traditional format of question–response–evaluation described by Cazden (1988). Reading instruction was modified to more closely match the topic associating style of local students speech called *talk story* in which students build on and respond to topics collaboratively rather than in a strict turn-taking sequence (Speidel, 1987).

As a result of the instructional change in discourse styles, children performed better on measures of academic engagement (Au & Mason, 1981), greatly improved their reading scores, and developed their language abilities in both English and Pidgin. Cazden (1988), Foster (1989, 1992), and Piestrup (1973) found similar positive effects of familiar ways of speaking on African American children's ability to successfully engage in instructional dialogue.

Gee (1996) and Michaels (1991) have shown the other side of the coin, that children's use of home discourse styles at school have led to miscommunication and negative teacher evaluations and limited children's full participation in educational interaction. These results and those described above broaden the range of what is usually looked at when language difference in the classroom is considered. Language differences beyond surface level grammar and vocabulary exist, and instructional modifications made with this awareness can have great results.

In addition to the studies of discourse-level difference that have come out of the KEEP program, the significant financial resources of the Kamehameha schools have made it possible to do additional studies concerning Pidgin and education issues. Of particular interest are studies dealing with the question of interference—the often asserted but never demonstrated assumption that children's Pidgin interferes with their ability to acquire English. Actually, Kamehameha researchers found positive correlations between students' abilities in Pidgin and in English and found "no empirical support for the 'trade-off' notion" (DOE, 1988, p. 27).

Pidgin Activism and Recent Developments

In 1987, the Hawai'i Department of Education Planning and Evaluation Branch was asked to find out the extent to which Pidgin was spoken at school. They found themselves unable to accomplish the task because "there exists no standard, unambiguous set of agreed-upon features or markers of pidgin English." At the time there did exist linguistic descriptions of Pidgin (Bickerton, 1977; Bickerton & Odo, 1976; Carr, 1972; Reinecke, 1935/1969/1988; Sato, 1985; Tsuzaki, 1966, 1969). It may be the case that these writings were not in a form educators could easily use. Now there is a grammar available in a form specifically intended to be accessible to teachers and other non-linguists. The grammar (Sakoda & Siegel, 2003) is intended to inform them of the systematic nature of the grammar of Pidgin (not "anything goes" as many believe) and the ways in which it differs from English.

Additional developments include: the establishment of the Sato Center at the University of Hawai'i dedicated to the collection and dissemination of information about Pidgin; the language varieties network, an internet resource for students to learn about Pidgins and Creoles around the world; and Da Pidgin Coup, a group of Pidgin activists and researchers involved in activities such as teacher training, conference presentations, the production of a position paper on Pidgin and education, and providing support for research on Pidgin and Pidgin-related issues such as education.

Conclusion

Progress has been made in Hawai'i in the attitudes and institutional responses to Pidgin in the educational arena. However, we have not yet seen here the types of programs designed for Pidgin speakers that would raise awareness of language differences while respecting both Pidgin and English. Segregating language usage to different domains began when children were told to leave their languages at home and come to school to become assimilated. Language is part and parcel of the whole human being and leaving one part outside the classroom door is impossible to do without causing mental and emotional distress. Ultimately, the decision to believe in the worth of many languages will not only change our social and political structures, it will also return us to the ecologically sound values of the *aloha* spirit where affiliation is balanced with achievement.

QUESTIONS FOR DISCUSSION AND REFLECTIVE WRITING

1. Eades and Jacobs argue that the *appropriateness* approach reinforces standard language ideology, especially in educational settings. How would you respond to their argument?

2. What strategies can be used within and beyond the classroom to address what the authors describe as Pidgin speakers' "schizophrenic attitude" toward their language—"yes, I love my culture and language, and yes my language is terrible."

3. Imagine a classroom that used the *language awareness* approach as suggested by the authors. What would such a classroom look like? What kinds of attitudes, approaches, and activities would transpire there?

ACKNOWLEDGMENTS

We would like to thank our good friends and colleagues who have made many helpful suggestions on drafts of this paper: Joy Kobayashi, Ricky Jacobs, Kent Sakoda, and Jeff Siegel. Any remaining errors are entirely the writers' responsibility.

REFERENCES

Anon. (1921). A new course of study. *Hawaii Educational Review, 10*(1), 1–24.
Au, K., & Mason, J. (1981). Social organization factors in learning to read: The balance of rights hypothesis. *Reading Research Quarterly, 17*(1), 115–152.
Beck, N. B. (1940). The 'Spich' problem in Hawai'i. *Hawaii Educational Review, 28*(9), 261–262, 282.
Berry, R., & Hudson, J. (1997). *Making the jump: A resource book for teachers of Aboriginal students.* Broome: Catholic Education Office of Western Australia.
Bickerton, D. (1977). *Change and Variation in Hawaiian English. Vol. 2: Creole Syntax.* Honolulu: Social Sciences and Linguistics Institute, University of Hawaii.
Bickerton, D., & Odo, C. (1976). *Change and Variation in Hawaiian English. Vol. 1: General Phonology and Pidgin Syntax.* Honolulu: Social Sciences and Linguistics Institute, University of Hawaii.
Boggs, S. (1985). *Speaking, relating and learning: A study of Hawaiian children at home and at school.* Norwood, NJ: Ablex.
Carr, E. B. (1972). *Da kine talk: From pidgin to standard English in Hawaii.* Honolulu: University Press of Hawaii.
Cazden, C. (1988). *Classroom discourse.* Portsmouth, NH: Heinemann.
Chock, E., Lum, D., Miyasaki, G., Robb, D., Stewart, F., & Uchida, K. (Eds.). (1978). *Talk Story: An anthology of Hawaii's local writers.* Honolulu, HI: Petronium Press/Talk Story.
Chock, E., Harstad, J., Lum, D., & Teter, B. (Eds.). (1998). *Growing up local: An anthology of poetry and prose from Hawai'i.* Honolulu: Bamboo Ridge Press.
Da Pidgin Coup. (1999). *Pidgin and education: A position paper.*
De Bose, C. (1992). Codeswitching: Black English and standard English in the African-American linguistic repertoire. In C. Eastman (Ed.), *Codeswitching* (pp. 157–167). Exeter, UK: Short Run Press.
DOE (Department of Education). (1988). *Literature review: Research findings on students' use of Hawaii creole (pidgin) English and relationships with Standard English and school achievement in Hawaii.* Honolulu: Department of Education.
Dotts, C., & Sikkema, M. (1994). *Challenging the status quo: Public education in Hawaii 1840–1940.* Honolulu, HI: Hawaii Education Association.
Eades, D. (1995). *Aboriginal English.* Sydney: Board of Studies (Aboriginal Literacy Resource Kit series).
Fairclough, N. (1992). The appropriacy of appropriateness. In N. Fairclough (Ed.), *Critical language awareness* (pp. 33–56). London: Longman.
Fordham, S. (1999). Dissin' "the Standard": Ebonics as guerrilla warfare at Capital High. *Anthropology and Education Quarterly, 30*(3), 272–293.
Foster, M. (1989). It's cookin' now: A performance analysis of the speech events of a Black teacher in an urban community college. *Language in Society, 18*(1), 176–206.
Foster, M. (1992). Sociolinguistics and the African-American community: Implications for literacy. *Theory into Practice, 31*(4), 303–331.

Gee, J. (1996). *Social linguistics and literacies: Ideology in discourses* (2nd ed.). London: Taylor & Francis.

Hara, M. (1998). *Fourth grade Ukus. Growing up local.* Honolulu, HI: Bamboo Ridge Press.

Hargrove, E., & Sakoda, K. (1999). The hegemony of English or Hau kam yu wen kawl wat ai spik ingglish wen you no no waz. *Bamboo Ridge, 75,* 48–70.

Hawai'i. (2000). *State of Hawai'i Facts and Figures.* Retrieved June 11, 2002, from http://www.hawaii.gov/dbedt/facts/statefact.html

Javar, D. (1998). Shame and the first day of college. In E. Chock, J. Harstad, D. Lum, & B. Teter (Eds.), *Growing up local: An anthology of poetry and prose from Hawai'i* (pp. 293–294). Honolulu, HI: Bamboo Ridge Press.

Kawamoto, K. (1993). Hegemony and language politics in Hawai'i. *World Englishes, 12*(2), 193–207.

Leong, S. (2000). *Attitudes towards Hawai'i Creole English: An interpretive qualitative study.* Unpublished Master of Arts Scholarly Paper, University of Hawai'i.

Lippi-Green, R. (1997). *English with an accent: Language ideology and discrimination in the United States.* London and New York: Routledge.

Lum, D. (1990). *Pass on, no pass back.* Honolulu, HI: Bamboo Ridge Press.

Lum, D. (1997). *Local genealogy: "What school you went?": Stories from a Pidgin culture.* Unpublished doctoral dissertation, University of Hawai'i.

Menacker, T. (2004). *Pidgin at school.* Unpublished doctoral dissertation research, University of Hawaii at Manoa.

Michaels, S. (1981). "Sharing time": Children's narrative styles and differential access to literacy. *Language in Society, 10*(3), 423–442.

Pablo, J., Ongteco, B., & Koki, S. (2000). *A historical perspective on Title VII Bilingual Education projects in Hawaii.* Honolulu, HI: Pacific Resources for Education and Learning.

Piestrup, (1973). *Black dialect interference and accommodation of reading instruction in the first grade.* (Monographs of the Language Behavior Research Laboratory, No. 4). Berkeley: University of California.

Reinecke, J. (1969). *Language and dialect in Hawai'i: A sociolinguistic history to 1935.* Honolulu, HI: University of Hawai'i Press.

Reinecke, J. (1988) (c.1969) (c.1935). *Language and dialect in Hawai'i: A Sociolinguistic History to 1935.* Honolulu, HI: University of Hawaii Press, Social Science Research Institute.

Roberts, S. (2002, January). *The role of style and identity in the development of Hawaiian Creole.* Paper presented at Linguistics Society of America/Society for Pidgin and Creole Linguistics Conference, San Francisco.

Rogers, T. S. (2002, October 31). *Poisoning Pidgin in the park.* Presentation at the Department of Second Language Studies, University of Hawaii at Manoa.

Romaine, S. (1994). Hawai'i Creole English as a literary language. *Language in Society, 23*(4), 527–554.

Rynkofs, J. T. (1993). *Culturally responsive talk between a second-grade teacher and Hawaiian children during writing workshop.* Unpublished doctoral dissertation, University of Michigan.

Sakoda, K., & Siegel, J. (2003). *Pidgin grammar: An introduction to the Creole language of Hawai'i.* Honolulu, HI: Bess Press.

Sato, C. (1985). Linguistic inequality in Hawai'i: The post-Creole dilemma. In N. Wolfson & J. Manes (Eds.), *Language of inequality* (pp. 255–272). Berlin: Mouton.

Sato, C. (1989). A nonstandard approach to Standard English. *TESOL Quarterly, 23*(2), 259–282.

Sato, C. (1991). Sociolinguistic variation and language attitudes in Hawai'i. In J. Cheshire (Ed.), *English around the world: Sociolinguistic perspectives* (pp. 647–663). Cambridge: Cambridge University Press.

Siegel, J. (1992). Teaching initial literacy in a pidgin language: A preliminary evaluation. In J. Siegel (Ed.), *Pidgins, creoles and nonstandard dialects in education* (Occasional Paper No. 12, pp. 53–65). Melbourne: Applied Linguistics Association of Australia.

Siegel, J. (2000). Substrate influence in Hawai'i Creole English. *Language in Society, 29*(2), 197–236.

Speidel, G. (1987). Conversation and language learning in the classroom. In K. E. Nelson & A. van Kleek (Eds.), *Children's language: Vol. 6* (pp. 99–135). Mahwah, NJ: Lawrence Erlbaum Associates.

Stueber, R. (1991). An informal history of schooling in Hawai'i. In *To teach the children: Historical aspects of education in Hawai'i* (pp. 16–35). Honolulu: Bernice Pauahi Bishop Museum.

Tamura, E. H. (1994). *Americanization, acculturation, and ethnic identity: The Nisei generation in Hawaii.* Urbana, IL: University of Illinois Press.

Tomita, A., & Sawyer, J.-M. (1996). *Retail managers' perceptions of tape recorded speech samples of male and female Hawai'i Creole English and standard English speakers.* Bachelor of Arts thesis, University of Hawai'i.

Tonouchi, L. (2001). *Da Word.* Honolulu, HI: Bamboo Ridge Press.

Tonouchi, L. (2002). *Living Pidgin: Contemplations on Pidgin culture.* Kaneohe, Hawai'i: Tinfish Press.

Tsuzaki, S. (1966). Hawaiian-English: Pidgin, creole, or dialect? *Pacific Speech, 1*(2), 25–28.

Tsuzaki, S. (1969). Problems in the study of Hawaiian English. *Working Papers in Linguistics, No. 3, 1*(2), 25–28.

Warner, S. N. (1999). Hawaiian language regenesis: Planning for intergenerational use of Hawaiian beyond the school. In T. Huebner & K. Davis (Eds.), *Sociopolitical perspectives on language policy and planning in the USA* (pp. 313–332). Amsterdam: John Benjamins.

Watson-Gegeo, K. (1994). Language and education in Hawai'i: Sociopolitical and economic implications of Hawai'i Creole English. In M. Morgan (Ed.), *Language and the social construction of identity in creole situations* (pp. 101–120). Los Angeles: Center for Afro-American Studies, UCLA.

Wolfram, W., & Christian, D. (1989). Dialect diversity in America. In *Dialects and education: Issues and answers* (pp. 1–23). Englewood Cliffs, NJ: Prentice Hall Regents.

Wong, L. (1999). Language varieties and language policy: The appreciation of Pidgin. In T. Huebner & K. Davis (Eds.), *Sociopolitical perspectives on language policy and planning in the USA* (pp. 205–222). Amsterdam: John Benjamins.

HISPANIZED ENGLISH

The English of Latinos from a Plurilingual Transcultural Angle: Implications for Assessment and Schools

Ofelia García
Teachers College, Columbia University

Kate Menken
The City College of New York, CUNY

KEY POINTS

- Complex sociolinguistic context and language use of English-speaking US Latinos.
- Dynamic linguistic practices of US Latinos characterized as *plurilingualism.*
- Need to rethink dichotomies and traditional categories of bilingualism.
- Challenges to the narrow scope of language in high-stakes testing.
- Ways to bridge the gap between language use and assessment.

INTRODUCTION: US LATINOS BEYOND SPANISH

Latinos in the United States (US) are an important component of our national identity. Not only do people of Latino descent make up a large percentage of the US population (13%, according to the 2000 Census), but they have been a founding presence, albeit a marginalized one, in the forging of this nation's sociocultural and sociohistorical landscape. Despite both the massive presence of US Latinos today, the role that they historically played in the expansion and development of the United States, and the rapid growth that they will experience in the 21st century, US Latinos seem to catch national attention only as poor and uneducated Spanish speakers.

Language has played, and continues to play, a very important role in how we view US Latinos. The expansion of United States borders into Mexico and later into the Caribbean put Anglophones in close contact with Spanish speakers whose lands were claimed as US territories. The English language policy imposed in schools of the Southwest and Puerto Rico during the years of US expansion attempted to eradicate Spanish and speed up the language shift of Spanish-speaking children to English (see Academia Puertorriqueña de la Lengua Española, 1998 for Puerto Rico; Corona & García, 1996; Hernández-Chávez, Cohen, & Beltramo, 1975 for the southwest; and Pérez, 1982 for Cuba).

More than a century later, we continue to use Spanish as the identity category of US Latinos and simultaneously support language policies in school that eradicate Spanish. We view Spanish as the characteristic of Latinos that has to be eliminated, even when they are English speakers. In speaking of educational failure and poverty, we focus on those who speak Spanish only because we continue to have faith in the power of English monolingualism for all, without understanding on the one hand, issues of language loyalty, language identity, and intergenerational language memory that go beyond the here and now, and on the other hand, issues of racism and linguicism (for more on linguicism, see Phillipson, 1992; Skutnabb-Kangas, 2000).

Acknowledging that there are English-speaking or even bilingual Latinos would bring us closer to understanding the transculturation and bi/multilingualism of the United States. The educational issues facing Latino children today go beyond simply teaching them English or teaching those who are English Language Learners[1] (ELLs), and bring us face to face with the realization that as a nation we have failed in truly educating the majority of our citizens—those who speak English in bidialectal or bilingual contexts (Rumbaut & Portes, 2001).

This chapter is an attempt to make visible the English speaking Latino, bilingual and not, and to look at the languages of Latinos beyond the Spanish category. We analyze the complex sociolinguistic context of US Latinos that calls for ways of thinking about language beyond dichotomies or traditional categories of bilingualism. In light of this sociolinguistic complexity, the chapter examines the role that standard English plays in education today, especially as it is used in high-stakes assessment. We look at the disparate ways in which Latinos use English in their homes and communities when compared to the way in which English is used in standardized testing,

---

[1]Latino and other language minority students in need of language support services to succeed in English-medium classrooms are referred to as English Language Learners (ELL) in this document.

and the impact this difference has on the lives of Latinos. We conclude by proposing ways in which schools may help bridge those distances.

ENGLISH/SPANISH: PLURILINGUALISM IN A TRANSCULTURAL CONTEXT

Of the 35,305,818 Latinos in the United States in 2000, 72% of those who speak Spanish report strong English proficiency while just 10% speak only Spanish, making English a very important language for US Latinos (U.S. Census Bureau, 2000). Yet little scholarly attention has been paid to the English of US Latinos, despite warnings since 1980 of this gap. Chicano English is the English spoken by the largest group of US Latinos (Fought, 2002; Peñalosa, 1980), and the influence of Spanish phonology on Chicano English, particularly in Los Angeles, has received the greatest research attention (MacDonald, 1989; Santa Ana, 1993, 1996). Sociolinguists have also shown the role of the speech setting, taking into account regional, generational, social and community-specific factors on what has been established to be Chicano English (Bayley, 1994; Santa Ana, 1993).

The overall lack of interest in varieties of English other than US standard academic English has characterized our scholarly literature until recently, a deficit which this volume, among others, tries to address (see especially, Nero, 2001; Wolfram, Temple Adger & Christian, 1999). Only African American Vernacular English has been given the prominence it deserves (Baugh, 2000; Rickford, 1999; Smitherman, 1986). The disinterest is indicative of our naïve monolingual assumptions that languages other than English are foreign, and that speakers who undergo language shift leave behind all traces of their first language, using English in exactly the same way as those for whom the standard English of school has always been the language of the home.

On the other hand, the Spanish of US Latinos has received increased attention in the last two decades, especially since the publication of *Spanish in the United States* (1982) by Amastae and Elías-Olivares, and the development and institutionalization of an annual conference on Spanish in the US. The scholarship on US Spanish among different groups, focusing mainly on Spanish as a contact dialect, is extensive and growing.[2] This growing body of research reflects an acknowledgement of the use of Spanish in US society, as immigration from Latin America increases and the number of Spanish-speaking Latinos continues to grow.

---

[2]Some other scholars who have made substantive contributions to US Spanish scholarship are: Garland Bills, Margarita Hidalgo, Eduardo Hernández Chavez, Mary Ellen García, Carol Klee, John Lipski, Francisco Ocampo, Luis Ortiz, Ricardo Otheguy, Shana Poplack, Ana Roca, Carmen Silva Corvalán, A. Jacqueline Toribio, Lourdes Torres, Guadalupe Valdés, Daniel Villa, and Ana Celia Zentella, among others.

Traditional disciplines run the risk of seeing a reality only from their perspective. It has often been in nontraditional interdisciplinary programs such as Chicano Studies, Puerto Rican Studies, Latino Studies, or Bilingual Education, where the angle of the US Latino speaker has been adopted, expanding the lenses used to study one or the other language of US Latinos, and looking at the complex language use in US Latino literature (Aranda, 2000; Taylor, 1999) and communities (Anzaldúa, 1999; Bayley & Schecter, 2003; González, 2001; Otheguy, García & Roca, 2000; Poplack, 1983; Schecter & Bailey, 2002; Urciuoli, 1996; Zentella, 1997). This scholarship acknowledges the dynamism of US Latino speech communities, where multiple varieties of both English and Spanish are used, where members of dominant and nondominant groups, often speakers of nonstandard varieties of both US English and Latin American Spanish, communicate with one another. This occurs within and across communities that use different features of different languages (or even different languages) within a lifetime and intergenerationally. To capture this dynamic bilingualism–multidialectism, we use the term *plurilingual* in this chapter.[3]

This scholarship also acknowledges the *transculturation* of US Latinos in the sense given to us by Cuban ethnologist, Fernando Ortiz in his *Contrapunteo Cubano del Tabaco y del Azúcar* (1940/1978). Transculturation goes beyond the concept of simple acculturation and multiculturalism; it implies the creation of new cultural phenomena. Malinowski explains in the prologue of *Contrapunteo*: "It is a process in which both parts of the equation are modified. A process in which a new reality emerges, compounded and complex; a reality that is not a mechanical agglomeration of characters, *not even a mosaic*, but a new phenomenon, original and independent" (p. 4, our emphasis and translation). US Latinos, often transnational and comfortable being in borderlands and across borderlands, are situated in a complex linguistic and cultural context, using their plurilingualism as they attempt to negotiate a transcultural context. This more inclusive and expansive view of the languages of US Latinos, without compartmentalizing the English and/or the Spanish language experience, helps us understand the challenges that the English of assessment poses for all Latinos.

LANGUAGES IN CONTACT, CONTINUUM, AND DISCONTINUUM IN SCHOOLS AND SOCIETY

In the United States, much attention has been paid to the acquisition of English by Latinos over the last forty years, in both educational research and policy. Since the passage of the first Bilingual Education Act by Con-

---

[3]The term plurilingualism has been used by Michael Clyne (2003) to capture the dynamics of the variability that bilinguals exhibit in Australia, differing from two double monolinguals and is increasingly used in the European Union.

gress in 1968, politicians and educators, as well as the general public, have debated the merits of using only English, or English and Spanish, to educate Latino children who enter US schools without sufficient English language proficiency. We have seen the proliferation of educational programs to teach English to these children, some insisting that only English be used, others using the children's mother tongue temporarily and even throughout the child's education. Although bilingual programs are widespread, English as a second language (ESL) programs are prevalent; as such, the majority of English Language Learners spend their day in schools where English is the only medium of instruction (National Center for Education Statistics, 1997). The debate that sometimes pits those who support English-only instruction against those who believe in the use of Spanish in instruction is indicative of the lack of sociolinguistic understanding of how US Latinos actually use language. The debate, rooted in the standard English monolingual angle of US language policy and carried out mostly through education, focuses on whether Latinos are to be English monolingual speakers or bilingual speakers of standard English and standard Spanish. But much more is involved. The increasingly transcultural context in which US Latinos currently live demands that we adopt a more dynamic model of bilingualism and bidialectism that takes into account the *language contact* situation and the complex *linguistic continuum,* as well as the *discontinuities,* in which US Latinos participate.

The academic dichotomy of Spanish on the one hand and English on the other, using classical models of monolingualism and bilingualism, with some in the group speaking one or the other standard and others speaking both, is too simple to characterize the sociolinguistic situation of US Latinos today. US Latinos have complex histories and relationships to the United States. Some are descendants of those living in US territories that were once Spanish speaking, and others are victims of a colonial relationship in Puerto Rico and imperialistic policies in much of Latin America. Some US Latinos have been English speakers for generations and have undergone *language shift.* Others are in the process of *reversing their language shift* by studying what is now an ancestral language, while still others have only recently arrived in the United States and bring their Spanish to the US context (for more on language maintenance, language shift and reversing language shift, see Fishman, 1991, 2001).

US Latinos are a highly hybrid group sociolinguistically. Most US Latinos are not English Language Learners (ELLs) as the academic literature, especially on education, leads us to believe. For most US Latinos, English exists in *contact* with Spanish and many times in contact with nonstandard varieties of English, especially African American Vernacular English (AAVE) and Caribbean Creole English (CCE). Their Spanish many times shows evidence of contact with English, as well as with the many languages of Latin

America's indigeneous minorities. US Latinos come from increasingly diverse Latin American countries, joining Latinos who have been in the US for different generational periods. US Latinos come into contact with ethnolinguistic groups who speak languages other than English as well as different varieties of Spanish. But US schools insist that US Latino children, living and participating in homes and communities that are highly plurilingual, use only standard English in schools, and on occasion, only standard Spanish.

In the modern context of transculturation, especially in the urban centers where the majority of Latinos live, communication proliferates with speakers moving along a *bilingual and bidialectal continuum*, using linguistic resources from the other language or from other English varieties or Spanish varieties when needed and possible. Sometimes, speakers use *loanwords*, bringing both form and meaning from the other language. An example would be *Voy a hacer overtime* (pronounced [*oBertain*]) (I'm going to do overtime). Other times, they alternate languages or code-switch. *Calques*, meanings taken from words in the other language and borrowed without their corresponding word forms, are also prevalent in the language of bilinguals. An example would be *Está corriendo para alcalde* (He's running for mayor; see Otheguy, 1993; Otheguy, García, & Fernandez, 1989). US Latinos, whether bilingual or not, often participate in discourse that falls somewhere along the continuum between one language and the other.

US Latino literature written in English or Spanish about life in the US uses code-switching and calques as literary devices reflecting the oral discourse of many US Latinos (Aranda, 2000). However, schoolchildren are most often forced to write in standard English only and sometimes, when they are fortunate, in standard English and standard Spanish. Features of their spoken discourse along the bilingualism continuum are stigmatized and discouraged.

With the advent of the Internet in recent years and the global village it seeks to create, we have witnessed increased participation by many in literate discourse structures that were previously reserved for the elite. Chat rooms and electronic communication have, for the first time, allowed hybrid language varieties to be used in written communication. The explosion of the multidimensional written word and multimedia literacies, all used in simultaneous synchronous communication, has allowed for the public display of the linguistic continuum of US Latinos.

But Latino plurilingualism also involves *linguistic discontinuities*. Unlike bilingual situations where languages have equal power or where populations are stable, harsh English-only language policies in school create linguistic discontinuities between the home and the school, between children and parents, between modes of language use in individual children. Often parents speak only Spanish, while children speak English only. Other times only Spanish is spoken and allowed in the home, whereas only English is spoken and allowed in school. And children most often can understand Spanish well, can speak Spanish hesitantly, but cannot read or write it. Improved air travel and our global economy create much of the movement across national and linguistic borders that created Latino linguistic hybridity at the start, but now is responsible for other discontinuities. The question of length of residence in the United States is a difficult one for many Latinos. Many have to explain that they've been back and forth numerous times. Many Latino children are sent back to live in Latin America with grandparents and extended family for long periods of time so that parents can work in the US. Other Latino children are left behind after parents immigrate to the US. Many move back and forth with families whose social circumstances change with work opportunities. The picture that emerges here is a sociolinguistic context for Latinos in the 21st century that goes beyond Spanish or English, encompassing instead a dynamic plurilingual context where there is contact between languages and varieties, where speakers move along a continuum developmentally as they engage in second language acquisition, language shift and reversing language shift, and where speakers experience linguistic discontinuities as they go in and out of different geographic spaces and social domains.

WHEN THE TEST IS WHAT COUNTS: THE LANGUAGE OF ASSESSMENT IN 21ST-CENTURY US

US schools have responded to this more expansive sociolinguistic situation of US Latinos (and of other ethnolinguistic groups in the United States) by adopting more narrow definitions of academic language, this time assessed in standard English only by high-stakes tests that focus on literacy. The change has been subtle, but significant. Most academic language assessments in the late 20th century focused on reading comprehension, asking students to answer multiple-choice questions. Although language minority and second dialect students never did well in standardized assessments of reading, the receptive language skills that these exams tapped were more easily acquired by those who spoke English as a second language, who spoke varieties of English other than the standard, or who used language in the complex ways just outlined. Written essays, which require productive skills, were most often used by classroom teachers only for internal assessment and evaluation.

But recent decades have brought about changes in our conception of knowledge and the ways in which it is acquired. The United States, and other countries, created and adopted educational standards for each grade level, providing a set target to measure student growth and thereby a means of accountability for that growth (for an insightful analysis of the consequences of the US educational standards movement for poor and minority populations, see Ohanian, 1999). New performance-based standardized assessments, developed in an effort to measure student attainment of the standards that had been set, started tapping students' multi-faceted use of literacies, including making sense of graphic, literate and technological texts. But despite the complex use of literacies that new technologies require, schools and standardized assessments continue to depend on traditional skills of writing in standard English as the vehicle to evidence complex understandings that only multimedia literacies may, in fact, encompass.

At the same time as assessments have neatly partitioned standard English from more dynamic language use, testing itself has become more important than ever before. Assessment for accountability purposes is a pivotal theme in current standards-based education reforms, cutting across much of the legislation passed by Congress in recent years. US mandates such as *Goals 2000* (H.R. 1804, 1994), Title I, and most recently Title III of the Elementary and Secondary Education Act (as amended in 2001) require that standardized assessments apply to all students, placing great emphasis on the inclusion of English Language Learners. With this new emphasis on the inclusion of all students as part of evolving accountability systems, and the visibility of test scores in the public and political eye, performance by Latino students on assessments greatly impacts the evaluation of a teacher, school, or school system (García, 2003; Menken, 2000, 2001, 2005).

Standardized tests also now carry higher stakes than ever before for individual students in most states, as they are used as the primary criteria for high school graduation, grade promotion, and placement into tracked programs (Heubert & Hauser, 1999). In 2001, 25 states required high-stakes tests for graduation, up from 18 the prior year. But the tests that count are in standard English, and were developed for the assessment of native-English speakers—not plurilingual students.

In the case of students who use English differently from standard English speakers, and those who lack English proficiency, the test in itself is an assessment of their knowledge of standard English, and thus an unfair measure of what they know. One of the standards for educational and psychological testing developed by the American Psychological Association (APA), the American Educational Research Association (AERA), and the National Council of Measurement in Education (NCME) in 1985 says: "for a nonnative English speaker and for a speaker of some dialects of English, every test given in English becomes in part a language or literacy test" (APA/AERA/NCME, 1999, Standard no. 13). Likewise, Wiley & Lukes (1996) point out how a lack of proficiency in standard English negatively impacts speakers of nonstandard varieties, using tests as the sorting mechanism to position these students at the low end of a social hierarchy that values the standard.

We seem to be in a bind. On the one hand, we have raised our expectations and made school systems accountable for language minority students, but on the other hand, we have failed to develop fair assessments that can distinguish what students know from the way in which English is used by plurilingual students.

ASSESSMENT IN SCHOOLS OF THE MULTILINGUAL APPLE

As one of the most multilingual cities of the world (García & Fishman, 1997/2001), New York City offers a case in point. An examination of its policy regarding assessment and high school graduation may help us understand the disparity between language use in society and language use in assessment. It can also shed light on the grave societal impact of this disparity, as educators develop ways of helping language minority students show that the standards have been met.

The New York City Department of Education reports that as of December 2002 the total school enrollment was 1,087,255 children, of whom thirty-eight percent were Latinos and twelve percent were English Language Learners (ELLs). In 1995, the New York State Board of Regents raised curriculum and graduation standards, requiring that all students pass five core Regents examinations in English, mathematics, global history and geography, US history and government, and science, in order to graduate. All of these exams are highly literacy-based, regardless of the content area. Unlike the majority of states in the US (Rivera & Stansfield, 2000), New York State does permit the use of native-language assessments for content-area subjects. Translated editions of the Regents Examinations in all core areas required for graduation are available in Spanish, Korean, Chinese, Haitian-Creole and Russian. Despite the fact that translations of the content examinations are offered for students who have been in US schools less than three years, the English Regents examination, a two-day six-hour exam, is required by all students to graduate from New York City high schools (New York State Department of Education, 2003). The English Regents exam is the accountability mechanism of the four English Language Arts Standards which require that students read, write, listen and speak for: (1) information and understanding, (2) literary response and expression, (3) critical analysis and evaluation, and (4) social interaction.

The English Regents exam also includes an essay, written in standard English, that is given twice the weight as the multiple-choice questions. The directions for the essay portion of the August 2002 English Regents exam read, "Guidelines: . . . Be sure to follow the conventions of standard written English." The exam makes explicit that evaluation of students' writing will be based not only on their ability to convey knowledge, but rather on their ability to do so in standard English. We know that productive language, whether written or spoken, reveals the dynamics of language contact and discontinuities in ways that receptive language, whether listening or reading, seems to mask. Therefore, an exam that burdens writing will negatively affect plurilingual students.

Data pertaining to graduation and dropout rates offer a glimpse of the seriousness of this issue for all Latinos. The New York State Department of Education has four-year completion outcomes for the Class of 2002. According to this data, Latino students had the lowest graduation rate (41.1%) and the highest dropout rate (26%) of all ethnic/racial groups in New York City. Performance rates were even poorer for ELLs, with a graduation rate of just 30.3% and a dropout rate of 31.5%. After a decade-long decline, dropout rates for Latinos and ELLs have increased in recent years, a trend that is directly linked to the new graduation testing policy (Del Valle, 2002; New York City Department of Education, 2001).

The statistics provided in the preceding passages paint a dire picture of how the current emphasis on high-stakes testing impacts Latino plurilingual students, whether ELLs or not, exposing disparities that must be addressed. Although the first stage of improving our educational systems is to expose those problem areas of inequity and disparity, to do so alone is not enough. We need solutions. We turn now to ways in which schools can help young people, and especially US Latinos, to succeed.

BEYOND THE CHALLENGES: POSSIBILITIES

In our discussion above, we have argued that there is a discontinuity between the actual language use of US Latinos and definitions of success in public schools that are based on standard English proficiency, creating a new set of educational challenges that need to be addressed. The demand for standard English is most acute where standardized testing is concerned, because of the gatekeeper role such tests currently play. We now offer possibilities for helping Latino students acquire the standard English that is required for them to succeed, and we suggest ways that schools and educators must also change to meet the needs of these students.

Given the standard English language policy that has been implicitly adopted in New York State, it is imperative that we do better at teaching standard English to ELLs and speakers of nonstandard varieties, while also seeking a space for the bilingual/bidialectal continuum in school. Many educators today insist that standard English and academic discourse be explicitly taught to language minority students (Delpit, 1998; Langer, 1991;

Rogoff, 1990; Scarcella, 2002). Ways must be found to engage language minority students in meaningful written discourse, extend their use of language, require that they attend to form, and give them the respectful audience and practice they need to develop the advanced English literacy that schools in the 21st century require.

In the case of Latino students, instead of just focusing on student development, teachers must also consider possibilities for meeting their students half way. We must look for ways of being in the borderlands with language minority students, and so increase more authentic interaction and heteroglossia (Bakhtin, 1981). This requires continual interaction and negotiation of meaning, whereby all voices are heard, thus creating a "third space" for Latino students in US schools (Gutierrez, Rynes, & Larson, 1995).

García and Traugh (2002) have described ways of transforming the education of urban bilingual students. The pedagogy that García and Traugh have called "of the borderlands," and that they have used successfully in expanding understandings as well as developing standard English, put the students' and the faculty's different English voices alongside each other, and alongside the academic text written in standard English. The pedagogy holds, and makes visible, the range of differences—conceptual differences, as well as cultural and linguistic ones. Both students and faculty describe, in a disciplined fashion, using language carefully and non-judgementally, and without any interruptions from either the instructor or other students, what has struck them about the readings or the ideas being discussed. Students are encouraged to share and read specific passages, to contribute details, and to use images and stories from their own lives, experiences and understandings, in sharing their reactions. This process encourages speakers to cut across abstractions and generalities. It gives all students an opportunity to participate, and to hear each other's voices, as well as the writer's, although passing is allowed. As a result of the discipline, slowness, and inclusiveness of the process, it builds over a time a safe, equitable, and collaborative classroom environment, in which individual understandings and voices, including those of the faculty member, are enlarged and amplified. As conceptual, cultural and linguistic understandings expand, ideas for collective action are generated, and individual voices acquire understanding of other varieties. Not only do language minority students gain bidialectal ability while acquiring a standard English voice, but faculty also become more knowledgeable of their students' many different English varieties, increasing their ability to teach these students. The attention given to detail, as well as to language, coupled with the respect for different voices and opinion, expands possibilities for students. This pedagogy of the borderlands has connections to poststructural feminist pedagogies, insisting that all class participants, including the instructor, be engaged in constructing knowledge as they develop a voice that is continuously shifting, as individuals connect their own experiences and voices with those in the academic readings and in the social structures in which they're positioned (For more on poststructural feminist pedagogies, see Tisdell, 1998).

A tool in carrying out this pedagogy of the borderlands is the use of *double-entry journals*. As students write their thoughts and experiences alongside those of the academic texts they are reading and from which they copy, they attend to the reading, to the words and the form, and to their own thinking (Berthoff, 1995; Traugh, 2002). As teachers read the students' work and listen to the particularity of their stories, they pay attention to form as well as to what the student is saying. This kind of writing results in students' ability to make connections with texts, infer messages, extend meanings, and think independently, as they develop ways of using informational, literary, analytical and social language. It also makes it possible for teachers to gain understandings of students' ways of using language in order to construct meaning, building upon the language use of their Latino students as a resource in their education. Double-entry journals is one way of extending students' writing in standard English and achieving the intersubjectivity of their voices and language.

Many schools have also shown much creativity in helping plurilingual students meet the new English standards. In some New York City high schools, the response to testing reforms and demand for standard English has been to develop the advanced Spanish literacy of Latino students—with promising results. Believing that native language literacy skills transfer to the second language, a high school in the Bronx has greatly improved scores by Latino ELLs on the English Regents exam by increasing the opportunities for these students to formally study Spanish in school. The Spanish *Advanced Placement (AP)* class is a way to teach informational, literary, analytical and social language, the language skills needed for the English Regents. When offered to native Spanish speakers, it has also been found to bridge the distance between students' language abilities and the language use of the English Regents exam. Because of the success at this high school, where Spanish AP courses are taught in combination with intensive ESL, other Bronx high schools have now begun implementing this approach and offering their Latino students intensive Spanish studies (Shapiro, 2001). If this approach were to take hold and be developed, even in elementary schools, NYC schools would be supporting and developing advanced literacy in standard Spanish. This would do much to connect some of the linguistic gaps and discontinuities in which Latino children's lives are now lived. Not only would the children's English, alongside their Spanish, be improved, but US society would have much to gain from this greater plurilingualism.

Despite educational efforts (with limited creativity), the challenges faced by language minority students are great. It is important to continue to seek assessment alternatives. Although the New York Commissioner of Education recently rejected a bid by nontraditional schools to substitute individually tailored projects for the English Regents (Keller, 2000), there are alternative assessments suitable for Latino students both in the classroom and on a wide scale that are worth exploring. Portfolio assessments offer one example, and have been used at schools in Philadelphia to successfully evaluate performance by bilingual education students who are classified as "English-dominant," yet do not have the English proficiency necessary to display their knowledge of content-area subjects in English-medium standardized tests. Portfolios can be implemented on a large scale as well, and efforts to do so are currently underway across Vermont and Delaware, with promising results for speakers of nonstandard varieties of English and English Language Learners (Northeast Islands Regional Educational Lab, 1999).

CONCLUSION

The United States today reflects not the immigration of our past history, but the greater flow of people, information, goods, and services within and across national boundaries that is evident in the world. But yet, the approach to language that we continue to follow in schools mirrors that of the past where language is perceived as monolithic, and standard English occupies most of the space. When this educational approach does not work, we impose accountability measures, using standard English literacy as the only measure of educational success.

In the transcultural context of the 21st century, success will be increasingly measured by the ability to use multiple languages and multiliteracies, including multimodal technologies. Because the use of standard English may be the most demanded literacy for citizens worldwide, it is essential that US schools do a better job of ensuring that all our citizens have this advanced literacy. We must find ways of doing so that use the multiplicity of languages and literacies in which the world communicates. For US Latinos, this means understanding the plurilingual context in which they live, and the circumstances of language contact in continuum and discontinuum. US schools must take some responsibility to ensure that Latinos have access to the full continuum of their plurilingual repertoire, and that their languages are not subject to the great discontinuities which the present educational policy intensifies. Assessment of languages and literacies must respect the difference between knowledge and standard English use. Only then can we hope to provide the educational opportunities that are the makings of a democratic society, and become a nation with highly advanced English literacy that is equitably distributed, where varieties other than the standard and languages other than English are respected and valued.

QUESTIONS FOR DISCUSSION AND REFLECTIVE WRITING

1. García and Menken paint a complex picture of the language practices of US Latinos that includes language contact, language shift, reverse language shift, and linguistic discontinuities. To what extent does this picture challenge prevalent language attitudes and policies towards Latinos?

2. Should assessment for Latinos be allowed in something other than the standard variety of English or Spanish? If so, in what contexts? If not, give reasons.

3. What are the likely effects (short-term and long-term) of high-stakes testing for language minority students and their teachers?

REFERENCES

Academia Puertorriqueña de la lengua española. (1998). *La enseñanza del español y del inglés en Puerto Rico. Una polémica de cien años.* San Juan de Puerto Rico.

Amastae, J., & Elías-Olivares, L. (1982). *Spanish in the United States.* Cambridge, MA: Cambridge University Press.

Anzaldúa, G. (1999). *Borderlands. La Frontera. The new mestiza* (2nd ed.). San Francisco: Aunt Lute Books.

APA/AERA/NCME. (1999). *Standards for educational and psychological testing.* Washington, DC: American Psychological Association.

Aranda, L. V. (2000). The languages US Latino literature speaks. *Proceedings of the National Association of African American Studies and National Association of Hispanic and Latino Studies: 2000 Literature monograph series.* Houston, Texas. Retrieved September 3, 2002, from www.edrs.com/members/sf.cfm?AN-ED454008

Bakhtin, M. M. (1981). *The dialogic imagination.* Austin: University of Texas Press.

Baugh, J. (2000). *Beyond Ebonics: Linguistic pride and racial prejudice.* New York: Oxford University Press.

Bayley, R. (1994). Consonant cluster reduction in Tejano English. *Language Variation and Change, 6,* 303–326.

Bayley, R., & Schecter, S. R. (Eds.). (2003). *Language socialization in bilingual and multilingual societies.* Clevedon, UK: Multilingual Matters.

Berthoff, A. (1995). Dialectical notebooks and the audit of meaning. In T. Fulwiler (Ed.), *The journal book* (pp. 11–18). Portsmouth, NH: Heinemann.

Corona, D., & García, O. (1996). English in Cuba: From the imperial design to the imperative need. In J. Fishman, A. Conrad, & A. Rubal-Lopez (Eds.), *Post-imperial English: Status change in former British and American colonies, 1940–1990.* Berlin: Mouton de Gruyter.

Clyne, M. (2003). *Dynamics of language contact.* Cambridge: Cambridge University Press.

Delpit, L. (1998). The politics of teaching literate discourse. In V. Zamel & R. Spack (Eds.), *Negotiating academic literacies: Teaching and learning across languages and cultures* (pp. 207–218). Mahwah, NJ: Lawrence Erlbaum Associates.

Del Valle, S. (2002). *A briefing paper of the Puerto Rican legal defense fund on the new English regents exam and its impact on English Language Learners.* New York: Puerto Rican Legal Defense and Education Fund.

Fishman, J. A. (1991). *Reversing language shift*. Clevedon, Avon: Multilingual Matters.

Fishman, J. A. (Ed.). (2001). *Can threatened languages be saved?* Clevedon, Avon: Multilingual Matters.

Fought, C. (2002). *Chicano English in context*. Hampshire: Palgrave MacMillan.

García, O. (2003). Nouvelles espérances et barrières dans le domain de l'éducation aux États-Unis. Hommes et Migrations (France) no. 1246 (Novembre–Décembre, 2003), pp. 17–27.

García, O., & Fishman, J. A. (Eds.). (1997/2001). *The multilingual apple: Languages in New York City*. Berlin: Mouton de Gruyter.

García, O., & Traugh, C. (2002). Using descriptive inquiry to transform the education of linguistically diverse US teachers and students. In L. Wei, J. M. Dewale, & A. Housen (Eds.), *Opportunities and challenges of bilingualism* (pp. 311–328). Berlin: Mouton de Gruyter.

González, N. (2001). *I am my language: Discourses of women and children in the borderlands*. University of Arizona Press.

Gutierrez, K., Rynes, B., & Larson, J. (1995). Script, counterscript, and underlife in the classroom: James Brown versus Brown v. Board of Education. *Harvard Educational Review, 65*, 445–471.

Hernández-Chávez, E., Cohen, A., & Beltramo, A. (Eds.). (1975). *El lenguaje de los Chicanos: Regional and social characteristics of language used by Mexican Americans*. Washington, DC: Center for Applied Linguistics.

Heubert, J., & Hauser, R. (Eds.). (1999). *High stakes: Testing for tracking, promotion, and graduation*. National Research Council. Washington, DC: National Academy Press.

H.R. 1804, 103d Cong. (1994). (enacted). *Goals 2000: Educate America Act*.

Keller, B. (2000, February). N.Y. chief deals blow to alternative-assessment plans. *Education Week, 2*. Retrieved September 3, 2002, from http://www.edweek.org/ew/articles/2000/02/02/21altern.h19.html

Langer, J. (1991). Literacy and schooling: A sociolinguistic perspective. In E. H. Hiebert (Ed.), *Literacy for a diverse society* (pp. 9–27). New York: Teachers College Press.

MacDonald, M. (1989). The influence of Spanish phonology on the English spoken by United States Hispanics. In P. Bjarkman & R. Hammond (Eds.), *American Spanish pronunciation: Theoretical and applied perspectives* (pp. 215–236). Washington, DC: Georgetown University Press.

Menken, K. (2000). What are the critical issues in wide-scale assessment of English language learners? *NCBE Issue Brief No. 6*. (2000, September). Washington, DC: National Clearinghouse for Bilingual Education. [Online] Available: http://www.ncbe.gwu.edu/ncbepubs/issuebriefs/ib6.pdf

Menken, K. (2001, May/June). When all means all: Standards-based reform and English language learners. *NABE News, 24*(5).

Menken, K. (2005). *When the test is what counts: How high-stakes testing affects language policy and the education of English language learners in high school*. Unpublished doctoral dissertation, Teachers College, Columbia University, New York.

National Center for Education Statistics. (1997). *1993–94 Schools and staffing survey: A profile of policies and practices for limited English proficient students: Screening methods, program support, and teacher training*. Washington, DC: U.S. Department of Education, Office of Educational Research and Improvement.

Nero, S. (2001). *Englishes in contact. Anglophone Caribbean students in an urban college*. Cresskill, New Jersey: Hampton Press.

New York City Department of Education, Division of Assessment and Accountability. (2001). *The class of 2001 four-year longitudinal report and 2000–2001 event dropout statistics*. New York: Author. [Online] Available: http://www.nycenet.edu/daa/reports

New York State Department of Education, Office of Curriculum, Instruction, and Assessment. (2003). *Regents and high school diploma/graduation requirements*. Section 100.5 of the Regulations of the Commissioner of Education Relating to General Education and Diploma Requirements. [Online] Available: http://www.emsc.nysed.gov/part100/pages/1005a.html

Northeast Islands Regional Educational Laboratory at Brown University. (1999). Creating large-scale portfolio assessments that include English language learners. *Perspectives on policy and practice*. Providence: Author. [Online] Available: http://www.lab.brown.edu/public/pubs/PolPerELL.pdf

Ohanian, S. (1999). *One size fits few. The folly of educational standards*. Portsmouth, NH: Heinemann.

Ortiz, F. (1978). *Contrapunteo cubano del tabaco y el azúcar* [Tobacco and Sugar: A Cuban counter point]. Caracas, Venezuela: Ayacuho. (Original work published 1940).

Otheguy, R. (1993). A reconsideration of the notion of loan translation in the analysis of US Spanish. In A. Roca & J. Lipski (Eds.), *Spanish in the United States: Linguistic contact and diversity* (pp. 21–41). Berlin: Mouton de Gruyter.

Otheguy, R., García, O., & Fernandez, M. (1989). Transferring, switching, and modeling in West New York Spanish: An intergenerational study. *International Journal of the Sociology of Language, 79*, 41–52.

Otheguy, R., García, O., & Roca, A. (2000). Speaking in Cuban: The language of Cuban Americans. In S. McKay & S. Wong (Eds.), *New immigrants in the United States* (pp. 165–188). Cambridge: Cambridge University Press.

Peñalosa, F. (1980). *Chicano sociolinguistics: A brief introduction*. Rowley, MA: Newbury House.

Pérez, L. (1982). The imperial design: Politics and pedagogy in occupied Cuba, 1899–1902. *Cuban Studies/Estudios Cubanos, 12*, 1–18.

Phillipson, R. (1992). *Linguistic imperialism*. Oxford: Oxford University Press.

Poplack, S. (1983). Intergenerational variation in language use and structure in a bilingual context. In C. Rivera (Ed.), *An ethnographic sociolinguistic approach to language proficiency assessment*. Avon, England: Multilingual Matters.

Rickford, J. R. (1999). *African American Vernacular English*. Malden, MA: Blackwell.

Rivera, C., & Stansfield, C. (2000). *An analysis of state policies for the inclusion and accommodation of English language learners in state assessment programs during 1998–1999*. Washington, DC: The George Washington University, Center for Equity and Excellence in Education.

Rogoff, B. (1990). *Apprenticeship in thinking: Cognitive development in social context*. New York: Oxford University Press.

Rumbaut, R., & Portes, A. (Eds.). (2001). *Ethnicities: Children of immigrants*. Los Angeles: University of California Press.

Santa Ana, A. O. (1993). Chicano English and the nature of the Chicano language setting. *Hispanic Journal of Behavioral Sciences, 15*(1), 3–35.

Santa Ana, A. O. (1996). Sonority and syllable structure in Chicano English. *Language Variation and Change, 8*(1), 63–89.

Scarcella, R. (2002). Some key factors affecting English learners' development of advanced literacy. In J. Mary & M. Colombi (Eds.), *Developing advanced literacy in first and second languages* (pp. 209–226). Mahwah, NJ: Lawrence Erlbaum Associates.

Schecter, S. R., & Bayley, R. (2002). *Language as cultural practice: Mexicanos en el norte*. Mahwah, NJ: Lawrence Erlbaum Associates.

Shapiro, C. (2000, March 21). *Ensuring the success of English language learners: A school wide effort*. Presentation at the Bronx High School Principals Meeting for the Bronx Superintendent's Office, Bronx, New York.

Skutnabb-Kangas, T. (2000). *Linguistic genocide in education—Or worldwide diversity and human rights?* Mahwah, NJ: Lawrence Erlbaum Associates.

Smitherman, G. (1986). *Talkin and testifyin: The language of Black America*. Detroit, MI: Wayne State University Press. (Original work published 1977)

Taylor, P. (1999). Bronzing the face of American English: The double tongue of Chicano literature. In T. Hoenselaars & M. Buning (Eds.), *English literature and the other languages* (pp. 255–268). Amsterdam: Rodopi.

Tisdell, E. (1998). Poststructural feminist pedagogies: The possibilities and limitations of feminist emancipatory adult learning theory and practice. *Adult Education Quarterly 48,* 139–156.

Traugh, C. (2002, March). Inquiry as a mode of renewal: Imagining the possibilities of circumstance. *CUE Point of View, 1.*

Urciuoli, B. (1996). *Exposing prejudice: Puerto Rican experiences of language, race, and class.* Boulder, CO: Westview Press.

U.S. Census Bureau. (2000). QT-P16 Language spoken at home: 2000. *Census 2000 Summary File 3.* Washington, DC: Author.

Wiley, T., & Lukes, M. (1996). English-only and standard English ideologies in the U.S. *TESOL Quarterly, 30*(3), 511–537.

Wolfram, W., Temple Adger, C., & Christian, D. (1999). *Dialects in schools and communities.* Mahwah, NJ: Lawrence Erlbaum Associates.

Zentella, A. (1997). *Growing up bilingual: Puerto Rican children in New York.* Malden, MA: Blackwell.

Chapter 9

Tex Mex, Metalingual Discourse, and Teaching College Writing

Michelle Hall Kells
University of New Mexico

KEY POINTS

- Longitudinal study of Mexican-origin college students.
- Raising awareness of Tex Mex, the vernacular of many South Texans.
- Myths and attitudes towards Tex Mex.
- Approaches to teaching composition to Mexican American students.
- Promoting metalingual discourse to confront language attitudes.

In January 2003, the Census Bureau announced that US "Hispanic" populations currently surpass African American populations in size and constitute the largest minority group in the United States. The porosity of our southernmost borders, the impact of the North American Free Trade Agreement, and the fifty-year legacy of Mexico–U.S. transnational migration patterns are among the key factors responsible for the dramatic rise in Hispanic populations, the result of which is a reconfiguring of the sociolinguistic landscape of the United States. In particular, the complex social, economic, and political border both uniting and separating the US from Mexico continues to fuel the migration of Mexicans and Latin Americans to the US, and impacts public policy, commerce, local social structures, as well as the US educational system. Consequently, Mexican-origin students represent one of the fastest growing and increasingly ethnolinguistically complex student populations in US colleges today.

Like Puerto Rican, African American, and Anglophone Caribbean students, Mexican American college students challenge traditional educational structures and pedagogies. Specifically, the language of many South Texas Mexican Americans, *Tex Mex*,[1] has complicated simplistic definitions of English and Spanish, and has spawned an array of myths and attitudes that affect language teaching and learning. In a broader sense, the presence of Mexican American students and ethnolinguistically diverse students in college and university English Studies programs across the nation forces us to question prevailing attitudes and stances toward the discursive practices, the linguistic codes, genres, and views of literacy they bring to the classroom. The need to facilitate these new student groups prompts us to reflect on the discourses we privilege in our classrooms, and question how literacy education impacts our students' sense of cultural identity.

Against this background, this chapter will examine approaches to teaching and language awareness that take into account language attitudes with specific reference to Mexican American students. Drawing on the findings from my own longitudinal study of Mexican-origin college students, I will foreground some of the most disabling myths about Tex Mex and propose strategies for teaching future teachers of English how to dismantle these myths and successfully facilitate the process of academic discourse acquisition. Additionally, I will enlarge my discussion of language myths to address broader issues of linguistic racism and offer one classroom practice that helps students reflect on the implications of linguistic prejudice.

TEX MEX: THE ANGUISH OF DEFINITION

Much of the literature on Mexican-American educational issues falls under the category of bilingual education with the presumption that English is the second language. Findings from my 1996–1997 longitudinal study problematize the assumption that the majority of Mexican American bilingual college students are Spanish-dominant and point to the linguistic heterogeneity of South Texas Mexican American college students. Most of the stu-

---

[1] I have adopted the term *Tex Mex* to reflect the self-ascribed speech practices of South Texas bilinguals. With dramatic demographic shifts in progress, it is not uncommon to hear Tex Mex spoken in the streets of San Antonio, Texas as well as in other corners of the nation: Charlotte, North Carolina, Birmingham, Alabama, Seattle, Washington, and Chicago, Illinois. Historically the term Tex Mex was applied by Anglo-English speaking groups to describe the cultural and linguistic practices of Mexican-origin (Tejano) populations in Texas. Current use of the term Tex Mex by Mexican-origin groups reflects a pattern of self-ascription and reappropriation, complicating the historically pejorative semantic value of the label. Cross-cultural language attitudes span a broad continuum ranging from linguistic pride to ambivalence. Recent evidence suggests that Tex Mex functions as a solidarity marker among bilingual speakers. For further discussion of the social value of Tex Mex see Kells (2004).

dents in my study (N = 195) claim English (or border varieties of English) as their first language (Kells, 2002). However, to define this group ethno-linguistically as English monolinguals would be too reductive. The majority of Mexican-origin students speak two language varieties: *Chicano English* and *Chicano Spanish*. (See García and Menken chap. 8, this volume for a fuller discussion of the complex linguistic behavior of US Latinos.)

As noted earlier, the common, self-ascribed term for South Texas Mexican American speech practices is *Tex Mex*. Significantly, this term is an historically pejorative label imposed by the dominant Anglo society. Student response patterns from Mexican Americans and Anglo Americans suggest that Tex Mex is regarded as a kind of linguistic corruption of English and Spanish by both groups. Moreover, on both sides of the US–Mexico border, Tex Mex carries negative social value and speakers of Tex Mex find themselves censured in both US English and Spanish classrooms (Villa, 2002). Nevertheless, for Mexican-origin students in South Texas, Tex Mex represents an important self-ascribed language practice. Even as a marked code, speakers acknowledge Tex Mex as part of their linguistic repertoire. Over fifty percent of South Texas college students claim to speak Tex Mex (Kells, 2002).

If we apply the concept of a creoloid continuum, Tex Mex falls within a broad spectrum between Spanish and English (Lipski, 1993; Rickford, 1985). For some speakers, Tex Mex more strongly reflects English. For others, Tex Mex more strongly reflects Spanish. In any case, Tex Mex incorporates some level of inter- and intrasentential code-switching. With intersentential code-switching, speakers may speak a number of sentences or discourse units in one code then switch to the other language. With intrasentential code-switching, speakers alternate words in English and Spanish in the same sentence or communicative event. In addition to code-switching, the linguistic repertoire of Tex Mex speakers includes lexical features specific to the region that are neither codified English nor Spanish morphemes such as *lonche* (lunch), *parkear* (to park), and *taipear* (to type). Nonstandard Spanish lexical items such as *pader* (*pared*), *sia* (*silla*), and *antonces* (*entonces*) likewise appear in this variety. Tex Mex is characterized by a number of structural features including a tendency toward simplification through vowel reduction and the loss of word final syllables in such Spanish lexical items as *pos* (*pues*); *quiere* (*quere*); *ta* (*esta*); *pa* (*para*).[2] The lexical inventory, morphosyntactic features, and code-switching practice distinguish Tex Mex from other hispanicized varieties of English or anglicized varieties of Spanish.

Significantly, in spite of its marked status, Tex Mex operates as an important solidarity marker, helping to establish and maintain social access

---

[2]For a detailed examination contrasting *Chicano Spanish* from *Mexicano Spanish*, see Hidalgo (1987) and Lope Blanch (1987).

among speakers.[3] Tex Mex, therefore, is more than code-switching. Its distinct lexicon and morphosyntactic features distinguish it from other border varieties of English and Spanish. Although sociolinguists debate its status as a dialect, the prevalence of self-ascribed Tex Mex users demands closer consideration within the academy. As an examination of language attitudes, a full descriptive linguistic analysis of Tex Mex exceeds the scope of this discussion. However, studies over the past twenty-five years on Chicano English and Chicano Spanish point to the categorical quandary of Tex Mex or what Baugh (1984) calls "the anguish of definition" (Amastae & Elías-Olivares, 1982; Bills, Hudson, & Hernández-Chávez, 2000; Doviak & Hudson-Edwards, 1980; Durán, 1981; Lipski, 1985; Martínez, 2002; Peñalosa, 1975, 1980; Penfield, 1984; Sánchez, 1983; Wald, 1984).[4]

Baugh (1984) argues that the process of linguistically teasing out Chicano English from Chicano Spanish remains a tenuous enterprise because of the great range of variation between these related codes. The earliest attempts to define the parameters of *Spanglish* began in the mid-1970s with Acosta-Belén (1975), Barker (1975), Bills and Ornstein, (1976), Gingrás (1974), Lance (1975), and Valdés-Fallis, G. (1976). *El diccionario del español de Tejas* compiled by Galván and Teschner (1975) represents an early attempt to codify this regional Spanish variety. In that same period, Barker (1975) and Acosta-Belén (1975) chronicled the "widespread negative attitudes towards its use" and the feelings of "inferiority" and "alienation" by its users.

Jacobson (1978) attempted to simplify the discussion on defining Tex Mex and Spanglish by reducing Tex Mex to solely a code-switching phenomenon. Velásquez (1995), however, challenged this kind of linguistic reductionism, arguing that Spanglish in its multifarious forms represents a productive code in and of itself. My observations of South Texas Mexican American bilinguals reflects Velásquez's claim that Tex Mex functions as a third code by combining two distinct linguistic systems and evolving into its own innovative language practice. I agree with Velásquez that sociolinguistics needs to recognize speakers' self-ascribed language practices— even if such broad notions of language variation complicate the anguish of definition.

_____

[3]A more detailed examination of the rhetorical dimensions of Tex Mex and code-switching are explored in Kells (2004).

[4]The terms *Chicano English* and *Chicano Spanish*, applied to these border language varieties by sociolinguistic researchers of the 1960s–1980s, do not represent local language naming practices. Chicano English and Chicano Spanish are not widely used or recognized among the speakers of these border language varieties. Rather these terms index the political and scholarly perspectives of the researchers of this period. Only a very small percentage of South Texas Mexican Americans today adopt the label *Chicano/a* to represent their ethnolinguistic identity and political position. The majority self-ascribe Tex Mex to describe their bilingual language practices.

TEX MEX AND METALINGUAL REFLECTION
IN THE COMPOSITION CLASSROOM

My findings over the course of five years of quantitative and qualitative research of Tex Mex-speaking college students reveal not only the complexities involved in defining their language, but also the fact that ethnolinguistic identity is closely tied to language attitudes and myth subscription.[5] Hispanic English-dominant bilinguals, Hispanic Spanish-dominant bilinguals, Hispanic English monolinguals, Anglo English monolinguals all subscribe to a number of language myths and dialect misconceptions. Language misconceptions may contribute to self-fulfilling prophesies of failure in English studies classes. The most disturbing finding in my research is the high degree of negativism that bilingual Mexican Americans exhibit toward Tex Mex as a language practice. It appears that many users adopt the attitudes of the dominant culture toward their language varieties.

Excerpts from the following journals of three South Texas first year composition Mexican American bilingual students map the complexities of their sociolinguistic contexts from personal perspectives:[6]

> Martín Alaniz: South Texas is mainly composed of bilingual people: Spanish and English. Some know how to manipulate both languages better than others. Many people get mad when they listen to a hispanic speak their Spanish all wrong. I admit that sometimes I get frustrated when hispanic people pretend to be only monolingual; in this case, pretending to only speak English. I understand that some do not really know how to speak one or the other language well. Sometimes I get tongue tied speaking English. I use to hate to speak English because I would be scared to say the wrong words.

This student articulates a common theme of ambivalence and uncertainty about using Spanish as a marked code. He poignantly illustrates the communicative dilemma facing speakers of stigmatized language varieties. Martín expresses his own resentment toward bilinguals who refuse to use Spanish in public settings as well as admits his own discomfort shifting to English in these situations. He aptly captures the "damned if you do,

---

[5]I conducted a longitudinal study in 1996–1997 at a South Texas university comprised of over 75% Mexican-origin college students. I used random sampling methods to identify the ethnolinguistic features of first-year composition students and correlate language attitudes and myth subscription. A complete description of the research methods and findings are available in Kells (2002).

[6]Students who participated in this study gave formal permission to publish their journal responses. I have given pseudonyms to protect the identity of the respondents. I have transcribed journal entries without correction or the notation (sic) for nonstandard orthographic features.

damned if you don't" scenario facing speakers of Tex Mex. The following journal entries further illustrate the challenges bilinguals often face:

> Yvette Lira: It does not matter where you come from if you learn (to) speak Spanish before you learn to speak English you are pointed out as being a poor Mexican American who cannot communicate or speak and understand anything. Which is not true. Lots of Spanish speaking people understand English but have a harder time trying to speak it.

> Terese Camacho: People assume that if you speak Spanish or Tex Mex you are not very educated. I really feel it is wrong and inhuman to be so cruel. People should judge from the heart and not from their eyes. For instance, I remember this young girl from Mexico who came to the United States to receive an education in our school. She was treated with disrespect and was verbally bashed every day. If she was not ridiculed about being poor or Mexican, she was ridiculed about her accent. I never realized how mean people could actually be till I saw the tears in her eyes after class.

> Jacob Flores: Monolinguals don't understand what it is like to know and speak two languages. They figure that it is lack of education or ignorance because they don't know how it is to be bilingual. When a person is bilingual it is very easy to speak the two languages at the same time. For example, Mexicans usually tend to speak Spanish and English words in a conversation. That is what we refer to as Tex Mex. It is common and we as speakers accept it. Monolinguals, on the other hand, may think it uneducated.

The college composition classroom needs to become the site of these kinds of discussions. The problem for many English teachers, the majority of whom are monolinguals, is how to facilitate productive metalingual discourse without exacerbating alienation (Dean, 1989). The personal narrative informed by the descriptive perspective of sociolinguistics can promote valuable classroom dialogue about language ideologies.

The observations of one Anglo English monolingual South Texas composition student reflect one such opportunity for classroom discussion about stereotypes and linguistic prejudice:

> S. Walker: I don't think people are unintelligent when people code-switch. Sometime I might if they have an accent. Yes, I know that is wrong. People probably perceive people that do code-switch ignorant because they think they should be able to speak English if they are in America. Plus, people have an inner prejudice that is automatically in them that society makes them have. T.V., media, and your parents also push it into you.

This student describes the internalization and diffusion of language prejudices through her writing. The exercise begins as internal deliberation about herself and evolves into social critique. Another Anglo monolingual student chronicles her exposure to linguistic prejudice in a South Texas high school:

> Sarah McGehee: I saw evidence of this rejection of cultural dialect in my high school classrooms. . . . All of the English teachers in my high school were white and through the years of writing assignments and oral presentations, I noticed a difference in the way that my work was graded in comparison to the way that some of my Mexican friends' work was graded. . . . [M]any of the corrections and comments that our teachers added to my friends' work pertained to the "cultural" style of self-expression. Speaking Spanish was almost forbidden, and any insertion of Tex Mex words or phrases in class work would constitute a failing grade.

Recognizing and verbalizing the inequities are essential steps toward changing the inequities. Teachers of composition to ethnolinguistically diverse students exercise a critical role in literacy education and have the power to implicitly (even if not explicitly) alienate writers from not only the academy but from themselves. However, an understanding of linguistic belief systems can help teachers and students recognize disabling fictions about ethnolinguistic identity. The cultivation of metalingual awareness and dialogue about language ideologies in composition classes are necessary to facilitate learning and academic discourse acquisition. Incorporating opportunities to articulate the unspoken beliefs about different language varieties such as those stated above allows students and teachers to openly confront linguistic racism.

The problem of linguistic racism is not limited to the remote outposts of South Texas. The terrain of the US educational system is populated by ethnolinguistically diverse students who do not fare well in the prescriptivist project of English Studies, not only because of their bidialectalism or bilingualism, but even more significantly, because of their Englishes (Baugh, 2000; Heller, 1999; Heller & Martin-Jones, 2001; Meier, 1989; Pennycook, 2000). Like Anglophone Caribbean students who are inappropriately placed in courses for nonnative speakers of English, Mexican-origin students claim native speaker proficiency in English, yet frequently find themselves labeled as nonnative speakers, and even worse, remedial. The majority who are placed in remedial writing courses never complete their college degree while less than half even successfully complete the first year composition sequence (Kells, 1995). A common explanation for high placement rates of Mexican Americans in remedial Composition courses rests on the claim of L1 (Spanish) interference. However, that assertion is called into question when the ethnolinguistic identity of this student population is more closely examined. The majority of the students in the South Texas university I examined are English-dominant bilinguals or what Lipski (1993) calls *transitional bilinguals*. For most, English (or, more precisely, border varieties of English) is their first language, not Spanish (Kells, 2002). The gatekeeping function of the college English classes too often results in sanctioned forms of institutionalized discrimination through which only those speakers whose language variety most closely approximates the idealized code gain entry into academe. Speakers of all other varieties of English, in turn, must negotiate various portals of provisional entree through ESL or remedial programs.

The issues related to English bias and linguistic discrimination are far reaching with national and global implications as English becomes the first, if not the most common second language of communities around the world (Blommaert, 1999; Canagarajah, 1999; Hall & Eggington, 2000; Hornberger, 1998; Huebner & Davis, 1999; Muller, 1996; Phillipson, 1992; Wolfson & Manes, 1985). The new racism, argues Villanueva, is "competitive racism." "That folks of Color don't achieve the same status of Whites in equal numbers (or comparable ratios) becomes part of racial pathologies, replete with a list of 'if only' statements," Villanueva contends.[7] "If only they'd stop whining and get to work." And we might add, "If only they'd speak correct English." But what is the standard by which we measure native-speaker of English competence? This question is especially problematic in sites like South Texas where students claim English, Spanish, and Tex Mex as their primary languages. As Nero (2001) observes, the distinction between native and nonnative speaker of English is becoming increasingly blurred. Thus it appears that while the literary canon has undergone significant revision over the past two decades to include global literatures in English, an equivalent reassessment of the privileging of the monolithic concept of "English" does not appear to be a debate that will soon yield structural change.

To transform college and secondary school writing classrooms into productive sites for academic discourse acquisition demands reevaluation at multiple levels. Not only do we need to question how we are teaching students of English, we need to interrogate how we are teaching teachers of English. One way to help teachers in this process is to train them in facilitative ways of analyzing their students' language. Like Nero (2001), I maintain that the analysis of students' language performance in colleges and universities must include examination of the historical and sociocultural contexts within which the student's language and literacy practices have emerged. A commitment to critical pedagogy demands that we respond to the growing population of immigrant and traditionally excluded student groups and expand the scope of the teaching of composition to include recognition of the full range of students' linguistic repertoires. But we can't stop there. We need to embed discussions about language use in

---

[7]Cited in Smitherman and Villanueva (2003, p. 3).

context—the sociological, political, and culture milieux of speaking. Moreover, we need to be concerned by the alienation of Latino students from education, especially higher education, as evidenced by national-level rates of low retention and low graduation among Mexican-origin and other Latino student populations.[8]

Until very recently, inquiry that examines the immediate and long-range consequences of stigmatizing students' language practices has been limited. The exodus of Mexican-origin and Latino students from secondary schools and higher education appears to be linked to issues of ethnolinguistic identity and language attitudes (Kells, 1999, 2002; National Center for Public Policy and Higher Education, 2000; Romo & Falbo, 1996; Valdés, 1992, 1996; Valenzuela, 1999). Without new sociolinguistic and applied linguistics research connecting language attitudes to literacy practice, our understanding of the role of ethnolinguistic identity in the retention of Mexican American students at the college level will remain speculative and superficial.[9] Furthermore, understanding our students' beliefs and attitudes remains critical to framing appropriate and effective classroom practice.

FROM RESEARCH TO CLASSROOM PRACTICE

While descriptive research about the linguistic features of the speech practices of Mexican-origin students is necessary and productive to linguistic analysis, equally, if not more, important to us as teachers of composition, is inquiry focusing on extra-linguistic features such as students' attitudes toward their own language varieties as well as their attitudes toward the target code of the academy. Recent findings published by the Conference of College Composition and Communication Language Policy Committee delineate the need for the training of English teachers at all levels in Language Awareness and American Dialects. The 2000 "Language Knowledge and Awareness Survey Final Report" underscores the need for courses in the teacher education curriculum that examine languages in contact and reach beyond the traditional History of the English Language syllabus.[10] Among their recommendations, the committee asserts: "Teachers should remain distinctly conscious of their covert attitudes toward their students' language

---

[8]To respond to the gap in current pedagogical literature see Kells, Balester, and Villanueva (2004).

[9]A recent review of research in sociolinguistics and composition studies over the past ten years reveals the underexamination of the problems of language attitudes and ideologies among Mexican American bilinguals in college contexts. See Bizzell, Herzberg, and Reynolds (2000).

[10]CCCC Language Policy Committee. Language knowledge and awareness survey, Final Report, 2000. www.ncte.org/cccc/

and the impact of those attitudes 'upon the academic achievement of those students' " (p. 32). Teacher education in English studies at all levels needs to include critical approaches to language and linguistics.

In this regard, despite decades of debate and dispute, we remain fixated on questions of standardization whenever we attend to issues related to educational access of linguistic minority students. The heteroglossia of diverse student populations (their non-standard English varieties, bilingualism, and bidialectalism) is frequently examined and treated pathologically as a linguistic deficit. Although the aim of language education is to enlarge students' linguistic repertoires (expanding their use of codes, genres, and media), when dealing with diverse students, the focus is to reduce and minimize class features and ethnic markers. After decades of dismal retention and graduation rates of Latino students across the nation, it is time to reassess this approach. If we start the process of academic discourse acquisition by fixing and removing, we have shaken if not severely undermined the already-whole and intact linguistic system of the individual learner.

The bilingualism and bidialectalism of diverse college students are not the primary problems in academic discourse acquisition. The problems rest with negative language attitudes (outside and inside the academy as well as within teachers and students). The social stigmas attached to users of low prestige language varieties is one of the greatest impediments to effective approaches to education. The language varieties themselves are functional linguistic systems. The attitudes about these language varieties are dysfunctional. Although we are increasingly acknowledging this fact at a theoretical level in scholarly venues, we have given little guidance to front-line teachers as to what constitutes facilitative practice for diverse college writers.

Composition Studies has only recently begun to address the impact of language attitudes on writing (Balester, 1993; Gilyard, 1991, Guerra, 1998; Kells & Balester, 1999; Kells, Balester, & Villanueva, 2004; McKay & Hornberger, 1996; Severino, Guerra, & Butler, 1997; Silva & Matsuda, 2001). Although the national conversation on students' rights foregrounds the need to recognize the value of students' heritage languages, we have yet to define what that means in terms of practice in Composition and English studies (Smitherman, 1999).

It is this disconnect that moved my own research program over a five-year trajectory from quantitative, experimental, ethnographic, and qualitative designs toward classroom practice. Because few secondary and college-level English teachers are part of the conversation on ethnolinguistic diversity issues, I see the undergraduate curriculum as a critical juncture for attitude formation. As such, I restructured the Introduction to Linguistics course at Texas A&M University (spring 2001), interweaving structural and functional linguistics with applications for teaching writing. Introduction to Linguistics is the avowed dreaded course in the English major curriculum, frequently avoided until the final year or semester of the under-graduate program. Besides wanting to find a way to make the syllabus more relevant and less onerous, I wanted to address issues related to the grow-ing presence of Mexican-origin students in our schools. After surveying the student population of 150 undergraduate students (95% Anglo) in my two sections of the Introduction to Linguistics, I implemented an applied dimension to the syllabus in the form of what I call the "Linguistics Narra-tive Journal."

Because I wanted to encourage students to write what they wanted to say and not what they thought I wanted to read, I followed a very liberal grad-ing criteria. Journal entries were assessed on length only. Each of the ten journal entries had to be one and a half (word-processed) pages respond-ing to the readings with their own reactions. I did not grade for content or for writing conventions such as spelling, punctuation, etc. In brief, they were rewarded for simply doing the reading and writing. The Linguistics Narrative Journal represented only fifteen percent of the course grade, however. Sixty percent of the course grade rested on four major exams fo-cusing on analytical linguistics principles and problem solving exercises. It was an ambitious syllabus because they did everything required in the tradi-tional general linguistics course as well as the journal.

My hope was to provide the opportunity for critical reflection to my stu-dents, the vast majority of whom will become teachers in elementary, sec-ondary, and even college settings. My argument for incorporating the Lin-guistics Narrative Journal into the syllabus rested on the claim that the experience of engaging in metalingual discourse (in writing and class dis-cussion) would endure long after they had forgotten how to do phonetic transcription. According to the description on my course syllabus, the aim of the Linguistics Narrative Journal was "to focus on issues facing future teachers of English and language studies: language varieties and attitudes, usage and standardization, communicative competence, sociogeographic distribution, and language acquisition." I wanted this course project to re-flect one of the key missions of the Texas A&M Department of English: to educate and train English teachers for elementary, secondary, and post-secondary positions.

Furthermore, the need to educate future teachers about the myths and stigmas of Tex Mex as a language practice is especially critical in terms of re-tention of Mexican American students in the Texas educational system. So-cioeconomically, Mexican Americans represent the fastest growing poverty group in the state and nation. Mexican American college students are more likely to be placed in remedial writing programs, to fail first-year composi-tion, and to drop out of the educational system than their Anglo counter-parts. To educate my linguistics students about these realities, I assigned readings from *Attending to the Margins: Writing, Researching, and Teaching on the Front Lines* (Kells & Balester, 1999), linking the themes of the chapters on marginalized writers to concepts such as linguistic variation, descriptivism, language universals, acquisition, phonology, language shift, contact, and the historical development of English.

The success of the course exceeded my expectations. I will provide a few excerpts from the 150 journals generated in this course. Every student submitted a Linguistics Narrative Journal (even those "A" students who could have held onto their course average without it). The retention and success rates in my Introduction to Linguistics courses were higher than previous semesters. Attendance and participation remained strong. Even in a lecture format for more than 100 students, discussion was productive and enthusiastic. At Texas A&M University where tradition is spelled with a capital *T* and verges on the sacred, I anticipated significant resistance to the undergirding principles of the course: the equality, creativity, and changeability of all languages. I knew I would be challenging some cherished beliefs about the purity and superiority of English. The anticipated backlash did not happen. By approaching language variation and change through the descriptive principles of linguistics, students were able to make the next logical step and realize that language varieties like Tex Mex are the natural result of language contact and change in progress. Three Anglo writers reflect on the readings and connect the issues to their own experiences:

> Anthony Nading: Bilingual students, those that speak both Spanish and English, seem to think that Tex Mex is an inferior form of both Spanish and English. This is prevalent in Houston. In Houston, there is a large and steadily increasing population of Mexican American students. It is a cultural stereotype that Tex Mex is inferior. People in Houston who speak Tex Mex are usually less likely to get jobs when they are as equally qualified as a white person. Teachers need to learn that it is becoming necessary for them to adapt to social change and adapt their teaching styles as well. It is now important that teachers address the linguistic division that occurs within the classroom. Students who are bilingual will feel pushed aside unless the teacher can make strides to help incorporate them into the learning process.

> Monica Withers: Teachers unconsciously perpetuate language myths and prejudices inside the English classroom because they are teaching *English* classes, and that simple act leads to their unconscious bias against other dialects (and languages). . . . Teachers can confront these misconceptions by talking to the students about it, and making them aware of these language myths. Educate the students so that the idea of change begins to spread.

> Mark Danforth: As a native Texan raised in West Texas where many Hispanics reside, I have personally heard Tex Mex spoken by Mexicans. I'll admit that until taking this class, I viewed Tex Mex as a lower class language. I suppose I thought this not only because my teachers looked down upon their style of language, but because I always had the opinion that Americans, no matter

previous nationality, should speak "proper English," despite the fact that I knew that my style of language per se was "improper." I had always thought that the Mexicans just didn't care about what was proper. This chapter helped me to realize my own stereotypes of Tex Mex and how other people viewed this style of Spanish. It was amazing to me that people of Spanish descent even thought that Tex Mex sounded ignorant. . . . Now I see that educated young Mexican Americans are degraded for speaking Tex Mex and persuaded to change to fit the white norm.

Of the 150 students in these two Introduction to Linguistics courses, there were only eight Mexican American students. This underrepresentation of Mexican American students is reflective of the demographic of Texas A&M University as a predominantly white, middle class student population. Although the lack of representational diversity at this flagship institution has been the focus of a number of university symposia and initiatives, substantive change remains slow. One Mexican American student examines her experiences and perceptions of Tex Mex:

> Angela Barajas: Having lived in South Texas, I understand well the differences in language that occur there. I do not think students' language attitudes are very malleable. Each language is seen as a social status. What languages you speak in social situations had a large effect on how others would categorize others. Spanish was never spoken in class, and was actually frowned upon. However, when in a social situation such as lunchtime or in between classes, Spanish was commonly heard. The language you spoke during this time, however, greatly reflected on what other people's opinions of you were. For example, those speaking Spanish were stereotyped as the "wet backs" or those of a lower class. Those ones who spoke Tex Mex were considered "Cholos" which is a term that refers to the gangsters or the guys who always get into fights. Those that spoke English were the popular or smarter students. Spanish seemed to be an inferior language. Even worse was the use of Tex Mex because it was considered to be used by those of lower education and prestige.

Angela's experiences suggest that Tex Mex not only signifies class and race but citizenship. Ethnolinguistic identity functions as an index of social position. She articulates how language codes access and belonging.

Cultivating critical approaches to language studies and incorporating metalingual discourse into the English studies curriculum are integral not only to teacher education but to entry-level college writing courses as well. The educational future of ethnolinguistically diverse students such as Angela can certainly be impacted by their experiences in English courses. One might argue that their presence in these courses moves us to reconsider the role of the Department of English in the US educational system. In many ways, the ethnolinguistic heterogeneity in college classrooms complicates the very notion of a Department of English. It gives us pause to wonder if our universities of the future will be more accurately termed Departments of Englishes.

Still, at each level of the US educational system, emerging writers need opportunities to explore, critique, manipulate, and circulate language. But we need English courses that do more than strive to standardize language practice. We need English courses that facilitate academic discourse acquisition as well as critical thinking. Above all else, we need English courses in which not only privileged student populations excel, but historically-excluded students thrive. To achieve this, the prescriptive aims of English and Composition Studies must be attenuated by the descriptive insights of sociolinguistics. Moreover, the disciplinary divisions between Composition Studies and linguistics must be bridged. Inviting students into academic discourse through metalingual reflection and linguistic narratives can help to pave the way for critical language awareness and increased consciousness of the many communicative spheres to which they belong (or hope to belong).

QUESTIONS FOR DISCUSSION AND REFLECTIVE WRITING

1. Hall Kells (citing Velásquez) describes Tex Mex as a "third code" (neither English nor Spanish). Do you agree with this assessment? How does this characterization of Tex Mex compare and contrast with other language varieties such as Caribbean Creole English or West African Pidgin English?

2. Working with a partner, discuss and write about your reaction to the attitudes towards Tex Mex reflected in the excerpts from student journals in this chapter. How might those attitudes be constructively drawn upon in a composition classroom?

3. The author of this chapter proposes metalingual reflection through journal writing as a means of bridging the "prescriptive aims of composition studies" and the "descriptive insights of sociolinguistics." In a small group or as a whole class, examine the challenges and possibilities that can emerge by bridging these two disciplines in the classroom.

ACKNOWLEDGMENTS

My gratitude to Peter Elbow and the participants in the 2001 Symposium on Dialects of English at the University of Massachusetts, Amherst for their guidance and encouragement in the writing of this essay.

REFERENCES

Acosta-Belén, E. (1975). "Spanglish:" A case of languages in contact. In M. Burt & H. Dulay (Eds.), *On TESOL '75: New directions in second language learning, teaching, and bilingual education* (pp. 151–158). Washington, DC: Teachers of English to Speakers of Other Languages.

Amastae, J., & Elías-Olivares, L. (Eds.). (1982). *Spanish in the United States: Sociolinguistic aspects.* New York: Cambridge University Press.

Balester, V. (1993). *Cultural divide: A study of African-American college-level writers.* Portsmouth, NH: Heinemann-Boynton/Cook.

Barker, G. C. (1975). Social functions of language in a Mexican–American community. In E. Hernández-Chavez, A. D. Cohen, & A. F. Beltramo (Eds.), *El lenguaje de los Chicanos: Regional and social characteristics used by Mexican Americans* (pp. 170–182). Arlington, VA: Center for Applied Linguistics.

Baugh, J. (1984). Chicano English: The anguish of definition. In J. Ornstein-Galicia (Ed.), *Form and function in Chicano English* (pp. 3–13). Rowley, MA: Newbury.

Baugh, J. (2000). Transforming the politics of schooling in the U.S: A model for successful academic achievement for language minority students. In J. K. Hall & W. G. Eggington (Eds.), *The sociopolitics of English language teaching* (pp. 104–116). Tonawanda, NY: Multilingual Matters.

Bills, G., & Ornstein, J. (1976). Linguistic diversity in Southwest Spanish. In J. D. Bowen & J. Ornstein (Eds.), *Studies in Southwest Spanish* (pp. 4–16). Rowley, MA: Newbury.

Bills, G., Hudson, A., & Hernández-Chávez, E. (2000). Spanish home language use and English proficiency as differential measure of language maintenance and shift. *Southwest Journal of Linguistics, 19*(1), 11–27.

Bizzell, P., Herzberg, B., & Reynolds, N. (2000). *The Bedford bibliography for teachers of writing* (5th ed.). New York: Bedford/St. Martin's Press.

Blommaert, J. (Ed.). (1999). *Language ideological debates.* Berlin: Mouton de Gruyter.

Canagarajah, A. S. (1999). *Resisting linguistic imperialism in English teaching.* Oxford: Oxford University Press.

Dean, T. (1989). Multicultural classrooms, monolingual teachers. *College Composition and Communication, 40,* 23–37.

Doviak, M. J., & Hudson-Edwards, A. (1980). Phonological variation in Chicano English: Word-final (z)-devoicing. In E. L. Blansitt & R. V. Teschner (Eds.), *A festschrift for Jacob Ornstein* (pp. 82–96). Rowley, MA: Newbury.

Durán, R. (Ed.). (1981). *Latino language and communicative behavior.* Norwood, NJ: Ablex Publishing Corp.

Galván, R., & Teschner, R. (1975). *El diccionario del español de Tejas.* Silver Spring, MD: Institute of Modern Languages.

Gilyard, K. (1991). *Voices of the self: A study of language competence.* Detroit: Wayne State University Press.

Gingrás, R. C. (1974). Problems in the description of Spanish–English intrasentential code-switching. In G. Bills (Ed.), *Southwest area linguistics* (pp. 167–174). San Diego: San Diego State University, Institute for Cultural Pluralism.

Guerra, J. C. (1998). *Close to home: Oral and literate practices in a transnational mexicano community.* New York: Teachers College Press.

Hall, J. K., & Eggington, W. (Eds.). (2000). *The sociopolitics of English language teaching.* Tonawanda, NY: Multilingual Matters.

Heller, M. (1999). *Linguistic minorities and modernity: A sociolinguistic ethnography.* New York: Longman.

Heller, M., & Martin-Jones, M. (Eds.). (2001). *Voices of authority: Education and linguistic difference.* Westport, CT: Ablex.

Hidalgo, M. (1987). Español mexicano y español chicano: Problemas y propuestas fundamentales. In T. A. Morgan, J. F. Lee, & B. Van Patten (Eds.), *Language and language use* (pp. 166–193). Lanham, MD: University Press of America.

Hornberger, N. (1998). Language policy, language education, language rights: Indigenous, immigrant, and intercultural perspectives. *Language in Society, 27,* 439–458.

Huebner, T., & Davis, K. A. (Eds.). (1999). *Sociopolitical perspectives on language policy and planning in the USA.* Philadelphia, PA: John Benjamins.

Jacobson, R. (1978). The social implications of intersentential codeswitching. In R. Romo & R. Paredes (Eds.), *New directions in Chicano scholarship* (pp. 227–256). La Jolla: Chicano Studies Program, University of California, San Diego.

Kells, M. H. (1995). *Basic writing: A gateway to college for Mexican Americans of South Texas.* Masters Thesis, Texas A&M University–Kingsville, University of Michigan Press.

Kells, M. H. (1999). Leveling the linguistic playing field in first-year composition. In M. H. Kells & V. Balester (Eds.), *Attending to the margins: Writing, researching, and teaching on the front lines* (pp. 131–149). Portsmouth, NH: Heinemann-Boynton/Cook.

Kells, M. H. (2002). Linguistic contact zones in the college writing classroom: An examination of ethnolinguistic identity and language attitudes. *Written Communication, 19*(1), 5–43.

Kells, M. H. (2004). Understanding the rhetorical value of Tejano codeswitching. In M. H. Kells, V. Balester, & V. Villanueva (Eds.), *Latino/a discourses: On language, identity and literacy education* (pp. 24–39). Portsmouth, NH: Heinemann-Boynton/Cook.

Kells, M. H., & Balester, V. (Eds.). (1999). *Attending to the margins: Writing, researching, and teaching on the front lines.* Portsmouth, NH: Heinemann-Boynton/Cook.

Kells, M. H., Balester, V., & Villanueva, V. (Eds.). (2004). *Latino/a discourses: On language, identity, and literacy education.* Portsmouth, NH: Heinemann-Boynton/Cook.

Lance, D. M. (1975). Spanish-English code-switching. In E. Hernández-Chavez, A. D. Cohen, & A. F. Beltramo (Eds.), *El lenguaje de los Chicanos: Regional and social characteristics used by Mexican Americans* (pp. 138–153). Arlington, VA: Center for Applied Linguistics.

Lipski, J. M. (1985). *Linguistic aspects of Spanish–English language switching.* Tempe: Arizona State University Center for Latin American Studies.

Lipski, J. M. (1993). Creoloid phenomenon in the Spanish of transitional bilinguals. In A. Roca & J. M. Lipski (Eds.), *Spanish in the United States: Linguistic contact and diversity* (pp. 155–182). New York: Mouton.

Lope Branch, J. (1987). Problemas de morfología dialectal en el español de Texas. In T. A. Morgan, J. F. Lee, & B. Van Patten (Eds.), *Language and language use* (pp. 97–107). Lanham, MD: University Press of America.

Mártinez, G. A. (2002). Colonial lag, social change, and ethnolinguistic identity in South Texas, 1791–1910. *Southwest Journal of Linguistics, 21*(1), 119–135.

Meier, K. (1989). *Race, class, and education: The politics of second-generation discrimination.* Madison: University of Wisconsin Press.

McKay, S. L., & Hornberger, N. (Eds.). (1996). *Sociolinguistics and language teaching.* Cambridge: Cambridge University Press.

Muller, K. E. (Ed.). (1996). *Language status in the post-Cold War era.* Lanham, MD: University Press of America.

National Center for Public Policy and Higher Education. (2000). *Measuring up 2000.* Available from http://www.highereducation.org

Nero, S. (2001). *Englishes in contact: Anglophone Caribbean students in an urban college.* Cresskill, NJ: Hampton Press.

Peñalosa, F. (1975). Chicano multilingualism and multiglossia. In E. Hernández-Chavez, A. D. Cohen, & A. F. Beltramo (Eds.), *El lenguaje de los Chicanos: Regional and social characteristics used by Mexican Americans* (pp. 164–169). Arlington, VA: Center for Applied Linguistics.

Peñalosa, F. (1980). *Chicano sociolinguistics.* Rowley, MA: Newbury.

Penfield, J. (1984). The vernacular base of literacy in Chicano English. In J. Ornstein-Galicia (Ed.), *Form and function in Chicano English* (pp. 71–82). Rowley, MA: Newbury.

Pennycook, A. (2000). Educational malpractice and miseducation of language minority students. In J. K. Hall & W. G. Eggington (Eds.), *The sociopolitics of English language teaching* (pp. 89–103). Tonawanda, NY: Multilingual Matters.

Phillipson, R. (1992). *Linguistic imperialism.* Oxford: Oxford University Press.

Rickford, J. R. (1985). Standard and non-standard language attitudes in a creole continuum. In N. Wolfson & J. Manes (Eds.), *Language of inequality* (pp. 145–160). New York: Mouton.

Romo, H. D., & Falbo, T. (1996). *Latino high school graduation: Defying the odds.* Austin: University of Texas Press.

Sánchez, R. (1983). *Chicano discourse: Socio-historic perspectives.* Rowley, MA: Newbury.

Severino, C., Guerra, J. C., & Butler, J. E. (Eds.). (1997). *Writing in multicultural settings.* New York: Modern Language Association.

Silva, T., & Matsuda, P. K. (2001). *On second language writing.* Mahwah, NJ: Lawrence Erlbaum Associates.

Smitherman, G. (1999). CCCC's role in the struggle for language rights. *College Composition and Communication, 50*(3), 349–376.

Smitherman, G., & Villanueva, V. (Eds.). (2003). *Language diversity in the classroom: From intention to practice* (pp. 1–6). Carbondale: Southern Illinois University Press.

Valdés, G. (1992). Bilingual minorities and language issues in writing. *Written Communication, 9,* 85–136.

Valdés, G. (1996). *Con Respeto: Bridging the distances between culturally diverse families and schools: An ethnographic portrait.* New York: Teachers College.

Valdés-Fallis, G. (1976). Codeswitching and language dominance: Some initial findings. *General Linguistics, 18,* 90–104.

Valenzuela, A. (1999). *Subtractive schooling: U.S. Mexican youth and the politics of caring.* Albany: State University of New York.

Velásquez, M. D. G. (1995). Sometimes Spanish, sometimes English: Language use among rural New Mexican Chicanas. In K. Hall & M. Bucholtz (Eds.), *Gender articulated: Language and the socially constructed self* (pp. 421–446). New York: Routledge.

Villa, D. (2002). The sanitizing of U.S. Spanish in academia. *Foreign Language Annals, 35,* 220–230.

Wald, B. (1984). The status of Chicano English as a dialect of American English. In J. Ornstein-Galicia (Ed.), *Form and function in Chicano English* (pp. 60–70). Rowley, MA: Newbury.

Wolfson, N., & Manes, J. (Eds.). (1985). *Language of inequality.* New York: Mouton.

Part VI

WEST AFRICAN PIDGIN ENGLISH

IV

WEST AFRICAN PIDGIN ENGLISH

West African World English Speakers in U.S. Classrooms: The Role of West African Pidgin English

Christa de Kleine
College of Notre Dame, Baltimore

KEY POINTS

- Widespread academic underachievement of speakers of nonstandard varieties of English.
- Assessment and placement of Anglophone West African students.
- Analysis of salient grammar-related errors in West African students' writing.
- West African Pidgin English (WAPE) influence in the written language of West African students.
- Contrastive analysis approaches; distinguishing between developmental and interference errors.

INTRODUCTION

In recent years, public school systems in urban areas in the United States, especially on the East Coast, have experienced a significant increase in students who hail from the anglophone part of West Africa, in particular Ghana, Sierra Leone, Nigeria and Liberia (cf. Crandall & Greenblatt, 1998; Sewell, 1997; Sewell, Rodriguez-McCleary & Staehr, 2003). A disproportionate number of West African World English-speaking students struggle to perform at grade level in school, particularly those at the secondary level.

This chapter attempts to provide a better understanding of a key factor in the underachievement of West African students that has been overlooked or underemphasized until now (cf. Crandall, 1995; Scott, 2003; Sewell 1997): their unique English language background, which includes West African Pidgin English (WAPE).

Students who speak a variety of World English often experience serious language-related challenges in the US classrooms (Adger, 1997; Crandall, 2003; de Kleine, forthcoming; Narvaez & Garcia, 1992; Nero, 2001; Pratt-Johnson, 1993; Sewell, 1997; Sewell, Rodriguez-McCleary & Staehr, 2003). Despite (often extensive) exposure to English in their home countries, including in education, their (standard) English language development is typically insufficient to perform at grade level in US classrooms. To remedy this problem, World English speakers are sometimes placed in special education classes or, more frequently, in ESL programs. Neither has proven adequate for them. World English-speaking students already possess a certain amount of English upon arrival in the US; as a result, either their receptive skills tend to exceed their productive skills, as noted by Nero, this volume, or, in cases of students with low literacy development, their oral skills are more developed than their written skills (Crandall, 2003; Sewell, 1997, 2003; Sewell, Rodriguez-McCleary, & Staehr, 2003). Placement in classrooms with traditional ESL students is undesirable and inefficient, as it fails to build on existing linguistic knowledge.

A fairly extensive amount of research is available on World English-speaking students in educational settings requiring standard English, primarily in the form of research on Creole English-speaking students from the Caribbean in the UK and North America (cf. Coelho, 1991; de Kleine, forthcoming; Edwards, 1979, 1986; Nero 2001), as well as in the Caribbean itself (Christie, 2001; Craig, 1999). However, no in-depth research has been conducted to date on West African students in English-speaking countries outside of Africa (Scott, 2003). This chapter is a first attempt to examine in detail the nature of the linguistic issues that this student population faces in American classrooms. Based on an analysis of the writings of West African students enrolled in an ESL program in a large urban school district (with excellent services for limited English proficient students), this chapter argues that the language-related problems encountered by the English-speaking West African student population are primarily rooted in the unique variety of World English that they bring to the classroom, in the form of pidginized or creolized English. Preparing these students for the linguistic demands of today's classroom, and indeed, society at large, requires pedagogical approaches very different from those typically employed in the ESL classroom—approaches that can only be developed if we understand the nature of the language-related challenges these students experience in the educational system of this country. Before discussing the present study, an overview of the use of English in West Africa and the challenges faced by nonstandard variety speakers in standard English classrooms is necessary.

BACKGROUND

The use of English in West Africa has a long history dating back to 1530 (Angogo & Hancock, 1980). The spread of English along the coast of West Africa was largely the result of British colonization, with the exception of English use in Liberia, where it resulted from the resettlement of slaves from the American South (Holm, 1989; Todd, 1983). The history and use of English in West Africa is complex, and has resulted in different kinds of English that continue to exist in West Africa to date. On the one hand, restructured varieties, both pidginized and creolized, developed probably as early as the 17th century, when English traders started setting up families with local African women, first in the areas now known as Gambia, Sierra Leone and Ghana (Holm, 1989). In the 18th century, primarily as a result of the British playing a dominant role in the slave trade, the use of restructured English continued to spread in West Africa, including to Nigeria and Cameroon. In addition, in 1787 freed African slaves from England set up a colony in Sierra Leone, and in the 1820s freed slaves of African origin returned from North America to establish a similar colony of freed slaves in Liberia (Holm, 1989; Todd, 1983). These developments fueled the development of restructured English in West Africa further. Today, as a result of past colonization, restructured varieties of English—varieties that possess grammatical structures that are often quite different from standard (American or British) English as a result of pidginization and/or creolization, but which use a lexicon that is largely drawn from English—are found in all of the officially English-speaking countries of West Africa.

Although there are certainly differences between the varieties of restructured English in West Africa (cf. Angogo & Hancock, 1980; Banjo, 1997, Elugbe & Omamor, 1991; Holm, 1989; Huber, 1999; Singler, 1981, 1997), they are all considered to be part of the Atlantic group of English pidgins and creoles that, together with the English-based creole languages found in the Caribbean, share common social and historical roots. As a result, they display significant linguistic similarities as a group, particularly with regard to the structure of the verb phrase, but certainly not limited to that.

The extent to which the restructured varieties of English in West Africa have remained pidgins (i.e., second languages), albeit typically in expanded form, or developed into creoles (i.e., first languages), varies by country and variety, and is not always clear. Indeed, as Holm argues, the distinction between pidgin and creole English is by no means clear-cut in West

Africa, as children often learn the (expanded) pidgin outside the home, and may use it so extensively in their lives outside their homes that it essentially becomes their primary language. When this happens on a large scale, it can result in creolization of the expanded pidgin. This has apparently occurred with Nigerian Pidgin English (Elugbe & Omamor, 1991; Jibril, 1997; Schnukal & Marchese, 1983), and may very well happen with Ghanaian Pidgin English as well, if its overall increased use is any indication (cf. Huber, 1999). Creolization may be of a more recent date in parts of West Africa, such as Nigeria, but the process of creolization goes back much further for Liberian English and Krio (spoken in Sierra Leone), and this is well-established in the literature (cf. Breitborde, 1988; Singler, 1997 for creolized English in Liberia; Jones, 1971 for Krio). Following McArthur (2003), the term West African Pidgin English (WAPE) will be used here for the various restructured varieties of English of West Africa, including those that have undergone creolization.

Regardless of whether it is primarily used as a first or second language—assuming that the distinction is a valid and useful one in West Africa—the use of WAPE is now clearly widespread, not only in Liberia (cf. Breitborde, 1988; Singler, 1997; Todd, 1983) and Sierra Leone (cf. Holm, 1989; Jones, 1971; Todd, 1983)—countries where WAPE has a relatively long history—but also in Nigeria, where it is now even used in the media, popular literature and even (unofficially) in education (cf., Bamiro, 1991; Elugbe, 1997; Jibril, 1997; Mann, 1996, 1997). In fact, commenting on its increased use in Nigerian society, Tagliamonte, Poplack & Eze (1997) explain that "the developing linguistic situation is that Nigerian Pidgin English is now the preferred means of communication amongst Nigerians of mixed ethnic groups in informal settings" (p. 105). In Ghana, too, where WAPE has long been stigmatized and its use therefore denied, WAPE has spread significantly, as a recent, highly detailed investigation of Ghanaian WAPE (Huber, 1999) clearly establishes.

Along with WAPE, in Ghana, Nigeria, Sierra Leone, Liberia and the Gambia, standard English remains in use as the official language in these countries. Except for Liberia, which uses American English as the model for standard English (Ngovo, 1998), all other anglophone countries in West Africa use British English as their model for the standard variety. Despite some dispute in the past regarding the issue of grammatical differences between British and West African varieties of standard English (cf. Sey, 1973; and American English in the case of Liberian English), there is now a growing acknowledgement that the various anglophone countries of West Africa have indeed developed their own standard English varieties. The differences are not restricted to a distinct phonology and lexicon, but include unique grammatical characteristics (Ahulu, 1994a, 1994b, 1995, 1998; Bamgbose, 1998; Gyasi, 1991; Ngovo, 1998).

SPEAKERS OF WORLD ENGLISH VARIETIES IN
STANDARD ENGLISH CLASSROOMS: AN OVERVIEW

Research has established overwhelmingly that there is a tendency for students who speak a variety of English different from standard English, especially creolized and pidginized varieties, to underachieve academically (Sato, 1989). AAVE speakers also fall into this category (as noted by Labov, 1995; Rickford, chap. 3, this volume; Rickford, 1999).

A number of reasons have been proposed for this tendency:

• Limited access to instruction since students understand the language variety used in the classroom only partially. Research suggests that for speakers of creolized varieties of English, the standard variety may be harder to understand than is generally assumed (de Kleine forthcoming; LeMoine, 2001; Nero, 2002; Reynolds, 1999; Sato, 1989; Smitherman, 2000; Winer, 1993, 1999).

• Poor preparation of most teachers in US classrooms to deal with this population (Adger, Snow, & Christian, 2002; Corson, 2001). One reason is they do not have in-depth knowledge of nonstandard varieties of English, unless they are themselves native speakers of one such variety. Thus, they may find it equally difficult to understand their nonstandard speaking students (cf. Narvaez & Garcia, 1992; Smitherman, 2000; Wheeler & Swords, 2001). This will impact instruction and academic performance negatively. This is especially true when teachers are unaware of their own lack of understanding.

• A wider gap to bridge between spoken and written language—a gap that typically manifests itself on the levels of phonetics, morpho-syntax, as well as semantics (Wolfram, Adger, & Christian, 1999). The gap between the student's nonstandard language variety vis-à-vis the language of the classroom also affects assessment. Currently most assessment procedures presume the use of standard English, with students being penalized for adhering to nonstandard, including World English, linguistic features (Kenkel & Tucker, 1989; Lowenberg, 2002). Such assessment practices clearly provide an additional impediment to academic success for non-standard English speakers. The overrepresentation of World English speakers, more specifically speakers of pidginized and creolized varieties, in special education classes in Canada (Scott, 2003) and the UK (Edwards, 1979) lends support to this viewpoint.

• Differences between the cultural discourse norms of nonstandard varieties and the standard school-based variety. Citing a large number of studies from very diverse communities, including nonstandard English speaking ones, Corson (2001) illustrates how discrepancies between the discourse norms favored in mainstream classrooms and children's home communities can have devastating effects on literacy development.

• Negative teacher attitudes and accompanying low expectations, as noted elsewhere in this volume. For example, a small-scale research project in Canada found that teachers expected less from Caribbean and West African students, with students regularly being "put back in grade, irrespective of their age and ability" and encouraged more often than others to take nonacademic classes (Scott, 2003).

• Challenges with regard to cultural assimilation, including a lack of familiarity with the school culture. For example, in a small study conducted in a large US school system, Sewell (1997) found that West African students were used to different teaching methodologies and often failed to understand teacher expectations. Likewise, Scott (2003), focusing on West African and Caribbean students in Canadian schools, describes these immigrant students' bewilderment at the lack of respect shown to teachers, and the different ways of disciplining students on the part of the teachers.

• Interrupted education. This factor should be considered with the West African student population in light of the recent political upheaval in parts of West Africa (and this will indeed be examined in this study later on). However the systematic underperformance of the diverse set of student populations reviewed earlier—where there is no history of interrupted education, but the main common characteristic is their nonstandard English language background instead—clearly points to the central significance of linguistic background in academic success.

THE PRESENT STUDY: BACKGROUND

The school system where we conducted the present study, located in the suburbs of the Washington D.C. area, began to see an influx of students from the anglophone part of West Africa in the mid 1990s: the number of students from this part of the world enrolled in grades 1–12 was only 14 in 1995, but by September 2003, it had grown to a total of 851, with every English-speaking country of West Africa represented.[1]

With experience having taught that World English-speaking students often do not have sufficient standard English proficiency to succeed in mainstream classrooms, the school district routinely assesses incoming immigrant students who come from officially English-speaking countries—even when they claim English as their home language (as they often do). Table

---

[1]Students from Cameroon, which is only part Anglophone, were excluded, as our data did not clearly establish whether students came from the English or French-speaking part. Total student enrollment in the school system in September 2003 was 163,399, with 19,921 students enrolled in ESL classes.

TABLE 10.1
LEP Designation and ESL Eligibility for Anglophone
West African Students, Grades 1–12

Country of Origin	Eligible for ESL	Designated LEP, Exited ESL	Non-LEP	Unknown	Total
Ghana	187	110	69	41	407
Liberia	64	16	5	31	116
Nigeria	19	16	18	34	87
Sierra Leone	136	36	36	27	235
The Gambia	5	0	1	0	6
TOTAL	411	178	129	133	851
Percentage	48.3%	20.9%	15.2%	15.6%	100%

10.1 shows that of the total of 851 students from anglophone West Africa enrolled in the district, 589 were designated *limited English proficient* (LEP), or 69.2% (columns 1 and 2 combined). Another 133 students had not received an initial language assessment, most likely as a result of erroneously having been identified as fully English proficient. There is, however, good reason to assume limited English proficiency in these cases, too (D. Sewell, personal communication, 2004). Adding these numbers to the total, a percentage that may be as high as 84.5 of all West African students appears to be lacking sufficient standard English language skills to cope with the linguistic demands of the US classroom.

Students that are designated LEP during initial assessment are offered ESL instruction when they enter the system (column 2, Eligible for ESL); this reflects the standard approach in this school system for students with insufficient scores on English language proficiency tests. After their scores on reading and writing tests are sufficient to exit the ESL program, they continue to be monitored for another two years, during which they are still considered LEP (and as such, for instance, remain entitled to accommodations on standardized tests, column 3, *Designated LEP, exited ESL*).

A survey conducted by the school system among ESL teachers in 2002, however, revealed that the placement of World English speakers in ESL classrooms, almost all of whom are from anglophone West Africa, was generally considered a poor fit (Sewell & Rodriguez-McCleary, 2002), thus echoing similar claims voiced elsewhere (Adger, 1997; Crandall, 2003; Narvaez & Garcia, 1992; Pratt-Johnson, 1993). The reason most frequently cited in the survey was that these students' oral language skills typically far exceed their written language skills, making appropriate placement difficult, as the county's ESL program assumes relatively comparable levels of all language skills. In the survey, ESL teachers indicated that while reading skills often did indeed present problems, with students sometimes having limited decoding skills and/or overall comprehension problems, the level of their writing skills was particularly worrisome. Specifically, grammar was considered an area of great challenge for these students. To illustrate, one teacher reflected:

> The content of their writing samples is full of knowledge; yet, the syntax might not meet standard expectations. (Sewell & Rodriguez-McCleary, 2002, p. 5)

Commenting on the writing skills of one particular World English-speaking student, another ESL teacher wrote:

> His English seems to be "baseless." He does not seem to understand patterns of words. He has ideas but no rules in the writing process . . . I feel as though I am trying to correct his bad English. (Sewell & Rodriguez-McCleary, 2002, p. 2)

Limited general academic skills were also believed to be an impediment to performing at age and grade level. It is unclear, though, to what extent poor performance in general content classes stemmed from students' substandard reading and writing skills, or lack of more general academic skills, i.e. whether they were rooted in linguistic or nonlinguistic factors. Irrespective of the underlying reasons for underperformance, though, the survey clearly revealed that the ESL program was unable to meet World English-speaking, i.e., West African, students' needs appropriately, with several teachers suggesting services specifically designed for these students.

The goal of the present study is to examine the actual written language production of World English-speaking West African students by analyzing grammatical errors, in an effort to better understand the linguistic problems of this student population. Such knowledge is required in order to be able to modify current ESL instruction for West African students in ways that will allow these students to receive the much needed full benefit of this type of remedial instruction.

AN ANALYSIS OF WRITING SAMPLES

The corpus for this analysis consisted of 98 writing samples produced by West African students from Ghana (46), Liberia (13), Nigeria (8) and Sierra Leone (31). The data were restricted to samples from secondary level students in grades 6 through 12, as these students were considered to have the most serious problems. Although some of the writings were samples collected as part of students' initial assessment to determine eligibility for ESL services and placement level, the majority of the samples were collected by ESL teachers from students who were already receiving ESL instruction.

The samples were produced by students placed in lower, middle and higher level ESL classes, as reflected in Table 10.2. (It has to be borne in mind, though, that ESL level placement is based on a composite score of which writing is only one part; thus, level of ESL placement cannot be equated to writing level proficiency. In reality, the level of writing ability tends to vary quite significantly within the 3 levels.) Table 10.2 also indicates the numbers of samples, including per country of origin.

Selection of the writing samples was random, with teachers and personnel at the Central Assessment office having been requested to submit writing samples by students from anglophone West Africa, without any further instructions regarding specifics of the samples. In addition, data were also collected on students' country of origin, number of years of schooling in the US (that varied from zero to eight years), number of years of schooling in the home country, language(s) used in the home, current grade level, and current ESL proficiency level.

All writing samples, that varied in length, consisted of essay-format responses to a prompt, such as "Describe a person you want to be like and tell why," "Write about a person in history you would like to meet and why," "Write about a time you helped someone or someone helped you," "Tell about your favorite place. Where is it? Why is it your favorite place?" and "What advice would you give your parents?"

Initial analysis of the corpus revealed—not surprisingly—that the writings displayed a number of areas of weakness, including vocabulary use, organizational structure, punctuation, spelling and grammar. Organizational structure and punctuation were typically presenting serious problems only for students enrolled in the lowest-level ESL classes, but grammar was an area of difficulty for all students, with every writing sample displaying at least several grammatical errors, and many error types having been produced repeatedly. Spelling errors were found in all but 6 samples, but the number of spelling errors per sample was on average much lower than the number of grammatical errors. These general observations then confirm the teachers' impressions identified in the survey: problems with grammar are the most prominent in the writings, providing the basis for the analysis that follows.

TABLE 10.2
Number of Writing Samples Analyzed
by Student's Country of Origin and ESL Level

Country of Origin	Lower ESL Level	Middle ESL Level	Higher ESL Level
Ghana	7	17	22
Liberia	3	7	3
Nigeria	3	1	3
Sierra Leone	12	9	10

Frequent Grammatical Errors

Detailed analysis of the writing samples revealed that there is significant uniformity among the patterns of grammatical errors encountered in the samples, patterns that are moreover observed with students placed at all ESL levels.

In the 98 writing samples analyzed, 19 types of grammatical errors were located in 3 or more writing samples. Not surprisingly, some patterns were encountered far more often than others. Interestingly, though, there was a clear divide between errors found in many samples vis-à-vis errors found in only a few samples, with 10 (out of 19) types of errors encountered in fewer than 10 writing samples (and in several cases far fewer), and the remaining 9 error types located in at least 18 samples, and often many more.

No further quantitative analysis was conducted with regard to errors identified in each individual writing sample. Such analysis could not be justified given that the writing prompts and length of the samples varied, each of which is likely to have influenced the opportunity to produce certain errors (e.g., a writing prompt asking students to describe advice they would give to their parents resulted in high numbers of *will* for hypothetical clauses (see the section "Incorrect Use of the Modal Verb *Will*"). However, the general tendency was clearly for the errors that occurred in many samples to also occur repeatedly within the same sample, thus making the divide between these two groups of errors even more pronounced.

In an attempt to isolate error tendencies among West African students, the account that follows below focuses on frequently encountered errors: those patterns of errors located in at least 18 of the writing samples. These include nine different types, most of which are related to the verb phrase or the noun phrase (with the sole exception of preposition use).

Noun-Related Errors

Plural Marking. A total of 60 out of 98 writing samples contained nouns that were not marked for plural, all in contexts that would have required such marking in standard American English, making this the grammatical error that appeared in the highest number of samples. These errors were by no means random and occurred exclusively in sentences where the context clarified the plural meaning, in most cases through the use of a quantifier:

1. all my relativeØ (G5 A)[2]
2. Six FlagØ [referring to Six Flags, an amusement park] (G11 B2)

---

[2]This code indicates the student's country of origin (G for Ghana, N for Nigeria, L for Liberia, and SL for Sierra Leone), followed by a randomly assigned student number, and the student's ESL placement level, with A corresponding to the lower level, B1 to the middle level, and B2 to the higher ESL level.

The following excerpt illustrates the alternation between marked and unmarked forms, depending on the presence of a quantifier in the noun phrase:

3. Oranges are sweet fruit. Everybody love oranges because of the smell and the color. It [is] one of the famous plantØ on earth. People can make many thing Ø from it. (SL 6 A)

In cases where no quantifier is present, these errors invariably appeared in contexts that left no doubt as to whether the reference was plural:

4. She has black hair and brown eyeØ (G9 B1)

It appears then that—for a number of students at least—plural marking is indeed rule-governed, with overt plural marking on the noun becoming unnecessary in these students' linguistic repertoires when either the overall context or a quantifier in the noun phrase obliterates the need to mark the head of the noun for plural. Not all writings displayed this type of rule-governed (albeit unlike standard American English) use of plural marking, though. Indeed, several of the writing samples created the impression of students being confused, with students alternating randomly between marked and unmarked forms, even when using the same noun phrase with identical reference:

5. I will give it to my parentØ because they are parents (G1 B1)

The impression of confusion is substantiated by hypercorrections found in the data, as in the following excerpt:

6. ... who [how] black's peoples [s crossed out, later added again] and white's people's should live together ... (N1A)

Some instances of what appear to be hypercorrections of plural noun forms could alternatively have been motivated by the students' treating the noun as a count rather than noncount noun. Although there are no vast grammatical differences between standard English in the UK and US vis-à-vis West Africa (cf. McArthur, 2003), the use of certain nouns in West African English as count nouns where standard British and American English treat these as noncount, is well-documented (Ahulu, 1998; Todd, 1983). For instance, the noun *advice* is a count noun in West African standard English, and this noun indeed appeared as such several times in the writing samples, in singular as well as plural form:

7. <u>the</u> advices that I will give my parents ... (SL1 B2)

8. ... such <u>an</u> advice to my parents ... (G22 B2)

Lack of Articles. Another very frequently encountered type of error is the lack of an article where standard American English requires one. The latter only allows the zero article for plural count nouns (e.g., *cars*), noncount nouns (e.g., *sugar*), and singular proper nouns (e.g., *William*). Ungrammatical zero articles were located in 34 writing samples, both where indefinite (9) as well as definite articles (10–11) would have been used in standard American English:

9. Miss T. have small eyes, Ø small mouth and Ø big head (SL11 A)

10. ... in Ø USA (G6 A)

11. She work hard for Ø money (L1 B1)

Zero article use where standard American English would have used an indefinite article is by far the most common error in the data. There appears to be no pattern to this error, and typically the writings that contain this error display correct indefinite article usage elsewhere. It is found both in noun phrases with specific reference as well as nonspecific reference.

The small number of instances where SAE would have required a definite article but none is used tend to reflect exceptions to general patterns of definite article use in standard American English. For instance, with noun phrases containing a definite article typically having specific reference (as in e.g., *I gave him the money*), the noun phrase *money* in the example above (11), which does not have specific reference, constitutes an exception to a more regular pattern. Similarly, since proper nouns, including country names, usually do not take an article, the required use of the definite article in the noun phrase *USA* in (10) forms an exception. It is presumably the irregularities of standard American English, then, that account for the small set of noun phrases lacking definite articles, with students applying more regular rules instead. A relatively high number of samples—a total of 20, including 12 that did not display the original error—contain hypercorrections with regard to article use, i.e, instances where students have used article forms where standard American English does not require them:

12. She issued our documents and <u>an</u> airline tickets (G13 B2)

13. I would like to visit Hawai'i because of <u>the</u> Pearl Harbor (G8 B2)

14. And my aunty buy for me <u>the</u> ice cream (SL9 A)

As the examples illustrate, hypercorrections are found with noncount nouns (14), proper nouns (13), and plural nouns (12).

Lack of Possessive. The third type of noun-related error in the data, encountered in 18 writing samples, is the lack of overt marking of possession in cases where standard American English uses the -'s inflection:

15. my best friendØ mother (GA 6)
16. this guyØ movies (L3 B2)
17. My motherØ name (SL12 A)

Verb-Related Errors

Lack of Subject–Verb Agreement. The most prominent error in the category of verb-related errors is the lack of subject–verb agreement that is found in 47 samples, often repeatedly within one sample:

18. . . . One thing I like about my father is he's strong. He's goes to work everyday, not a day he missØ. My father doØ som[e] activities in the house, he cookØ cleanØ and wishØ [washes] dishes. (L2 B1)
19. She participateØ in school activity . . . she doØ her heir [hair]. She keepØ the classroom clean, whenever a teache[r] is not in class she always goØ and callØ the teacher (SL12 A)

As with most other errors, they typically alternate with correct verb forms, as in *goes* in (18). As can be seen in both examples, this type of error affects both regular and irregular verbs. With this type of error, too, hypercorrections are found in the data, in a total of 15 writing samples, of which 9 did not contain the original error.

20. My parents always <u>tells</u> me about how some people can't have babies. (G1 B2)
21. There are some leaders that <u>uses</u> autocratic leadership styles to get work accomplished (SL5 B2)

Lack of Past Tense Marking. Another prominent error type in the data constitutes the failure to mark the verb phrase for past tense when reference is clearly to past time, in which case standard American English requires the verb to be marked. This error appeared in 45 samples.

22. He was 10 years old when his grand father dieØ (SL9 A)
23. They all helpØ me when I was little (G2 B1)

Most samples that contain this error also use many verb forms that are indeed correctly marked for tense. Consideration should thus be given to the possibility of another principle governing the marking of these verbs, as for instance seen in varieties of Caribbean Creole English where tense marking is determined by discourse patterns (cf. Winford, 2000). Alternatively, phonological rules influencing the deletion of final -*ed* could play a role, as Singler argues for certain varieties of Liberian Creole English[3] (Singler, 1981). It appears, however, that tense marking, or the lack thereof (in past contexts), is fairly random in the writings. As the following excerpt illustrates, lack of past tense marking affects regular and irregular verbs alike, suggesting that it is not simply influenced by a phonological rule pattern deleting -*ed*. Neither do discourse patterns appear to govern the—often frequent—switching back and forth between marked and unmarked forms:

24. Last year Christmas day I **went** to the beach with my brother and his friends, and we **began** to play football (soccer) and I begin to dribbling [dribble] the ball. This time **am** [I am] with the goalkeeper as the goalkeeper **saw** he **thought** I will kick the ball high. I just slam the ball and it is a goal. From there I **began** to swim and my friends come and **said** let us play ball in the water and we begin to play, I **ran** out of the water and **said** I am not playing anymore because I see my aunty, I ask my aunty to buy for me ice-cream and the ice-cream finish, she buy for me hamburger and soft drink and I eat everything, that is the happiest day in my life. (SL8 A)

In 20 writing samples hypercorrections of tense marking were encountered (of which 12 contained the original error as well). This relatively high number of samples with hypercorrections—higher than any other grammatical feature—suggests that tense marking in standard American English is an area of great difficulty and confusion for West African students. Most of the hypercorrected forms consist of *to*-infinitive forms, which are per definition not inflected in standard American English:

25. I decided that I was going to talked to some police officers (L4 B1)

Interestingly, hypercorrections are not restricted to verb forms, but extend to forms that have probably been misanalyzed as verbs (but see also footnote 4), as in:

---

[3]The deletion of word final -*ed* ($/d/$ or $/t/$) is indeed found in the data on adjectives and a few past participles as well, which suggests that phonological patterns may play some role. Examples of adjectives are "I was really **surprise**," "he was **determine**," "**love** ones"; past participle forms found similarly affected are "I would have **improve**," "it should be **base** upon," "a name **call** Darick." These errors are far less frequent in the data than past tense marking errors, including those of irregular past tense verbs.

26. If I could enter the capital [Capitol] or the white house and just take a <u>looked</u>. . . (L5 B1)
27. . . . live my <u>owned</u> life (SL 4 B1)

Incorrect Use of the Modal Verb **Will.**   In a total of 31 writing samples the modal verb *will* is used where standard American English dictates the use of *would.* Instances of incorrect use of *will* typically appeared in conditional sentences expressing an unreal condition[4] (cf. Palmer, 1986), as illustrated in the following sentence:

28. If my dreams came true, I **will** be so happy and I **will** not know what to do (L1 A)

Especially writing prompts presenting hypothetical scenarios elicited many such incorrect forms. For instance, when asked to reflect on what they would do if they had just been given $1000, one student wrote:

29. I **will** go to the store and buy lots of DVD movies. I **will** go buy a big screen stereo with big speaker's. I **will** tell worker's to build a pool outside my house. . . . After all that I **will** go to the store and buy 10 brand new car's (G2 B1)

Additional instances of modal *will* for standard American English *would* are found in structures that Celce-Murcia and Larsen Freeman (1999, p. 147) have labeled 'frozen' modal-like constructions, such as *would like to, would prefer to* and *would love to:*

30. He is the one I **will** like to be (SL7 B2)
31. I **will** prefire [prefer] to an English teacher (G7 A)

Quite unlike most other error types found in the data, the use of *will* for standard American English *would* is an error that is made quite consistently by many writers. In fact, in some writings *would* is never encountered, including in samples with many conditional sentences. In other words, overall there is much less alternation between correct and incorrect forms than seen with other error types. It appears that *would* in this modal function is not at all part of some writers' linguistic repertoires.

---

[4]These instances of *will* need to be distinguished from those carrying future tense, as in "we all thought something *will* happen to her" (N4 B2). Such instances of *will* are analyzed as verbs lacking past tense marking and are not included here.

Lack of a Form of **To Be.**   There are two types of sentences in which *to be* is occasionally found missing. In most instances—27 writing samples to be precise—it concerns a copular verb, as in the following examples:

32. It Ø always noisie [noisy] (G9 B2)
33. It Ø a market scene (N2 B2)
34. Even though you Ø the teacher . . . (SL4 B2)

Typically, the grammatical environment in which this error appears is one in which the absent copula is followed by either an adjective or a noun phrase, as the examples illustrate. In an additional 4 writing samples, the auxiliary verb *to be* is left out where the use of an *-ing* verb form in the verb phrase dictates its use in standard American English. Interestingly, in all but one instance, this is in a verb phrase with *going* as the main verb:

35. That is what I Ø gonna do (G15 B1)
36. The person that Ø going to fix the car . . . (SL1 B2)

Lack of Correct Preposition

The only frequent error not directly related to verb or noun phrases concerns incorrect preposition use, which appeared in a total of 30 writing samples. This was sometimes in the form of a preposition different from the one standard American English uses:

37. In [on] the other hand . . . (G8 B1)
38. . . . to be tolerant to [of] people (SL4 B2)

Most often though, students omitted a preposition where standard American English requires one:

39. . . . not to discriminate [against] us (SL10 B2)
40. I want to go [to] a party (SL3 A)
41. I want to provide them [with] as much things as possible (SL8 B1)

As these examples illustrate, by far the majority of the preposition errors concerned forms that had nonspatial reference, often occurring in idiomatic constructions that combined an adjective, verb or noun with a set preposition. In fact, students hardly ever produced errors in sentences where prepositions had a spatial, literal, meaning.

DISCUSSION

The ESL program in the school district where the research was conducted uses a number of criteria to assess writing skills, grouped in three categories: "composition," "written expression/sentence structure," and "mechanics/usage." "Composition" criteria include the development of a central idea, supported by appropriate details, and the use of multiple paragraphs; "written expression/sentence structure" focuses on the use of precise, descriptive vocabulary and varied sentence structure; the "mechanics/usage" criteria look at the use of correct punctuation and spelling, and overall grammatical correctness, with particular attention to "consistent control of adjectives, adverbs, pronouns, subject-verb agreement, and appropriate verb tenses" (Fairfax County Public Schools, 2002). Many writing samples did indeed fail to meet criteria in other categories as well, particularly in the form of spelling errors (many of which reflected West African English pronunciation), but the data showed that students from anglophone West Africa were placed in the ESL program for reasons that were disproportionally related to issues in the "mechanics/usage" category, with all 98 samples displaying grammatical errors, many of which appeared frequently. This then strongly suggests that the prevalence of grammatical errors has indeed played a significant role in West African students' limited English proficient designation, confirming the impressions of the ESL teachers surveyed earlier, who judged grammar to be an area of great challenge for these students.

Clearly, in order to be able to develop instructional strategies and materials for West African students that are more appropriate than those currently employed in ESL classes, a better understanding is needed of the underlying causes that have led to these students' language problems. Specifically, we need to understand which factor(s) can account for the grammatical errors that pervade these writing samples. In this context, the nature and depth of students' original English language background, as well as the potential role of their home language(s), if other than English, is significant.

The data collected for this project included students' (self-reported) home languages, represented in Table 10.3. Analyzed as a group, the linguistic background of the anglophone West African students is highly diverse, with a total of fourteen languages represented, including English. Given that students' home languages represent a large set of typologically distant languages, first language interference is unlikely to provide a powerful explanation for the overall patterns of errors identified in this research, certainly if we consider that the error patterns were found across different student populations. This is not to say that no L1 interference was present in the data; however, it is doubtful that L1 interference is a significant cause of the error types seen in the data.

TABLE 10.3
Self-Reported Home Languages by Country

Country	Home Languages	Number of Students
Ghana	Twi	42
	Akan	2
	Fanti	1
	Ga	1
Liberia	Sarpo	1
	Grebo	1
	Twi	1
	Creole/English	2
	English	8
Nigeria	Urhobo	1
	Hausa	3
	English/Creole	1
	Ibo	1
	Yoruba	1
Sierra Leone	Creole (or Krio)	23
	Creole/English	5
	Kono	1
	Creole/Temne	2

Note. The labels *Creole* and *Krio* refer to the same language variety in Sierra Leone. Although this language is typically referred to as Krio in the linguistics literature (cf. Holm, 2000; McArthur, 2003), most students used the term Creole.

It is for several reasons equally unlikely that the error types are primarily developmental, i.e., reflective of the second language acquisition process. First, it is clear from students' overall English language development that they had already been exposed to significant amounts of spoken, and to some extent written, English upon entering the school system in the US, as evidenced by their relatively large English vocabulary as well as their overall oral fluency. The types of errors identified here are generally not consistent with this level of (oral) language proficiency. For instance, lack of subject–verb agreement marking is characteristic of beginning level ESL students (Celce-Murcia & Larsen-Freeman, 1999). Likewise, at the more advanced levels, tense marking errors typically do not involve the incorrect use of the simple present when a simple past verb form is required; errors related to tense marking at the intermediate and advanced levels tend to center on the correct use of the simple past versus the present perfect instead (Parrott, 2000).

Plural marking, another frequently found error, is also not an error type that is generally persistent in intermediate and advanced ESL students' interlanguage (Parrott, 2000). Other errors, on the other hand, most notably possessive marking using 's, the lack of article use, and incorrect preposition use can indeed be found at different proficiency levels (cf. Celce-

Murcia & Larsen-Freeman, 1999; Parrott, 2000), and therefore could be developmental in nature. Although this possibility cannot be fully rejected, it seems a much less plausible explanation when we take into consideration the full set of errors, most of which are clearly not developmental. A more uniform, and thus convincing, explanation for the set of error types as a whole, as well as the persistence of these errors at higher proficiency levels, can be found in the influence of the variety of English that many of these students have been exposed to when growing up in West Africa.

In the cases of Liberian and Sierra Leonean students reporting Creole English as their home language, as most did (see Table 10.3), it can safely be assumed that this is a variety of Liberian English Creole or, in the case of Sierra Leonean students, Krio. In addition, as Liberia officially uses American English in education (Ngovo, 1998), students must have been exposed to that as well. Likewise, the linguistic repertoire of students from Sierra Leone has included Creole English (Krio), and in addition must have included standard English, though in this case a standard variety resembling British English. Determining linguistic background as it relates to English is less straightforward in the case of students from Nigeria and Ghana. Official policy in Nigeria requires English as a medium of instruction at the secondary school level only (Mann, 1996), with children's predominant home languages being used at the elementary level. Nevertheless, all seven Nigerian students in our research project reported having attended schools that used English as the medium of instruction from grade one. In Ghana, English is the medium of instruction after the first three years of elementary school (Obeng, 1997), although a recent report from the American Institutes of Research (Awedoba, 2001) shows that, in reality, English is used even in the lowest grades, largely as a result of textbooks being in English, and in some cases because teachers simply do not know the first language of the students well enough to use it as a medium of instruction. Thus, like the students from Nigeria, Ghanaian students, too, are likely to have been exposed to a fair amount of standard English in their classrooms back in West Africa.

Although standard English exposure through education is fairly easily established, exposure of Ghanaian and Nigerian students to WAPE can only be inferred. Yet, with WAPE being as prevalent as it is in West Africa in the countries where the students hail from, it is almost inevitable that students arriving here have had exposure to WAPE in their home countries.[5] It

---

[5]An additional complicating factor in determining West African students' linguistic background, as is the case with many countries where restructured (mostly creolized) varieties of English are used (as for instance in the Caribbean), is that there exists a continuum of dialects between the various standard varieties of English and WAPE (McArthur, 2003), blurring the distinction between the standard English and WAPE, thus making it even harder to assess their former English exposure in any precise way.

is quite conceivable that this exposure was much more intense than exposure to standard English, as the latter is restricted to the classroom, while the former tends to be used in many informal settings.

Closer analysis of grammatical structures found in WAPE (drawing primarily on detailed descriptions presented in Huber, 1999, Elugbe & Omamor, 1991, and Singler, 1981) presents additional evidence suggesting exposure to WAPE: these structures reveal remarkable similarities with the error types encountered most frequently in the writings, thus strongly suggesting that students' linguistic repertoires have indeed included WAPE. In fact, all major error types identified in this study reflect structures also found in WAPE, which will be discussed in detail in the remainder of this chapter.

The most frequently encountered error, the lack of plural marking, is a common feature of WAPE, where either the context typically clarifies the meaning (McArthur, 2003), or another element, usually a preceding quantifier, does so explicitly.

In WAPE, and also in standard varieties of West African Standard English (WASE) for that matter, article usage is different when compared to standard American English, and this may very well account for the frequent errors in the data with regard to article usage. In most Atlantic Creoles, overt articles, both definite and indefinite, tend to be used for noun phrases with specific reference, but the zero article is used for noun phrases that have generic (i.e., nonspecific) reference (Holm, 2000). This pattern is confirmed for Ghanaian Pidgin English (Huber, 1999), Liberian Creole English (Singler, 1981), and Nigerian English (Elugbe & Omamor, 1991).

Incorrect article usage may further have been fueled by article usage in WASE, as even local standard varieties in West Africa have a tendency to use the zero article in grammatical environments that would not allow this in standard American English (Ahulu, 1994b; Bamiro, 1995; Bokamba, 1992; Kirk-Greene, 1971).

Unlike errors related to article usage, which can potentially be traced to both WAPE and WASE, the lack of -'s to mark possession in a noun phrase is clearly rooted solely in WAPE, which typically uses juxtaposition to express possession, with the possessor followed by the entity possessed. Indeed, this feature is found in many varieties of pidginized and creolized English, in both the Caribbean and West Africa (Holm, 2000).

Some of the most significant differences between WAPE and standard American English lie with the verb phrase (cf. Huber, 1999), which is hardly surprising given that the structure of the verb phrase is generally considered central in distinguishing restructured varieties from their non-restructured lexifier languages (Holm, 2000). The data indeed show many errors in the students' writings that are related to the structure of the verb phrase. One basic characteristic of the verb phrase in WAPE is that it is generally not inflected for number, person, or tense and aspectual distinctions. As noted earlier, the context clarifies time reference (Winford, 2000). Thus, verbs have one invariant form only, with the categories of tense, mood and aspect expressed through the use of preverbal markers, a pattern found in most pidginized and creolized languages around the world.

Absence of the copular verb *to be* is another error type in the data that can be explained by the features of WAPE. As a matter of fact, copula absence is a feature deeply rooted in pidginized and creolized varieties of English, including in West Africa (cf. Huber, 1999). This is not to say that WAPE does not possess copular verb forms; in fact, it has several. However, whenever followed by an adjectival phrase, the verb *to be* tends to be absent. This has been attested in Krio, Ghanaian Pidgin English and Nigerian Pidgin English (Holm, 2000; Huber, 1999).

Another frequent error related to the verb phrase, as pointed out before, concerns the use of the modal verb *will* for *would*, found in conditional sentences in the writings, in addition to a handful of set phrases. Unlike all other forms discussed so far, though, this one does not seem widely used in WAPE. In fact, Singler (1981), which focuses on Liberian English, is the only source that attests this use of *will*, the predominant modal verb form for this function in WAPE being *go* (Huber, 1999). On the other hand, there is some evidence that this form may be used in at least some standard varieties of West African English. McArthur (2003) alludes to its use when he mentions *will* being used for *would* in Ghanaian Standard English (without specifying its particular grammatical role). The fact that this use of *will* is identified in writings of students from all four countries involved here, roughly to the same extent, suggests this may very well be the case.

Like the incorrect use of *will*, errors in prepositions can not be traced to WAPE as straightforwardly as all other error types. With the exception of Ghanaian Pidgin English (cf. Huber, 1999), there is simply not enough detailed information available on preposition use in WAPE varieties to establish a direct link between specific errors as manifested in the data and those in WAPE. Nevertheless, in general, the preposition inventory of pidginized and creolized English varieties tends to be significantly smaller as compared to standard English, with prepositions often having a wider semantic range than they do in standard English, resulting overall in a poor match between the latter and WAPE, thus creating opportunity for interference errors. Secondly, prepositions tend to have primarily spatial reference in restructured varieties, including in WAPE (cf. Huber, 1999). This pattern is indeed reflected in the data, with many preposition errors appearing in phrases with nonspatial reference, often occurring in idiomatic constructions that combine an adjective, verb or noun with a set preposition, as illustrated by the example: "In [on] the other hand."

Finally, it should be highlighted that preposition errors, unlike most other error types encountered frequently in the data, are notoriously persistent in the language of all ESL learners, including at the higher proficiency levels (Celce-Murcia & Larsen-Freeman, 1999). In the absence of clear patterns of specific preposition errors, then, including patterns cutting across student populations with different home language backgrounds, the influence of students' home languages other than WAPE varieties should also be considered with this error type.

Analyzed as a group, the errors provide convincing evidence that WAPE exerts a strong influence on the written language production of students from the anglophone part of West Africa, and, with literacy skills in standard English being a prerequisite for academic success in US classrooms, on overall academic achievement.[6] Furthermore, although WASE may underlie some of the students' error tendencies, as has been detailed, the significance of WASE on the whole seems much more limited than the influence of WAPE. In fact, most of the grammatical characteristics that set WASE apart from (American and British) standard English as they have been documented to date (Ahulu, 1994a, 1994b, 1995; Bamiro, 1995; Bokamba, 1992; McArthur, 2003) never appeared in the data, or did so very sporadically.

To date, publications dealing with the academic underperformance of students from the anglophone part of West Africa in American classrooms have emphasized interrupted formal education in students' home countries as a leading cause of students' literacy problems, in addition to social and cultural adjustment difficulties (Crandall, 1995; Crandall & Greenblatt, 1998; Scott, 2003; Sewell, 1997; Sewell, Rodriguez-McCleary, & Staehr, 2003). Although social and cultural adjustment are likely to have had some influence on students academic performance (as is typically the

---

[6]Additional evidence supporting the crucial role of WAPE on the error types identified in this study, and thereby written language production, comes from similar studies that have analyzed the writings of Caribbean Creole English-speaking students in US educational settings. In the study mentioned earlier that was conducted among Caribbean Creole English speakers in elementary and secondary schools in Baltimore, de Kleine (in press) found a set of error types that was remarkably similar to the one presented here. In fact, all prominent error types described here were isolated in that study as well, with the exceptions of preposition errors and errors of modal *will*, of which the latter is hardly surprising as the use of *will* in conditional sentences is not a feature of Caribbean Creole English. Furthermore, Nero's analysis of grammatical errors in the writings of Caribbean students enrolled at a college in New York City included the same set of errors identified here (Nero, 2001), with the exception of the two error types not found in de Kleine either. The impressive overlap of error types described in these studies and the present one provides strong support for the claim that the influence of the restructured varieties of English used in students' home countries is indeed a powerful factor in explaining the errors West African students produce in US classrooms, and by extension, the language-related problems they experience here.

case for any immigrant student), the present study sheds serious doubt on the claim that interrupted education is the central cause of West African students' writing problems. In fact, of the 98 students whose writings were analyzed for the present study—all of whom were enrolled in ESL it should be remembered—only 21 had experienced interrupted education, representing a percentage of 21.4%. The specific percentages by country are reported in Table 10.4. The fact that only a small number had had their education interrupted shows beyond any doubt that this factor—for the students involved in this study at least—cannot explain the writing problems of the group of West African students as a whole.

The findings in the present study indicate that the principal cause of students' literacy challenges lies elsewhere: their West African English language background, primarily in the form of WAPE, is interfering significantly with their production of standard American English. As conversations with assessment personnel and ESL teachers in the school system where the research was conducted revealed, the problem of extensive WAPE interference was often compounded by a lack of knowledge on the part of ESL educators regarding pidginized and creolized language varieties, in particular WAPE, including the fundamental differences between WAPE and standard American English. As a result, West African students' errors tended to be misanalyzed as developmental—quite an understandable misinterpretation, as these errors indeed superficially resemble developmental ones. Furthermore, when these errors are truly of a developmental nature—as they usually are with regular ESL students—they tend to be associated with relatively low-level proficiency skills. This, then, led teachers to the incorrect conclusion that the errors pervading the writings of so many West African students were indeed a reflection of an overall low level of English proficiency, a conclusion drawn often in spite of additional evidence suggesting the opposite, such as elaborate vocabulary use. In some cases teachers even maintained that many of the West African students were essentially illiterate—a claim clearly refuted by the writings analyzed for this study. The research here has only focused on West African students in ESL classes, but there is good reason to believe that West African students' writing problems may have been misunderstood by mainstream teachers as

TABLE 10.4
Percentage of Students With Interrupted Education by Country

Country	Students With Interrupted Education
Ghana	17.4%
Liberia	35.7%
Nigeria	12.5%
Sierra Leone	22.5%

well, given the widespread lack of knowledge about language variation among teachers in general (cf. Adger, Snow & Christian, 2002).

CONCLUSION

The present study has established the significance of linguistic interference, primarily in the form of WAPE, in the writings of students from the anglophone part of West Africa. Although factors related to cultural assimilation and particularly to interrupted education should by no means be ignored in our attempts to explain the academic challenges of West African students in US schools, the present study has provided evidence strongly suggesting that it is first and foremost these students' unique English language background that has undermined their standard English literacy development, and thereby overall academic achievement.

The typical ESL curriculum tends to be a poor fit for students from anglophone West Africa (Crandall, 2003; Sewell, 1997; Sewell, Rodriguez-McCleary, & Staehr, 2003). Our data from the school system tentatively confirmed this: many students had received ESL instruction for several years without being promoted to the next ESL level, in some instances up to as many as six (!) years. This is perhaps not entirely surprising given the current focus in many ESL classrooms on academic content, often at the expense of grammar instruction.[7] If West African students are indeed primarily at a disadvantage as a result of linguistic interference, as these findings suggest, then obviously the role of WAPE needs to be addressed in the classroom. It is hard to see how that can be done more efficiently than by providing explicit grammar instruction, contrasting WAPE features directly with standard English (in a meaningful context), so as to heighten students' awareness of the differences (for more information on specific pedagogical strategies within this approach, see Craig, 1999, and Winer, chap. 5, this volume). This will crucially have to include an in-depth analysis of WAPE (and possibly also WASE), followed by a comparison with standard American English. In addition, writing errors should generally not be left uncorrected; it is important, however, that correction occurs in the context of an overall contrastive analysis approach, as otherwise students may fail to understand why they have been corrected.

---

[7]In the Anglophone Caribbean, where the role of Creole interference in academic underachievement is well established (cf. Craig, 1999, 2001), a shift in the 1980s and 1990s in language education from a focus on meaning at the expense of a focus on form, i.e. grammar, has been linked to lower performance in education (Craig, 2001). Similarly, in Singapore, where many students' first language background includes a restructured variety of English, the trend of a stronger emphasis on communicative ability and content as opposed to language structure has been cited as the main cause of decreased writing ability among university students (Davie, 2003).

Furthermore, as Kaldor (1991) rightly points out, teaching standard English to speakers of nonstandard English "requires a great deal of tact and very sophisticated language educational skills on the part of the teacher" (p. 80). The teacher has to ensure that the nonstandard speaker is afforded the same educational opportunities that standard speakers receive, "while at the same time ensuring that no child is made to feel embarrassed about his/her [nonstandard] speech variety."

Undoubtedly, an important prerequisite for a contrastive approach is an understanding and appreciation of varieties of English on the part of (ESL) teachers, including an ability to distinguish between developmental and interference errors. Although such knowledge is currently lacking in many teachers, an increased acknowledgement in the field of TESOL that the nature and value of World English varieties merits special attention in teacher education programs is in this context very encouraging (TESOL, 2003).

QUESTIONS FOR DISCUSSION AND REFLECTIVE WRITING

1. This chapter lists a number of reasons—linguistic, attitudinal, and sociological—for the academic underachievement of speakers of nonstandard varieties of English. What steps might be taken by school districts to address each of these reasons?

2. Compare and contrast the linguistic and educational issues pertaining to West African students with two other groups discussed in this volume. Discuss your most striking findings.

3. De Kleine's study shows that grammar plays a disproportionately significant role in the placement and assessment of West African students. What are the consequences of this role? Work with a partner or group to design a unit that would address the grammatical issues pertaining to West African students.

REFERENCES

Adger, C. (1997). Issues and implications of English dialects for teaching English as a second language. *TESOL Professional Papers 3*. Retrieved March 5, 2003, from http://www.tesol.org/pubs/profpapers/adger1.html

Adger, C., Snow, C., & Christian, D. (2002). *What teachers need to know about language.* McHenry, IL: Delta Systems.

Ahulu, S. (1994a). How Ghanaian is Ghanaian English? *English Today, 38*, 25–29.

Ahulu, S. (1994b). Styles of Standard English. *English Today, 40*, 10–17.

Ahulu, S. (1995). Variation in the use of complex verbs in international English. *English Today, 42*, 28–34.

Ahulu, S. (1998). Grammatical variation in international English. *English Today, 56,* 19–25.

Angogo, R., & Hancock, I. (1980). English in Africa: Emerging standards or diverging regionalisms? *English World-Wide, 1,* 67–97.

Awedoba, A. K. (2001). *Policy dialogue and classroom-based research on Ghana's school language policy.* Retrieved January 20, 2004, from http://www.dec.org/pdf_docs/PNACL069.pdf

Bamgbose, A. (1998). Torn between norms: Innovations in World Englishes. *World Englishes, 17,* 1–14.

Bamiro, E. O. (1991). The social and functional power of Nigerian English. *World Englishes, 10,* 275–286.

Bamiro, E. O. (1995). Syntactic variation in West African English. *World Englishes, 14,* 189–204.

Banjo, A. (1997). On codifying Nigerian English: Research so far. In A. Bamgbose, A. Banjo, & A. Thomas (Eds.), *New Englishes. A West African perspective* (pp. 203–231). Trenton, NJ: African World Press.

Bokamba, E. G. (1992). The Africanization of English. In B. Kachru (Ed.), *The other tongue. English across cultures* (2nd ed., pp. 125–147). Urbana and Chicago: University of Illinois Press.

Breitborde, L. B. (1988). The persistence of English in Liberia: Sociolinguistic factors. *World Englishes, 7,* 15–23.

Celce-Murcia, M., & Larsen-Freeman, D. (1999). *The grammar book. An ESL/EFL teacher's course* (2nd ed.). Boston: Heinle and Heinle.

Christie, P. (Ed.). (2001). *Due respect. Papers on English and English-related creoles in the Caribbean in honour of Professor Robert Le Page.* Barbados: University of West Indies Press.

Coelho, E. (1991). *Caribbean students in Canadian schools* (Vol. 2). Markham, Ontario: Pippin.

Corson, D. (2001). *Language diversity and education.* Mahwah, NJ: Lawrence Erlbaum Associates.

Craig, D. R. (1999). *Teaching language and literacy. Policies and procedures for vernacular situations.* Georgetown: Education and Development Services.

Craig, D. R. (2001). Language education revisited in the Commonwealth Caribbean. In P. Christie (Ed.), *Due respect. Papers on English and English-related creoles in the Caribbean in honour of Professor Robert Le Page* (pp. 61–78). Barbados: University of West Indies Press.

Crandall, J. A. (1995). Reinventing (America's) schools: The role of the applied linguist. In J. E. Alatis (Ed.), *Linguistics and the education of language teachers: Ethnolinguistic, psycholinguistic, and sociolinguistic aspects* (pp. 412–427). Washington, DC: Georgetown University Press.

Crandall, J. A. (2003) They DO speak English: World Englishes in U.S. schools. *ERIC/CLL News Bulletin, 26,* 1–3.

Crandall, J. A., & Greenblatt, L. (1998). Teaching beyond the middle: Meeting the needs of underschooled and high-achieving immigrant students. In M. Basterra (Ed.), *Excellence and equity in education for language minority students: Critical issues and promising practices* (pp. 43–80). Chevy Chase, MD: Mid-Atlantic Equity Center.

Davie, S. (2003). Shocking grasp of English among JC students. *The Straights Times,* September 29, 2003. Retrieved on January 4, 2004, from http://straitstimes.asia1.com.sg/education/story/0,1870,212176,00.html

de Kleine, C. (in press). The acquisition of standard American English by speakers of Creole English: Interference in the writings of K–12 students in the Baltimore City public school system. In A. K. Spears & J. DeJongh (Eds.), *Black language in the U.S. and Caribbean: Education, history, styles and structure.*

Edwards, V. (1979). *The West Indian language issue in British schools. Challenges and responses.* London: Routledge and Kegan Paul.

Edwards, V. (1986). *Language in a black community.* San Diego: College-Hill Press.

Elugbe, B. O. (1997). Nigerian Pidgin: Problems and prospects: In A. Bamgbose, A. Banjo, & A. Thomas (Eds.), *New Englishes. A West African perspective* (pp. 284–299). Trenton, NJ: African World Press.

Elugbe, B. O., & Omamor, A. P. (1991). *Nigerian Pidgin. Background and prospects.* Ibadan, Nigeria: Heinemann.

Fairfax County Public Schools. (2002). *ESOL WRITING Rubric for Program Placement, Grades 4–12.* Falls Church, VA: Author.

Gyasi, I. K. (1991). Aspects of English in Ghana. *English Today, 26*, 26–31.

Holm, J. (1989). *Pidgins and creoles. Vol. 2. Reference survey.* Cambridge: Cambridge University Press.

Holm, J. (2000). *An introduction to pidgins and creoles.* Cambridge: Cambridge University Press.

Huber, M. (1999). *Ghanaian Pidgin English in its West African context. A sociohistorical and structural analysis.* Amsterdam: John Benjamins.

Jibril, M. (1997). The elaboration of the functions of Nigerian Pidgin. In A. Bamgbose, A. Banjo, & A. Thomas (Eds.), *New Englishes. A West African perspective* (pp. 232–247). Trenton, NJ: African World Press.

Jones, E. (1971). Krio: An English-based language of Sierra Leone. In J. Spencer (Ed.), *The English language in West Africa* (pp. 66–94). London: Longman.

Kaldor, S. (1991). Standard Australian English as a second language and a second dialect. In M. L. Tickoo & L. Makhan (Eds.), *Languages and standards: Issues, attitudes, case studies.* (ERIC Document Reproduction Service No. ED 347 798).

Kenkel, J. M., & Tucker, R. W. (1989). Evaluation of institutionalized varieties of English and its implications for placement and pedagogy. *World Englishes, 8*, 201–214.

Kirk-Greene, A. (1971). The influence of West African languages on English. In J. Spencer (Ed.), *The English language in West Africa* (pp. 123–144). London: Longman.

Labov, W. (1995). Can reading failure be reversed? In V. Gadsen & D. Wagner (Eds.), *Literacy among African-American youth* (pp. 39–68). Cresskill, NJ: Hampton.

LeMoine, N. (2001). Language variation and literacy acquisition in African American students. In J. L. Harris, A. G. Kamhi, & K. E. Pollock (Eds.), *Literacy in African American communities* (pp. 169–194). Mahwah, NJ: Lawrence Erlbaum Associates.

Lowenberg, P. (2002). Assessing English in the expanding circle. *World Englishes, 21*, 431–435.

Mann, C. (1996). Anglo-Nigerian Pidgin in Nigerian education: A survey of policy, practices and attitudes. In T. Hickey & J. Williams (Eds.), *Language, education and society in a changing world* (pp. 93–106). Clevedon, UK: IRAAL/Multilingual Matters. (ERIC Document Reproduction Service No. ED 397 662).

Mann, C. (1997). *Language, mass communication, and national development: The role, perceptions and potential of Anglo-Nigerian Pidgin in the Nigerian mass media.* Paper presented at the 3rd International Conference on Language in Development, Langkawi, Malaysia. (ERIC Document Reproduction Service No. ED 412 740).

McArthur, T. (2003). *Oxford guide to World English.* Oxford: Oxford University Press (paperback version).

Narvaez, D. H., & Garcia, M. L. (1992). *Meeting the needs of newly-arrived West Indian students in New York public schools.* National Origin Unit, Equity Assistance Center, Baruch College, CUNY. (ERIC Document Reproduction Service Center No. ED359307).

Nero, S. (2001). *Englishes in contact. Anglophone Caribbean students in an urban college.* Cresskill, NJ: Hampton Press.

Nero, S. (2002). Englishes, attitudes, education. *English Today, 18*, 53–56.

Ngovo, B. (1998). English in Liberia. *English Today, 54*, 46–50.

Obeng, S. G. (1997). An analysis of the linguistic situation in Ghana. *African Languages and Cultures, 10*, 63–81.

Palmer, F. (1986). *Mood and modality.* Cambridge: Cambridge University Press.

Parrott, M. (2000). *Grammar for English language teachers.* Cambridge: Cambridge University Press.

Pratt-Johnson, Y. (1993). Curriculum for Jamaican Creole-speaking students in New York City. *World Englishes, 12,* 257–264.

Reynolds, S. B. (1999). Comprehension problems between American standard English and Hawaii Creole English in Hawaii public schools. In J. Rickford & S. Romaine (Eds.), *Creole genesis, discourse and attitudes: Studies celebrating Charlene Sato* (pp. 303–319). Amsterdam: John Benjamins.

Rickford, J. R. (1999). Language diversity and academic achievement in the education of African American students—An overview of the issues. In C. T. Adger, D. Christian, & O. Taylor (Eds.), *Making the connection. Language and academic achievement among African American students* (pp. 1–20). McHenry, IL: Delta Systems and Washington, DC: Center for Applied Linguistics.

Sato, C. J. (1989). A nonstandard approach to standard English. *TESOL Quarterly, 23,* 259–282.

Scott, J. L. (2003). English language and communication: Issues for African and Caribbean immigrant youth in Toronto. In P. Anisef & K. M. Kilbride (Eds.), *Managing two worlds: The experiences and concerns of immigrant youth in Ontario.* Retrieved November 17, 2003, from http://ceris.metropolis.net/Virtual%20Library/education/scott1.html

Schnukal, A., & Marchese, L. (1983). Creolization of Nigerian Pidgin English. *English World-Wide, 4,* 17–26.

Sewell, D. (1997, June/July). World English speakers in ESL classes: Not a perfect match. *TESOL Matters, 7*(1), 22.

Sewell, D., & Rodriguez-McCleary, B. (2002). *ES, MS, & HS ESOL teachers responses to World English survey 3/02.* Unpublished manuscript.

Sewell, D., Rodriguez-McCleary, B., & Staehr, D. (2003). Working with World English-speakers from the Outer Circle. *WATESOL News, 34,* 1–2, 10.

Sey, K. (1973). *Ghanaian English.* Basingstoke: Macmillan.

Singler, J. V. (1981). *An introduction to Liberian English.* Peace Corps/Michigan State University, African Studies Center.

Singler, J. V. (1997). The configuration of Liberia's Englishes. *World Englishes, 16,* 205–231.

Smitherman, G. (2000). *Talkin' that talk: Language, culture, and education in African America.* New York: Routledge.

Tagliamonte, S., Poplack, S., & Eze, E. (1997). Plural marking patterns in Nigerian Pidgin English. *Journal of Pidgin and Creole Languages, 12,* 103–129.

TESOL. (2003). *TESOL/NCATE program standards. Standards for the accreditation of initial programs in P-12 ESL teacher education.* Alexandria, VA: Author.

Todd, L. (1983). The English language in West Africa. In R. Bailey & M. Gorlach (Eds.), *English as a world language* (pp. 281–305). Ann Arbor: University of Michigan Press.

Wheeler, R. S., & Swords, R. (2001). *"My goldfish name is Scaley" is what we say at home: Code-Switching—A potential tool for reducing the achievement gap in linguistically diverse classrooms.* Paper presented at the Annual Meeting of the National Council of Teachers of English in Baltimore, MD. (ERIC Document Reproduction Service No. ED 461 877).

Winer, L. (1993). Teaching speakers of Caribbean English Creoles in North American classrooms. In A. W. Glowka & D. M. Lance (Eds.), *Language variation in North American English: Research and teaching* (pp. 191–198). New York: Modern Language Association.

Winer, L. (1999). Comprehension and resonance. English readers and English Creole texts. In J. R. Rickford & S. Romaine (Eds.), *Creole genesis, discourse and attitudes: Studies celebrating Charlene Sato* (pp. 391–406). Amsterdam: John Benjamins.

Winford, D. (2000). Tense and aspect in Sranan and the creole prototype. In J. McWhorter (Ed.), *Language change and language contact in pidgins and creoles* (pp. 383–442). Amsterdam: John Benjamins.

Wolfram, W., Adger, C. T., & Christian, D. (1999). *Dialects in school and communities.* Mahwah, NJ: Lawrence Erlbaum Associates.

Part VII

ASIAN ENGLISHES

Chapter 11

Indian Versus American Students' Writing in English

Anam K. Govardhan
Western Connecticut State University

KEY POINTS

- Background of English language teaching in India.
- Error analysis of American and Indian students' writing.
- Discourse analysis and discussion of American and Indian students' writing.
- Comparison and contrast of key rhetorical differences between American and Indian students' writing in English.
- Suggestions for American teachers to help Indian students writing in the US.

INTRODUCTION

Indian Students constitute the largest foreign student population in the United States. In the 2003–2004 academic year, 79,736 or 13.9% of the total number of foreign students in the US were from India (*Open Doors 2003*). A majority of Indian students (79%) pursue graduate programs leading to Master's and doctoral degrees with their popular majors being business, engineering, computer science, physical and life sciences, and social sciences in that order. Indian students' preference for the US is not only based on the high quality education available here but also due to Indian students' familiarity with the English language and western educational system.

ENGLISH IN INDIA

English Christian missionaries started teaching English in their schools around 1813; in fact, they prepared students to pursue higher education in the universities the British started in India in 1857 (Ravindran, 2003). Lord Macaulay was instrumental in introducing English as the medium of instruction in the universities in India in 1857. In the beginning, the curriculum in schools and colleges reflected the British government's need for English educated Indians to play a supporting role to the British in India and elsewhere. By the end of the 20th century, English became a part of the long list of Indian languages. Like other Indian languages, English is being increasingly used today in "imaginative and creative contexts" (Kachru, 1986).

India's multilingual society needed a link language to unite the population. English served that purpose before and after independence from Britain in 1947. The Indian Constitution of 1950 ensured the use of English along with Hindi as a link language, and the Official Languages Act of 1963 permitted the use of English for an indefinite period (Chaudary, 2001). It is the sole medium of instruction in all post-secondary institutions though regional Indian languages are offered as the medium of instruction in state-run institutions at the school level. However, even at the school level, most Indian parents prefer to send their children to private institutions that offer instruction in English. Today more than 350 million Indians use English in their daily lives. English is the language of business, commerce, banking, science and technology, etc. India also boasts of the third largest publisher of English language books in the world (Chaudary, 2001). Indians writing in English have won the Nobel Prize for literature, the Booker Prize, the Pulitzer Prize, just to name a few. India also has the largest circulated English daily in the world today—*The Times of India*.

ENGLISH LANGUAGE TEACHING IN INDIA

English language proficiency of Indian students varies widely depending on where they were schooled. Students who attend English medium schools have no problem communicating in English, but the same cannot be said of those who attend regional language medium schools. English language teaching has also not been geared fully to meet the challenges of the growing number of children attending schools and colleges in the country. Although a few English language teachers have had the benefit of attending the premier English language training institutes, most of the English language teachers have little or no training in teaching English. To compound the problem, there is a "wide-spread and deeply rooted assumption among teachers that the *only* problems which students have in composition are *linguistic* problems—chiefly, the problems of syntax. The 'teaching' of composition rarely amounts to anything more than the remedial teaching of grammar" (Das, 1978, p. 60). The emphasis on teaching mechanics of expression and preparing students for the essays based on texts leave no room for students to develop the discovery process and purposive expression. The products of such a system in India have problems communicating with their peers, teachers, and expressing their ideas in either speaking or writing (Chakraverty & Gautum, 2000). The problem is compounded further by the absence of any textbooks on rhetoric and composition. The result is that English instructors depend on their own intuition and experience to teach English.

The status of teaching composition in India has not changed very much over the years. On the very well-established pattern of teaching composition, Bhatia (1977) observes that "the teacher introduces a topic, writes an outline on the blackboard with or without student-participation, and the students are expected to develop the theme into a full-fledged composition" (p. 59).

Aware of the lack of training of Indian students in western rhetorical tradition, institutions in the United States, Canada and other countries require Indian students to prove their English language proficiency by taking tests like the TOEFL, TSE, etc. Even when they comply with the language proficiency requirements, they are required to take additional English language proficiency tests for placement purposes as soon as they arrive at US institutions. In the regular writing classes, when the instructors notice the rhetorical differences between the American and Indian student writing, they hardly know how to address them.

This chapter is based on a study attempting to bring out the linguistic and rhetorical differences between Indian and American student writing and suggest ways to address them. The study involved the collection of information about writing tasks, selection of writing samples, training graders/raters, scoring student writing samples, selecting linguistic and rhetorical tools for analyses, interpretation and comparison of analyses, identifying areas of similarities and dissimilarities, highlighting their implications for teaching, and finally suggesting measures to bridge the gap between American and Indian student writing in English.

PREVIOUS RESEARCH

Discourse analysis of native and non-native speakers of English has not elicited much interest in academic circles in the United States, and that explains why there is not much information available in the libraries. For example, Kaplan's (1966) study on the differences in writing between native and non-native speakers of English remains the most influential in the field. According to Kaplan, the rhetorical patterns in English are based on the linear Platonic–Aristotelian thought patterns. Several studies (Hinds, 1983; Kachru, 1988) following Kaplan confirm that differences exist in the rhetorical patterns of native and non-native speakers of English. As for India, though the British had been in India for well over 300 years, their influence on the Indian thought patterns is not very significant. In addition, in the absence of teaching western rhetorical models and strategies associated with them, Indian students seem to depend on the Sanskrit tradition, which is synonymous with Indian rhetorical tradition.

Kachru (1988) cites extensive studies (Das Gupta, 1975; Heinmann, 1964; Pandharipande, 1983) on Indian rhetorical tradition to suggest that Indians tend to think in "a circle or a spiral of continuously developing potentialities, and not on a straight line of progressive stages," and the Indian concept is cyclic, and its logic syllogism is non-sequential.

DATA FOR THE STUDY

This author has chosen his host institution for the collection of American student writing samples. He administered a writing task in the freshman writing program and collected nearly 350 American student writing samples. During his trip to India in 2001 and 2002, the author visited colleges in Bombay, Hyderabad, and Madras and administered the same writing task in the freshman classes and collected about 200 Indian student writing samples. Inviting volunteers among his colleagues who teach writing, the author conducted calibration sessions to help them become familiar with the Test of Written English holistic scoring guide (the TOEFL and TSE Bulletin 1993–94). The student-writing samples were scored twice by the trained graders, and when the difference in score was more than one, a third grader was asked to look at the writing sample. After the scoring exercise was over, the writing samples were pooled together based on the scores, and six student writing samples each from American and Indian students representing the range of scores from 1 to 6 were chosen for linguistic and rhetorical analyses. The author used error analysis and T-Unit analysis forming linguistic analyses, and F-unit analysis forming rhetorical analysis. Finally, he also looked at the writing samples from the point of view of their success in fulfilling the descriptors mentioned in the ETS's *Test of Written English Scoring Guide*, namely, addressing the task, development, organization, syntactic complexity, coherence, diction, grammar, punctuation, and mechanics.

Error analysis was used to identify the types and patterns of errors that could be associated with the essays placed in the upper half (scores ranging from four to six) and lower half (scores ranging from one to three). Likewise, the T-unit analysis was used to show the differences between the two different levels of essays in handling complex syntactic structures. F-Unit analysis was used to bring out the differences in the rhetorical qualities. In order to do so, two sets of student writing samples both American and Indian, one with scores of six and the other with scores of three, were chosen for comparison.

ANALYSIS OF WRITING SAMPLES

Error Analysis

Since the quality of student writing can be affected by the kinds of errors a student commits in writing, each of the student writing samples was closely examined to identify six different categories of errors based on the paradigm suggested by Kroll (1990). They are outlined in Table 11.1 below.

Results and Discussion

The information provided in Table 11.1 does not conclusively prove the differences in writing quality between upper and lower half student writing samples. Although the length of the essays belonging to the upper half (494 words in IN 57 and 503 words in AM 322) and lower half (380 words in IN

TABLE 11.1
Results of Error Analysis of Both American
and Indian Student Writing Samples

Student #	Score	# of Words	Sentence Structure	Verb Centered	Reference	Word Level	Article	Punctuation	Total
Upper Half									
IN 57	6	494			1		1	2	4
AM 322	6	503	2			5		4	11
Lower Half									
IN 62	3	380	6	1		8		1	16
AM 200	3	419	4			6	1	2	13

Note. IN = Indian Student; AM = American Student.

62 and 419 words in AM 200) provides a superfluous distinction between them, the distribution of errors in the upper (4 in Indian student writing and 11 in American student writing) and lower half papers (16 in Indian student writing and 13 in American student writing) throw some light on their respective qualities. For example, the lower half papers have serious errors like the following:

Indian Student 62:

Sentence 10: India's gupta age is called Golden age because of the rich culture has existed that time (Sentence Structure).

Sentence 15: This was the time situation in olden times (Sentence Structure).

Sentence 21: Like for females: they have also become challengable their way of dressing, their conversating languae etc. has changed which shows that they are trying to modernize themselves (Sentence Structure).

American Student 200

Sentence 11: End of commercial (Fragment).

Sentence 15: More examples, women half dressed standing next to cars, eating cookies, drinking soda its everwhere (Fragment).

Sentence 17: Although it is changing . . . slowly (Fragment).

On the other hand, the errors in upper half papers are mostly in punctuation and mechanics, as in:

Indian Student 57

Sentence 4: vedic instead of Vedic (Capitalization)

Sentence 9: sister-in-laws instead of sister-in-law's (Apostrophe)

Sentence 12: such tradition instead of such a tradition (Omission of article a)

American Student 322

Sentence 5: Many of the songs in this particular category are about male rock stars who see themselves as the main dish on a menu (Punctuation—comma before who).

Sentence 6: They act as though they have thousands of silicone enhanced women just drooling over their mouth watering success (Punctuation: omission of a hyphen between silicone and enhanced).

Sentence 7:   The worst part of all this is the males egotistical attitude (Punctuation—Omission of apostrophe for males').

The examples from both sets of student writing suggest that while the errors in upper half papers are mostly performance based errors, the errors in the lower half papers are more serious and likely to obscure the meaning. Likewise, the frequency of error distribution seems to be one of the criteria for assigning a writing sample to the lower half. For example, student writing sample IN 57 has 494 words with four errors, i.e. one error for almost 126 words, and therefore received a score of six. On the other hand, student writing sample IN 62 has 380 words with 16 errors, i.e., one error for nearly 24 words, and therefore received a score of three. However, the error pattern does not exist in the case of the American student samples, for example, AM 322 that received a score of six has 503 words with 16 errors, i.e., one error for nearly 31 words, and likewise American student sample AM 200 has 419 words with 13 errors, i.e., one error for nearly 32 words.

Although error analysis provides some insight into the type and frequency of errors in the writing samples belonging to the two levels, it is not conclusive enough to differentiate the writing quality among them. Therefore T-unit analysis is employed as a supplement to the error analysis to evaluate the quality of student writing.

T-Unit Analysis

T-unit analysis, developed by Hunt (1964) has been used extensively to measure the overall syntactic complexity of both speech and writing samples (Gaies, 1980). The T-unit is defined as consisting of a main clause plus all subordinate clauses and nonclausal structures that are attached to or embedded in it (Hunt, 1964). Hunt claims that the length of a T-unit is parallel to the cognitive development in a child and thus the T-unit analysis provides an intuitively satisfying and stable index of language development. The T-unit's popularity is due to the fact that it is a global measure of linguistic development external to any particular set of data and allows for meaningful comparison between first and second language acquisition. Monroe (1975) has suggested that the process of T-unit lengthening and the stages in that process are consistent in both L1 and L2 acquisition. In both L1 and L2, the writer begins by combining sentences using coordination; in the next stage, he uses subordination; finally he learns to use sentence-embedding and clause reduction.

T-unit analysis has been successfully used by Larsen-Freeman & Strom (1977) and Perkins (1980) as an objective measure to evaluate the quality of ESL student writing. T-unit measures used in this study include words per composition, sentences per composition, T-units per composition, error-free T-units per composition, words in error-free T-units per composition, T-unit length, and ratio of errors versus T-units per composition. Of particular interest in this study is the relationship between these objective measures and the holistic assessments that have resulted in upper half and lower half scores. The information gathered from the analysis is furnished below.

Results and Discussion

From the information available in Table 11.2, the following conclusions can be drawn about the quality of the essays:

a. The total number of words per essay are greater for the upper half group than the lower half.

b. The average number of words per T-Unit is also larger in upper half than in the lower half papers in Indian student writing, but the same cannot be said about American student writing.

c. The ratio of error-free T-units versus total T-units also presents a mixed picture; for example, while the distinction is very glaring between the upper half and lower half Indian student writing samples (1: 0.22 versus 1:0.71), there is no distinction between the upper half and lower half American student writing samples (1:0.42 versus 1:0.42).

The T-unit analysis shows that the length of upper half essays tend to be longer with more error-free T-units than the lower half papers, and likewise, the length of sentences in upper half papers tend to be longer than the sentences in the lower half papers. The following sentence from an upper half American student writing sample (322) has two T-units with two main clauses and two dependent clauses with 26 words in it:

TABLE 11.2
Results of T-Unit Analysis of Indian
and American Student Writing Samples

Variable	IN 57	AM 322	IN 62	AM 200
Score	6	6	3	3
Total number of words	494	503	380	419
Total number of sentences	18	30	29	25
Total number of T-units	22	30	29	26
Total number of error-free T-units	18	21	17	18
Average number of words in a T-unit	22.45	16.77	13.1	16.1
Ratio of error free T-units: T-units with error	1:0.22	1:0.42	1:0.71	1:0.42

Let us first have a look at makeup commercials, one that stands out in my mind has us guessing how old these beautiful women really are. (Sentence Structure—Comma Splice) (1 ET) (2 M and 2 D).

Similarly, the following sentence from an upper half Indian student writing sample (57) has just one T-unit consisting of 36 words—one main clause and two dependent clauses:

Social Reformers like Raja Ram Mohan Roy, writers like Shoba De, Mirnal Pande and inspirational people like Mother Teresa have made great efforts to prove that all people are equal, no matter what their gender is (1 T-Unit— one main clause and two dependent clauses).

On the contrary, lower half papers in both American and Indian student writing samples are far shorter than the above two sentences. For example, the average sentence of American student writing sample (200) belonging to the lower half has only 16.1 words per sentence and his Indian counter- part (62) has only 13.1 words per sentence. Therefore, the above findings also confirm Ney's (1966) observation that a higher number of error-free T- units in a composition is indicative of a better quality of writing because it shows a writer's ability to handle subordination, coordination, and embed- ding successfully, and his or her ability to clarify, elaborate, or exemplify his or her ideas in clear and error-free T-units. However, the results also raise questions about relying too much on errors as a factor in distinguishing the quality of student papers, because both the upper and lower half American student writing seem to have an almost identical ratio of T-Units with er- rors. In spite of some superfluous advantages, T-unit analysis cannot ex- plain how the various sentences in a composition hang together or how co- herence is achieved in writing. The author therefore tried to supplement the above linguistic analyses of the student writing samples with rhetorical analysis.

Rhetorical Analysis

Halliday and Hasan (1976) have acknowledged that continuity between sentences is not the whole of coherence. According to them, "the organiza- tion of each segment of a discourse in terms of its information structure is also part of its texture no less important than the continuity from one seg- ment to another" (p. 299). Similarly, Van Dijk (1985) has observed that "the meaningfulness of discourse resides not only at this local level of im- mediate clause and sentence connections but also at a global level" (p. 115). Coherence is also achieved through a reader's successful interaction with a text and how well it fulfills the reader's expectations about using the appropriate modes of discourse. The readers' expectations in this study have been enunciated in the holistic scoring scale. The descriptors in the holistic scoring used to rate the student writing samples reflect an emphasis on theme and topic development, rhetorical organization of ideas, coherence, and audience awareness. Such emphases are understandably difficult to address in discrete linguistic analyses discussed earlier in this chapter.

As stated earlier, the unity of a text depends on more than a mere collection of sentences. Although there is inherent difficulty in stating what makes an essay click as an exemplary one, it can be reasonably assumed that a good essay will have the following: a thesis statement, narrow focus with controlling idea(s), definite purpose, clearly identifiable audience, details in support of the thesis statement, syntactic complexity, deft use of cohesive devices/transitions, and an appropriate organization (framework or format). Linguistic analyses are not sufficient to describe the above features in a text. Therefore, the student writing samples were subjected to F-Unit analysis to describe the writing quality beyond the sentence level.

F-Unit Analysis

Lieber (1980) and Lindeberg (1985a) came up with the functional unit (F-unit) analysis to study the rhetorical purposes of F-units in a discourse and how F-roles are pieced together. Unlike the Functional Sentence Perspective (FSP), which allows the examination of adjacent pairs of sentences in terms of given/new, and topic/comment, F-unit analysis studies large stretches of discourse and focuses on the rhetorical functions.

An F-role, according to Lieber (1980), refers to clauses or clause equivalents that serve an identifiable rhetorical function in a written discourse. Lindeberg (1985b) defines an F-role as a means to "express the developmental relationship between one functional unit and a preceding or subsequent (not necessarily adjacent) functional unit, naming the function of the unit in the textual context" (p. 330).

The F-units have self-explanatory function roles (F-roles) and are often led by cohesive ties, which signal F-roles. For example, the tie "because" signals the F-role of "reason," "nevertheless" signals the F-role of "contrast," and "thus" may signal the F-role "result." An F-role sequence generally begins with an "assert" and is followed by "specify" or "expansion." The F-roles "result" or "summarize" occupy the last position in an F-role sequence. Lindeberg (1985a) justifies F-unit analysis as it provides the freedom needed to deal with L2 student writing, some of which may not conform to the accepted English syntax. It also provides quantitative evidence to measure patterns of coherence rather than simply describing them (Connor 1984; Tirkkonen-Condit, 1984). This author also finds that an analysis of F-roles helps to show how the underlying meaning of individual functional units contributes to the coherence of a text. Functional role analysis also allows a greater flexibility in examining student writing, which may have many errors in structure and punctuation. In this study, the author has identified "assert," "specify," "cause," "result," "summarize," "contrast," and "expansion" as major functional roles, as used in a similar study (Govardhan, 1994). The results of functional role analysis of the data are summarized in Table 11.3.

Results and Discussion. The distribution of F-roles across the different levels of student writing reveals that:

a. Whereas the mere number of F-roles only indicates a writer's ability to express ideas, it is the length of F-role sequence that demonstrates a writer's ability to develop ideas and link those ideas together. The writing samples in the upper half clearly demonstrate that they have fewer F-role sequences (5 and 6 for IN 57 and AM 322 respectively) than the lower half writing samples (13 and 7 for IN 62 and AM 200 respectively) indicating that the writers in the lower half tend to introduce ideas but fail to clarify, expand or elucidate them;

b. In addition, the average number of F-roles per F-role sequence is higher in the upper half writing samples (1:6.3 and 1:5.0 for IN 57 and AM 322 respectively) than in lower half writing samples (1:2.9 and 1:3.4 for IN 62 and AM 200 respectively) indicating that the upper half writing samples that have a larger number of F-roles in an F-role sequence demonstrate the writers' ability to narrow down the topics and provide specific examples or supporting details for the development of ideas. The longer F-role sequences also help the writers to achieve coherence in the essays; the following examples of longer F-role sequences will illustrate my point:

TABLE 11.3
Distribution of F-roles in American
and Indian Student Writing Samples

Writing Samples	IN 57	AM 322	IN 62	AM 200
Score	6	6	4	3
F-role sequences in the essays	5	6	13	7
F-roles in the essays	32	30	38	24
One-role sequences	1		4	1
Two-role sequences	1		1	1
Three-role sequences		2	1	1
Four-role sequences			3	3
Five-role sequences and more	3	4	3	1
Ratio of F-roles for one F-role sequence	1:6.3	1:5	1:2.9	1:3.4

Indian Student 62 (Sentences 1–8)

S1. It is ever growing and diverse, and therefore her people follow many rituals, beliefs and customs (Clarify+Expansion).

S2. Although India, as a developing country, does allow the woman to reach the same level as a man does—on a family level or at one's work place, it has been accepted only in the metropolitan cities and other urban areas (Clarify+Expansion).

S3. The people, who live in rural towns and villages, are yet to accept the status of a woman as equal to that of a man (Contrast)

S4. Such a notion has been among those who have a very strong sense of tradition ever since the vedic times (Clarify).

S5. Even the epics like the Ramayana and the Mahabaratha depict women as delicate ornaments, who need men to protect them (Expansion).

S6. While the woman is kidnapped, it is her husband, lover or some good hearted handsome stranger, who comes to her rescue (Specify+Specify)

S7. The same has been shown today, in the Indian theatre (Specify)

S8. A woman, who tries to avenge her sister's rape and murder and has the killer convicted, is not accepted by the masses, as much as a man, who avenges his brother's and sister-in-laws death and family destruction (Expansion+Expansion).

American Student 322 (Sentences 17–25)

S17. Lastly we have movies to enhance our stereotypes of men and women. (Assert)

S18. I think a perfect example is "pretty woman." (Specify)

S19. In this movie, Julia Roberts plays a gorgeous prostitute. (Specify)

S20. How much closer to a subject can we get? (Clarify)

S21. Predictably, the male star, Richard Gier plays an extremely wealthy and successful business man looking for love and on the rebound. (Specify)

S22. Of course, Richard is Julias night in shining armor. (Clarify)

S23. You know, the kind that disguises her as upper class and parades her around like his new and overpriced sports car. (Clarify)

S24. I am beginning to resent myself for watching this movie more than once. (Clarify)

S25. At any rate, "Pretty Woman" is the perfect example of how movies portray men as success objects and women as sex objects. (Clarify)

c. Longer F-role sequences bring about cohesion and unity in an essay and contribute to successful interaction between the reader and the text, but shorter F-role sequences violate the pattern of development suggested by D'Angelo (1974) as well as the given/new principle of the Functional Sentence Perspective, because shorter F-role sequences create gaps in communication between the reader and the text. Further, shorter F-role sequences are generally assertions, which are not fully expanded or explained, and therefore the ideas introduced in them remain undeveloped or unsubstantiated, leaving the reader to make inferences and necessary connections. The following examples will exemplify this aspect of writing:

Indian Student 62 (Sentence 1–3)

S1. Before stating my views on this topic <u>I would like to thank you sir</u> (Assert).

S2. Firstly I am proud as a citizen of India to give my opinion in my country's culture (Assert).

S3. India has got a rich culture (Assert).

American Student 200 (Sentences 5–8)

S5. These messages might not openly exploit women and praise men. (Assert)

S6. An example would be that new whirlpool commercial where they are trying to market washing machine saying its whisper quiet and compact. (Specify)

S7. You can go about your other business with no worry. (Assert)

S8. They have this lady preparing dinner and being interrupted by the doorbell and the phone. (Assert)

The present study reiterates several previous studies that have confirmed the relationship between the length of F-role sequence and coherence in writing. For example, Neuner (1987) observed that cohesive chains in good essays were sustained over a larger portion of a text. These chains contribute to the development, fullness, and intensity of their subjects. Similarly, Stotsky (1983) found writers of high-rated essays "creating longer semantic units, placing a large number of these units in cohesive relationships, and establishing a portion of the text" (p. 287). The lack of longer F-role sequences in low-rated essays confirms the findings of Connor (1984) that low-rated essays lack the sequential development of assertions and thereby the coherence.

This study also finds that the relationship of F-roles within an F-role sequence is established not only by overt cohesive ties but also by semantic relationships that are unmarked by cohesive ties. For example, both the reference (pronominal) and conjunction ties on the one hand, and lexical ties such as same word repetition, synonyms and near synonyms on the other, help achieve coherence in the texts. However, in the upper half papers, the use of a semantic strategy to establish the relationship between the F-roles within an F-role sequence has been noted, a strategy that is normally associated with good writers and older writers (Haswell, 1989).

In addition, this study finds the upper half American and Indian students samples using the hierarchical structure, which the previous studies (Longacre, 1976; McKoon, 1977; Meyer, 1975; Tannen, 1987) have shown to facilitate readers' positive interaction with a text. Tannen (1987) has noted that the structure or frame of a discourse reveals to the listener/reader what to expect in it. Likewise, Kintsch (1974) and Thorndyke (1977) have demonstrated the influence of generalized story structures or frames on readers' comprehension. Jones (1977) and Pike (1967) have used a model of the referential hierarchy of language in their analysis of thematic structures to describe hierarchical content organization and explain its effect on readers' comprehension of theme.

As identified by Jones, theme highlighting devices in expository prose are:

1. Order of sentences within paragraphs (topic sentence followed by supporting details).
2. Order of words within a sentence (topic/comment).
3. Special constructions: passives, relative clauses, rhetorical questions, topicalization.
4. Cohesive devices: reference, conjunction, and lexical collocation.

In a similar study, Hult (1982) used Jones' model to study persuasive essays written by high school students to determine differences between the high-skilled and low-skilled writers in terms of hierarchical organization of arguments, discourse structure, and devices used to highlight themes. Her studies confirm that high-skilled writers produce high quality essays that have adequate, unified, and coherent argument, and global organization. They also show greater control over syntactic or grammatical theme-marking devices and have fewer unconventional paragraphs or unrelated themes. The study also confirms that the high-skilled writers and readers share the same expository frame. It is this frame that allows the readers to evaluate those essays favorably. Hult schematized the content organization in student essays to provide a visual display of theme dominance. In her model, a tree diagram displays theme at the highest level of the tree structure, main arguments and summation at the second level (topic sentences in a paragraph), and supporting points at a lower level of generality as either proceeding in a subordinate or a coordinate sequence. The main arguments are developed through exemplification, clarification, and substantiation.

The thematic analysis concentrates on how students highlight themes, provide background information, supply supporting points, and finally, how they use any other devices to contribute to the hierarchical organization of arguments. Thematic analysis conducted in this study is based on

Hult's (1982) study of theme dominance in student essays. This study has adapted Jones' (1977) tree diagram for illustrative purposes.

Hult (1982) proposes the term *main argument* to identify the highest level in the tree diagram. The main argument may include one or more points within a paragraph. That is, the main argument is a paraphrase of one or more points. In addition to the main argument, there are: *clarifying support points* (C.S.), which are subordinate and therefore used to clarify preceding points; *enumerative support points* (E.S.), which are coordinated to each other and are used to elaborate through enumerating examples at a parallel level of specificity; and *closing arguments* (C.A.), which are generally found at the end of an essay or at the end of a main argument sequence. The term *point* is used instead of *sentence* as sometimes one sentence may have two points or one point may be extended over more than one sentence.

Often, a main argument resembles the traditional *topic sentence* of a paragraph; however, this, too, can extend over more than a single sentence. The writing sample of the student with the identification number 57 is analyzed and presented in Diagram 11.1 as an example of the thematic analysis conducted for the study. First, the sentences have been rephrased for the purposes of identifying the main arguments, clarifying support points, and enumerating support points. In keeping with Hult's (1982) framework, points are labeled as clarifying support points (C.S.), and enumerating support points (E.S.).

The student writer, IN 57, has explicitly highlighted the theme, produced three clearly identifiable main arguments, followed them except one with clarifying and enumerating support points, and concluded the essay with a closing argument. The main arguments are supported by clarifying or enumerating support points ranging from none for the main argument number 2 to eight for the main argument number 1. All points contribute to the logical progression of ideas in the essay. Thus the author of the essay has generally exhibited a grasp of the topic and an awareness of the structure of an expository essay, both of which are essential for the purpose of persuading the reader.

Likewise, the writing sample of AM 322 has highlighted a theme, supported by five clearly identifiable main arguments and a concluding argument, all of which are followed by supporting points. The main arguments are strengthened by supporting points ranging from two for main arguments 1 and 3 to eight for main argument number 5. In addition, the coherence of the essay is achieved by linking each of the main arguments logically. Though the development of main points is not uniform, the reader can see from the diagram 11.2 that the essay AM 322 is more fully developed than the essay IN 57.

On the other hand, the thematic analysis of the writing sample of student IN 62 in diagram 11.3 clearly shows a lack of development of ideas.

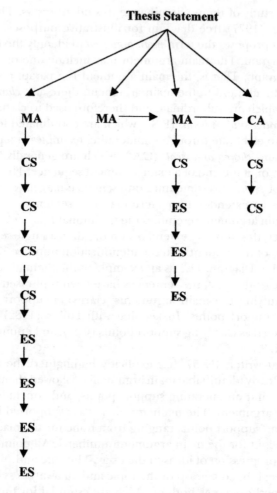

Diagram 11.1.   Thematic analysis of Indian student 57 (score 6).

The student has introduced six main arguments, of which three received just one supporting point, one received four, another one five and the last one eight supporting points. The student leaves three main arguments undeveloped. Further, the arguments introduced are not related to the task attempted, and therefore not connected together.

Similarly, the writing sample AM 200, which also received a score of three, has introduced six main arguments and one concluding argument (see diagram 11.4). However, the sample fails miserably as the main arguments are not adequately developed. For example, out of the six main arguments, one does not receive any supporting points, another received just one supporting point, three main arguments received only three support-

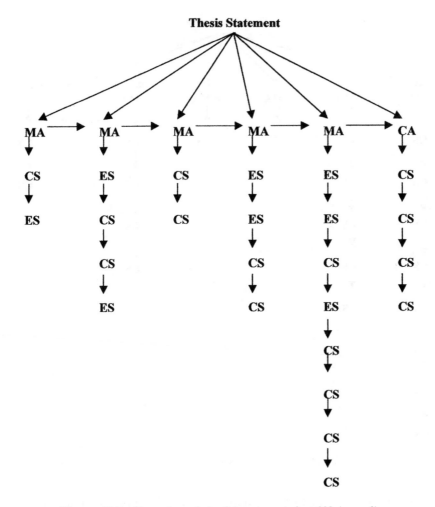

Diagram 11.2. Thematic analysis of American student 322 (score 6).

ing points each, and finally, only one main argument received five support-ing points. The uneven development of the main arguments and uncon-nected main arguments naturally lead to the weakening of the overall structure of the essay and its resultant negative effect on reader's interac-tion with the essay.

Results and Discussion of Thematic Analysis

From the details furnished in Table 11.4, it is not difficult to notice the distinct qualities of the upper half essays. Likewise, the following conclu-sions can also be drawn based on the details in the above table:

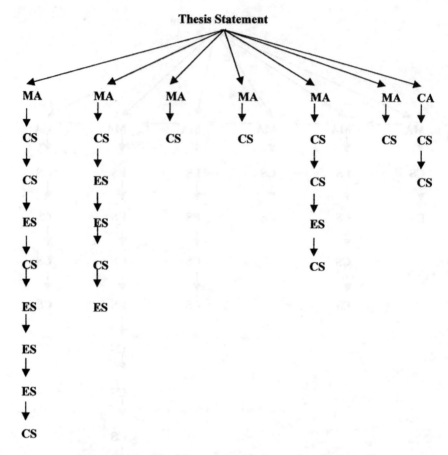

Diagram 11.3.   Thematic analysis of Indian student 62 (score 3).

a. In the upper half essays, an average of 3.02 supporting points follow one main argument, which is 0.36 more than the essays in the lower half.

b. The number of main arguments, clarifying support points, and enumerating support points is consistently higher in the writing samples belonging to the upper half papers than the lower writing samples. On average, the difference ranges from 1.12 to 2.12 points. Each main argument in the upper half essays is followed by 1.68 clarifying supporting points and 1.34 enumerating supporting points compared to 1.63 and 1.03 in lower half essays. The distribution of main and supporting arguments clearly shows that the upper half essays concentrate on the development of ideas introduced in the main arguments with sufficient details, whereas the lower half essays tend to

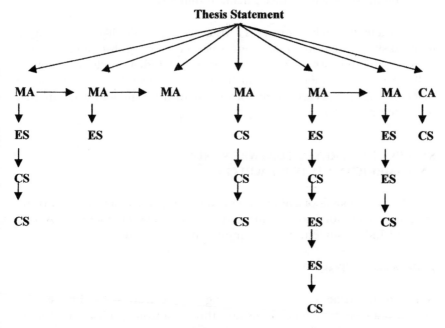

Diagram 11.4. Thematic analysis of American student 200 (score 3).

TABLE 11.4
Thematic Analysis of Indian and American Student Writing Samples

Variable	IN 57	AM 322	IN 62	AM 200
Score	6	6	3	3
Number of main arguments	3	5	6	6
Number of clarifying support points (C.S.)	7	12	12	8
Number of enumerating support points (E.S.)	6	12	8	7
Total number of closing arguments (C.A.)	1	1	1	1
Total number of supporting points for CA	2	4	2	1
Average number of clarifying support points for one main argument	1:2.33	1:2.4	1:2	1:1.33
Average number of enumerating support points for one main argument	1:2	1:2.4	1:1.33	1:1.17
Average number of supporting points for each main argument	1:4.33	1:4.8	1:3.33	1:2.5

introduce new arguments before fully exploiting or elaborating on the previously introduced main arguments.

The thematic analysis presents a visual image of a well-grounded argument. It shows the distinct differences between the highly-rated and lowly-rated essays and also between American and Indian student rhetorical styles. A western reader is more inclined to favor a student writing sample that conforms to the classical rhetorical modes and argument structure that he or she is familiar with.

SALIENT DIFFERENCES BETWEEN INDIAN AND AMERICAN STUDENT WRITING

Based on the analysis of twenty Indian and twenty American student writing samples, this author finds that major differences between upper half American and Indian student writing samples are as follows:

Addressing the Task

Although the American student writing sample (AM 322) addresses the task with a clearly defined thesis and three controlling ideas, the Indian writing sample (IN 57) does not address the task directly ("stereotypes of men and women perpetuated by the advertising, movies and television, and music videos"); instead, the Indian writer takes a circular route of first orienting the reader by providing an historical perspective of the role of women in Indian society ("India is a country which has a very rich culture and heritage . . . The people who live in rural towns and villages are yet to accept the status of a woman as equal to that of a man), and then, tries to elaborate the ideas with clear-cut examples. The lower half papers from both American and Indian student samples fail to address the task adequately; they introduce three supporting ideas that stand alone without any elaboration, illustration, or connectivity to the thesis statement.

Theme

The American student (AM 322) introduces the theme by asking a question and answering himself/herself and thus, creates curiosity among readers, but the Indian student (IN 57) creates an historical context for the discussion of the discrimination of the females in the male dominated society, marks the theme only vaguely, and thereby sends mixed signals to the reader. Since the readers' interaction with the text is only possible when their expectations are met with, the Indian student paper contributes to the lack of involvement of the readers with the text.

Audience Awareness

The American Student (AM 322) shows his/her awareness in the first sentence itself, anticipates the readers' expectations on the issue, and addresses them adequately using the generalized story structures or frames of discourse (topic sentence followed by supporting details). On the other hand, the Indian student (IN 57) assumes that the reader needs to know the background about India and the place of Indian women in Indian society, and therefore, spends most of the allotted time creating a platform from which to address the task. For a western reader unfamiliar with Indian style of writing, Indian student writing (IN 57) reads like rambling ideas that are only tangentially related to the task at hand. Among the lower half papers, American student writing sample (AM 200) shows audience awareness clearly by directly addressing the reader (Sentence 3: "You might say that the music you listen to doesn't do that, the movies and/or ads you see don't either").

Development

The upper half papers show consistent development of the main points with supporting points at the rate of 1:4.8 for AM 322 and 1:4.33 for IN 57, but the rate is 1.2.5 for AM 200 and 1:3.3 for IN 62 indicating the lack of development of ideas and thereby affecting the readers' satisfactory interaction with the text.

Organization

Although both the American student papers (322 and 200) conform to the traditional American hierarchical organization of ideas and five-paragraph structure of the essay with introduction, body, and conclusion, the Indian student papers (57 and 62) lack similar organization, instead using a long introduction to provide a historical context and showing inadequate development of ideas in the body of the essay.

Syntactic Complexity

As for the syntactic complexity of the upper half papers, the Indian student paper IN 57 shows greater syntactic variation (18 sentences, 22 T-Units, 494 words, 23 independent and 23 dependent clauses) than the American student paper AM 322 (30 sentences, 30 T-Units, 503 words, 32 independent and 16 dependent clauses) testifying to the fact that Indian students are capable of writing more complex and longer sentences than their American counterparts. Both the lower half papers—the Indian student paper IN 62 (29 sentences, 29 T-Units, and 380 words 32 main clauses and 10 dependent clauses) and the American student paper AM 322 (25 sentences, 26 T-Units, 419 words, 27 main clauses and 11 dependent clauses)—show inconsistent facility in syntactic variety, as exemplified by one-clause sentences that are often choppy.

Coherence

Both AM 322 (81 cohesive ties, namely 29 references, 3 conjunctions, and 43 lexical) and IN 57 (88 cohesive ties, namely 36 references, 4 conjunctions, and 48 lexical) have used mostly adverbials for smooth transitions between sentences and paragraphs. Although AM 322 succeeds in achieving greater cohesion by using subtle semantic coherence by adhering to the traditional western five-paragraph hierarchical structure and theme-marking devices, IN 57 does so in a more circular way with a long introduction setting up the argument, historical examples, and implicit theme-marking devices. Among the lower half papers, AM 200 uses fewer cohesive ties, namely 24 references, 6 conjunctions, 14 lexical ties but uses the American organizational structure (five-paragraph—introduction, body, and conclusion) to achieve coherence. On the other hand, IN 62 uses 35 references, 4 conjunctions, and 63 lexical ties but fails to achieve coherence due to the lack of a definite organizational structure.

Special Construction

Both AM 322 and IN 57 use relative clauses and complex sentences. However, only AM 322 has successfully used rhetorical questions, short sentences, and even fragments with great effect. The absence of the syntactic variety in the lower half papers—both Indian and American, indicate their developing linguistic competence.

CONCLUSION: SUGGESTIONS FOR ADDRESSING THE DIFFERENCES IN INDIAN STUDENT WRITING

Since Indian students have been exposed to the English language extensively through the media, classroom instruction, and almost every walk of life in India, they have adequate proficiency in the English language, which is also confirmed by their scores on the TOEFL, TSE, GRE, GMAT, etc. However, it is undeniable that their writing is markedly different from American student writing, not at the grammatical level but at the rhetorical level. The differences in Indian student writing, as this writer has shown, can be traced not only to cultural thought patterns but also to lack of training in American rhetorical tradition. Therefore, instead of brushing aside

Indian student writing as "non-linear," "incoherent, "circular," "wordy," "full of clichés," etc., writing teachers in US institutions should consider adopting a positive attitude toward Indian student writing. Teachers could focus on helping Indian students understand the hierarchical argument structure of the American rhetorical tradition, the importance of rhetorical strategies, the awareness of audience, and finally, writing as a process. Since Indian students are not ESL students in the traditional sense, this author is confident that they will be quick to seize the opportunity to make the necessary adjustments in their writing to conform to the American rhetorical tradition as they have a very strong motivation to excel in their studies.

QUESTIONS FOR DISCUSSION AND REFLECTIVE WRITING

1. Imagine you are a student recently arrived from India. What might your attitude be toward an American writing class?

2. In a small group, discuss the implications of Govardhan's analysis of American and Indian students' writing for placement and assessment of both groups.

3. Working with a partner, look at the suggestions for teaching writing to Indian students offered by Govardhan. How would you modify these suggestions to be appropriate for your teaching context?

REFERENCES

Bhatia, A. T. (1977). Theory of discourse and the teaching of English composition to undergraduate students. *CIEFL Bulletin, 13*(2), 59–70.

Chakraverty, A., & Gautum, K. (2000). Dynamics of writing. *Forum, 38*(3), 22–24.

Chaudary, S. (2001). ELT in India: 400 years and still going strong. *IATEFL, 163*, 13–14.

Connor, U. (1984). Cohesion and coherence in English as a Second Language students' writing. *Papers in Linguistics: International Journal of Human Communication, 17*, 301–316.

D'Angelo, F. J. (1974). A generative rhetoric of the essay. *College Composition and Communication, 25*, 388–396.

Das, B. K. (1978). An investigation of some advanced skills of composition. *CIEFL Bulletin, 1*, 43–62.

Das Gupta, S. N. (1975). Philosophy. In A. L. Basham (Ed.), *A cultural history of India* (pp. 111–123). Oxford: Clarendon Press.

Gaies, S. J. (1980). T-Unit analysis in second language research: Applications, problems, and limitations. *TESOL Quarterly, 10*(3), 53–60.

Govardhan, A. K. (1994). *A discourse analysis of ESL student writing*. Unpublished doctoral dissertation, Northern Illinois University.

Halliday, M. A. K., & Hasan, R. (1976). *Cohesion in English*. London: Longman.

Haswell, R. H. (1989). Textual research in coherence: Findings, intuition, application. *College English, 51*, 305–319.

Heinmann, B. (1964). *Facets of Indian thought*. London: George Allen and Unwin.

Hinds, J. (1983). Contrastive rhetoric: Japanese and English. *Text, 3*, 183–195.

Hult, C. A. (1982). *Frames, content organization, and themes in student expository essays: An analysis of discourse structure.* (ERIC Document Reproduction Service No. 235 482).

Hunt, K. W. (1964). *Grammatical structures written at three grade levels.* Urbana: National Council of Teachers of English.

Jones, L. K. (1977). *Theme in English expository discourse.* Lake Bluffs, IL: Jupiter.

Kachru, B. (1986). *The alchemy of English: The spread, functions and models of non-native Englishes.* Oxford: Pergamon Press.

Kachru, Y. (1988). Interpreting Indian English expository prose. Issues and developments in English and applied linguistics. *Ideal, 3,* 39–50.

Kaplan, R. (1966). Cultural thought patterns in intercultural education. *Language Learning, 16,* 1–20.

Kintsch, W. (1974). *The representation of meaning in memory.* Hillsdale, NJ: Lawrence Erlbaum Associates.

Kroll, B. M. (1990). What does time buy? ESL student performance on home versus class compositions. In B. Kroll (Ed.), *Second language writing: Research insights from the classroom* (pp. 140–154). Cambridge: Cambridge University Press.

Larsen-Freeman, D., & Strom, V. (1977). The construction of a second language index of development. *Language Learning, 27*(1), 123–134.

Lieber, P. A. (1980). Cohesion in ESL students' expository writing: A descriptive study. New York University. *Dissertation Abstracts International, 41*(2A), 0657.

Lindeberg, A. (1985a). Cohesion, coherence patterns, and EFL essay evaluation. In N. E. Enkvist (Ed.), *Coherence and composition: A symposium* (pp. 67–92). Abo, Finland: Research Institute for the Abo Akademi Foundation.

Lindeberg, A. (1985b). Abstraction levels in student essays. *Text, 5,* 327–346.

Longacre, R. E. (1976). *An anatomy of speech notions.* Lisse: de Ridder.

McKoon, G. (1977). Organization of information in text memory. *Journal of Verbal Learning and Verbal Behavior, 16,* 247–250.

Meyer, B. J. F. (1975). *The organization of prose and its effects on memory.* Amsterdam: North Holland Publishing Company.

Monroe, J. H. (1975). Measuring and enhancing syntactic fluency in French. *French Review XLVIII, 6,* 1023–1031.

Neuner, J. (1987). Cohesive ties and chains in good and poor freshman essays. *Research in the Teaching of English, 21,* 92–105.

Ney, J. W. (1966). Review of grammatical structures written at three grade levels. *Language Learning, 16,* 230–235.

Open Doors 2003: Report on International Educational Exchange. Retrieved on November 1, 2004 from http://www.iie.org

Pandharipande, R. (1983). Linguistics and written discourse in particular languages: Contrastive studies: English and Marathi. *Annual Review of Applied Linguistics, 3,* 118–136.

Perkins, K. (1980). Using objective methods of attained writing proficiency to discriminate among holistic evaluations. *TESOL Quarterly, 14*(1), 61–69.

Pike, P. (1967). *Language in relation to a unified theory of the structure of human behavior.* The Hague: Mouton.

Ravindran, T. (2003). *English for engineers—An alternative syllabus for engineering colleges in Tamilnadu.* Doctoral dissertation submitted to Anna University, Chennai, India.

Stotsky, S. (1983). Types of lexical cohesion in expository writing: Implications for developing the vocabulary of academic discourse. *College Composition and Communication, 34,* 430–447.

Tannen, D. (1987). Repetition in conversation as spontaneous formulaicity. *Text, 7*(3), 215–243.

Thorndyke, P. W. (1977). Cognitive structures in comprehension and memory of narrative discourse. *Cognitive Psychology, 9,* 77–110.

Tirkkonen-Condit, S. (1984). *Towards a description of argumentative text structure.* Paper presented at the Second Nordic Conference of English Studies, Abo, Finland.

TOEFL and TSE bulletin. (1993–94). Princeton: Educational Testing Service.

Van Dijk, T. A. (1985). Semantic discourse analysis. In T. A. Van Dijk (Ed.), *Handbook of discourse analysis (2)* (pp. 103–136). London: Academic Press.

Chapter 12

A Transplant Takes Root: Philippine English and Education

Ma. Lourdes G. Tayao
University of the East Recto, The Philippines

KEY POINTS

- Discussion of the emergence of Philippine English (PE) as a variety of General American English (GAE).
- Demographic patterns of Asian (including Filipino) immigrants in the U.S., and their English language proficiency.
- Phonetic, lexical, and grammatical differences between PE and GAE.
- Problems encountered by Filipinos in understanding GAE speakers.
- Suggestions for improving listening, reading comprehension and writing skills of PE-speaking students.

> *The architects of . . . each strand of Asian English have molded, reshaped, accul-*
> *turated, redesigned—and by doing so—enriched what was a Western medium.*
> —Braj. B. Kachru (1997, p. 23)

With globalization, English has surfaced as the dominant language in use in business, geopolitics, and international communication. As such it has ceased to be owned solely by the native speakers of the language who belong to the inner circle of English users.[1] Their ownership of the language

---

[1] Kachru's Concentric Circle model of users of English shows the *Inner Circle* to consist of those whose native language is English, e.g., Britain, America, etc.; the *Outer Circle* comprising those from English colonized countries who have "developed, institutionalized, and nativized varieties of English," e.g., India, Hong Kong, Singapore, the Philippines; and the Outermost (also referred to as the *Expanding Circle*) made up of those from countries where English is not used extensively for example, China, Korea, and Japan.

is now shared with non-native speakers of English belonging to the outer and expanding circles of users of English. Moreover, sociopolitical developments have brought about changes in language attitudes. Objections have been raised to a monolithic standard of language performance in English resulting in the acceptance of the different varieties of English taking shape and evolving in different parts of the world. On the other hand, globalization has also resulted in migrations and in an increased movement of labor workforce from the outer and expanding circles of users of English to English-speaking countries. Therefore, to enhance international communication, an awareness of the varieties of English cannot be overemphasized. This chapter seeks to provide information concerning Philippine English and what might be done to enable speakers of that variety to cope linguistically in an English-dominant context.

Philippine English (PE), which has evolved through the years, is a variety of *General American English* (GAE) that is used extensively in different domains by educated Filipinos throughout the Philippines. It started out as a result of linguistic imperialism when America annexed the Philippines from Spain in 1898 and established the public school system teaching English and using it as a medium of instruction in all subjects. The decision to have just one language, namely English, as official language and to propagate its use through the school system stemmed from the fact that the Philippines, being multilingual, did not have at that time a single *lingua franca.*

What started out as linguistic imperialism gave way to Type A macroacquisition where multilingual speech communities in the Philippines learned English in schools with native speakers initially serving as teachers using the direct method of teaching the language. The standard then was General American English. In time, however, Filipino teachers majoring in English assumed the role of mentors and with developments in applied linguistics, English was taught as a Second Language (ESL) based on a contrastive analysis of General American English and the different Philippine languages. For a time, the audio-lingual method was used with emphasis placed on the spoken language and pattern drills. GAE continued as the standard, and deviations from it were stigmatized.

However, with the political independence of the country in 1946 and the growing sense of nationhood came the issue of linguistic identity. This paved the way for the adoption of a Bilingual Education Policy in which Filipino, the country's emerging national language, was accorded equal official language status as English. The two were used as a medium of instruction in schools with specific domains allocated to each of them. The domains for English included science, mathematics and English, while all the other subjects were to be taught in Filipino.

In the meantime, Philippine English, affected by all those factors—reduced exposure to, and use of English in schools, an increased sense of nationalism, a lack of learning resources and good models in English, etc.—continued to evolve as an autonomous variety of General American English but this time with "its own self-contained system and its distinct accent" (McKaughan, 1993, p. 52, cited in Bautista, 2000a).

That GAE as a transplanted language had indeed taken root but was in the process of being reshaped, acculturated and redesigned as PE was pointed out by T. Llamzon, a noted Filipino linguist, who pioneered in establishing the existence of Standard Filipino English as early as 1969. Llamzon (1997) describes three distinct sociolinguistic varieties of Philippine English: the acrolect variety, which closely approximates General American English, the mesolect variety, which shows deviations from the phonological structure of GAE but is nonetheless acceptable to educated Filipinos, and the basilect variety, where "the speaker's ethnic tongue forms the sustratum" (p. 47). Using a lectal approach, he underscores the fact that ". . . when educated Filipinos speak to their fellow Filipinos, they speak English the Filipino way. This way they retain something of their identity" (p. 43).

THE NEED FOR A DESCRIPTION
OF PHILIPPINE ENGLISH

Among the Asian countries, the Philippines ranks high in the number of its immigrants to, and in the size of its labor workforce in, English-speaking countries such as the United States, Canada, Australia, and the United Kingdom. These Filipino immigrants and workers use one of the three sociolinguistic varieties of Philippine English. This chapter gives first of all the demographic patterns of immigration of Filipinos to the United States. It then illuminates some phonetic, lexical and grammatical deviations of PE from GAE, and describes the problems in understanding spoken and written English encountered by speakers of PE in the hope that this might help clarify interactions in English involving Filipinos. Finally, it suggests measures to improve the listening, reading comprehension, and writing skills of PE speakers. This could serve as resource material for teachers of Filipino learners of English particularly in the United States, which has a large Filipino immigrant population, and in Canada, Australia, and other countries where English is the *lingua franca.*

What Do the Demographics Reveal of the Filipino
Population in the United States?

The Asian and Pacific Islander Americans (API) demographics (Hendriksson, 2002) reveal Asian and Pacific Islander Americans to be the "fastest growing racial group in the United States with a 95% increase from 1980 to

Asian American Population

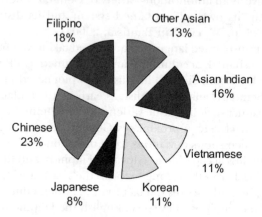

FIG. 12.1   Asian and Pacific Islander American Demographics.

1990, and a 48% increase since 1990." Figure 12.1 shows that, as per US Census 2000, Filipinos were the second largest group constituting 18% of the Asian American population in the United States.

The demographics of immigration consider likewise the English language proficiency of these immigrants, 40–50% of whom have limited English proficiency. Table 12.1 displays the percentages of Asian and Pacific Islander groups with limited English proficiency—those who do not speak English well (or at all) and those who are linguistically isolated in the sense that no one above 14 in the household speaks English well.

In school, students who come from homes where a language other than English is spoken are assessed for their English language proficiency. Those who do not meet the criteria are classified as "English learners." Based on statistics from the California Department of Education, it should be noted that among English learners "although the Philippines ranked relatively high as an immigrant-sending country, yet Filipino ranked only as the fifth or sixth most common non-English language used" (Tafoya, 2002, p. 5). This may be attributed to the change in the composition of the immigrants. "Whereas Filipino immigrants before 1965 were mostly rural workers with limited education, after the passage of the 1965 Immigration and Nationality Act, a significant number of highly educated professionals and urban dwellers began emigrating from the Philippines" (Mangiafico, 1988, cited in Tafoya, 2002, p. 4). Moreover, the Philippines has a bilingual education policy that stipulates the teaching of English as a second language in schools. However, the variety of English used by most Filipinos is Philippine English, which as pointed out earlier, has deviations from General Ameri-

TABLE 12.1
Asian or Pacific Islander Language Spoken
at Home and Ability to Speak English: 1990

Nationalities	Speak Asian or Pacific Islander Language at Home	Do Not Speak English "Very Well"	Linguistically Isolated
Total Asian	65.2%	56.0%	34.9%
Chinese	82.9	60.4	40.3
Filipino	66.0	35.6	13.0
Japanese	42.8	57.7	33.0
Asian Indian	14.5	31.0	17.2
Korean	80.8	63.5	41.4
Vietnamese	92.5	65.0	43.9
Cambodian	95.0	73.2	56.1
Hmong	96.9	78.1	60.5
Laotian	95.6	70.2	52.4
Thai	79.1	58.0	31.8
Other Asian	21.0	49.9	30.2

Note. Linguistic isolation refers to persons in households in which no one 14-years old and over speaks only English and no one who speaks a language other than English speaks English "very well."

can English on which it is based, necessitating a description of those contrasting features, as exemplified in the following sections.

PHONETIC FEATURES

Consonants

Since the Philippines has no fewer than 87 ethnic groups, each with a distinct language of its own, and since one's native language has been found to affect one's acquisition of a target language, it might be said that there would be regional differences in accents even among users of PE depending on the speaker's ethnic tongue. The description given here, however, pertains to the three sociolect varieties of PE, namely, the acrolect, mesolect, and basilect.

Generally speaking, the consonants of the three varieties of PE vis-à-vis those of GAE fall into three broad categories. The first category is made up of PE consonants that have equivalent forms in GAE. Belonging to this group are the consonants produced with the sounds / p, b, t, d, k, and g/. It must be pointed out, however, that the aspiration of / p, t, and k / in syllable initial stressed position as in *pay* /p^{h}ey/; *take* /t^{h}eyk/; *keep* /k^{h}iyp/ which is evident in GAE, is present but rare among the acrolect group, and not evident in the mesolect and basilect varieties (Tayao, 2004, p. 83). Other GAE consonant sounds also present in all three varieties of PE are / m, n, and ñ; l, and w and y/.

The second category is composed of consonants in GAE not found in PE (absent categories). Among the absent categories are GAE consonants /f/, /v/, soft th as in bath and hard th as in bathe. The consonants /f/ and /v/ are present in the acrolect and mesolect varieties but absent in the basilect except among speakers of Philippine languages like Ibanag, which has those consonant phonemes in their phonetic inventory. With the basilect group of speakers, /p/ and /b/ are substituted for /f/ and /v/ respectively.

The soft th and hard th are likewise absent categories in the basilect variety and for that matter in most Philippine languages. They are substituted with the consonants /t/ and /d/ respectively in the basilect variety. Acrolect and mesolect speakers produce the soft and hard th sounds as such only in focused and deliberate speech.

It might be pointed out therefore that English sounds not found in the phonetic inventory of Philippine languages would pose difficulty for Filipino learners of English. These absent categories are taught through the use of minimal pairs of words, which differ only on the critical sound. Here are examples of minimal pairs for the /t/ and soft th sound contrast and the /d/ and hard th sounds:

/t/	soft th	/d/	hard th
tie	thigh	dough	though
tin	thin	dine	thine

The third category is made up of only one PE consonant, namely, /s/ which is called a sibilant because of its hissing sound. In contrast, GAE has six distinct sibilants. This is an example of a split category where one sound in the native language has several different distinct sound equivalents in the target language as shown in Figure 12.2 below:

Sibilant in PE	Sibilants in GAE	
	/s/ 'bus'	/z/ 'buzz'
/s/ ⎫	/sh/ 'seashore'	/Z/ 'seizure'
⎭	/ch/ 'cheap'	/dZ/ 'jeep'

FIG. 12.2. Sibilants in PE and in GAE.

All of the sibilants are present in the acrolect variety of PE. Among the mesolect group of speakers, /z/, /sh/, or /Z/ are pronounced accordingly in word initial but not in word medial nor in word final position. Thus, initial /z/ in *zero* is pronounced as such but is rendered /s/ in final position as in *buzz*. On the other hand, except for /s/, all the other sibilants are absent in the basilect variety and for that matter in most Philippine languages.

Vowels

Vowels, too, are grouped into categories, the first of which is made up of PE vowels with equivalents in GAE. For the acrolect and mesolect groups, these are / *A, E, i, o, u* / with the diphthong /ey/ in PE as the equivalent of /e/ as in *bait* in GAE. For the basilect group whose native language has only three vowels, their PE vowels are /A, i, u /.

The second group of vowels is composed of absent categories. Since vowel length is not a distinctive feature of most Philippine languages, the distinction between GAE long and short vowels (e.g. *beat/bit* and *pool/pull*) is observed by the acrolect and mesolect groups only in focused and deliberate speech. Otherwise, among the mesolect group, the long and short sounds are used interchangeably. And with the basilect group, the long vowel sounds in *beat* and *pool* are used for their short counterparts in *bit* and *pull* respectively.

There are also short GAE vowel sounds that are absent in Philippine languages. Among these are the open *o* sound in *bought* for which all three groups use *o* as in *boat* instead, the *schwa* sound in *but* that the acrolect group produces as such but which is rendered /A/ as in *bar* by the mesolect and basilect groups, and the / / sound in *battle* that is pronounced /A/ as in *bottle* by all three groups.

Other Distinguishing Features Between PE and GAE

Other phonetic features that distinguish PE from GAE are the absence of consonant clusters as well as differences in intonation, stress, and juncture or pausing patterns. In keeping with the final intonation patterns in most Philippine languages, one of the stable features noted in PE is the use of the final rising–falling intonation in statements and the final rising intonation in questions. The former is true to the GAE intonation pattern for statements, but not with the latter. In GAE the final rising intonation is generally used in yes–no questions whereas the final rising–falling intonation is used in *wh-* questions, in yes–no tag questions seeking confirmation, and in statements.

Where word stress is concerned, some words stressed on the first syllable in GAE are found to be stressed by all three PE groups on the second syllable (e.g., *colleague, govern, menu, precinct*). On the other hand, words like *bamboo, committee, dioxide, utensil,* and *percentage,* which are stressed on the second syllable in GAE, are stressed by the PE basilect group on the first syllable; the two other groups stress the second syllable.

Regarding words with primary and secondary stress on the first and third syllables in GAE, (e.g. *adolescence, antecedent, rehabilitate, commentary, complimentary,* and *documentary*), the first four are stressed on only one syllable by all three PE groups, the second syllable for the first three words and the first syllable for the fourth. With the acrolect group, the last two words—*complimentary* and *documentary*—are stressed on the first and third syllables following GAE pronunciation, but the other two groups stress them only on the third.

Other GAE word stress patterns not found in PE are contrasts made between number words ending in *-teen* and those ending in *-ty* (e.g. *thirty* vs. *thirteen*), between words that may be used as nouns or as verbs (a *rebel* vs. to *rebel*), noun constructs in contrast to verb constructs (a *drop*out vs. to drop *out*), noun constructs as contrasted with adjective + noun combinations (*sewing* machine vs. sweet-smelling *flowers*).

LEXICAL FEATURES OF PHILIPPINE ENGLISH

The term *Filipinisms* is used to refer to lexical items peculiar to PE. Studies on the lexicon of PE classify these *Filipinisms* in varied ways. Casambre (1986) identifies four nativization or indigenization devices used by nonnative speakers "to manipulate the target language to suit their need to express themselves in the context of their cultural milieu" (p. 39). These devices are: *peculiar derivations* resulting from extended use of patterns of word affixation in the target language; *special meanings* given to GAE words as a reflection of the speaker's cultural milieu; *new coined expressions* to meet the exigencies of the speaker's experience; and *loan translations* or *calquing* where English is used to express feelings and thoughts peculiar to the nonnative user's milieu.

Bautista (1997), on the other hand, makes reference to what lexicographers cite as the various ways a lexicon develops and the forms that result in the process. One way is the "normal expansion of a term" due either to extensions or adaptations of meaning or to a shift in part of speech. Another is the "preservation of items which have become lost or infrequent" in other varieties. Still another is through "coinage" where new words or phrases are invented based on analogies of word affixation patterns found in the target language; the reduction or clipping of terms; the use of acronyms in lieu of words and expressions; the invention of totally new innovative terms or neologisms; compounding; and combining an English element with a borrowed one. Finally, the lexical inventory of PE has been enriched by "borrowing" from different languages with which it has come into contact. Bautista points out that whereas the first three processes, namely expansion, preservation, and coinage, result in lexical items that are English in form, the last one, borrowing, produces items akin to the source languages from which they were borrowed. The appendix shows the classification and examples of some terms cited by Bautista as peculiar to PE.

In addition to the inventory of words resulting from the processes of lexical development mentioned by lexicographers, there are also cases where lexical items in English are given additional special meanings in PE different from their meanings in GAE, resulting in false cognates. A few of the lexical items cited by Casambre are listed here:

Lexical Items	Meaning in GAE	Additional Meaning in PE
*salvage	the act of saving anything from a shipwreck, fire, danger, etc.	to waylay and kill persons
*hostess	a woman who entertains guests	a taxi** dancer employed to dance with customers for a fee
*manager	an executive in charge of an establishment or a team	a person who pays the bill when a group eats at a restaurant

**A *taxi dancer* is defined as a lady employee in a club or bar who is paid to dance with a customer who singles her out.

Finally, there are paired lexical items such as *come* vs. *go, bring* vs. *take* that are at times used interchangeably in PE, and *open* and *close* that are used in lieu of *turn on* and *turn off* when referring to appliances and utilities.

THE GRAMMATICAL FEATURES OF PHILIPPINE ENGLISH

In a videotape entitled, *Varieties of American English: Social and Specialized Groups*, the discussants, Shuy and Preston (1977), point out that variations in pronunciation in the different social varieties of American English are not stigmatizing. Nor are differences in lexicon. The former only serves to distinguish one group from another while the latter just requires the receiver of a message to determine the equivalent of an unfamiliar term in his own variety to make sense of what was told him. It is differences in grammatical features that are less acceptable and serve to mark a speaker as lower class or uneducated (as noted by Nero in the introduction to this volume). And where transplanted languages are concerned, these deviations could mark them as a bastardized form of the source language.

Deviations from the GAE norm on the use of grammatical categories have been noted in a number of studies: Alberca (1978), Casambre (1986), Gonzalez (1982, 1984), Gonzalez and Alberca (1978), and Pena (1997) to name a few. Presented here, however, are those cited by Bautista (2000b) as possible features of Standardized Philippine English with references made to other deviations mentioned in the earlier studies.

Using as a database written texts in the Philippine component of the International Corpus of English (ICE) and focusing on deviations from the GAE norm, Bautista (2000b) describes the status and some grammatical features of PE in an attempt to define Standard Philippine English. Care was taken in the analysis of the data to ascertain that variations were not performance/typological errors but could be called features, or on the way to becoming features, of Standard Philippine English. For a deviation to be considered as such, it must be widespread, systematic and rule-governed, and used by competent users of the language. A distinction was also made between a categorical rule that may not be broken and a variable one that is open to variable application. The grammatical categories investigated in the study were subject–verb agreement, articles, prepositions, tenses, mass and count nouns, and pronoun–antecedent agreement.

Two types of deviations noted in subject–verb agreement were, first, those resulting from the use of special nouns (collective, mass, amount, clausal) as subject of the sentence, examples of which are as follows:

1. The *audience await* [awaits] the swordfights eagerly . . .
2. . . . a visibly impressed *public have* [has] been coming to view the imposing structure . . .
3. Wet-milled spray-dried U.S. rice *flour form* [forms] aggregates of 30–50 uM spheres.

A second type of deviation stems from the presence of intervening prepositional phrases. Examples cited by Bautista are as follows:

4. Liquidity *problems* of rural banks on a massive scale *is* [are] being experienced for the first time.
5. The shortest *path,* as well as the distance, *are* [is] easily obtained with standard graph theory algorithms.

In the second example, the intervening expression is signaled by *as well as.*

A third group of subject–verb deviations include expletive constructions that were labeled "*There* sentences" but to which might be added *It* as well, and the inverted sentences and predicative nominatives that required the writer to be concerned with structures before and after the verb. For example:

6. There *exists* [exist] some basic *roadblocks* to compromise, roadblocks that are legal and moral.

Still another deviation stemmed from failure to note the antecedent in a relative clause resulting in a lack of concord between subject and verb. Per-

formance/typological errors in subject–verb agreement for which no plausible explanation could be given were also presented but were not considered a part of the variable rules of Philippine English.

Among the deviations in article usage found in the data was the omission
of the article (e.g. the indefinite article *a/an* before count nouns; whether
abstract or concrete):

7. A loan availed by * [a] bona fide Pag-ibig member . . .

or the omission of the definite article *the* to indicate specific reference:

8. . . . since *[the] mid-fifties, computers have been used in industrial
    process . . . control.

It was pointed out that what seems to have become standard in PE was the
non-use of articles to mark *majority*:

9. *[A] Majority of the public school teachers do not want to serve as
    poll officials in the May elections.

Another deviation was the use of articles even when they are not called for,
that is, before plural and mass nouns:

10. The president directed Cayetano to give him *a [Ø] feedback on the
     matter.

Still another was the use of the wrong article e.g. where *a/an* (not *the*)
should be used at the first mention of a noun and *the* at the succeeding
ones:

11. The MILF . . . has been fighting for *the [a] separate Islamic state
    since 1978.

Bautista points out that variable use of articles could be a feature of Standard Philippine English.

Concerning grammatical words, deviations from GAE are most apparent
in the use of prepositions in PE. This is because of the limited number of
prepositions in most Philippine languages compared to GAE. Among those
that present difficulty are: prepositions that occur with given verbs, nouns,
adjectives to signify different meanings; prepositions that collocate with a
given set of words; and contexts that require the use, and others that call for
the non-use, of prepositions. For the first type, PE makes use of prepositions other than the ones called for in those contexts in GAE. For the second type, the prepositions in the paired items are at times used interchangeably in PE. And for the third type, either substitutions are made or

prepositions are used even when these are not called for. Examples of these three types are shown below. The GAE equivalents are given in parentheses for the first type where prepositions other than those called for in GAE are used in PE:

a. contribute in (contribute _to_) have control of (control _over_)
   focused in (focused _on_)   capability for/ of (capability _to+ verb_)
b. _on_ the farm—_in_ the city   _on_ paper—_in_ the notebook
c. to cope _up_ with (cope _with_)

Bautista (2000b) notes that "patterns for prepositional usage in PE will take some time to form and so in the meantime, prepositional choice may well be idiosyncratic in Standard Philippine English" (p. 56).

Where tenses were concerned, deviations were found resulting from failure to stay within one axis of orientation corresponding to the moment of reference—past or present. The data revealed the use of the simple present or the present perfect instead of the simple past. The former was true to verbs in the subordinate clauses of reported speech where the verb in the main clause was in the past tense. The latter, on the other hand, was preferred even in cases where specific past time dates were given, for example:

12. But it was only in 1510 that a more authentic epidemic _has been_ [was] described.

In the case of modals, preference was shown for the past forms (_could, would_) even when the present form (_can, will_) was called for:

13. Demoloc and Kilalag have a population of 7,450 and 3,570 respectively (. . . Municipal Census 1989). These sitios _could_ [can] be reached by transportation via a rough, steep . . . road.

And in condition–result sentences, both clauses in PE made use of the future tense instead of using the simple present in the condition clause.

Mass/count noun deviations were of three types. One was using mass nouns as count nouns—marking them with the articles _a/an_ or _the_ or giving them the plural form; another was using mass nouns as collective nouns with the plural form of the verb; and the third was using the quantifiers _less/ much_ to mark count nouns. Examples of mass nouns that are pluralized are _equipments, researches, floodings_. Examples mentioned by Bautista of using the plural form of the verb with a collective noun and using the quantifier _much_ to mark count nouns are seen in these sentences:

14. Other _information_ from observers . . . _were_ [was] also documented.
15. . . . so _much_ [many] passenger _jeepneys_ and _buses_ ply the area.

To account for these deviations, Platt et al. (1984; as cited in Bautista, 2000b) contend that:

> ... the conversion of mass nouns to count nouns is not so much a case of overgeneralization (applying a rule too widely) as much as it is a case of reclassification (in this case, viewing the referents of the nouns in a different way) ... thus, in Standard Philippine English, *equipment* is reclassified as referring to an *item of equipment*; *research* as referring to a *research study* or *report*. (pp. 64–65)

Bautista also contends that this shift is an area where PE along with the other New Englishes could introduce innovations.

For deviations in pronoun–antecedent agreement—of which three types were noted, namely, lack of agreement in number, in gender, and between determiner and noun—both Gonzalez (1985, p. 200) and Bautista (2000b, p. 66) point out that these reveal an acquisitional deficiency and are performance errors. They break a categorical rule and cannot be accepted as a feature of Standard PE.

Other deviations noted were word order and using transitive verbs intransitively. The former included placement of adverbs of time, which in GAE usually occupies sentence-initial or sentence-final position; the placement of single-word and/or phrasal adverbs of manner, which usually come after the direct object and/or before the adverb of place; and the placement of frequency or mid-position adverbs

16. ... Solicitor General Ricardo Galvez *yesterday* said [said yesterday]

Included, too, as a deviation in word order is the use of the inverted instead of the natural order in *wh-* embedded questions in reported speech. For Bautista, some of the deviations in the placement of adverbs may not actually be deviations, but only "infelicitous use of the language" (p. 67). Examples of transitive verbs used intransitively are:

17. *Did you enjoy?; I cannot afford; I don't like.*
    Gonzalez (1992, p. 766 as cited in Bautista, 2000b, p. 34)

CHALLENGES FACED BY PE SPEAKERS UNDERSTANDING GAE SPEAKERS

Listening

The phonetic and stress pattern differences noted earlier in this chapter often create listening problems for Filipinos interacting with native speakers or listening to what is said in GAE. Among them are the speed with which utterances are made and the de-stressing of vowels in unstressed syllables. English, being a stress-timed language, puts emphasis only on the word or syllable given primary stress in each breath group. All the other words or syllables in that breath group are de-emphasized and are therefore said rapidly and are not articulated as clearly, making it difficult for a listener not used to stress-timed rhythm to make out what was said. Since Philippine languages are syllable-timed where syllables are articulated clearly, and all vowels—even those in unstressed syllables—are given full value and are not de-stressed, all three sociolinguistic groups of PE experience difficulty in keeping up with and understanding what is said by native speakers of English, as shown in Figure 12.3:

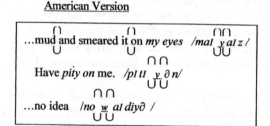

FIG. 12.3.   A comparison of the blends and pauses used by speakers of GAE and PE.

Another listening problem stems from failure to discriminate between contrasting sounds in English since those sounds are absent from the phonetic inventories of most Philippine languages. Those absent categories constitute difficulties not only in the recognition but also in the production of words containing those sounds. For example, vowel length is not a distinctive feature in Philippine languages. Hence, Filipinos experience difficulties in distinguishing between minimal pair contrasts like *beat/bit* and *pool/pull* in English. The same might be said about failure to note stress patterns in English resulting in confusion between the *-ty* and *-teen* numbers (e.g. *thirty/thirteen*) where the former is stressed on the first syllable and the latter on the second syllable. This is also true for sentence stress especially among the basilectal group. Failure on their part to note stress as a signal of the expected response to a query or a command results in failure to respond accordingly. One can imagine such a scenario taking place in a classroom resulting in a PE-speaking student's misunderstanding her GAE-speaking teacher. In a classroom, for example, where the teacher asked a student to read aloud the selection on page thirteen of the textbook, the student started to read the selection on page thirty resulting in the following interaction:

Teacher: What are you reading?

Student: What you asked me to. The selection on page thirty.

Teacher: I said *thirteen* not *thirty*

APPROACHES AND TECHNIQUES USED TO DEVELOP SKILL IN LISTENING TO ACADEMIC TEXTS IN ENGLISH

Varied approaches are used to develop listening comprehension skills. For short texts, the *whole text repeated approach* patterned after *Sound English* is utilized. In this approach, a different task targeting a specific listening skill goes with each repetition of the text. The *Tune in, Question, Listen, Respond (TQLR)* approach designed by the Science Research Associates as well as listening CLOZE and listen and draw exercises are also used with short listening texts.

For longer texts the *sectional approach* is utilized. Here, long texts are broken up into sections with questions raised after each section to simulate the processing of the text as it unfolds and to develop skill in anticipating and predicting what is to follow. Still another approach for long texts is Collins' *Stage-by-Stage approach* which has proven to be especially useful in developing note-taking skills. This comes in three stages with a listening comprehension exercise for each stage. Stage one is usually a summary of the entire lecture. This is followed by an extended version in Stage two and then by the full-blown text in the last stage.

READING PROBLEMS IN ENGLISH AMONG FILIPINOS

Among the causes cited for reading comprehension problems in English, as far as Filipinos are concerned, are the shifts in thrusts and policies concerning language instruction. In the 1950s language was deemed to be mainly oral with the written form serving as a mere graphic representation of the spoken language. This gave rise to the audio-lingual approach to language teaching with emphasis placed on language learning. Reading in English was in fact postponed to a later time after the pupils had gained some basic knowledge of English, else they would not understand the texts they were reading. Hence "content learning was being sacrificed for language learning" (Gonzalez, Jambalos, & Romero, 2003, p. 21).

A reaction to this was the Philippine community school movement that endorsed developing initial literacy in the native language. Although this found support in UNESCO, which recommended the use of the native language in education especially in the beginning stage, the lack of materials in the vernacular posed a problem to its widespread implementation. The need to develop beginning literacy in one's native language was in fact later proven to be theoretically sound by Cummins in his interdependence hypothesis of bilinguals (Cummins & Swain, 1986). Cummins pointed out that there will be a transfer of skills provided that the learner is in a supportive environment and is highly motivated.

The Philippine Bilingual Education Policy in the 1970s, later revised in the 1980s, stipulates the use of the vernaculars as auxiliary languages for instruction in Grades 1 and 2 with English and Filipino taught as subjects in those grades. These then become the medium of instruction in specified subjects from Grade 3 onward. However, the content area texts that have to be read are in either of those two languages, but with literacy skills not yet in place, problems of reading comprehension arise.

The de-emphasis of literacy skills was also evident in the attempt of teachers to integrate all four macro-language skills as well as the elements of language in the English lesson. The reading and literature texts were not taught primarily to develop reading comprehension skills and literary appreciation. They served mainly as a take-off for the introduction of the grammar points.

Other factors that might be cited as causes for reading comprehension problems in GAE are reduced time devoted to reading instruction, the lack of learning resources (e.g. textbooks, supplementary reading materials, reading skill builders, etc.), and the lack of training for teachers in reading. Hence reading comprehension of GAE texts remains a problem for many Filipino school children. National achievement tests for elementary school children have found them to be deficient in the ability to: decode meanings of words through context clues, note details and locate answers to *how/why* questions, perceive cause–effect relationships, give the possible effect of a given cause, and distinguish between fact and opinion.

MEASURES THAT HAVE BEEN TAKEN TO IMPROVE READING COMPREHENSION SKILLS IN ENGLISH

Considering that the Philippine Bilingual Education Policy seeks to develop proficiency in both Filipino and English, and since content area texts are in either of the two languages depending on the domain allocated to them, studies continue to be undertaken on how best to make Filipino learners biliterate. Although the issue of developing initial literacy in one's native language has been settled, the phasing in and development of reading skills in English and Filipino at the beginning level have yet to be resolved. In a study of the effects of bilingualism on literacy development,

Ocampo (2004) points out that "a revision of the sequence and rate of language and literacy instruction of English and Filipino is necessary to better achieve the goals of the Philippine Bilingual Education policy" (p. 1). According to Ocampo:

> The speed of learning found for Filipino word reading suggests that more time can be spent on the development of complex literacy skills in Filipino instead of spending equal amounts of time in teaching Filipino and English word reading skills. (p. 6)

Reading in the intermediate and higher grades, on the other hand, is mainly concerned with making sense of information-dense textbooks in science and mathematics. These texts call for academic language proficiency; hence the present curriculum focuses on content-based instruction where language and content learning are integrated. This goes well with the discourse or text-based approach in language learning, which underscores the text structure and language realizations in different genres.

Finally, realizing that more time is needed to develop literacy skills, the present curriculum has increased the time allotment for the basic skill subjects. Being aware of the need to develop autonomous learners, reading instruction now focuses on strategy training in problem identification and in the selection of strategies to apply to meet the problem and make sense of a text.

HOW MIGHT WRITING SKILLS OF THE THREE PE GROUPS BE DEVELOPED?

Developing functional literacy is one of the basic goals of education. Speaking a language is innate to humans and every person will learn to speak a native language even without instruction, but not so with the written language. One has to be taught to read and write.

Since writing has to do with the production of texts, a discourse or text-based approach to developing writing skills is recommended. In this respect, the reading–writing connection will have to be established with the reading texts serving not only as models of text structure but also as input for content. Among the key concepts to be developed in a writing class are the following:

1. *Different text types* such as exposition, description, personal recounts, instructions, definition, visual–verbal relationships.
2. *Different text structures* or macro-discourse patterns such as Problem–Solution (PSn) or Topic–Restriction–Illustration (TRI).

3. *Generic structures* of different genre or text types.

4. *Micro-discourse signals* intended to establish meaning relationships intra- or intersententially such as cause–effect, addition, comparison and contrast, sequence (time or space), etc.

5. *Cohesive devices* such as pronouns, repetition of keywords, connectors, etc. that will make a sentence stick to the preceding one.

6. *Types of sentences* (e.g. key idea—topic sentence, thesis statement—support sentences, transition word or sentence and restatement) classified according to the role they play in the text.

7. *Awareness of the intended reader* so that one can suit the language, style, and formality level to his needs and expectations.

Whereas the text-based or discourse approach to writing focuses on writing as a product, another approach to the development of writing skills could focus on writing as a recursive process. This is made up of several stages. The first stage, namely the *pre-writing stage* consists of choosing a topic, brainstorming about it, then narrowing down the topic. In the second stage, that is, the *drafting stage*, the writer goes over the words, phrases, and concepts that he or she came up with in the brainstorming stage, and groups together those that go together. Keeping in mind the objective of the writing piece, the student then writes out in complete sentences what he/she wants to put across, making use of cohesive devices and signals to establish coherent relationships between the ideas he/she puts down in writing. In the third stage, the *revising stage* self- and then peer editing is done with the use of guide questions prepared by the teacher. Some such questions would be as follows:

1. Is there any sentence that you think could be moved elsewhere?
2. Is there any sentence that may be deleted?
3. Is there any sentence that is in need of follow-up sentences to make it clearer?
4. Is there a need for signals to establish meaning relationships between the ideas you put down?
5. Is there a need for a transition word or sentence to make the flow from one key idea to another smooth and effortless?
6. Is there a need for a restatement to highlight a point?

For narratives and descriptions, pictures may be used as an aid to enable students to come up with a text. The step-by-step composition process in *Picture Talk* has been found to help linguistically disadvantaged students produce a text. They start with just listing words that name items in the picture. The words are grouped into nouns, verbs and modifiers. These are then put together in phrases to name the facts obvious in the picture. If it is a narrative, the student uses his imagination, makes inferences and observes story grammar (i.e. setting, characters, situation, problem, attempted solutions, result and evaluation) and comes up with a story based on the picture. He/she then narrates another similar incident as an application of the insight obtained from the initial tale.

If, on the other hand, it is a description, then attention could be called to space order in the sequencing of the details (starting from the general moving on to the specifics), use of single-word, phrasal, and clausal modifiers, and finally to one's reaction to the scene.

HOW MIGHT PROFICIENCY IN THE USE OF ENGLISH BE ASSESSED?

Global and task-based communicative tests have been recommended as a means of assessing one's command of the language since these will require the students to make use of what they know of the language to accomplish the task. One such test is the CLOZE test where systematic deletions are made on a given text and the students are asked to supply the deleted items to reconstruct the passage. This will require the students to make use of both reading and language skills.

Nominalization exercises can also be used as formative tests to determine if students can recast sentences without changing the meaning of the utterance. They are to change the verb to a noun, supply a verb that will collocate with it, change the adverbial to adjectival modifiers to go with the noun formed, and make other minimal changes called for while retaining the original meaning of the sentence. Tests on grammatical well-formedness and appropriateness can likewise be given for the students to single out what is not acceptable in a set of sentences These would determine linguistic and sociolinguistic competence.

For a listening test, students can be asked to listen to a text and then determine the speech event (where one is likely to listen to it), who is being addressed, who is the speaker, the objective of his talk, and his attitude towards the topic. For a speaking test, visuals such as a vicinity map may be given to the students for them to give directions on how to get from one place to another. For a reading or a writing test, the students may be asked to transcode the concepts in a text to a schematic diagram or vice versa, from a diagram to a written text. Journal writing may also be used for students to reflect on and write down personal growth experiences that took place that day and the insights he/she gained in the process.

SOME REACTIONS TO PE

It might be pointed out that because Filipino learners of English have greater exposure to the formal academic variety of English used in schools and textbooks, it is not surprising that the acrolect and mesolect varieties of PE have been viewed as bookish and pedantic by native speakers of English. This is because of the formality level of PE used by Filipinos even in informal gatherings. However, in situations calling for the use of basic interpersonal communication skills, the Filipino's choice of words, idioms, and even sentence constructions has been considered unusual by native speakers of English. Instead of saying, "Let's go to . . ." they would say "Let's proceed to . . ." Instead of saying "puke" or "throw up" they would say "vomit" or "wretch." With developments in sociolinguistics, however, awareness of formality levels as well as distinctions between the spoken and written code and the restricted and elaborated forms are now being taught in schools.

A POSTSCRIPT ON LANGUAGE TRANSPLANTS

This chapter started out with a quotation from Braj B. Kachru (1997) to the effect that:

> The architects of . . . each strand of Asian English have molded, reshaped, acculturated, redesigned—and by doing so—enriched what was a Western medium. (p. 23)

To this must be added the observation made by Bautista (2000b) that studies of transplanted languages should focus not only on divergences from the source norm but should also move from deviations to innovations. In this way eventually, broad generalizations can be made about what makes the transplant, in this case, the New Englishes "distinct from, and yet one with the established Englishes" (pp. 81–82).

QUESTIONS FOR DISCUSSION AND REFLECTIVE WRITING

1. With the widespread use of English resulting from globalization, and the rise of different varieties of English such as PE, what language policy should schools adopt concerning the comprehension, production, and assessment of English. Give reasons for your answer.

2. Given the three varieties of PE, what pedagogical approaches might be most effective in enhancing the cognitive academic language proficiency (CALP) of speakers of each variety?
3. Tayao notes that "the acrolect and mesolect varieties of PE have been viewed as bookish and pedantic by native speakers of English." How does this compare or contrast with your own view of PE, and of other varieties of English discussed in this volume?

APPENDIX
Nativization Processes and Classification
of Lexical Items Peculiar to PE

Nativization/Indigenization Process	Items in the Source Language	Resulting Items in Philippine English
A. Normal expansion 1. Extensions or adaptations of meaning	*Popular brand names of products *Adaptations of meaning	_colgate_ for toothpaste _pampers_ for disposable diapers _cut-rite_ for waxed paper _bath_ (take a shower) from GAE (in a bathtub)
2. Extending word-derivation patterns	*Addition of affixes to change a noun or an adjective to a verb	_operationalize_ _water cannoning_ _leap frogged_
B. Preservation of items lost or infrequent in other varieties	*Archaic-sounding items limited or no longer in use in GAE	_by-and-by_ _wherein_ _wherefore_
C. Coinage 1. Analogies of word affixation patterns in GAE	*Actor-marking affixes _er_ and _ist_ *Adjective-marking affix _al_	_carnapper_ from [kidnap + _er_], _holdupper_ from [holdup + _er_], reelection_ist_, rally_ist_ master_al_ after doctor_al_
2. Reductions	*Clipping or shortening words	_aircon_ for airconditioning unit _kinder_ for kindergartener
3. Acronyms	*Using only the initial letters	_CR_ for comfort room (toilet) _DI_ for dancing instructor
4. Innovations	*Coming out with new terms (neologisms)	_promdi_—"from the province"
5. English Compounds	*Combining two English words	_captain ball_—captain of a basketball team
6. Mixed compounds	*Combining an English term with a borrowed one	_common tao_ (ordinary Filipino) _sari-sari store_ (small variety store in the neighborhood
D. Borrowing	Adopting from others	_despedida_ from Spanish

REFERENCES

Alberca, W. L. (1978). *The distinctive features of Philippine English in the mass media.* Unpublished doctoral dissertation, University of Santo Tomas, Manila.

Bautista, Ma. L. (1997). The lexicon of Philippine English. In Ma. L. Bautista (Ed.), *English is an Asian language: The Philippine context* (pp. 49–72). Australia: Macquarie Library Pty. Ltd.

Bautista, Ma. L. (2000a). Studies of Philippine English in the Philippines. *Philippine Journal of Linguistics, 31*(1), 39–65.

Bautista, Ma. L. (2000b). *Defining standard Philippine English: Its status and grammatical features.* Manila: De La Salle University Press.

Casambre, N. G. (1986). What is Filipino English? *Philippine Journal for Language Teaching, 14*(1–4), 34–49.

Cummins, J., & Swain, M. (1986). *Bilingualism and education: Aspects of theory, research and practice.* New York: Longman.

Gonzalez, A. (1982). English in the Philippine mass media. In J. Pride (Ed.), *New Englishes* (pp. 211–226). Rowley, MA: Newbury House.

Gonzalez, A. (1984). Philippine English across generations: The sound system. *DLSU Dialogue, 20*(1), 1–26.

Gonzalez, A. (1985). *Studies on Philippine English.* Singapore: SEAMEO Regional Language Centre.

Gonzalez, A., & Alberca, W. L. (1978). *Philippine English. of the mass media* (preliminary edition). Manila: De La Salle University Research Council.

Gonzalez, A., Jambalos, T., & Romero, Ma. C. S. (2003). *Three studies on Philippine English across generations: Towards an integration and some implications.* Manila: Linguistic Society of the Philippines.

Hendriksson, M. (2002). *Asian and Pacific Islander American demographics.* United States Environmental Protection Agency.

Kachru, B. (1997). English as an Asian language. In Ma. L. Bautista (Ed.), *English is an Asian language: The Philippine context* (pp. 1–23). Australia: Macquarie Library Pty. Ltd.

Llamzon, T. (1969). *Standard Filipino English.* Quezon City: Ateneo de Manila University Press.

Llamzon, T. (1997). The phonology of Philippine English. In Ma. L. Bautista (Ed.), *English is an Asian language: The Philippine context* (pp. 41–48). Australia: Macquarie Library Pty. Ltd.

McKaughan, H. (1993). Toward a standard Philippine English. *Philippine Journal of Linguistics, 24*(2), 41–55.

Ocampo, D. J. (2004, April). *Effects of bilingualism on literacy development.* Compendium of Full Papers of the 2nd International Convention on Language Education. Philippine Association for Language Teaching. Manila: Philippines.

Pena, P. S. (1997). Philippine English in the classroom. In Ma. L. Bautista (Ed.), *English is an Asian Language: The Philippine context* (pp. 87–102). Australia: Macquarie Library Pty. Ltd.

Shuy, R., & Preston, D. (1977). *Varieties of American English: Social and specialized groups.* [A Video Presentation]. United States Information Agency.

Tafoya, S. M. (2002). The linguistic landscape of California schools. *California Counts: Population Trends and Profiles, 3*(4), 1–16.

Tayao, Ma. L. G. (2004). The evolving study of Philippine English phonology. *World Englishes, 23*(1), 77–90.

Conclusion

Shondel J. Nero
St. John's University

Many of the salient themes that have emerged throughout this volume—
language spread and variation, language attitudes, linguistic identities,
standard language ideology, language and power—are evident in the society at large. We can all agree, for example, that English does not sound or
look the same in the various places where it is spoken, even if it is mutually
understandable to its diverse speakers. Thus, there is a wide variety of people who claim English-speaking identities. We might also agree that standardized forms of English (indeed of any language) are generally privileged, and that nonstandard varieties are concomitantly stigmatized. Yet, it
is in the educational arena, specifically in the classroom, where these
themes converge, often in creative tension with each other. In fact, the
chapters in this volume collectively underscore a series of evolving tensions
that emanate from language spread and change, and challenge us to confront them in education. The tensions as I see them are: (a) a *static* versus a
dynamic view of language (Matsuda, 1997), (b) the need for (or impulse towards) norms/standards versus a desire for diversity or alternative stances,
(c) the ambivalent attitude of simultaneously celebrating and denigrating
the vernacular.

STATIC VERSUS DYNAMIC VIEW OF LANGUAGE

In the introduction to this volume, I referred to Brutt-Griffler (2002) who
argued that one of the most significant aspects of macroacquisition theory
is the idea that speech communities have taken English and made it their

own, changing the language in the process. This is inevitable; a language takes on a life of its own wherever it is used, even if it is imposed from the outside. Yet, we hold tenaciously to a monolithic view of English (especially in education), so that we are often surprised when our students claim an English-speaking identity even if they do not speak a North American or British variety of English. Even within American varieties of English, speakers of AAVE or Tex Mex are stigmatized because their language defies a static view of English as being only the standardized American or British variety. Tayao (chap. 12, this volume) shows us clearly how Philippine English evolved out of a set of historical circumstances to become its own variety ranging from the basilect to the mesolect to the acrolect. De Kleine, for her part in chapter 10, points out the dynamic use of English among West Africans, ranging from Pidgin to standard West African English. The static view of language is an attempt to not only define language, but to control its structure and use—an attempt that has historically failed. Linguists have long taken as axiomatic the (seemingly contradictory) notion that language is rule-governed and variable. Language, in fact, can only serve its fundamentally communicative function to the extent that it is able to self-regulate and at the same time adapt to the needs of its users. For this reason, language use is inherently dynamic.

The speakers of English we will confront in twenty-first century classrooms, then, will reflect this linguistic dynamism. The diversity of their backgrounds (with population movement we can expect they will be from anywhere in the world) will be reflected in their claim to, and investment in, multiple linguistic identities as well as their particular varieties and uses of English, thereby pushing the boundaries of a static view of language. They will also claim ownership of English. So, for example, in the U.S., a teacher might encounter a student who identifies herself as a native speaker of Caribbean English rather than as a nonnative speaker of American English. This framing has implications for teaching. The chapters in this volume suggest that a contrastive but additive approach to language teaching seems to be more effective. In other words, build on a student's linguistic repertoire (the language/dialect he or she claims, knows, and uses) rather than focus on how much he or she misses the mark (the target language/dialect).

NORMS/STANDARDS VERSUS DIVERSITY/ ALTERNATIVE STANCES

The authors in this volume also wrestle with how to affirm linguistic and cultural differences within the prescriptivist project of education that still foregrounds standards/norms as benchmarks for measuring academic success. This tension is articulated in chapter 1, where Kachru challenges us to rethink, or one might say retool, the goals of English Language Teaching (ELT). The underlying question is: What should be the goals of ELT in different parts of the world where English is spoken? Kachru clearly rejects the historical and continued preference for an exonormative approach to language teaching and learning in places like India (i.e., striving for British or American standards in speech, writing, and publishing). Rather, she argues for standards/goals more relevant to the local setting, and more inclusive curricula, methodologies, and materials. The issue is, of course, not clearcut, because the needs and goals of the diverse speakers and learners of English worldwide vary. For example, some learners will remain in their local milieu and will only need to use English in a limited way while others may aspire to higher education in Western countries, in which case familiarity with British or American varieties of English and norms would be appropriate (as noted by Govardhan, chapter 11). It might be the case that more flexible goals or standards are necessary to accommodate learners' various needs, but Kachru is correct in at least challenging the presumed goals of ELT.

A related issue raised in this volume is the extent to which the value placed on acquiring a narrowly defined variety of standard English in school is in conflict with other standard varieties and/or nonstandard varieties that students use in their daily lives. Siegel takes up this issue in chapter 2, by arguing through carefully articulated evidence *against* the notion that vernacular use in the classroom detracts from the acquisition of standard English. Indeed, one of the central concerns of the public in the Ebonics "firestorm," as Rickford describes it in chapter 3, was the widespread (mis)perception that African American students were going to be taught in Ebonics, thereby putting their acquisition of standard English in jeopardy. Through a careful analysis of the Oakland Unified School District's (OUSD) Resolution itself, Rickford shows that the goal of the OUSD was not to teach Ebonics, but rather to help African American children acquire and master Standard English, while maintaining respect for their vernacular through a contrastive analysis approach. Delpit (chap. 4) also shows in very practical ways that linguistic and cultural diversity can be affirmed while acknowledging the power of, and teaching, a standard variety of English. Eades and her colleagues in Hawai'i (chap. 7) critically analyze the focus on standard English and the attempted ban of Pidgin in the classroom through what they call the *appropriateness* argument. Their discussion of Hawaiians who are testing the boundaries of appropriateness in various contexts might be recast as a call for widening the parameters of what can be considered acceptable/normal/standard language by giving legitimacy to alternative language varieties. In each case, albeit from slightly different approaches, the authors are, in fact, challenging the sense of a *linguistic trade-off* that some language minority students are made to feel—that is to say, they must *give up* (the limitations of) their vernacular in order to *gain* (the benefits of acquiring) a standard variety of English. These authors are confident that a linguistic balance, or *bidialectalism*, is both desirable and possible for students.

Many educators, too, are grappling with finding the right balance between the ethnic/linguistic diversity that is present and will continue to grow in their classrooms, and the real life pressure to enforce standards (linguistic and otherwise) that is part and parcel of the educational system. Nowhere is this more evident than in the "Standards" Movement in assessment, palpably manifested in high-stakes testing. García and Menken in chapter 8 eloquently capture the disparity between the language of high-stakes testing (basically standardized academic English) and the language use of many linguistically diverse students, which ranges from nonstandard varieties of English to languages other than English. Thus, there's a great divide between prescribed and actual language use, creating a challenge for assessment. Despite classroom practices that might accommodate alternative assessment such as the use of portfolios, it is the preparation for high-stakes tests to which teachers must dedicate most of their time, lest they and their students suffer serious consequences. And to the extent that every test is in a sense a language test, as argued by scholars such as Abedi, Hofstetter and Lord (2004), O'Malley and Valdez Pierce (1996), and others, linguistically diverse students are at a decided disadvantage in high-stakes testing. Nonetheless, the focus on meeting standards continues to be a critical component in our current educational system, and so the tug-of-war between standardized and alternative assessment remains, for now, work in progress.

CELEBRATING AND DENIGRATING THE VERNACULAR

"Folk linguistics" tells us that the vernacular is to be despised and discouraged at all costs, particularly in school, but the reality of language use tells us otherwise. Winer, for example, in chapter 5, notes that the rise of nationalism in Caribbean nations following the granting of independence was reflected in the embracing and increased use of the vernacular (Creole) as a mark of true Caribbean identity. Yet, there's a sense that Creole is both good and bad; it is good for in-group community identity and solidarity; and bad for public linguistic identity because its speakers are stigmatized.[1]

---

[1]Pratt-Johnson (chap. 6, this volume) describes the prejudicial attitudes towards Creole that many Jamaican students encounter in New York City public schools. Hall Kells (chap. 9) describes the stigmatization of Tex Mex by others and its own speakers, even as they use it to forge a unique South Texas identity.

Thus it is not appropriate for use in school. It is usually the speakers of Creole or nonstandard varieties of English themselves that hold most fiercely to that dual belief—with good reason. Our society still privileges standard varieties of English, or, more precisely speakers thereof, and as noted above, academic success, as measured by assessment instruments of any real consequence, is still largely predicated on proficiency in standard English. It is the reason, as Hoover (1978) notes, why African American parents are almost unanimous in their desire for their children to master standard English, even as many of those very children exhibit strong affiliation with African American Vernacular English as a mark of group identity.

DIRECTIONS FOR FUTURE RESEARCH

Given the tensions articulated above, it is clear that the authors in this volume raise more questions than answers, and by so doing leave ample room for continued and promising research. Some of the areas that might be considered for future research in light of the foregoing discussion are:

- The extent to which language variation and change will continue to complicate language standards, language attitudes, linguistic identities, language pedagogy, and assessment.
- The ways in which the interaction of speakers of various varieties of English will affect the language use of each group, e.g., how will the interaction of Tex Mex and AAVE speakers affect the language of each group?
- Building on alternative models of linguistic categorization, such as those proposed by Leung, Harris, and Rampton (1997) that move beyond the limitations of the native/nonnative dichotomy, and critically addressing the range and complexity of linguistic behavior of English speakers worldwide.
- Exploring alternative language acquisition theories that take into account multiple linguistic identities.
- Examining how educational systems in host countries with large immigrant populations such as the U.S. or Canada respond to cultural/linguistic diversity in terms of teacher preparation, familiarizing themselves with the educational systems of sending countries, pedagogy and assessment practices.

It is hoped that this volume will serve as a springboard for embarking on such critically important research, as a means of addressing some of the more vexing questions in our field.

REFERENCES

Abedi, J., Hofstetter, C., & Lord, C. (2004). Assessment accommodations for English language learners: Implications for policy-based empirical research. *Review of Educational Research, 74*(1), 1–28.

Brutt-Griffler, J. (2002). *World English: A study of its development.* Clevedon, UK: Multilingual Matters.

Hoover, M. (1978). Community attitudes toward Black English. *Language in Society, 7,* 65–87.

Leung, C., Harris, R., & Rampton, B. (1997). The idealised native speaker, reified ethnicities, and classroom realities. *TESOL Quarterly, 31*(3), 543–560.

Matsuda, P. (1997). Contrastive rhetoric in context: A dynamic model of L2 writing. *Journal of Second Language Writing, 6*(1), 45–60.

O'Malley, J. M., & Valdez Pierce, L. (1996). *Authentic assessment for English language learners: Practical approaches for teachers.* Englewood Cliffs, NJ: Addison-Wesley.

Contributors

Christa de Kleine is Associate Professor of Education/TESOL at the College of Notre Dame, Baltimore, Maryland.

Lisa Delpit is Executive Director of the Center for Urban Education & Innovation at Florida International University. Among her publications are *Other people's children: Cultural conflict in the classroom* (1995), *The Real Ebonics Debate: Power, Language, and the Education of African-American Children* (co-edited with Theresa Perry, 1998), and *The Skin That We Speak: Thoughts on Language and Culture in the Classroom* (co-edited with Joanne Kilgour Dowdy, 2002).

Diana Eades is Honorary Fellow, Languages, Cultures and Linguistics, at the University of New England, Australia.

Ofelia García is Professor in the Department of International and Transcultural Studies at Teachers College, Columbia University. García has published extensively in the areas of sociology of language, bi/multilingual education, the education of immigrant students, especially Latino students, and US Spanish. With Joshua Fishman she co-edited *The Multilingual Apple: Languages in New York City* in 2001.

Anam K. Govardhan is a professor in the English department at Western Connecticut State University and a Coordinator of the ESL program. He has previously taught ESL in India and Nigeria. His articles have appeared in leading journals like the *TESOL Quarterly*, and the *CIEFL Bulletin*. He has written and produced nearly 150 lessons on teaching English language skills for TV stations in India and Malaysia.

Ermile Hargrove is an independent educational consultant in Hawai'i for schools and other agencies that provide educational services to children, youth, and adults. A speaker of Pidgin (Hawai'i English Creole), she is an active participant in keeping the language alive and an advocate for the Pidgin language.

Suzie Jacobs was formerly Professor of English at the University of Hawai'i in Honolulu and now resides in Atlanta. Her co-authored book on classroom writing and talk is entitled *Mindful of Others: Teaching Children to Teach* (Heinemann, 1994).

Yamuna Kachru is Professor Emerita of Linguistics at the University of Illinois at Urbana-Champaign. Her numerous publications include a book entitled *World Englishes in Asian Contexts*, co-authored with Cecil L. Nelson, scheduled for publication in 2005 from Hong Kong University Press.

Michelle Hall Kells is Assistant Professor in the Rhetoric and Writing program at the University of New Mexico. Kells launched *Attending to the Margins: Writing, Researching, and Teaching on the Front Lines* (Heinemann, 1999) with Valerie Balester. A second, *Latino/a Discourses: On Language, Identity, and Literacy Education* (Heinemann, 2004) co-edited with Valerie Balester and Victor Villanueva focuses on teaching writing to diverse student populations.

Terri Menacker is a doctoral student in Second Language Studies at the University of Hawai'i at Manoa. Her areas of interest are language minority education and multilingualism in individuals and society.

Kate Menken is Assistant Professor of Bilingual Education and TESOL in the School of Education at the City College of New York, City University of New York. Her research interests are in the areas of language policy, bilingual education, standardized testing and assessment, and national education reform.

Shondel J. Nero is Associate Professor of TESOL in the School of Education at St. John's University in Queens, New York. She has published several articles and is the author of *Englishes in Contact: Anglophone Caribbean Students in an Urban College* (Hampton Press, 2001). Her research interests include ESL, teaching standard English as a second dialect, Caribbean Creole English, sociolinguistics, and language and identity.

Yvonne Pratt-Johnson is Professor of TESOL at St. John's University in Queens, New York. She has conducted extensive research in teaching dialect-different students both in the United States and abroad.

John R. Rickford is the Pritzker Professor of Linguistics at Stanford University. He has published numerous articles, and several books, including *Dimensions of a Creole Continuum* (Stanford, 1987), *Spoken Soul: The Story of Black English* (with Russell Rickford, won American Book award, 2000), and *Language in the USA: Themes for the Twenty-first Century* (with Ed Finegan, 2004).

Jeff Siegel is Associate Professor of Linguistics at the University of New England (Australia) and Associate Researcher at the University of Hawai'i. He is author of *Language Contact in a Plantation Environment: A Sociolinguistic History of Fiji* (Cambridge, 1987), editor of *Processes of Language Contact: Studies from Australia and the South Pacific* (Fides, 2000) and co-author of *Pidgin Grammar: An Introduction to the Creole Language of Hawai'i* (Bess Press, 2003).

Ma. Lourdes G. Tayao is Professorial Lecturer in the Graduate School at the University of the East Recto, Manila, Philippines. She has authored several books on language and reading currently in use in private and public schools in the Philippines, and articles on language teaching published in local and international journals.

Lise Winer is Associate Professor of Second Language Education in the Faculty of Education at McGill University, Montréal, Québec, Canada.

Author Index

Subject Index